ACCESSIBILITY, TRADE AND LOCATIONAL BEHAVIOUR

To my parents, always accessible

Accessibility, Trade and Locational Behaviour

Edited by
AURA REGGIANI
Department of Economics
Faculty of Statistics
University of Bologna
Italy

Routledge
Taylor & Francis Group
LONDON AND NEW YORK

First published 1998 by Ashgate Publishing

Reissued 2018 by Routledge
2 Park Square, Milton Park, Abingdon, Oxon, OX14 4RN
711 Third Avenue, New York, NY I 0017, USA

Routledge is an imprint of the Taylor & Francis Group, an informa business

A Library of Congress record exists under LC control number: 98073399

ISBN 13: 978-1-138-35139-4 (hbk)
ISBN 13: 978-0-429-43530-0 (ebk)

Contents

Figures, maps and tables

Contributors

Michel Beuthe
Faculté Universitaire Catholiques de Mons
Group Transport & Mobility
161 Chaussée de Binche
B 7000 Mons
Belgium

Johannes Bröcker
Faculty of Traffic Sciences
University of Technology
D-01062 Dresden
Germany

Antje Burmeister
INRETS-TRACES
20, rue Elisée Reclus
59650 Villeneuve d'Ascq
France

Domenico Campisi
Institute of System Analysis and
Computer Science, C N R
Viale Manzoni 30
00185 Rome
Italy

Kristian Colletis-Wahl
Centre for European Evaluation
Expertise Tour Suisse (C3E)
1 bd. Vivier Merle
69443 Lyon Cedex 03
France

Laurent Demilie
Faculté Universitaire Catholiques de Mons
Group Transport & Mobility
161 Chaussée de Binche
B 7000 Mons
Belgium

Paul Drewe
Faculty of Architecture
Delft University of Technology
P.O. Box 5043
2800 GA Delft
The Netherlands

Valerie Dupuis
Faculté Universitaire Catholiques de Mons
Group Transport & Mobility
161 Chaussée de Binche
B 7000 Mons
Belgium

Ulla M. Forslund-J.
Royal Institute of Technology
Regional Planning KTH
10044 Stockholm
Sweden

Massimo Gastaldi
Institute of System Analysis and
Computer Science, C N R
Viale Manzoni 30
00185 Rome
Italy

Hideo Hashimoto
Faculty of Economics
Osaka University
1-7 Machikaneyama-cho
Toyonaka
Osaka 560
Japan

Veli Himanen
VTT Communities and Infrastructure
P.O. Box 1902
FIN-02044
VTT
Finland

Börje Johansson
Royal Institute of Technology
Regional Planning KTH
10044 Stockholm
Sweden

Ben Janssen
NEA Transport Research and Training
Branch Office Tilburg
Schouwburgring 91
5038 TK Tilburg
The Netherlands

Bart Jourquin
Faculté Universitaire Catholiques de Mons
Group Transport & Mobility
161 Chaussée de Binche
B 7000 Mons
Belgium

Rico Maggi
Facoltà di Scienze Economiche
Università della Svizzera Italiana
Centrocivico
Via Ospedale 13
CH-6900 Lugano
Switzerland

Dino Martellato
Department of Economics
University of Venice
Ca' Foscari, Fondamenta
S. Giobbe
I-30100 Venice
Italy

Peter McGregor
Fraser of Allender Institute
Department of Economics
University of Strathclyde
100 Cathedral Street
Glasgow G4 0LN
Scotland

Toshihiko Miyagi
School of Regional Studies
and Department of Civil Engineering
Gifu University
1-1 Yanagido
Gifu 501-11
Japan

Karin Müller
Socio-Economic Institute
University of Zürich
Haldenbachstrasse 44
CH-80006 Zürich
Switzerland

Peter Nijkamp
Department of Regional Economics
Free University
De Boelelaan 1105
1081 HV Amsterdam
The Netherlands

Simo Pasi
Office for Official Publications
of the European Communities
2, rue Mercier
L-2895 Luxembourg
Luxembourg

Remigio Ratti
Istituto di Ricerche Economiche
Centrocivico
Via Ospedale 13
CH-6904 Lugano
Switzerland

Aura Reggiani
Department of Economics
Faculty of Statistics
University of Bologna
Piazza Scaravilli, 2
40126 Bologna
Italy

Pierfrancesco Reverberi
Department of Production
Systems and Computer Science
University of Rome 'Tor Vergata'
Via della Ricerca Scientifica
00133 Rome
Italy

Takaji Suzuki
Faculty of Engineering
Department of Civil Engineering
Gifu University
1-1 Yanagido
Gifu 501-11
Japan

J. Kim Swales
Fraser of Allender Institute
Department of Economics
University of Strathclyde
100 Cathedral Street
Glasgow G4 0LN
Scotland

Roger Vickerman
CERTE
Keynes College
The University of Kent at Canterbury
Canterbury
Kent CT2 7NP
England

Wai Fai Tsang
Department of Regional Economics
Free University
De Boelelaan 1105
1081 HV Amsterdam
The Netherlands

Ya Ping Yin
Fraser of Allender Institute
Department of Economics
University of Strathclyde
100 Cathedral Street
Glasgow G4 0LN
Scotland

Preface

The drastic spatio-temporal changes currently taking place in transportation and mobility patterns necessitate a complete rethinking of the accessibility 'concept', conceived in the Regional Science and Transport Economics literature as the very core of cost-based theories and spatial interaction models.

It therefore seems timely to revisit – theoretically, methodologically and empirically – the conventional concepts and measures of accessibility, by considering their relevance in the framework of new emerging paradigms, such as networks, dynamics, complexity.

Of particular interest are new research questions, exploring the relationships between accessibility and the new space-economy, accessibility and connectivity/functioning of the networks, accessibility and dynamic location effects.

This volume is mainly the result of a special session on these issues, organized by the editor in Tokyo, in May 1996, as part of the World Conference of the Regional Science Association.

The organization of the whole conference was undertaken by the Japan Section of the Regional Science Association, under the direction of Professor Hirotada Kohno (University of Tsukuba). Thanks to his efforts the congress turned out to be a great success. Professor Kohno showed just how seriously the subject of Regional Science in general, and accessibility measures in particular, was taken by impressing us with a magnificent opening ceremony, honoured by the presence of the Emperor and the Empress of Japan, and by making very efficient local arrangements to facilitate our own proceedings.

The present volume thus brings together the various contributions of the special session on 'Accessibility, Trade and Locational Behaviour' from scholars actively involved in research in the field, with the aim of investigating the multiplicity of new accessibility dimensions, mainly in relation to the dynamic processes of trade and industrial location. Without the scientific output of all these authors and their willingness to participate in the Tokyo Conference, this book could not have been produced. Furthermore, the editor wishes to thank all referees for their careful cooperation in the refereeing process.

In addition, she would like to give special thanks to Professor Peter Nijkamp, who enthusiastically supported, both intellectually and practically, the idea of organizing such a big session in the Far East and who led the way – regarding the logistics of this 'opus' – in showing how to overcome the considerable distance 'barrier'.

Thanks also go to Mrs. Dianne Biederberg (Contact Europe, Amsterdam) for her skilful copy editing and capable assistance in coordinating the wordprocessing of the manuscript, as well as to Mrs.

Evelina Kaneclin (Milan) for her artwork in the preparation of various material during the editing process and to Mrs. Patricia Ellman (Amsterdam) for her excellent suggestions concerning the English of the introductory part of the text.

Last, but not least, the editor wishes to express her gratitude for the financial support from her home institution, particularly the Italian 'Progetto Finalizzato Trasporti 2' project no. 97.000.264.PF74, under the umbrella of the Italian National Research Council (CNR), and the 40 and 60 percent projects sponsored by the Italian Public Ministry (MPI), as well as from the EU/TERMINET project.

Aura Reggiani

February 1998
Bologna/Milan/Amsterdam

1 Accessibility, Trade and Locational Behaviour: An Introduction

AURA REGGIANI

1.1 The Accessibility Concept: A Brief Review

'Accessibility' is a well-known term used by scientists, experts and laymen, particularly in the literature of regional and transport research where the concept of accessibility has played a major role for several decades.

This concept came to the fore in the 1950s after the rigorous legitimation of gravity theory by Isard at the First Regional Science Meeting in 1954 (for an historical review of gravity theory/spatial interaction models, see Nijkamp and Reggiani 1992). One of the first foundation stones for the use of accessibility 'theory' can be found in Hansen (1959), who defined accessibility as the *potential of opportunities for interaction* (p.73). The quantification as well as the formulation of a theoretical structure for this concept has assumed various forms in the course of its history (Martellato et al. 1998).

Table 1.1 shows the various formal definitions of accessibility – mainly used in the regional science literature – and implicitly underlines how accessibility has been related in the past to the concepts of *nearness, proximity, ease of spatial interaction, potential of opportunities for interaction, or potentiality of contacts with activities or supplies* (Weibull 1980, p. 54). In other words, accessibility was considered a *property of configurations of opportunities for spatial interaction* (Weibull 1980, p. 53).

In this context, it is evident that, despite the various theoretical formulations displayed in Table 1.1, accessibility always emerges – in its analytical form – as the *potential of opportunities*:

$$Acc_i = \sum_j D_j \, f(c_{ij}) \qquad (1.1)$$

where Acc_i defines the accessibility of some reference point (origin i), D_j is a measure (or weight) of opportunities/activities in j, and $f(c_{ij})$ is the impedance function from i to j. Consequently this interpretation of accessibility has always governed the scientific literature.

Table 1.1 Conventional measures and formulations of accessibility: a concise review

Conventional Accessibility Measures	Analytical Formulations	Authors
Potential of Opportunity	$Acc_i = \sum_j D_j e^{-\beta c_{ij}}$ (1)	Hansen 1959; Ingram 1971; Wilson 1971; Domanski 1979; Weibull 1980; Bröcker 1989; Bruinsma & Rietveld 1993 a,b, 1998; Rietveld &; Nijkamp 1993; Forslund & Johansson 1993; Suarez 199; Bibby & Capineri 1997
Physical Measure	$Acc_i = \sum_j c_{ij}$ (2) or $Acc_i = \sum_j W_j c_{ij}$ (3)	Wachs & Kumagai 1973; Vickerman 1974; Mattson & Weibull 1981; Moretti 1985; Cattan 1992; Gutiérrez & Urbano 1996
Utility	$Acc_i = \ln \sum_j D_j e^{-\beta c_{ij}}$	Neuberger 1971; Wilson 1976; Williams 1977; Leonardi 1978; Williams & Senior 1978; Ben-Akiva & Lerman 1979; Leonardi & Tadei 1984; Bröcker 1989; Forslund & Johansson 1993
Inverse Function of Competition	$Acc_i = \frac{1}{A_i}$ (4)	Wilson 1982; Fotheringham 1983; Reggiani 1985a; Matthes 1994
Joint Accessibility	$Acc_i = \sum_j Acc_j D_j e^{-\beta c_{ij}}$ where $Acc_j = \sum_k D_k e^{-\gamma c_{jk}}$	Domanski 1979; Fotheringham 1986; Reggiani 1985b; Nijkamp & Reggiani 1992
Dynamic Accessibility	$Acc_i(t) = \frac{1}{A_i^{*}(t)}$ (5)	Nijkamp & Reggiani 1988

Surveys: Vickerman 1974; Domanski 1979; Pirie 1979; Weibull 1980; Bruinsma & Rietveld 1993a; Isquierdo & Monzon 1993; Vickerman 1994, 1995; Vickerman et al. 1995; Martellato et al. 1998; Rietveld and Bruinsma 1998.

Notes to Table 1.1

1 D_j is a measure of opportunities/activities in j.
2 c_{ij} is the impedance factor (distance, time, cost, generalized cost, etc.).
3 W_j is a weight related to location j.
4

$$A_i^* = \frac{1}{\sum_j D_j e^{-\beta c_{ij}}}$$

is the calibration factor in a spatial interaction model.
5

$$A_i^*(t) = \frac{1}{\sum_j B_j^* D_j e^{-\beta c_{ij}}}$$

where $B_j^* = B_j G_j$, B_j is the usual (dynamic) calibration factor and G_j a dynamic accessibility factor.

In 1979, Domanski (p. 1190) stated: 'By accessibility I mean the *possibilities* of using the opportunities that the economic, social, cultural and political facilities and institutions provide.' These opportunities may concern employment places, medical care centres, production places, shops, parks, etc., each particular type of opportunity having relevant attributes such as distance, mode of transport, travel time/cost, supply capacity, price, quality, congestion, queuing time, etc. According to model (1.1) the concept of 'potential of opportunities' includes a certain measurement of the opportunities at destination j, discounted (in relative or absolute value) by the spatial distance (travel/time/cost) of j from some reference point (origin) i (see again Martellato et al. 1998).

However, a closer examination of this conventional concept of accessibility shows how the concept of potential of opportunities could be better interpreted in the framework of the *utility* concept (the potential/expected utility of reaching (accessing) a certain place or a fixed amount of resources, or making a choice) on the basis of the fundamental works by Ben-Akiva and Lerman (1979), Domencich and McFadden (1975), and Leonardi (1978,1985) (see again Table 1.1 and Table 1.2).

It should be noted that Neuberger (1971), Williams and Senior (1978) and Wilson (1976) had already interpreted the inverse balancing factor of a spatial interaction model as an indicator of the *economic benefit* of facility size:

$$\frac{1}{A_j} = Acc_i = \sum_j D_j \exp(-\beta c_{ij}) = \sum_j D_j \exp(u_{ij}) \tag{1.2}$$

where

$$u_{ij} = v_{ij} - \beta c_{ij} \tag{1.3}$$

represents the net gain/benefit consisting of a component v_{ij} (referring to the value of accessing i) minus communication costs c_{ij} (including also congestion/saturation costs), while ß is a cost-sensitivity parameter.

In this framework the substitution of the words 'potential utility' for the word 'possibilities' in Domanski's definition above could be the first relevant step towards bringing new perspectives to the accessibility concepts/theories/methodologies developed so far.

1.2 Accessibility and the New Space Economy

1.2.1 Introduction

In this era of globalization leading to important socio-economic and (geo)-political changes, the new position of transport/communication provokes many intriguing policy and research questions, which can roughly be interpreted under the broad umbrella of *'transport sustainability'* (Nijkamp and Van Geenhuizen 1997; Reggiani 1997).

In this context, the new (physical and non-physical) accessibility flows and forms are coming to the fore as driving forces/trends behind globalization and the new spatial/ environmental developments ranging from local to transnational scales (Van Veen-Groot et al. 1998).

It is well known that a strategic choice for reducing the economic/social/ environmental/energy cost of the currently increasing mobility concerns the issue of *intermodality* (in both the passenger and freight transport sectors) at all levels of the transport/information organization. Intermodality – with a view to its related *interoperability* and *interconnectivity* factors – leads to what is known as the 'Inter-transport Matrix'[1], which also raises interesting research questions regarding *new concepts and approaches* in transport systems analysis and modelling efforts that are able to cope with future transport/economic/spatial problems (from both the demand and supply side) (see again Reggiani 1997).

1.2.2 New Concepts in the Space Economy

One of these new approaches is the *network* concept, embedding not only the physical morphological structure, but also the *functioning* of the network itself, connecting modal points in the underlying structure with a view to efficient operations via organized linkage patterns (see Dupuy 1993).

A related question is then whether – methodologically – the network dimension is 'captured' by the conventional accessibility concept displayed in formulation (1.1), or alternatively, how much the functioning of the network is influenced by the new forms of accessibility (e.g. the Internet, fast modes, etc.).

Another relevant concept which has recently attracted a great deal of attention is the dynamic complexity concept and hence the related '*complex network*' concept.

Nijkamp and Reggiani (1998) show the potential/limitations of this approach, with reference to the methodologies and empirical applications actually available in the space-economy, where the evolutionary complex forms of networks need to be predicted and evaluated. In this context, accessibility certainly plays a crucial role in both *slow* dynamics, characteristic of the supply side (e.g. infrastructure, facilities/locational developments), and *fast* dynamics, typical of the user side (e.g. demand mobility/communication patterns).

It is then clear that the conventional approach of static accessibility used so far (see Section 1.1) is a sort of 'operational' instrument able to 'decodify' the dynamic development of accessibility in the spatial complex networks.

The emerging question is whether new measures of accessibility could be able to adjust or incorporate this 'discrepancy' between slow and fast network dynamics (i.e. supply/demand), as well as between slow and fast spatial economic networks (e.g. different market structures in the core/periphery), for the better functioning of these interdependent networks.

Starting from the above considerations, the present volume aims to present new 'thoughts' and 'reflections' in this field, from three main perspectives: theoretical, methodological, and empirical. The next section contains an overview of the book with reference to the general theoretical background already provided in Sections 1.1 and 1.2.

1.3 New Accessibility Measures and Aspects: Theories, Methodologies and Empirical Analyses

1.3.1 Introduction

Regional Science has always been marked by a strong quantitative and model orientation. In particular, 'Location theory makes up the heart of regional science. Both theoretically and empirically, numerous contributions have been made in this framework in order to study the "where" and the "why there" of human activities, in regard to both firms and households. *Theoretically*, traditional location theory à la Weber and Lösch has been developed much further, by investigating spatial synergies (e.g. industrial complexes), spatial dynamics (e.g. innovation behaviour of firms, migration behaviour of households), and complex spatial systems (e.g. entropy and gravity models, (micro -)simulation analysis)' (Boyce et al. 1991, p. 2).

If we conceive of accessibility as expressed in formulation (1.1), its strong connection with the above-mentioned theories becomes straightforward, since the related analytical structure (see again equation (1.1)) is strictly linked to both the microeconomic theory of discrete choice models (i.e. logit models) and the macrosystem theory of entropy (i.e. spatial interaction models). Given the 'universal' role of logit/spatial interaction analysis in most (even dynamic) models adopted so far in Regional Science and Spatial Economics (see Anas 1983; Nijkamp and Reggiani 1992), it is not surprising to find the formal 'constancy' of the accessibility expression (1.1) emerging from the theoretical formulations displayed in Table 1.1.

Table 1.2 Accessibility, trade and locational behaviour: new measurements and frameworks

Theoretical Frameworks: Measurements of Accessibility	Methodological Frameworks: Locational Behaviour and Trade	Empirical Frameworks: European Freight Transport Networks
dynamic network accessibility (Chapter 2)	infrastructure characteristics for locational behaviour (Chapter 6)	logistic accessibility (Chapter 12)
functional/axiomatic accessibility (Chapter 3)	useful density of locational network economies (Chapter 7)	institutional accessibility (Chapter 13)
behavioural/economic accessibility (Chapter 4)	spatial integration of commodity and labour markets (Chapter 8)	institutional accessibility (Chapter 14)
	spatial equilibrium of trade (Chapter 9)	institutional accessibility (Chapter 15)
differential economic/ geographic accessibility (Chapter 5)	circularity dimension of organizational proximity (Chapter 10)	environmental accessibility (Chapter 16)
	regional active space (Chapter 11)	spatial/statistical accessibility (Chapter 17)

In a 'network' perspective with dynamic and complex, often uncertain, socioeconomic-physical characteristics, expression (1.1) probably models the steady-state of the network evolution (see Section 1.2.2). However, it could be interesting to evaluate if and in what situations the aforementioned accessibility/location theories need a complete 'network' framework, with reference also to methodological and empirical analyses.

In this context, the aim of the present book is to explore three main items/questions:

- *Theoretically*: Can we conceive of a dynamic complex accessibility able to also take into account the feedback effects of the networks?
- *Methodologically*: Is accessibility the cause and/or the effect of locational dynamic behaviour and trade economies?
- *Empirically*: Is accessibility a relevant 'latent' variable in the new spatial/organizational configurations of European freight transport networks?

Consequently, the individual contributions of the volume have been arranged according to three related main sections:

A) Theoretical Frameworks: Measurements of Accessibility
B) Methodological Frameworks: Locational Behaviour and Trade
C) Empirical Frameworks: European Freight Transport Networks

Table 1.2 gives the key points of each chapter within the basic structure of the book.

1.3.2 Theoretical Frameworks: Measurements of Accessibility

Part A is developed as follows. Martellato and Nijkamp (Chapter 2) suggest a new definition of accessibility taking into account the capacity of infrastructure and the intensity of use in a road network where users are classified in distinct groups. In particular, the authors show that accessibility may essentially be conceived of as an indicator for the steepness of the relationship between the traffic flow and the corresponding price.

Bröcker (Chapter 3) demonstrates the links between the economic potential formulation of accessibility and a spatial computable general equilibrium (CGE) model by calibrating his model for a system of 276 European regions. His work thus offers a fundamental theoretical economic framework for conventional accessibility indicators.

Miyagi and Susuki (Chapter 4) give a general definition of accessibility based on the axiomatic systems of accessibility and then show that the functional conventional form of accessibility can be compatible with the axiomatic system.

Finally, Vickerman (Chapter 5) concludes Part A of the book by considering the problems of accessibility in peripheral regions and by arguing that conventional measures fail to adequately identify the real constraints on peripheral regions and hence the economic effects of differing market structures. He then explores a few case studies in order to illustrate the issues discussed.

It seems clear from all these first contributions that there is a common effort to overcome the conventional accessibility formulations by moving towards new approaches embedding the dynamic economic effects of different market structures and network characteristics.

1.3.3 Methodological Frameworks: Locational Behaviour and Trade

The first contribution of Part B is by Forslund (Chapter 6). She addresses the issue of industrial location dynamics by comparing the regional location of economic activities. She adopts a niche model of leaders/followers where accessibility is incorporated – as an infrastructure attribute – in the resource capacity of a region for a certain economic/industrial sector. An empirical analysis is also presented here with reference to the relevance of high education intensity for the pattern diffusion of leads and lags in the joint Sweden-Norway area.

A further contribution to location dynamics is given by Johansson (Chapter 7), who also presents a theoretical analysis of accessibility, differentiated into intraregional and interregional accessibility. Accessibility is here determined by interaction costs and density of economic activities in a certain region, and hence is considered as a fundamental attribute of the economic milieu. Furthermore, Johansson emphasizes scale and agglomeration effects as driving forces for location decisions, by means of both theoretical and empirical analyses (with reference to Sweden). A follow-up, referring to the (quasi-) dynamic analysis of jobs location, is also presented.

McGregor (Chapter 8) then provides a further link between accessibility and spatial computable general equilibrium (CGE) models (see also Chapter 3). In particular, McGregor interprets accessibility as the spatial integration of both commodity and labour markets. He deals with the macroeconomic consequences – with reference to the real effects of both demand and supply disturbances – of these two key aspects of increasing accessibility (spatial integration of commodity markets/labour mobility) by means of numerical simulation analyses based on a CGE model parametrized with data from Scotland (UK).

A CGE model is again adopted by Hashimoto (Chapter 9) in order to develop a trade model – between two countries – here formulated as a non-linear complementarity programming model. Furthermore, this chapter also includes comparative static studies analysing the impact of trade polices, such as import tariffs, export taxes, export subsidies, import quotas and grants, as well as transportation costs. It is then clear that this model could also be used for simulating further trade policy and accessibility cost scenarios.

The next contribution is by Burmeister (Chapter 10) who considers the new role of transport infrastructure in regional development. She introduces the spatial dimension – in the network approach to production systems – through the concept of the circulatory dimension of proximity, thus overcoming the traditional accessibility concept of spatial propinquity. The determinants of proximity are as much the infrastructure (as a generic resource for circulation) as the organization and the degree of control of flows of goods, information and people.

In the same spirit Ratti (Chapter 11) continues the discussion on the relationship between space and innovation, by arguing that space, far from being a simple passive support, becomes an active element in the explanation of territorial development processes. He thus speaks of 'regional active space' by attributing to this concept the role of a true paradigm as well as an answer to the local-global debate. The regional active space is then presented as the result of different mutually interrelated regulation processes: the functional spaces of firms (market, production, and support space) together with the rules and the governance of the territoriality. We can then assume that different 'dimensions' of accessibility lead to the active space.

1.3.4 Empirical Frameworks: European Freight Transport Networks

The final part of this volume (Part C) is devoted to the empirical analysis of the emerging European freight transport networks, where accessibility – conceived of as 'institutional' access/barrier – is surely a relevant 'latent' variable.

Drewe and Janssen (Chapter 12) open this section by discussing the actual and future positioning of ports with the rise of product channel and transport logistics. They argue – in this framework – for a change from 'tonnage' to chains and value adding, as well from physical to logistic accessibility, and consequently for the transition from a competitive world of ports to a strategic cooperation of ports, based on complementarities. The analysis was carried out with reference to the North-Western European ports (Rotterdam, Hamburg, Le Havre, etc.)

Synergy and complementarity acting against conflicts and competition are also tackled by Pasi and Himanen (Chapter 13) with reference to the identification of the relationships between the main actors involved in the transport of goods between the Nordic Countries and the European mainland. Here accessibility – together with safety, sustainability and efficiency – is shown to be a goal of the road administration, 'different' for the four Nordic countries (Finland, Sweden, Denmark, Norway).

The Transalpine network – with reference to the impact of the Swiss 'barrier' of the 28-tonne weight limit for freight transport – is analysed in the following chapters. Müller and Maggi (Chapter 14) present an economic study whose theoretical framework follows a hedonic approach in order to identify the price effects of regulation. Their empirical results validate that the Swiss 28-tonne weight limit causes additional costs and price increases for Transalpine truck transport. These results indicate that in general the prevailing policy proposal relating to freight transport in Europe, i.e. the taxing of heavy vehicles, is a valid alternative to quantitative restrictions for promoting rail and intermodal transport.

Demilie, Dupuis, Jourquin and Beuthe (Chapter 15) present a multimodal freight transportation network model with the aim of analysing the above-mentioned problem of trucking regulation in Switzerland. The effects of the restriction are measured on the basis of a cost-minimizing analysis of transport flows between Italy and the rest of Europe. The network analysis is based on the Transeuropean network of roads and railways, and the chapter focuses on the substitution effects between road and rail, and on the choice of itineraries for bypassing Switzerland. The results again show that this restriction of 28-tonne weight reduces road freight transport on Swiss territory.

Intermodal substitution between rail and truck is also discussed by Campisi, Gastaldi and Reverberi (Chapter 16), but in an environmental perspective with reference to the Italian freight transport system. In particular, the authors estimate a Barnett translog cost function for a three-input transportation model. They also present numerical simulations with the aim of evaluating environmental benefits ensuing from the introduction of a given pollution tax in the Italian rail-truck competition. Their results show yet again that a tax policy tends to redistribute transport modal choice towards the more ecological rail systems.

Reggiani, Nijkamp and Tsang (Chapter 17) make a final contribution to this topic of the competition/substitution problem between rail and road in the European freight transport system, by analysing new network models able to forecast spatio-temporal patterns of different transport economic scenarios. They carry out sensitivity analyses – based on a comparative approach between logit and neural network models – in order to investigate the expected consequences of a rise in transport costs, due, for example to a European environmental tax on freight costs. The results highlight the sustainability of the two adopted approaches and thus the possibility of offering a 'range of values' to policy actors.

1.4 Conclusions

The conclusion drawn from this concise overview of the book is that not only has accessibility – and its relationships with locational behaviour and trade – not lost its 'traditional' importance, but it is also becoming a fundamental research issue for transport network economics. This volume brings together multiple dimensions of accessibility, mainly related to a dynamic (complex) economic network framework ranging from theoretical and methodological approaches to empirical studies. As a whole the various chapters show the 'richness' of the accessibility concept as well as its 'fruitfulness' in being a common 'basis' for analysing the emerging socio-transport-economic phenomena. In this context Spatial Economics and Regional/Transportation Science can be helpful for providing solid theoretical and methodological foundation and for developing both novel analytical insights and empirical contributions for future research.

Acknowledgement

The author is grateful for the financial support of the Italian CNR project n° 97.000.264.PF74 as well as the 40 percent and 60 percent MPI projects.

References

Anas, A. (1983), 'Discrete Choice Theory, Information Theory and the Multinomial Logit and the Gravity Models', *Transportation Research B*, vol. 17, no. 1, pp. 13–23.

Ben Akiva, M. and Lerman, S.R. (1979), 'Disaggregate Travel and Mobility Choice Models and Measures of Accessibility', in Hensher, D.A. and D.R. Stopher (eds), *Behavioural Travel Modelling*, Croom Helm, London.

Bibby, P. and Capineri, C. (1997), 'From Networks to Regional Development: Representations of Italian Regional Disparities', in Capineri, C. and P. Rietveld, (eds), *Networks in Transport and Communications*, Ashgate, Aldershot, pp. 193–215.

Boyce, D.E., Nijkamp, P. and Shefer, D. (eds) (1991), *Regional Science. Retrospect and Prospect*, Springer-Verlag, Berlin.

Bröcker, J. (1989), 'How to Eliminate Certain Defects of the Potential Formula', *Environment and Planning A*, vol. 21, pp. 817–30.

Bruinsma, F. and Rietveld, P. (1993a), 'Accessibility of Cities in European Infrastructure Networks: A Comparison of Approaches', *Research Memorandum 1993-18*, Department of Regional Economics, Free University, Amsterdam.

Bruinsma, F. and Rietveld, P. (1993b), 'Urban Agglomerations in European Infrastructure Networks', *Urban Studies*, vol. 30, no. 6, pp. 919–34.

Cattan, N. (1992), 'Air and Rail Accessibilities and Attractivities of European Metropolis', Paper presented at the 6th World Conference on Transport Research, Lyon.

Domanski, R. (1979), 'Accessibility, Efficiency and Spatial Organization', *Environment and Planning*, vol. 11, pp. 1189–206.

Domencich, T. and McFadden, D. (1975), *Urban Travel Demand: A Behavioural Analysis*, North Holland, Amsterdam.

Dupuy, G. (1993), 'Networks', *Flux*, vol. 11, pp. 42–7.

Forslund, U. and Johansson, B. (1993), 'Assessing Road Investments. Accessibility Changes, Cost benefit and Production Effects', ISRN KTH/RO/AR–93/2-SE, Royal Institute of Technology, Stockholm.

Fotheringham, A.S. (1983), 'A New Set of Spatial-Interaction Models: The Theory of Competing Destinations, *Environment and Planning*, vol. 15, pp. 15–36.

Fotheringham, A.S. (1986), 'Modelling Hierarchical Destination Choice', *Environment and Planning A*, vol. 18, pp. 401–18.

Gutiérrez, J. and Urbano, P. (1996), 'Accessibility in the European Union: The Impact of the Trans-European Road Network', *Journal of Transport Geography*, vol. 4, no. 1, pp. 15–25.
Hansen, W.G. (1959), 'How Accessibility Shapes Land-Use', *Journal of the American Institute of Planners*, vol. 25, pp. 73–6.
Ingram, D.R. (1971), 'The Concept of Accessibility: a Search for an Operational Form', *Regional Studies*, vol. 5, pp. 101–7.
Isquierdo, R. and Monzon, A. (1993), 'Capacité des Infrastructures et Accessibilité aux Reseaux. La Croissance du Transportation en Question', 12e Symposium International sur la Théorie et la Pratique dans l'Economie des Transports, Conférence Européenne des Ministres des Transports, CEMT-ECMT, Paris.
Leonardi G. (1978), 'Optimum Facility Location by Accessibility Maximizing', *Environment and Planning A*, vol. 10, pp. 1287–305.
Leonardi, G. (1985), 'Equivalenza Asintotica tra la Teoria delle Utilità Casuali e la Massimizzazione dell'Entropia', in Reggiani, A. (ed.), *Territorio e Trasporti*, F. Angeli, Milan, pp. 29–66.
Leonardi, G. and Tadei, R. (1984), 'Random Utility Demand Models and Service Location', *Regional Science and Urban Economics*, vol. 14, pp. 399–431.
Martellato, D., Nijkamp, P. and Reggiani, A. (1998), 'Measurements and Measures of Network Accessibility', in Button, K., Priemus, H. and P. Nijkamp (eds), *European Transport Networks*, E. Elgar, Glos, (forthcoming).
Matthes, N. (1994), 'Allocation of Mobile Communication Flows. From Micro-Economic Demand Theory to a Gravity Model', *The Annals of Regional Science*, vol. 28, no. 4, pp. 395–409.
Mattson, L.-G. and Weibull, J.W. (1981), 'Competition and Accessibility on a Regional Labour Market', *Regional Science and Urban Economics*, vol. 11, pp. 471–97.
Moretti, A. (1985), 'Le Misure dell'Accessibilità e le sue Utilizzazioni Territoriali', in Moretti, A. and A. Reggiani (eds), *Sperimentazioni e Analisi Comparate Riferite alla Misura di Acessibilità*, CLUP, Milano, pp. 25–52.
Neuburger, H. (1971), 'User Benefit in the Evaluation of Transport and Land Use Plans', *Journal of Transport Economics and Policy*, vol. 5, pp. 52–75.
Nijkamp, P. (1995), 'From Missing Networks to Interoperable Networks', *Transport Policy*, vol. 2, no. 3, pp. 159–67.
Nijkamp, P. and Reggiani, A. (1988), 'Entropy, Spatial Interaction Models and Discrete Choice Analysis: Static and Dynamic Analogies', *European Journal of Operational Research*, vol. 36, pp. 186–96.
Nijkamp, P. and Reggiani, A. (1992), *Interaction, Evolution and Chaos in Space*, Springer-Verlag, Berlin.
Nijkamp, P. and Reggiani, A. (1998), *The Economics of Complex Spatial Systems*, Elsevier, Amsterdam.
Nijkamp, P. and Van Geenhuizen, M. (1997), 'European Transport: Challenges and Opportunities for Future Research and Policies', *Journal of Transport Geography*, vol. 5, no. 1, pp. 4–11.

Pirie, G.H. (1979), 'Measuring Accessibility: a Review and Proposal', *Environment and Planning A*, vol. 11, pp. 299–312.
Pooler, J. (1995), 'The Use of Spatial Separation in the Measurement of Transportation Accessibility', *Transportation Research A* , vol. 29, pp. 421–27.
Reggiani, A. (1985b), 'Il Sistema della Mobilità in Lombardia: Sperimentazioni di Modelli di Interazione Spaziale con Riferimento alla Misura di Accessibilità', in Reggiani, A. (ed.), *Territorio e Trasporti*, Franco Angeli, Milan, pp. 214–27.
Reggiani, A. (1997), 'Towards New Models and Approaches in a European Transport Perspective', *Journal of Transport Geography*, vol. 5, no. 1, pp. 55–6.
Reggiani, A., (1985a), 'L'accessibilità nei Modelli di Interazione Spaziale', in Moretti, A. and A. Reggiani (eds), *Sperimentazioni e Analisi Comparate Riferite alla Misura di Accessibilità*, CLUP, Milan, pp. 5–24.
Rietveld, P. and Nijkamp, P. (1993), 'Transport and Regional Development', in Polak, J. and A. Heertje (eds), *European Transport Economics*, pp. 130–51.
Rietveld, P. and Bruinsma, F. (1998), *Is Transport Infrastructure Effective?*, Springer-Verlag, Berlin.
Suarez, C.G. (1995), 'Measuring Accessibility of Peripheral European Regions', *Paper presented at the ISINE/COST Conference*, Lausanne.
Sweet R.J. (1997), 'An Aggregate Measure of Travel Utility', *Transportation Research B* , vol. 31, no. 5, pp. 403–16.
van Veen-Groot, D., Van Delft, H. and Nijkamp, P. (1998), 'Globalization', *International Transport and the Global Environment, The Identifications of Trends and Driving Forces*, TEST Project Report, Free University, Amsterdam.
Vickerman, R.W. (1974), 'Accessibility, Attraction and Potential: a Review of Some Concepts and Their Use in Determining Mobility', *Environment and Planning A*, vol. 6, pp. 675–91.
Vickerman, R.W. (1994), 'Regional Science and New Transport Infrastructure', in Cuadrado Roura, J., Nijkamp, P. and P. Salva (eds), *Moving Frontiers*, Avebury, Aldershot.
Vickerman, R.W. (1995), 'Accessibility and Peripheral Regions', in Coccossis, H. and P. Nijkamp (eds), *Overcoming Isolation*, pp. 29–40.
Vickerman, R.W., Spiekerman, K. and Wegener, M. (1995), 'Accessibility and Regional Development in Europe', Paper presented at the NECTAR Conference, Espinho (Portugal).
Wachs, M. and Kumagai, T.G. (1973), 'Physical Accessibility as a Social Indicator', *Socio-Economic Planning Science*, vol. 7, pp. 327–456.
Weibull, J.W. (1980), 'On the Numerical Measurement of Accessibility', *Environment and Planning A*, vol. 12, pp. 53–67.
Williams, H.C.W. (1977), 'The Generation of Consistent Travel-Demand Models and User-Benefit Measures', in Bonsall, P.W., Hills, P.J. and M.W. Dalvi (eds), *Urban Transportation and Planning*, Abacus Press, Tunbridge Wells, pp. 161–76.
Williams, H.C.W. and Senior, M.L. (1978), 'Accessibility, Spatial Interaction and the Spatial Benefit Analysis of Land Use - Transportation Plans', in Karlqvist,

A., Lundqvist, L., Snickars, F. and J.W. Weibull (eds), *Spatial Interaction and Planning Models*, North-Holland, Amsterdam, pp. 253–87.
Wilson, A.G. (1971), 'A Family of Spatial Interaction Models and Associated Developments', *Environment and Planning A*, vol. 3, pp. 1–32.
Wilson, A.G. (1976), 'Retailers' Profit and Consumers' Welfare in Spatial Interaction Models', in Masser, I. (ed.), *Theory and Practice in Regional Science*, Pion, London, pp. 42–59.
Wilson, A.G. (1982), *Transport Location and Spatial Systems, School of Geography*, University of Leeds, Leeds.

Note

1. 'In this matrix, *interoperability* refers mainly to operational and technical uniformity that allows actors and operators to use and link various layers or components of a transport network. *Interconnectivity* is in particular concerned with horizontal coordination of and access to networks of a different geographical coverage. Finally, *intermodality* addresses the issue of a sequential use of different transport modes in the chain of transport. The Inter-Transport Matrix depicts essentially the integrating capabilities of various actors in the context of various ways of generating an added value in combined/coordinated network infrastructure' (see Nijkamp 1995, p. 164).

Part A
Theoretical Frameworks: Measurements of Accessibility

2 The Concept of Accessibility Revisited

DINO MARTELLATO AND PETER NIJKAMP

2.1 The Strategic Importance of Transport Accessibility

Our modern space economy offers many challenges and opportunities for regions, cities and firms in all countries. In the emerging European network, the spatial and functional position on networks and the benefits from network use are increasingly regarded as crucial success factors for regions, cities and firms. In this context, spatial accessibility plays a prominent role. In analyzing the impact of transportation on the economic performance of different regions and urban areas, there is a need to use an operational and measurable index of accessibility in space. Before focusing on this issue, we will first illustrate the importance of accessibility (research).

There is a long tradition in the available literature which recognizes the capacity of infrastructure to influence land use in a region or an urban area and even the level of (standard) economic performance indicators such as the unemployment rate or the growth rate. In Hansen (1959), for instance, there is an early attempt to investigate the relationship between the transport network on the one hand and the spatial structure of the economy on the other. It is obvious that more distant markets provide diminishing opportunities to economic agents, and therefore the provision of a new transport infrastructure and the regulation of land use are bound to change the likelihood of contacts between these agents and thus the degree of accessibility. Accessibility has played for several decades a major role in regional and transport research. More recent research has also focused on the relationship between urban form and (passenger) transport leading inter alia to the observation that in a compact city – where housing is dense and jobs are kept in the metropolitan area (Van Geenhuizen et al. 1994) – the use of public transport is higher and the consumption of gasoline lower than in decentralized metropolitan areas where jobs and houses are more dispersed. But also other issues, related e.g. to priority setting in infrastructure policy, come increasingly to the fore. For example, the enormous investments made in the last few decades in the construction of modern motorways have called the attention of various economists for the relationship between accessibility and growth performance of different regions. Dodgson (1974) and Linneker and Spence (1992), for example, have investigated the effects on accessibility and growth of the M62 motorway and the M25 London Orbital Motorway, respectively, while Cheshire (1990) was able to identify a significant contribution of improvements in road-based accessibility infrastructure (as a result of the extension of the EC during the 1980s) to changes in the economic performance of 100 European Functional Urban Regions.

New transport technologies (e.g. telematics systems, Maglev) which are at present being developed and which may contribute to energy efficiency, air pollution abatement or simply to transport system's efficiency are obviously expected to lead to a revival of the interest in the concept of accessibility (see also Martellato et al. 1995). New telecom networks may also be able to change the relative attractiveness of different cities as locations for specific industries and services. The pace of deurbanization – or the start of counter-urbanization – seems to be very much dependent on new networks. The accessibility changes perceived by entrepreneurs and households may hence drastically influence the spatial scene of society. There is thus certainly much scope for a thorough investigation of the accessibility concept.

In the past, accessibility has often been studied in the same analytical framework as trade barriers. As tariff barriers have a clear negative impact on trade across borders, it has long been recognized that their removal may change accessibility in a significant way. Keeble et al. (1982), for instance, have investigated the effects on regional accessibility of successive enlargements of the European Economic Community which have taken place from the sixties to the eighties. They found that the Community enlargements changed geographical accessibility, but it was not evident whether at the end the core periphery disparities were reduced or not.

In analyzing the accessibility effect of new networks, several caveats have to be taken into consideration. Bruinsma and Rietveld (1993), for instance, compared three different approaches for assessing accessibility and pointed correctly out that, although accessibility is generally believed to be an important – or even crucial – location factor, it is also true that many complementary factors are likely to affect the locational choices of entrepreneurs. There is however, clear empirical evidence from a number of studies based on broad surveys among individual entrepreneurs that stress the critical role of accessibility. According to the above mentioned authors, an investigation based on entrepreneurs' behavioural preferences – as revealed by decisions to relocate or not to relocate and to hire or not to hire more workers etc. – should be preferred to stated preferences in order to extract valid conclusions.

Besides conventional studies on the role of impediments in locational behaviour, it is note-worthy that recently new forms of transport improvement measures based on economic principles such as user charge principle have been proposed as a tool for coping with accessibility problems. In this context, road pricing systems – and other forms of road traffic regulation – have been much debated lately. If their welfare effects are already well understood (see, e.g. Emmerink et al. 1994; Verhoef et al. 1993), their impact on spatial accessibility is difficult to predict, and has certainly not yet been thoroughly investigated. It is furthermore not certain, whether the existing implementation problems (including public acceptance and social support) of such new policies can be solved. This means that it is not certain whether road pricing will be adopted on a large scale by many European cities in the next few years. Clearly, road pricing can anyway change the current pattern of relative road accessibility much in the same way as new infrastructure investments, high speed technology adoption and spatial economic integration can do. What we also have to bear in mind is that new road traffic regulations can be the result of a local policy authority decision and may concern only – or mainly – the intraurban policy scale. This means that changes in accessibility induced by regulations such as road pricing may be observed at a low geographical scale of analysis.

The above short list of illustrative examples serves to show the importance of the impact of new infrastructure investments, new technology adoption, spatial economic integration and public regulation on accessibility and hence on the economic performance of regions and cities. But the quantitative importance of this relationship is difficult to assess, because the uneven performance of regions and cities depends on a number of other factors as well. The assessment of the impact of the various factors listed above on accessibility is a complex undertaking for several reasons.

First, there are many definitions of accessibility and many ways of measuring it. The basic concept of accessibility of a location or site contains various aspects. Any specific location offers opportunities to agents who have chosen it. In principle, they can reach other locations and thus interact with other agents, but these opportunities are dependent on distance, prices of transport services, average transportation time (and time preference), and spatial position in a network. In this sense, it is clear that accessibility is an important argument in an actor's utility (or benefit) function.

Secondly, phenomena like economic integration and regulation entail the solution of political problems; they are sometimes slow to be accomplished, but can quickly be stopped. Other factors like infrastructure construction, new technology adoption and locational decisions often require large amounts of irreversible investment. This represents a sunk cost that a private firm would normally tend to forego or postpone, especially in the case of high risk and a low degree of competition in the market. This implies, in turn, that the installed transport capacity and the overall transport service demand of firms tend to change little, at least in the short run, when prices change. It is indeed well known that transport demand – being the expression of mobility needs resulting from production locations and human settlements – is mainly an indirect and derived demand. In the short run, the demand for transport services does usually not strictly depend on prices, even though one can imagine a transport demand curve relating services demanded to prices. In the short term, it seems plausible that – only to a certain extent – the mode composition of transport demand, the route choice and the time scheduling are more sensitive to relative prices.

In the third place, transport capacity and transport demand by firms are almost never in equilibrium. Seasonality of demand and peakloads imply by necessity both spare capacity and congestion. The well known relatively low profitability of transport activities implies a bias against the allocation of sufficient urban area to transport infrastructure and may thus lead to an insufficient supply of transport services. The existence of regulated prices and non-contestable markets and the concern for a sustainable environment bring about once more a structural capacity shortage. In conclusion, lack of accessibility appears to be a major bottleneck in infrastructure policy.

2.2 Measuring Accessibility

Accessibility is not an unambiguous concept. Many different definitions of accessibility and many ways to measure it can be found in the literature (see for a survey Pirie 1979; Isquierdo and Monzon 1993; Martellato et al. 1995; Vickerman 1995). The basic concept of accessibility of a location, as incorporated in many currently used indicators, seems to contain two different and complementary aspects. Any location in space offers economic possibilities to actors who have chosen it. Economic agents located in two different places can interact inter alia by physical movements. In doing so, they must however also make some effort, because in order to bridge geographical distance they must spend time – which obviously has a cost – and pay the service price. The time spent depends in turn, on velocity, density and congestion in the transport network at hand.

Both aspects, opportunities and effort, must be considered as a mutual relationship, and hence as elements of the definition of accessibility. It is plausible to assume that rational agents prefer the most accessible locations. Clearly, such a choice depends of course on the activities concerned. In general, we may argue that the agents' utility function will have as arguments at least both the positive opportunities and the effort costs of the location. They will not change their current location when the perceived utility – i.e. the net benefit – is at its maximum.

This economic concept of accessibility has evolved from previous and less operational concepts. These are related to a mere topological definition – where accessibility is inversely related to distance or to the cost to bridge it – or to the (unweighted) number of possibilities open to agents in a given location. In the latter case, accessibility is directly related to the number of potential interactions with agents located elsewhere.

If we assume that output cannot grow without an adequate growth in transport activities, i.e. without a proportional increase in physical movement of people, freight transport and communications, it is plausible that the volume of transport must increase – at least in the long run – more than its price. This means that the net benefit – i.e. economic accessibility - will increase. By the same token, two urban regions will gain a comparative advantage over other urban regions by simply increasing the relative number of possible interactions open to them at given costs and (or) by reducing their cost of movement. This simply means that the net benefit – i.e. economic accessibility – of agents located in those two urban areas will increase, because in that area firms will be encouraged to increase employment and production, with transport costs being lower and profits higher.

Traditional indicators of economic expansion, for a specific transport mode, usually employ a gravity function. The latter can be related to the well known potential function. This can clearly be seen by considering the following relationship between the number of actual trips between two spots, $_i$ and $_j$, and the gravitation force between them:

$$T_{ij} = \Gamma(D_i D_j / f(C_{ij})) \qquad (2.1)$$

where T_{ij} is the number of observed trips or shipments between $_i$ and $_j$, which is a function $\Gamma(.)$of the interaction possibilities which are proportional to the two disjoint masses D_i and D_j, weighted by a function f(.) of transport costs C_{ij}. The function f(.) is normally taken to be an exponential impedance function. We will return to this function later on.

By assuming that Γ has normally an inverse, we can rearrange terms and write a relationship between the potential and the gravitation index:

$$\Gamma^{-1} (T_{ij}) / Di = D_j / f(C_{ij}) \qquad (2.2)$$

By extending the previous function to all n networked urban areas, one obtains a relationship between actual and potential transport flows, for any urban region $_i$:

$$A_i = \Sigma_j(\Gamma^{-2} (T_{ij}) / D_i) = \Sigma_j (D_j / f(C_{ij})) \qquad (2.3)$$

The accessibility index A_i and the transport potential, which appears at the RHS of the equation, are then both related to actual flows T_{ij} through the function Γ.

Before focusing more on the economic accessibility (2.3), it is useful to consider a different representation of the cost (or, as we have called it, the effort component). In this particular case, accessibility is related to the average cost which agents incur to have access to city $_i$. It is a weighted average of n different costs, where the weights are relative potentials and adding to one. The cost accessibility is then:

$$C_i = \Sigma_j (C_{ij} [D_j / f(C_{ij})] / \Sigma_j (D_j / f(C_{ij})) \qquad (2.4)$$

It is worth noting that in this case accessibility has been defined by using potentials (which are relatively easy to measure) and costs. Usually, $f(C_{ij})$ is an exponential impedance function whose parameter is higher than 1.

A different, and probably polar, definition of accessibility can be obtained by stressing the second component, i.e. the number of possibilities which are really open to agents located in city $_i$. In this particular case, accessibility is defined by summing over $_j$ the masses in the n cities in equation (2.3), after defining the impedance function as follows:

$f(C_{ij}) = 1$, when C_{ij} < cost threshold (2.5a)

$f(C_{ij}) = 0$, when C_{ij} > cost threshold

or:

$f(C_{ij}) = 1$, when t_{ij} < time threshold (2.5b)

$f(C_{ij}) = 0$, when t_{ij} > time threshold

We notice that accessibility is defined here as the sum of those masses that fall below a critical threshold level of cost or time for city $_i$.

All three definitions given above share an inadequacy, however. In equations (2.3), (2.4), (2.5.a and 2.5.b), accessibility is assumed to be always a decreasing function of cost (or time) and this may be unsuitable for an index which must be related to a measurable variable.

Transport cost is not always easy to measure, because it includes, besides the unit price of transport service, a price of time. The first component has probably a quite large variation between individuals and firms. If one sticks to time only – as is the case for equation (2.5.b) – a similar argument holds; time may be a relevant variable for some individuals and firms, but not for all.

In the following section we will explore the relationship between total cost and service price. We will show that impedance and effort can be represented by means of a function of the unit price of transport service, an indicator which can be measured more easily than total unit cost or time.

2.3 The Impedance Function and the Cost of Movement

In this section we will consider the factors which, while related to the effort actors have to make to move themselves or commodities, should enter the formalization of the spatial impedance function and thus the accessibility index.

In the previous section we have implicitly defined impedance as a function of transport costs, $f(C_{ij})$. Our aim here is to focus on the elements which make up the cost of movement, defined in a broad sense. We will consider the cost elements as arguments in the same function $f(C_{ij})$ and thus in the accessibility index adopted.

All transport modes imply not only a payment of a monetary price, but also a non-monetary cost. Motorways are not always paid for when used by car drivers. For example, the charge per car and per kilometre is the highest in Austria, especially for lorries. It is lower in countries like France and Italy (about one tenth of the Austrian lorry unit toll). The Dutch, German and English motorways are toll free. Congestion which generates costs to the users of transport modes, is higher when the price is low and vice versa, other things being equal. It then seems necessary to add the cost of congestion to the monetary price. The congestion cost is dependent on the direct (or additional travel) time involved, the scheduling delay (e.g., change in departure time) and the risk of accidents.

The first obvious cost element is the unit price, which is the monetary component of travel cost. This includes also a non-monetary element, which is an opportunity cost related to the time spent in moving people and commodities over one unit of space and to the value of one unit of time. The second cost component varies in time and among agents, because the time required is related to congestion present at a certain point in time, in the mode and on the route concerned. It also varies among individuals and firms because of differences in the value attached by them to a unit of time. The third element of cost is, of course, distance. It is trivial that the cost of a trip or shipment of a certain commodity with a given transport mode, from $_i$ to $_j$, decreases when monetary and non-monetary cost and distance are reduced.

This discussion can be summarized by defining the cost of movement from $_i$ to $_j$, with mode $_m$, as follows:

$$C_{ijm} = d_{ijm} (p_m + t_m v) \tag{2.6}$$

where d is distance, p the monetary price per unit of distance, t the total time required for bridging a unit of distance, and v the average price of one unit of time. In other words, tv is the opportunity cost of travel time. Risks and schedule delay have been omitted here, but will be considered in a following section. As the time required by using a specific mode depends on the prevailing level of congestion and hence on the price paid - a higher price means, at least in principle, better infrastructure -, it is possible to relate time (t_m) directly to travel demand density or congestion (g_m) and indirectly to price (p_m). Congestion is, in a static context with given capacity, an externality produced by an individual driver on each other driver. The implicit function reads as follows:

$$t_m = t_m (p_m, g_m) \qquad (2.7)$$

We have already argued that the level of congestion is inversely related to the price. It is also inversely related to time because this variable also enters the definition of transport costs, as given in (2.18). Making again use of an implicit function, this relationship can be stated as follows:

$$g_m = g_m (t_m, p_m) \qquad (2.8)$$

It is safe to assume that congestion increases the time delay:

$$d\, t_m / d\, g_m > 0$$

and that time delay feeds back on congestion:

$$d\, g_m / d\, t_m < 0.$$

The latter expression may be interpreted in terms of a tradeoff relation between travel delay and the price to achieve for a trip maker the same utility level (or to maintain the same demand level). As there is a positive price effect on congestion:

$$d\, g_m / d\, p_m < 0$$

we conclude that:

$$d\, t_m / d\, p_m = (d\, t_m / d\, g_m)\, (d\, g_m / d\, g_m) < 0$$

The impedance function which relates the effort to the transport cost can then be modified as follows:

$$f(C_{ijm}) = f(p_m + t_m\, v)\, d_{ijm}) \qquad (2.9)$$

By using (2.7) and (2.8) we can also write (2.9) as a nested implicit function:

$$f(C_{ijm} = f(p_m + t_m\, (p_m, g_m\, (t_m, p_m))\, v)\, d_{ijm})$$

or, more briefly, we have the following impedance function:

$$f = f(p, t, d, v). \qquad (2.10)$$

Assuming in a static context d and v constant, we will focus mainly on p and t. This is indeed a general way of formulating the impedance function, as it incorporates congestion – and thus monetary and non–monetary costs – as an argument. It makes clear nevertheless, that space impedance – and thus effort – depends ultimately on three variables: the price p_m, the imputed price v and the distance d_{ijm}. The relationship with the price p_m is a complex one, because the latter enters the definition of cost directly and indirectly, i.e. through the nested implicit function through which time depends on price.

A higher price implies a lower level of congestion and this in turn implies a lower travel time, but a lower travel time implies higher accessibility and thus a larger transport demand for the mode concerned. It is not clear, in the end, whether a given increase of price is always able to generate a reduction of travel time or impedance and thus of transport cost. A reasonable hypothesis seems to be possible, however. By decreasing the price of one particular mode (m), impedance in the mode concerned increases until a point is reached where the demand effect is strong enough to compensate for the negative price effect, thus making impedance to get higher. This occurs because, when the price rises, transport time goes down until it reaches a minimum.

In order to obtain a better insight and understanding of this point, we take distance (d) and time price (v) as given and totally differentiate in (2.10), to obtain:

$$df = f_p\,dp + f_t\,dt \tag{2.11}$$

where f_p and f_t are partial derivatives of the impedance function. Besides, dp and dt are the absolute change of price and time in mode m (index omitted). The change in price, which produces the direct effect f_p dp, is obtained when a toll (or the cost of running the infrastructure of the mode (m) concerned) is charged by public authorities (or by firms).

The effect connected with a change of transport time is best appreciated when we relate time to the demand-supply balance instead of to p (as is done in equations (2.7) and (2.8)). By doing so, we highlight the second, or indirect, relationship between impedance and price.

In what follows we will assume that the change of transport time is proportional to the balance between the change in transport demand (dD) and the change in installed transport capacity (dS), as follows:

$$dt = a(dD - dS) \tag{2.12}$$

where a is a constant and where the index m is omitted.

We will now consider the nature of the demand function more closely. The demand for transport services for mode (m) reflects the locational decisions already taken by agents (transport demand is indeed a derived demand), the level of economic activity in the system and the relative price of mode (m). As we have argued in the preceding section, locational decisions bear on the relative degree of accessibility (real or only perceived) of different locations. This means that the feedback effect from accessibility to transport demand is expected to operate in the long run. Infrastructure and relocation imply almost irreversible investments and can be conceived of as 'slow' variables.

As congestion and transport time are 'fast' variables, the opposite is true for the relation from transport demand to accessibility. The demand level determines also the degree of accessibility in the short period. It is indeed common knowledge that a traffic jam makes it impossible to reach in a reasonable time even the closest destination. However, one traffic jam – and even many repeated traffic jams – do not necessarily induce an agent to relocate.

In conclusion, one can safely assume that, in the short run, only the level of activity (y) and the relative price of mode (m) can change. All this can be summarized by the following demand function:

$$D = D(u, y) \tag{2.13}$$

The variable u is the ratio of the price of mode m (p_m) relative to the average price of other available modes (p_n), i.e.:

$$u = p_m / p_n \tag{2.14}$$

We substitute for u in (2.13) and totally differentiate to obtain:

$$du / u = dP_m / p_m - dp_n / p_n = p_m^o - p_n^o$$

and then the equation for the demand effect on impedance becomes:

$$dD = D_u\, u\, (p_m^o - p_n^o) + D_y\, dy \tag{2.15}$$

where p_m° and p_n° are the percentage change of the prices of the two competing modes. In addition, dy is the absolute change of the activity level in the system. The partial derivatives of demand are D_u and D_y.

At this stage we can substitute for dD in equation (2.12) and then for dt in (2.11). The resulting decomposition of the impedance change then reads as follows:

$$df = f_p\, dp_m + f_t\, a\, D_u\, u\, (p_m^o - p_n^o) + f_t\, a\, D_y\, dy - f_t\, a\, dS \tag{2.16}$$

This equation adds to the direct effect of a change in the price of mode (m) an indirect effect related to any change of relative prices as well as an income effect. These are, respectively, the first three items appearing in the RHS of the equation. The sum of the first two items is the net price effect we were discussing above. The sign of the net price effect – i.e. the sum of the first two items – is ambiguous, because the direct one is negative while that of the indirect one is positive. The sign of the net price effect on impedance change thus depends very much on where the transport system is in terms of transport price. We may clarify this point by equating, in equation (2.11), (df) to zero. A necessary condition for the impedance to reach a constant or invariant value is:

$$dt / dp = - f_p / f_t \tag{2.17}$$

Clearly, for a maximum value also the second-order conditions would have to be investigated. The sign of the income effect and the capacity effect, the last two RHS parts of equation (2.16), are obviously positive. A sensible conclusion then seems to be that an increase in the price p_m yields a negative effect on the impedance (i.e., a positive effect on accessibility), if the system is at a price lower than that implied by the preceding equation and vice versa.

Before concluding this section, it is worth noting that the discussion so far – and, particularly equation (2.11) – has recognized the fact that two basic factors of change, viz., prices of different transport modes and activity levels in the system, have an impact on accessibility, mainly through transport demand and in the short run. In the long run, infrastructure investments and any other event capable of bringing about a change in capacity also have an impact on accessibility (equation 3.6). Accessibility changes and location decisions impact on transport demand, time and thus accessibility only in the long run and rather smoothly.

2.4 Accessibility and Prices

In the previous section a general assessment of the various factors which influence the accessibility pattern has been offered, which might be sketched as follows in Table 2.1:

Table 2.1 depicts the expected impacts of various accessibility-related parameters. The last pair of factors change smoothly and their variations can be assessed only in the long run. Agents seem indeed inclined to delay their reactions to a changing environment, because of incomplete information available to them and because of various economic and non–economic costs implied by physical movement.

Distance and capacity change only when adequate investments are accomplished. These are largely sunk costs which often imply a long gestation and bear a high risk. Public and private agents usually respond to the irreversibility of decisions by postponing them. Private entrepreneurs however, may be compelled to pile-up capacity, leading sometimes even to excess capacity, to defeat competitors. Once performed, these investments cause distance and capacity to jump up and down, respectively. This means that given their very nature, these effects may appear as a short run issue. Changes in relative prices of transport modes, when realized by agents, and changes in the general activity level may generate an impact on accessibility, even in the short run.

Table 2.1 Impacts of various accessibility-related parameters

symbol		SHORT RUN	LONG RUN discrete changes	LONG RUN smooth changes
p	monetary price	*		
y	economic activity	*		
d	level		*	
S	distance		*	
v	infrastructure			*
	capacity			*
	time price			
	location decisions			

The available literature seems to focus mainly on the accessibility and the transport demand effects of factors such as capacity expansion, activity level and location. The preceding section has, instead, tried to highlight the critical role of prices. Thus, it makes sense to relate accessibility indices to prices and to other variables as well.

Turning back to the indices of accessibility defined in Section 2.2, it may be interesting to find out how changes of relative prices of transport modes are bound to interfere with the relative accessibility of urban regions or cities.

The effects of the last five factors in the list above are seemingly predictable and known. New capacity increases accessibility, and economic growth and dispersion of locations increase transport demand and decrease accessibility, other things being equal. We argue however, that changes of transport prices may instead yield unpredictable results. If the price attached to time is sufficiently high and demand is sensitive to prices, there is a range on which the price increase yields higher accessibility. Outside that range any price increase is bound to decrease accessibility.

The importance of the actual outcome might be judged by considering the expected effects on congestion and accessibility of much debated traffic restraints like road pricing, motorway tolling and other legal constraints on road use in terms of pricing policies (in the latter case the price may be thought to be extremely high or even infinite).

We will now adopt the accessibility index defined above in (2.3) and represented here for convenience with a mode dimension (m) added to it:

$$A_i = \Sigma_m \Sigma_j (\Gamma^{-1}_m (T_{ijm}) / D_{im}) = \Sigma_m (\Sigma_j (D_{jm} / f_m(C_{ijm})) \qquad (2.18)$$

When a change in some relative prices of modes occurs, there are changes in the perceived impedance over different transport modes and cities. The net outcome reflects the mixes of available modes and the differences of price attached to time in different cities. We argue that the profile of cost functions C_{ijm} is not necessarily the same in the successive cities, because the mix of agents - and hence the price attached to time - varies across cities. This will be illustrated by a simple example.

In the following example (see Figure 2.1) we consider four different cities (A, B, C, D) and two transport modes. All cities have both modes except C.

(J)	links	2	4	3
1				
(M)	modes	2	2	2
1				
	(JM)	4	8	5
1				

Figure 2.1 A simple spatial transport network

We assume that the masses of the cities are normalized to unity and we adopt the following simple specification for $f_m(C_{ijm})$:

$$f_m (C_{ijm}) = a_0 - a_1 u + a_2 u^2 \qquad (2.19)$$

The parameter a_0 reflects the existing location pattern, the current activity level, the distance and the installed transport capacity in the links between city $_i$ and any other city, for mode $_m$. The available infrastructure is also represented by the number of modes available (M) in a city, a variable appearing in equation (2.18). The other two parameters, a_1 and a_2, reflect the net price effect on the effort which agents must make in different nodes. An increase of the relative price u of the two modes yields a negative effect proportional to u and a positive effect that is proportional to the square of u. The two effects are equal, when $u^* = a_1 / (2a_2)$ and the impedance (accessibility) reaches an extreme value.

We furthermore normalize the city masses and consider the average accessibility in order to facilitate the comparison between nodes with a different number (M) of available modes and links (J). The accessibility index then is:

$$A_i = \Sigma_m \Sigma_j 1 / (JM (a_{lm} - a_{2m} u + a_{3m} u^2)) \qquad (2.20)$$

We have defined impedance as a function of relative prices only (see equations (2.10) and (2.16)); it may then be conceived of as a parameter that is typical of agents located in a node rather than a quality of a certain link. It follows from the preceding expression that we can also omit the sum over $_j$.

Accessibility is then simply the average impedance perceived by agents in node i for the different modes available over there:

$$A_i = (\Sigma_m 1 / (a_{lm} - a_{2m} u + a_{3m} u^2) / M) \qquad (2.21)$$

The parameters of our simple numerical network illustration are now supposed to be as follows (see Table 2.2).

Table 2.2 Hypothetical values of parameters in our spatial transport network

	A	B	C	D
set 1				
a_0	3	3	2.998	3.04
a_1	-0.05	-0.05	-0.05	-0.05
a_2	0.025	0.023	0.027	0.005
u*	1	1.086956	0.925925	5
set 2				
a_0	3	3.1		3.2
a_1	-0.06	0.06		-0.06
a_2	0.01	0.01		0.01
u*	3	3		3

It should be noted that the example in Table 2.2 is a partial example, as for the sake of simplicity it is assumed that $b_t = 0$, so that 2.16) does not apply in full. We may now depict the resulting values of the accessibility index for the illustrative modes under consideration. Figures 2.2 and 2.3 show the average accessibility for different sets of parameter values and the resulting average level of accessibility in relation to the relative price u, based on (2.20). If the price of mode 1, relative to that of mode 2, rises, accessibility per mode and city changes as well. This is an obvious result, but more important is the fact that the relative accessibility in each city, which is an average of available modes, undergoes a change which alters the urban ranking.

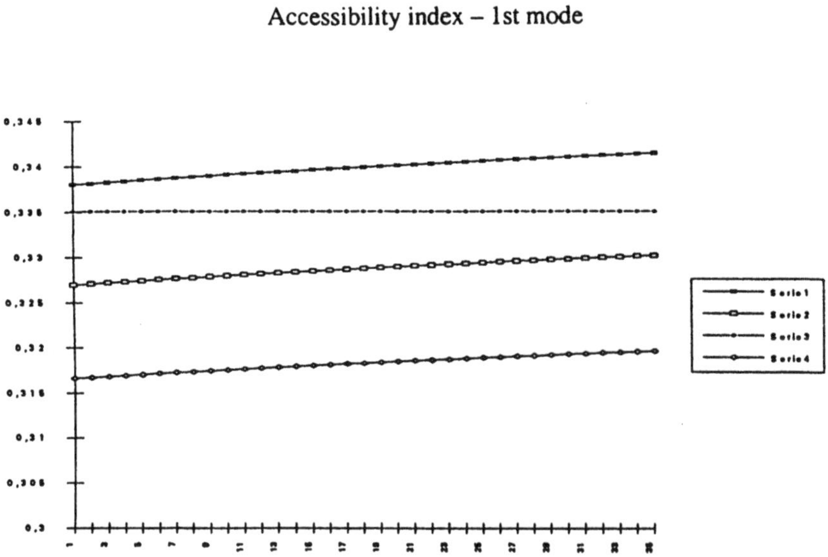

Figure 2.2 Values of accessibility index for different nodes and modes (set 1)

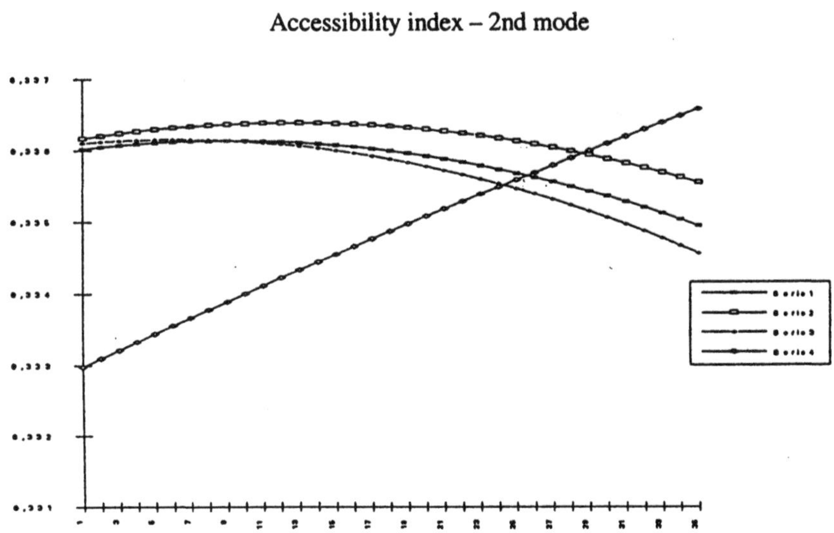

Figure 2.3 Values of accessibility index for different nodes and modes (set 2)

2.5 The Actual Accessibility Concept

So far we have been concerned with a gravitation (or aggregate) concept of potential accessibility in a transport system, where accessibility is related to the number of all potential interactions that agents located in any specific node perceive as possible by making some effort and by using some of the available transport modes. By adopting our definition (2.3) of accessibility in node $_i$, any increase of masses of the cities yields an increase of accessibility in the same node $_i$. This may not actually be the case, as a larger use of existing infrastructure implies a lower accessibility. We have already seen that the relation between potential accessibility and relative mode prices turns out to be nonlinear and spatially differentiated.

In the present section, we will offer a new approach, by focusing on actual accessibility – or cost of access – rather than potential accessibility. One might be more interested in the efficiency of the existing transport system per se or some of its nodes and links without paying attention to the potential interactions open to agents in specific locations.

Given a specific transport mode, the actual accessibility seems to be a concept more related to the actual costs of a trip or shipment, along a specific route, rather than to a weighted sum of all possibilities open to agents. The actual cost may refer to the monetary cost, or the value of time lost by congestion and the rescheduling time. In the following, we will only refer to road transportation, because congestion phenomena have in this case the highest importance.

A route between two distinct locations can be direct or indirect, and implies usually a combination of different links as well as the crossings of some urban areas or districts. We need then a definition suitable for measuring the ease of access to a network formed by links and nodes. Such a definition appears to be rather different from definitions of potential accessibility in the existing literature. In this case, we are not interested in aggregating over cities and modes, as done before by means of an impedance function. We aggregate instead over links and nodes, for a specific mode which is supposed to be a road. To find a suitable way of measuring the ease of road access, it seems sensible to focus on the possibility of choosing between alternative routes and time schedules that agents have. With regard to the various factors that may have an impact on accessibility, we now argue that distance, transport infrastructure, time price and locations can be assumed as given, at least in the short period.

Changes in relative prices of transport modes, when realized by rational agents, and changes in the general activity level exercise their impact on accessibility through demand, even in the short run. Implicitly, we take as given that the time required for a trip (or a shipment) and the schedule delay may be regarded as dependent on the degree of congestion, that is, on the various elements like route characteristics, route assignments, traffic composition and time schedule chosen by agents.

In the case of road transport this seems plausible from the fact that a regulation of the degree of congestion and pollution abatement can be obtained by either a tolling system or by rigid traffic restrictions, i.e. by imposing an infinite price on the road use. In order to establish a social optimum, public authorities regulate congestion by using prices in particular when capacity expansion is unfeasible or simply postponed. The reduction of travel time and the scheduled delay – or the improvement of the efficiency of the transport system – is a target which a public authority can indeed pursue even without changing transport capacity.

Prices can accomplish this task, even if road transport demand is rigid with respect to prices and transport costs. By changing the route and the time schedule, agents can try to minimize their travel costs. In the case of road networks, in particular congestion and regulations – and the related costs – are capable of interfering with the route choice and the time scheduling made by private car owners. If a bottleneck is foreseen and a driver can be late without much concern, he will be late, while a driver who cannot, will probably leave his home or working place earlier. We notice that we are making here an assumption different from that in the previous sections where prices were seen to influence demand.

We will offer now a simple illustration. We start from a hypothetical urban system formed by four nodes (A, B, C and D), where we assume that each city has four districts (e.g.: A_{11}, A_{12}, A_{21}, A_{22}; see Figure 2.4):

```
                        (A)____________(B)____________(D)____________(C)
                          \____________/ \____________/

(J)        links          2               2               3
      2
(M)        modes          1               1               1
      1
           districts      4               4               4
      4
```

Figure 2.4 A simple urban transport network

There are obviously many possible itineraries. Take the pairs of nodes A,B and A,C. One can travel directly from A to B, or vice versa. But to travel from A to C one can select the direct itinerary A,C or the indirect one A,B,C. In the latter case one has to consider the crossing of the urban area B. This is also the case when one leaves city A and enters C. The crossing of B can be made by using one of the various existing alternative combinations of urban segments. To reach B, from A, one might perhaps prefer AC plus CB.

What matters in the end is the cost of the travel to be defined in a moment. First, we will give some notation and list the various possibilities for the two pairs in our example:

C_{AB}	travel cost in the direct link A, B
C_{AC}	travel cost in the direct link A, C
C_{BC}	travel cost in the direct link B, C
C_{BB}	travel cost for crossing B
$C_{AB} + C_{BB} + C_{BC}$	travel cost in the indirect link A, C

By choosing particular ways of crossing cities, one can identify two possible complete itineraries out of the great many options available:

$C_{A12} + C_{AC} + C_{B11}$	itinerary A, B
$C_{A11} + C_{AB} + C_{B11} + C_{B12} + C_{BC} + C_{C21}$	itinerary A, C.

It may be possible to argue that in measuring actual accessibility only the effort matters, if we are interested in measuring the ease of access or the efficiency of the existing transport facilities. Some aspects which seem to be worth considering are the following:

- Travel costs change with the time required or the degree of congestion in a route.
- There are often many routes and itineraries available, and travellers choose rationally based on their guesses about the cost involved.
- There is an aggregation problem. If we use costs, we can solve it and aggregate over links and nodes; otherwise, we cannot.
- Only total costs matter, because the decision to move, has already been taken. We then focus on actual, not potential accessibility.
- The possibility of rescheduling is obvious. If there is congestion, a traveller arrives in time at his destination only by leaving earlier. Otherwise, he will be late.
- Costs are equal to operating costs and tolls (which might differ for different users), when the number of users is below a given capacity level. Above the capacity level they increase more than proportionally.
- There are heterogeneous drivers in relation to the motives of their decision to move (work, shopping, leisure, school, etc.) and to the type of occupation, etc. It seems however, more suitable to distinguish between fast car drivers, slow car drivers, and lorries. Congestion costs (time required and schedule delay) change when the mix of drivers changes, since there are cross-congestion effects.

To show the number of all possible itineraries in the example above, it may be helpful to consider the following table (the 'criss-cross table') where available links and city-crossings are arranged (see Table 2.4) and they are all equally feasible.

Travel costs are obtained by adding to the monetary component (the toll and the car operation cost) the non-monetary component. The latter is the time spent on travelling times the price of time plus the scheduling delay conveniently priced. The time spent on travelling is obtained by adding to the time required without congestion the time spent in traffic jams. The scheduling delay stems from changes in departure time.

There is a substantial amount of literature (e.g. Arnott et al. 1992, 1994; Henderson 1977; Vickrey 1969) assuming that travel costs are additive and linear in travel time and scheduling delay, at least in equilibrium. The maintained hypothesis is that the system is in equilibrium when no traveller can reduce his travel costs by altering the route and his travel time. In this case, travel costs of different groups of travellers are a linear function of the number of travellers, the normal time and the toll. It seems however more appropriate to assume a nonlinear relation and an elastic flow with respect to costs on a specific route. Changes in the road density, reassignment, rescheduling and carpooling are examples of phenomena capable of making, in regard to costs, the number of cars in a certain point and in a certain moment more flexible.

Table 2.4 A criss-cross table of the urban transport network

D	A	B	C	
A	A_{11} A_{12} A_{22}	AB	AC	
B		B_{11} B_{12} B_{22}	BC	
C			C_{11} C_{12} C_{22}	CD
D				D_{11} D_{12} D_{22}

A general impedance function relating travel costs to density, for a specific group (g) and for a given mode and route (r = AB, AC, BB, etc.), might be defined by adding to the specific monetary component p_{rg}, a new component related to the travel time and the schedule delay. It is safe to assume that, after a certain density threshold, the costs that any group of travellers incurs for waiting at a bottleneck and for the change in the departure time are an increasing (decreasing) function of density (velocity), given the characteristics of the route, its own peculiarities, the time schedule, and the mix of user groups.

The capacity limit, above which any flow increase implies congestion and thus extra travel time and rescheduling, has usually been investigated by traffic engineers (see, on this point also Nijkamp and Vleugel 1993). The number of vehicle-kilometres travelled by all vehicles in a particular route (r) without congestion is supposed to be equal to S_r. This is a measure of the flow level on route (r). The implicit function relating travel costs per kilometre to the flow level is:

$$C_{rg} = p_{rg} \qquad \text{when:} \quad \Sigma_{h=1,G} D_{rh} < S_{r*}$$

$$C_{rg} = p_{rg} + (\Sigma_{h=1,G} \Omega_{rgh}(D_{rh}) \quad \text{when:} \quad \Sigma_{h=1,G} D_{rh} > S_{r*} \qquad (2.22)$$

where G is the total number of groups of drivers and $\Omega' > 0$. The value of the implicit function Ω_{rgh} (D_{rh}) for a group 'g' different from group 'h' is the cross–congestion cost (i.e. the impact of group 'h' density on drivers of group 'g'), while for g = h the same function gives the own congestion effect (i.e. the impact of group 'g' density on the drivers of the same group). The presence of a private cost and a cost inflicted to others implies that C_{rg} is the marginal cost of a vehicle conditional to the mix of groups. This is further depicted in Figure 2.5a and 2.5b.

Figure 2.5 (panel a) below gives an example for two routes, r and s, respectively. Notice that the slope of any upward bending tail reflects the physical characteristics of the route, the weather conditions, the peculiarities of the group (g) concerned and the mix of groups which are found on the route. In our picture, the latter is assumed as given.

Accessibility, defined as ease of access to a certain route, is not constant. It also differs from one group of users to another. This means that it is bound to change with the mix of groups found on the road, and over time. By indicating by W_{rg} (t) the share of vehicles of group (g) in a certain moment (t) of time, one can define the average total marginal cost conditional to the traffic composition, i.e. to time as a weighted sum:

$$C_r(t) = \Sigma_{g=1,G} C_{rg} W_{rg}(t) \qquad (2.23)$$

By allowing the time index to change, the function describes the distribution of transport cost in relation to the composition of traffic flows, i.e. to time.

Turning now to Figure 2.5 (panel b), one can say that, from the point of view of group (g) and given a specific mix, the relevant routes (r) and (s) have different degrees of actual accessibility.

In Figure 2.5, at point S*, the costs on the two routes are equated, and there is no unused route (user equilibrium). However, accessibility is not at its maximum, so that the system is not at its optimum (i.e. the second Wardrop principle does not hold). With a flow below S*, route r is more efficient than route s, even there is some congestion. Above that limit, the opposite is true, in the time period (t). If the drivers of the group (g) are perfectly informed and behave rationally, they should choose route (r) for a flow lower than S*, and route (s) when the flow is above S*. At S*, the journey times on the two routes are equal and less than those experienced by any single vehicle on any unused route (this is Wardrop's first principle).

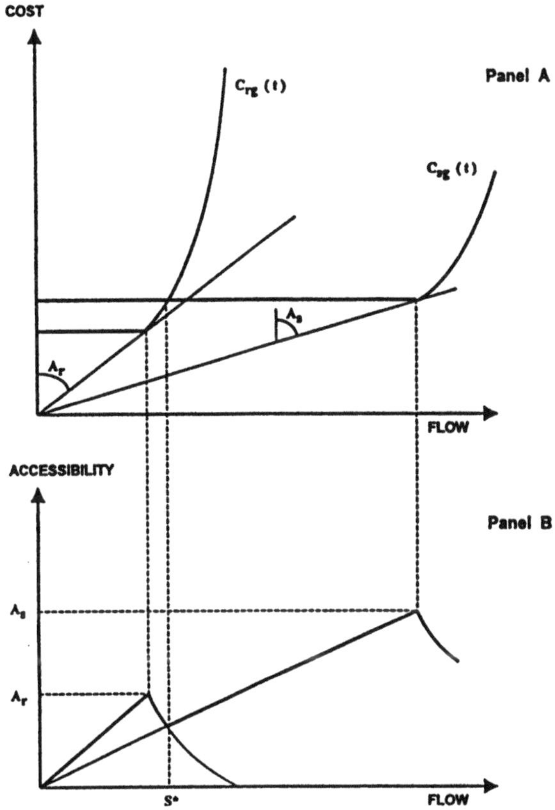

Figure 2.5 Cost and accessibility in relation to traffic flow

Assuming that this is the case, we can address the problem of measuring actual accessibility for the same group in the connection between nodes A and B. In doing so, we can observe that the rising cost that accompanies the flow increase above the capacity limit is essentially the consequence of the increase in the use of the resource time. In other words, above a critical number of vehicle-kilometres, any increase in the flow is accompanied by an increase of time, i.e. a reduction of velocity. It is surprising that the similarity between the (rising) production price of an industry and the (rising) travel cost on roads has not been recognized in the literature thus far. A road, the cars and the drivers deliver transport services incurring costs (some of which are imputed costs) much in the same way an industry does in its production activity.

The angle with the vertical axis spanned by any point in the envelope curve (heavily shaded in Figure 2.5, panel a.) indicates the average cost at which the actual user flow is routed. Above a certain threshold, the cost increases with the use, a phenomenon which resembles the increasing supply price at which a firm or a sector sells its output.

The bold curve corresponds to the optimal choice and entails a yes-no assignment pattern: i.e. everybody on route r until S* and every S-S* on route s, if demand is above that threshold. This would be an application of Wardrop's second principle. If this flow pattern is actually realized, then the profile of actual accessibility may easily be drawn. The angles are reported in panel b of the same figure which depicts the level of actual accessibility, under the stated assumption of a social optimum.

Each angle is the demand level divided by the cost defined above and gives the index of actual accessibility for the road link or crossing concerned and for the group concerned, given the mix of users. The elementary accessibility index is then:

$$A_{rg}(t) = \frac{D_{rg}(t)}{C_{rg}(t)} \tag{2.24}$$

By adopting the appropriate use shares as weights, we can aggregate over groups, in order to obtain the following accessibility index by route:

$$A_r(t) = \Sigma_{h=1,G} \frac{D_{rh}(t)}{C_{rh}(t)} \frac{D_{rh}(t)}{\Sigma_{g=1,\,G} D_{rg}(t)} \tag{2.25}$$

or, alternatively, the accessibility index by user group:

$$A_g(t) = \Sigma_{r=1,R} \frac{D_{rg}(t)}{C_{rg}(t)} \frac{D_{rg}(t)}{\Sigma_{r=1,R} D_{rg}(t)} \tag{2.26}$$

Notice that the first term appearing in both equations is decreasing with a road use exceeding the limit S_r, that is when the cost increase is more than proportional to the increase in use. Somewhere, the cost is simply the monetary price and in this instance the index is easy to measure. Above the capacity limit, it implies extra travel time and some schedule delay, which is more difficult to assess.

Accessibility is once again related to prices and costs, not only to capacity or use. As is apparent from panel b of Figure 2.5, it goes up and down. Points A_r and A_s are the only ones known. In general, it can be $A_r > A_s$ or vice versa, and actual accessibility is continuously moving below the two maxima. Accessibility may be very low, whatever the maximum. As users are not perfectly informed about the current congestion, nor are they rational, they may be found simultaneously on all routes of the criss-cross table. This occurs also, because they cannot coordinate their decisions. The co-ordination failure occurs, even if they were perfectly informed, since they cannot switch freely across routes. Aggregation is thus always necessary because the lack of information and coordination makes it unlikely that the optimal yes–no pattern of use does occur in practice.

By aggregating over groups and routes, one arrives as an index of overall accessibility, conditional to the mix:

$$A(t) = \Sigma_{h=1,G} \Sigma_{r=1,R} \frac{D_{rh}(t)}{C_{rh}(t)} \frac{D_{rh}(t)}{\Sigma_{g=1,G} \Sigma_{s=1,R} D_{sg}(t)} \qquad (2.27)$$

All stated indexes of accessibility are conditional on the mix of groups of users, as the cost component C_{rh} (h) is a function of traffic composition (equation (2.22)). Actual accessibility can indeed not be measured with a time invariant index, as is the case with other traditional indexes. It is thus obvious that the ease of access changes over time.

An absolute index on actual accessibility may perhaps be obtained by transforming the discrete index A(t) into a density function of accessibility and then by integrating over time. As a practical alternative, it seems plausible to adopt some approximated measure of the time profile of the accessibility index. As a further step towards a viable analysis one might only consider the lower value observed on the relevant segment, i.e. for each specific link or city-crossing. To get an assessment of actual accessibility of a route, from the point of view of one particular group of user, one has to consider usually more than one link and more than one node crossing. The lowest value (the minimum minimorum) assumed by the index at different segments may then give a rough indication of actual accessibility.

References

Arnott R., de Palma, A and Lindsey, R (1992), 'Route Choice with Heterogeneous Drivers and Group-specific Congestion Costs', *Regional Science and Urban Economics*, vol. 22, pp. 71–102.

Arnott R., de Palma, A. and Lindsey, R (1994), 'The Welfare Effects of Congestion Tolls with Heterogeneous Commuters', *Journal of Transport Economics and Policy*, May, pp. 139–61.

Bruinsma F. and Rietveld, P. (1993), 'Urban Agglomerations in Europe Infrastructure Networks', *Urban Studies*, vol. 30, pp. 919–34.

Bruinsma F. and Rietveld, P. (1993), *Accessibilities of Cities in European Infrastructure Networks: a Comparison of Approaches*, Research Memorandum 18, Vrije Universiteit, Amsterdam.

Cheshire P. (1990), 'Explaining the Recent Performance of the European Community Major Urban Regions', *Urban Studies*, vol. 27, pp. 311–33.

Dodgson J.S. (1974), 'Motorway Investment, Industrial Transport Costs, and Sub–regional Growth: A Case Study of the M62', *Regional Studies*, vol. 8, pp. 75–91.

Emmerink R., Axhausen, K.W., Nijkamp, and Rietveld, P. (1993), *Concentration, Overreaction, Market Penetration and Wardrop's Principles in an ATIS Environment*; Discussion Paper TI 93–229, Tinbergen Institute, Amsterdam.

Emmerink R., Nijkamp,P. and Rietveld, P. (1994), *How Feasible Is Congestion Pricing?*, Discussion Paper TI 94–62, Tinbergen Institute, Amsterdam.

van Geenhuizen M., Banister, D. and Nijkamp, P. (1994), 'Transport and Communication Technologies in Next Decades: Barriers to Adoption and Potential Impacts', Paper presented at 34th European Congress of the Regional Science Association, Groningen 23-26 August.

Hansen, W.G. (1959), 'How Accessibility Shapes Land Use', *Journal of the American Institute of Planners*, vol. 25, pp. 73–6.

Henderson V. (1977), *Economic Theory and the Cities*, Academic Press, New York.

Isquierdo R. and Monzon, A. (1993), *Capacité, des Infrastructures et Accessibilité, aux Reseaux; La Croissance du Tranportation en Question*, Conference Européenne des Ministres des Transports, 12me Symposium International sur la Theorie e la Pratique dans L'Economie des Transports, CEMT-ECMT, Paris.

Keeble D., Owens P. and Chris T. (1982) 'Regional Accessibility and Economic Potential in the European Community', *Regional Studies*, vol. 16, pp. 419–32.

Linneker B.J. and Spence, N.A. (1992), 'An Accessibility Analysis of the Impact of M25 London Orbital Motorway on Britain', *Regional Studies*, vol. 26, pp. 31–47.

Martellato D., Nijkamp, P. and Reggiani, A. (1995), *Measurement and Measures of Network Accessibility*; Discussion Paper, Tinbergen Institute, Amsterdam.

Nijkamp P. and Vleugel, J.M. (1993) 'Assessment of Capacity in Infrastructure Networks: A Multidimensional View', *Transportation Planning and Technology*, vol. 17, pp. 301–10.

Pirie G.H. (1979), 'Measuring Accessibility: A Review and Proposal', *Environment and Planning A*, vol. 11, pp. 299–312.

Verhoef E., Nijkamp P. and Rietveld P. (1993), *Second-best Regulation of Road Transport Externalities*; Discussion Paper TI 93–209, Tinbergen Institute, Amsterdam.

Vickrey W.S. (1969), 'Congestion Theory and Transportation Investment', *The American Economic Review* (Papers and Proceedings), vol. 59, pp. 251–61.

Walters A.A. (1977) 'Congestion', in Eatwell, J., Milgate, M. and P. Newman (eds), *The World of Economics – The New Palgave*, Macmillan, London, pp. 126–33.

3 Measuring Accessibility in a General Equilibrium Framework

JOHANNES BRÖCKER

3.1 Introduction

Indicators of accessibility have a wide range of applications in empirical research in transport economics and economic geography. As an example, comparing benchmark and counterfactual accessibility indicators is common practice in the evaluation of transport infrastructure investments. Accessibility indicators have also been widely used in regression analyses trying to figure out determinants of industrial location and regional growth. A further field of application is in the prediction of spatial effects of economic integration. The basic idea is that integration reduces economic distance and therefore favours regions gaining a comparatively large increase of input and output market accessibilities (Clark et al. 1969).

A typical measure of accessibility used in empirical research is the economic potential index. For a region r the potential P_r is defined as

$$P_r = \sum_s M_s\, f(c_{rs}).$$

M_s is the 'mass' in s, c_{rs} is the economic distance between r and s, and $f(c_{rs})$ is a decreasing function of distance. $f(c_{rs}) = \exp(-\beta c_{rs})$ or $f(c_{rs}) = c_{rs}^{-\partial}$ are typical specifications. If P_r measures a market potential, the mass variable M_s denotes the size of the market in s. The distance c_{rs}can be a composite of several components like out-of-pocket costs, time costs, tariffs and non tariff barriers to trade, and costs for bridging any kind of cultural distance.

Though the potential measure is a powerful tool in applied research, its theoretical underpinning remains obscure. Furthermore, it is by no means obvious, how a certain increase of the potential index resulting from a decrease of transport costs on a transport link, say, should be translated into economic meaningful quantities like income, employment or even welfare. It is therefore desirable to develop accessibility measures having a clear economic meaning, and being based on an explicit behavioural theory of economic interaction in space.

The aim of this chapter is to show how this could be done in the framework of a spatial computable general equilibrium model. The plan of the chapter is as follows. The design of the model is described in Section 3.2. Section 3.3 returns to the accessibility issue. It shows how the prices appearing in the model are related to economic potential indicators as well as to the theoretical concepts of welfare economics. Section 3.4 shows that the parsimonious design of the model allows for a calibration with a very limited data base. In fact, the information required for a potential analysis is almost sufficient for a calibration of the general equilibrium model. Section 3.5 presents results from an application of the approach to regional data for Europe. The chapter concludes by assessing the merits of the approach and hinting to possible extensions.

3.2 A Spatial Computable General Equilibrium Model

3.2.1 A Non-formal Introduction

A spatial computable general equilibrium model is characterized by the set of agents assigned to each region, by the technologies, preferences and endowments assigned to these agents, by the delineation of markets and by the market structure.

In our model there is a set of firms in each region producing a bundle of horizontally diversified goods, using labour, capital, and a composite good as inputs. There is a large number of brands making up this bundle of goods. For firms and households buying goods, different brands are imperfect substitutes. Firms supplying an individual brand act as monopolistic competitors. They maximize profits, taking the price responsiveness of demand for the offered brand into account. Market entry is free, and the number of brands offered in the market is endogenously determined by the condition that firms earn zero profits. The intermediate input of goods is composed of all the brands available on the market. All brands appear symmetrically in the production function. That means there is no preference for a specific brand. The marginal productivity of a single brand is decreasing, such that higher product diversity of inputs increases productivity.[1]

The factor payments of regional firms go to regional households expending their income on goods. Households have strictly convex preferences. Hence they prefer diversified over concentrated consumption bundles. The households in the model represent all final demand, including public consumption and investment.

The spatial dimension is introduced by assuming trade to be costly. Trading goods implies costs, which increase with the distance between producer and consumer.

We now describe this structure in formal terms.

3.2.2 *Firms*

We think of production as a two-stage process. In the first stage firms in a region r produce a homogeneous malleable good – called the 'raw output' – by a Cobb-Douglas production function (CD function), using labour, capital, and a composite good as inputs. Hence, for a price taking firm the minimal cost per unit raw output in region r is

$$p_r = \mu_r w_r^{\alpha} z_r^{\beta} q_r^{\gamma}, \qquad \alpha + \beta + \gamma = 1. \tag{3.1}$$

w_r, z_r and q_r denote the wage rate, interest rate and price of the composite good in region r, respectively. The parameters α, β and γ are the partial production elasticities. They equal the shares of labour, capital, and intermediate inputs, respectively, in the value of output. Due to limited information we have to assume these parameters are identical for all regions. Regional differences in the level of productivity are represented by the parameters μ_r. Note that given a constant input vector, the level of output is proportional to the inverse of μ_r. The parameters μ_r have to be calibrated. In our calibration we allow μ_r to vary between countries, but not between regions within a country. The reason is again lack of information: We use national data on GDP, which only allow for calibrating national μ-parameters.

In the second stage, firms take the raw output as an input for producing different brands of final goods.[2] For producing x units of a certain brand the firm requires f + vx units of raw output. This means that we assume a linear cost function, with f denoting fixed cost and v denoting variable unit cost, both expressed in terms of units of raw output. Using the Amoroso-Robinson relation, a profit maximizing firm will set the price

$$\pi_r = \frac{\sigma}{\sigma - 1} v p_r \tag{3.2}$$

for final goods, if it takes p_r as given. σ is the price elasticity of demand, which is assumed to be larger than unity. If free entry drives profits to zero, π_r must equal average costs. Hence

$$v + \frac{f}{x} = \frac{\sigma}{\sigma - 1} v.$$

Solving for x yields

$$x = \frac{f}{v}(\sigma - 1).$$

From this we obtain l_r, the number of brands produced in region r, as

$$l_r = \frac{X_r}{\sigma f}, \tag{3.3}$$

with X_r denoting the quantity of raw output in r.

A unit of the composite good is composed of individual brands according to a symmetrical index with constant elasticity of substitution (CES index). Expressing this in dual form means that q_s, the price per unit of the composite good in region s, equals

$$q_s = \left[\sum_r l_r \, (\pi_r \, \tau_{rs})^{1-\sigma} \right]^{\frac{1}{1-\sigma}}. \tag{3.4}$$

Here σ denotes the elasticity of substitution between different brands. $\tau_{rs} > 1$ is a markup factor representing costs for transferring goods from r to s. If the total number of brands is large (strictly speaking, if it is infinity), $-\sigma$ is the price elasticity of demand for an individual brand, the same which appears in 3.2.

3.2.3 Households

Households in region r earn an income y_r by renting out the services of the labour and capital, which they own, to regional firms. Due to limited information in the empirical application, we assume that all factor services used by regional firms come from regional households. That means there are no interregional flows of factor incomes. This is not realistic, in particular with regard to capital income, but there is no other choice, given the fact that the regional distribution of capital income is unknown.

Households spend this income totally for buying goods. They have symmetrical homothetic CES preferences over brands with elasticity of substitution σ, the same as in the aggregator for firms' inputs. Hence, if households in r earn the income y_r, then their attainable maximal utility is

$$u_r = y_r / q_r \,. \tag{3.5}$$

Relative changes of u_r equal Hicksian measures of relative variation, as shown below.

3.2.4 Costs of Interregional Trade

As already noted, trade costs are not just transport costs, but any kind of transport and communication costs, costs for overcoming trade barriers etc. We call them trade costs, for short. Usually trade costs are assumed to depend on the quantity of goods traded. Some costs of interregional transfer, especially costs of information exchange and insurance costs, depend on the value rather than the quantity traded, however. Letting trading costs depend on the value of trade makes the model much simpler, and we therefore prefer this assumption.

We introduce two kinds of trade costs: costs related to geographical distance, and costs for overcoming impediments to international trade. If region r belongs to country k and region s to country l, then the markup factor representing trade costs is

$$\tau_{rs} = \exp(\eta g_{rs})\, \delta_{kl}\, .$$

g_{rs} denotes geographical distance. η measures the costs per unit of distance as a share in the good's value. $(\delta_{kl} - 1) \geq 0$ is a tariff equivalent for all costs stemming from the fact, that a good has to be exported from country k to country l. These include tariffs, but also, and more important, all costs stemming from non-tariff barriers like costs due to language differences, costs for bureaucratic impediments, time costs spent at border controls and so forth. $\delta_{kl} = 1$ for $k = l$, of course, but it is suggested to be strictly larger than unity for $k \neq l$, even if countries k and l are both members of the EU.

We can express international trade impediments as distance equivalents. The distance equivalent of an impediment δ_{kl} is equal to $\log(\delta_{kl})/\eta$. Thus, we can write

$$\tau_{rs} = \exp(\eta c_{rs}) \qquad (3.6)$$

with the generalized distance

$$c_{rs} = g_{rs} + \log(\delta_{kl})/\eta.$$

In a general equilibrium one must specify, where trading costs are going. Any expenditure must appear as a proceed somewhere in the system. For the sake of simplicity, we assume that trading costs for goods arriving in s are paid to a 'transport service', doing the job by consuming composite goods and making no profit. In other words, expenditures for goods are partly used for buying the goods going into production and consumption, and partly for buying goods going into the transport service. We neglect tariff receipts, for the sake of simplicity.

3.2.5 Equilibrium

From the specified technologies, preferences and market structures we can now derive a general equilibrium for a closed static system of regions. Each region is endowed with a fixed amount of labour and capital owned by households residing in the region. Households spend all their factor income, maximizing their utility. Firms act under Chamberlinian monopolistic competition. Goods and factor prices as well as product diversity adjust until markets are cleared and profits are driven to zero.

The equilibrium system consists of the composite price equations (3.1) and (3.4) and three equilibrium conditions, one for the goods markets, one for the labour markets, and one for the capital markets. Denoting the output value as $V_r = X_r p_r$,, and using (3.2) and (3.3), equation (3.4) is written as

$$q_s = \left(\sum_r \phi V_r p_r^{-\sigma} \tau_{rs}^{1-\sigma} \right)^{\frac{1}{1-\sigma}} . \tag{3.7}$$

Constants are gathered in ϕ.

Goods market equilibrium requires that, for each region r, the output value V_r equals the value of demand for goods from region r. It is a bit tricky to see that this leads to the equations

$$V_r = \sum_s \frac{V_r (p_r \tau_{rs})^{-\sigma}}{\Sigma_t V_t (p_t \tau_{ts})^{-\sigma}} V_s . \tag{3.8}$$

To obtain this result, note that the CES form in (3.4) implies that d_{rs}, the demand for a single brand from r per unit of composite good bought in s, equals

$$d_{rs} = \left(\frac{q_s}{\pi_r \tau_{rs}} \right)^{\sigma} .$$

Hence, the share of region r in the value of demand in s equals

$$\frac{l_r d_{rs} \pi_r}{\Sigma_t l_t d_{ts} \pi_t} = \frac{V_r (p_r \tau_{rs})^{-\sigma}}{\Sigma_t V_t (p_t \tau_{ts})^{-\sigma}} .$$

Here we make use of the fact that π_r is proportional to p_r by (3.2), and that $l_r \pi_r$ is proportional to V_r by (3.3). Finally, if no income is transferred between regions, then the value of expenditures for goods in s equals V_s, because firms expend all their proceeds to buy intermediate goods, to pay trading costs or factor incomes. Payments for trading costs as well as factor incomes then themselves flow into outlays for goods.

Factor demands are easily obtained from (3.1) by Shephard's Lemma. Hence, equilibrium conditions for factor markets result as

$$L_r = \frac{\alpha V_r}{w_r} \tag{3.9}$$

and

$$K_r = \frac{\beta V_r}{z_r} . \tag{3.10}$$

The equilibrium model consists of equations (3.1), (3.7), (3.8), (3.9) and (3.10), jointly determining p_r, q_r, V_r, z_r and w_r for all r, given factor stocks L_r and K_r for all r.

3.3 Accessibility and Welfare

As already mentioned, the index u_r defined in equation (3.5) is the natural regional welfare index in this model. In a comparative static analysis regional incomes for the benchmark and the counterfactual are obtained from multiplying factor prices with factor endowments. Let u_r^b and u_r^c denote utilities in the benchmark and counterfactual solutions, respectively. Then

$$REV_r = \frac{u_r^c}{u_r^b} - 1$$

is the welfare gain in the counterfactual equilibrium, as compared with the benchmark, measured as the Hicksian relative equivalent variation. The relative equivalent variation is the equivalent variation, expressed as a share in the benchmark income. Similarly,

$$RCV_r = 1 - \frac{u_r^b}{u_r^c}$$

is the Hicksian relative compensating variation. It is the compensating variation expressed as a share in the counterfactual income. A compromise is the relative logarithmic variation, defined as

$$RLV_r = \log\left(\frac{u_r^c}{u_r^b}\right) .$$

All three measures approximately coincide, of course, if they are small, in the order of 0.1.

The welfare index depends on endowments, technologies and location. In order to isolate the effect of location, one could ask for the maximal real return on factors of production, which a representative firm could pay at different locations, provided the technology of this firm would be the same, wherever we locate it.

Let the firm's technology be defined by its cost function

$$p_r = \bar{\mu} w_r^{\alpha} z_r^{\beta} q_r^{\gamma} , \tag{3.11}$$

which is like (3.1), but with a constant μ.

We may think of this technology as a two-level nested CD function. In the lower nest the services of labour and capital are combined to a factor service with price m_r, in the upper nest this factor service jointly with the intermediate inputs produces the output. Hence, equivalent to (3.11), we write

$$m_r = (w_r^{\alpha} z_r^{\beta})^{\frac{1}{\alpha+\beta}}$$

for the lower nest, and

$$p_r = \bar{\mu} m_r^{1-\gamma} q_r^{\gamma}$$

for the upper nest. Thus we obtain the real factor return F_r as

$$F_r = \frac{m_r}{q_r} = \left(\frac{p_r}{\bar{\mu} q_r} \right)^{\frac{1}{1-\gamma}} . \tag{3.12}$$

Hence, F_r is an increasing function of p_r/q_r, which in turn is a combination of a demand and a supply potential:

$$p_r/q_r = S_r^{\frac{1}{\sigma-1}} D_r^{\frac{1}{\sigma}},$$

with supply potential

$$S_r = \sum_s \phi V_s p_s^{-\sigma} \exp[(1 - \sigma)\eta c_{sr}] \tag{3.13}$$

and demand potential

$$D_r = \sum_s b_s V_s \exp(-\sigma\eta c_{rs}). \tag{3.14}$$

b_s is an inverse potential:

$$b_s = \frac{1}{\Sigma_t V_t p_t^{-\sigma} \exp(-\sigma\eta c_{tr})}. \tag{3.15}$$

S_r and D_r are similar to standard market potentials. The modification in S_r is that supply in s is weighed by $p_s^{-\sigma}$. Supply counts less, the higher the price. Similarly, the modification in D_r is that demand is weighed by an inverse supply potential. Demand counts less, the higher the potential of competing supply. Note, however, that different distance functions appear in equations (3.13) and (3.14).[3]

It is also noteworthy that $p_r^{-\sigma}$ and b_s are the balancing factors of a doubly constrained gravity model describing the trade flows in the model. By equations (3.8), (3.15) and (3.6) the value of trade from r to s equals

$$t_{rs} - V_r p_r^{-\sigma} \exp(-\sigma\eta c_{rs}) V_s b_s. \tag{3.16}$$

In (3.8) and (3.15) t_{rs} must add up to V_r and V_s. Hence we get the two constraints

$$V_s = \sum_r t_{rs} \tag{3.17}$$

and

$$V_r = \sum_s t_{rs}. \tag{3.18}$$

3.4 Calibration

We calibrate the model for a system of 276 regions covering the whole of Europe and adding up to 36 countries. See Table 3.1 for the list of countries. The n-column in the table shows the number of regions in the respective country. As already mentioned, the model is calibrated to a very limited data base. We use data on population by region, interregional distances, and national GDPs. All data refer to the year

1994. Regional population data stem from various national sources. As they refer to different years, they are adjusted to national 1994 totals taken from PlanEcon and OECD statistics (PlanEcon Inc. 1995; OECD 1996). GDPs in purchasing power parity US dollars are taken from OECD statistics (OECD 1996) for the OECD countries and from PlanEcon (PlanEcon Inc. 1995) for the former socialist countries. At present distances are simply measured as the crow flies. Currently we are compiling generalized travel costs, which will be used instead in future.

Let us gather the parameters, which have to be calibrated:

- σ, the elasticity of substitution between brands in intermediate and final demand.
- η, the distance cost share per unit of distance.
- α, β, and γ, the production elasticities.
- δ_{kl}, the international trade impediments.
- μ_r, the inverse of the regional level of efficiency. As already mentioned, we assume $\mu_r = \mu_s$ if regions r and s belong to the same country. Hence, we have to calibrate parameters μ_l , $l = 1,\ldots, 36$, for our 36 countries.

The calibration procedure has to fix these parameters jointly with all endogenous variables of the model, which are the goods prices p_r and q_r, the factor prices w_r and z_r, and the values of regional output V_r and interregional trade t_{rs}.

We go through the parameter list step by step. Concerning σ and η, note that in (3.16) the product $\sigma\eta$ is the standard distance parameter of a doubly constrained gravity model with an exponential distance function. Estimates of this parameter, at least for international trade, are available from the literature. According to Bröcker and Rohweder (1990) this parameter is in the order of 1/5 per thousand kilometres for international trade. There is some evidence, however, that this figure underestimates the effect of distance on interregional trade for regions, which are much smaller than countries. An indication of this is that in the model of Bröcker and Rohweder, like in other gravity models of international trade, there is a significant positive neighbourhood effect, indicating that short distance trade is higher than predicted by the estimated distance function. Furthermore, we found that using the estimate $\sigma\eta = 1/5$ per thousand kilometres generates too low a distance sensitivity of interregional trade within Germany in our model.

In a different study using sectorally disaggregated data (Bröcker 1984) we found a considerably higher parameter for international trade in a range close to 1 per thousand kilometres, on average. Still, this seems to be too low an estimate. In our model, it would generate too large international trade flows, even if we set international trade impediments δ_{kl} to implausibly high values. Hence we use our estimate for road transportation flows between the regions of six EC countries for 1970 (Bröcker 1984). The data are a bit dated, but have the advantage of covering intranational and international flows by one model.[4] The estimate is $\sigma\eta$ = 4.6 per thousand kilometres. It generates more plausible international trade flows within our model.

Knowledge of $\sigma\eta$ still does not deliver information on σ and η separately. What can be said about η? If we only take mere transport costs into account, we would have to choose an η in the order of a few percent. Average transport costs in manufacturing industry are reported in the literature not to exceed 2 percent of sales value (McKinnon 1996). This would imply that σ is in the order of hundreds, which is virtually the same as perfect substitutability in interregional trade and therefore not plausible. Clearly, there are distance related trade costs other than transport costs, like costs of communication and face to face contacts required for establishing and maintaining trade relationships. Average logistic costs are estimated to range up to 20 percent of sales value (Weber 1987, p.38). On the one hand, some of them are not related to distance, but on the other hand, many distance related costs are not counted as logistic costs, like costs for face to face contacts. Furthermore, average distance in interregional trade is much less than a thousand kilometres, such that the cost per thousand kilometres is much higher than average costs. Hence, a higher value than 20 percent for η can be justified. We assume an η equal to 0.46 per thousand kilometres due to the fact, that it does not seem plausible to choose σ larger than 10. Hence, η = 0.46 per thousand kilometres and σ = 10 is our preliminary decision. It is open to further discussion.

The elasticities α, β and γ in the production function equal the shares of labour, capital, and intermediate inputs, respectively, in the value of output, as already mentioned. We take these shares from German national accounts, showing 26 percent for labour, 13 percent for capital and 61 percent for intermediate inputs.

Concerning δ_{kl}, we assume two categories of trade flows, EU trade and non EU trade. We regard all trade flows between countries 1 to 17 (see Table 3.1) as EU trade, though a few countries listed were not EU members in 1994 and two of them (Norway and Switzerland) are still not. Nevertheless, the agreements with these countries come close to membership, as far as commodity trade is concerned. In our estimates for interregional transportation flows in Europe (Bröcker 1984) we found a distance equivalent of 375 km for trade impediments between EC countries in 1970. Given our estimate of η = 0.46 per thousand kilometres, this corresponds to δ_{kl} = 1.19, that means to a 19 percent tariff equivalent. One might speculate that trade impediments have almost vanished in the internal market, but we would not accept a lower estimate, because ours is already rather low as compared to McCallum's (McCallum 1995) estimate of trade impediments between Canada and the US. According to our estimate, intranational trade is 5.6 times higher than border crossing EU trade, ceteris paribus. According to McCallum, trade within Canada is 22 times higher than trade across the Canada-US border, ceteris paribus. Taking our elasticity of substitution of σ = 10 this corresponds to a tariff equivalent of 36 percent.

Table 3.1 Accessibility and welfare, countries

	Country	n	p_r	q_r	F_r			u_r		
					mean	min	max	mean	min	max
1	Germany	36	1.07	0.93	1.44	1.16	1.59	1.29	0.96	1.48
2	France	22	1.03	0.97	1.19	0.69	1.51	1.20	0.55	1.66
3	Italy	20	1.03	0.98	1.17	0.82	1.36	1.16	0.70	1.43
4	Netherlands	12	1.03	0.97	1.18	1.04	1.24	1.15	0.97	1.23
5	Belgium	9	1.03	0.97	1.17	1.14	1.20	1.31	1.26	1.35
6	Luxembourg	1	0.98	1.02	0.91	.	.	1.85	.	.
7	Gr. Britain	35	1.05	0.96	1.30	0.70	1.48	1.16	0.48	1.37
8	Ireland	1	0.95	1.06	0.75	.	.	0.88	.	.
9	Denmark	3	0.98	1.03	0.88	0.86	0.90	1.25	1.20	1.29
10	Greece	13	0.93	1.09	0.67	0.48	0.80	0.58	0.36	0.74
11	Spain	16	0.99	1.02	0.94	0.73	1.10	0.83	0.58	1.04
12	Portugal	5	0.95	1.06	0.75	0.63	0.80	0.68	0.54	0.75
13	Finland	12	0.94	1.11	0.65	0.42	0.78	0.87	0.47	1.11
14	Norway	19	0.92	1.12	0.62	0.22	0.80	1.10	0.25	1.52
15	Sweden	24	0.95	1.07	0.75	0.39	0.83	0.98	0.40	1.14
16	Austria	5	0.99	1.01	0.95	0.94	0.98	1.22	1.20	1.27
17	Switzerland	7	1.01	0.99	1.07	1.04	1.11	1.50	1.44	1.57
18	Poland	9	0.98	1.05	0.82	0.74	0.91	0.31	0.27	0.36
19	Czech Rep.	4	0.96	1.05	0.80	0.77	0.82	0.52	0.50	0.54
20	Slovakia	3	0.93	1.10	0.63	0.59	0.66	0.37	0.33	0.39
21	Hungary	5	0.94	1.08	0.70	0.68	0.75	0.38	0.36	0.41
22	Romania	1	0.94	1.10	0.65	.	.	0.17	.	.
23	Slovenia	1	0.92	1.10	0.64	.	.	0.67	.	.
24	Croatia	1	0.92	1.10	0.62	.	.	0.32	.	.
25	Bosnia Herzeg.	1	0.88	1.16	0.48	.	.	0.13	.	.
26	Macedonia	1	0.86	1.19	0.43	.	.	0.14	.	.
27	FR Yugoslavia	1	0.91	1.12	0.59	.	.	0.15	.	.
28	Bulgaria	1	0.92	1.12	0.60	.	.	0.23	.	.
29	Belarus	1	0.96	1.07	0.75	.	.	0.31	.	.
30	Ukraine	1	0.97	1.07	0.79	.	.	0.18	.	.
31	Moldova	1	0.89	1.17	0.49	.	.	0.13	.	.
32	Russia	1	0.78	1.30	0.26	.	.	0.23	.	.
33	Albania	1	0.85	1.21	0.40	.	.	0.06	.	.
34	Estonia	1	0.90	1.15	0.53	.	.	0.38	.	.
35	Latvia	1	0.91	1.14	0.56	.	.	0.27	.	.
36	Lithuania	1	0.91	1.13	0.58	.	.	0.17	.	.

Trade impediments to non EU trade are presumed to be considerably higher than those for EU trade. Our guess is a distance equivalent of 600 km, leading to $\delta_{kl} = 1.32$, that means to a tariff equivalent of 32 percent. It implies that EU trade is 2.8 times higher than non EU trade, ceteris paribus. According to Bröcker and Rohweder (1990) trade within the EC was only 1.6 times higher than non EC trade in the western world in 1983, ceteris paribus. One has to take into account, however, that there are special impediments to trade with countries in transformation. Hence the higher EU effect of 2.8 is more plausible.

The remaining parameters μ_l for $l = 1,..., 36$ are found by solving a system of equations jointly determining these parameters as well as all endogenous variables, given the parameter values discussed in previous paragraphs. This system of equations fixes μ_l such that in the equilibrium solution the national GDP of a country l just equals the observed national GDP of this country.

For deriving this equation system, assume for a moment that the output values V_r are known for all r. It has already been noted that t_{rs} fulfils the equations of a doubly constrained gravity model (see equation (3.8) or equations (3.16), (3.17) and (3.18)):

$$t_{rs} = a_r V_r b_s V_s f_{rs} , \tag{3.19}$$

$$V_s = \sum_r t_{rs} , \tag{3.20}$$

$$V_r = \sum_s t_{rs} , \tag{3.21}$$

with $a_r = p_r^{-\sigma}$ and $f_{rs} = \tau_{rs}^{-\sigma}$ This system is well known to have a unique solution for t_{rs}, if f_{rs} is strictly positive.[5] It can be found by iterative scaling (Darroch and Ratcliff 1972).

The multipliers a_r and b_s are unique up to an arbitrary scaling factor. Hence, from

$$p_r = a_r^{-1/\sigma} \tag{3.22}$$

we obtain unique output prices p_r (up to an arbitrary scaling factor). Inserting this into (3.7) yields unique prices q_s for composite goods (again up to an arbitrary scaling factor). Fixing the scaling factors is just a matter of choosing units for the output and the composite good.

So far we have shown how to calculate goods prices, if output values are known. Now we show how to calculate output values, if goods prices are known. To solve the problem, we have to make two additional assumptions. First, we assume that the participation rate is constant over regions, such that L_r, the regional labour force, is proportional to population B_r, that means $L_r = \lambda B_r$, with participation rate λ. Second, we assume that z_r, the price of capital, is constant over regions. The first assumption is not too far from reality, and could easily be removed by using data on regional total employment rather than on population. These are more or less easily accessible. The second assumption could be justified by assuming perfect interregional capital mobility. This, however, is not realistic, in particular as far as eastern Europe is concerned. But even if we assume capital immobility away, we only could argue in favour of an equalized rate of return on tradable assets. The real rate of return on installed capital, which is meant by the variable z_r, can deviate from this equalized rate, because installing capital is costly and takes time (Hayashi 1982). These deviations would vanish in a long run steady state, but Europe in transition can hardly be assumed to move along a steady state. Hence, frankly speaking, it is again the lack of information forcing us to make this rather unpleasant assumption.

For a region r belonging to country l we obtain from equation (3.1)

$$w_r = \left(\frac{p_r q_r^{-\gamma}}{z^{-\beta} \mu_l} \right)^{1/\alpha} .$$

Here z denotes the constant price of capital. Hence, we conclude from (3.9) that

$$\begin{aligned} V_r &= \frac{L_r w_r}{\alpha} \\ &= \frac{\alpha}{\lambda} B_r w_r \\ &= \varphi_l \, B_r p_r^{1/\alpha} q_\rho^{-\gamma/\alpha} . \end{aligned}$$

Constants not varying over r within country l are gathered in φ_l. Now we make use of our knowledge about the national GDP, Y_l. We calibrate μ_l (or , φ_l which is a function of μ_l and several constants) such that the observed national GDP coincides with the model's national GDP. This implies

$$Y_l = (\alpha + \beta) \sum_{r \in C_l} V_r$$

$$= (\alpha + \beta)\, \varphi_l \sum_{r \in C_l} B_r p_r^{1/\alpha} q_r^{-\gamma/\alpha} ,$$

with C_l denoting the set of regions making up country l. This gives us φ_l, and therefore also V_r:

$$V_r = \left(\frac{Y_l}{\alpha + \beta} \right) \left(\frac{B_r p_r^{1/\alpha} q_r^{-\gamma/\alpha}}{\Sigma_{r \in C_l} B_r p_r^{1/\alpha} q_r^{-\gamma/\alpha}} \right) . \tag{3.23}$$

The calibration procedure runs as follows:

- Start with $p_r = q_r = 1\ \forall r$.
- Find V_r from (3.23).
- Solve equations (3.19) to (3.21) by iterative scaling.
- Calculate p_r by (3.22) and q_s by (3.7).
- Stop, if convergence is achieved, else go to 2.

3.5 Accessibilities in Europe

Figure 3.1 shows results for the accessibility indicator defined in equation (3.12). It is scaled to an average of unity. Tiny arrows in the figure point upwards. Accessibility ranges for countries are shown in Table 3.1. Accessibilities range from 0.26 for Russia to 1.57 for the German region Giessen. Hence, given the spatial distribution of markets, a representative firm in Giessen can pay to its factors more than seven times what it could pay in Moscow, if the technology used were the same in both locations. There are also considerable differences of accessibilities within developed regions. For example in Germany the highest accessibility (in Giessen) exceeds the lowest (in Schleswig-Holstein) by 37 percent. Even stronger differences exist within the Scandinavian countries, as expected. Accessibilities range from 0.22 in the very north of Norway to 0.8 around Oslo.

Besides the global maximum in Germany there exist high level local humps around Paris and London. Lower level local humps are observed in central Spain and northern Italy. Accessibilities sharply decline at the former iron curtain due to the assumption about East-West trade impediments. Impacts of other national borders are also visible. Austria, Switzerland, Belgium and Luxembourg suffer to some extent from a small country effect. Despite their geographical centrality they do not show the highest accessibilities. The same effect explains why the Baltic countries have lower accessibilities than their surroundings. The Balkans appear as a deep hollow in the accessibility landscape, because the countries are small and their output is extremely low. The local minimum is in Albania.

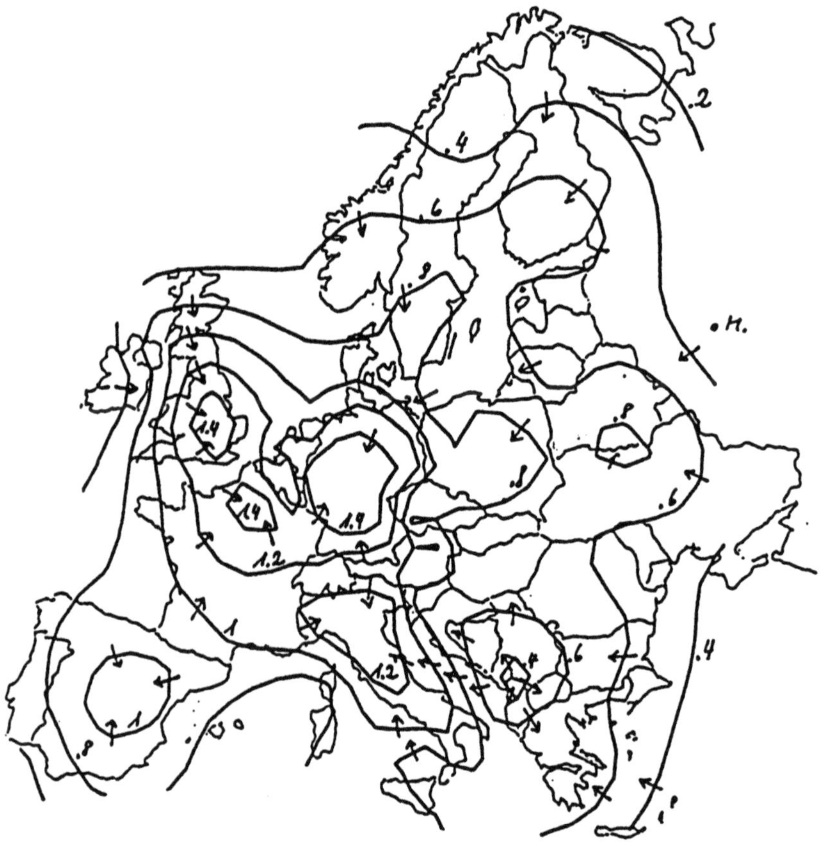

Figure 3.1 Accessibility contour of Europe

Table 3.1 also shows national ranges of utility as defined in equation (3.5), scaled to an average of unity. Utility ranges from 0.06 for Albania to 1.85 for Luxembourg. Hence, multiplying an Albanian's income by 32 makes him as well off as a person in Luxembourg.

3.4 Conclusion

It has been shown that a theoretically well founded accessibility index can be derived from a general spatial equilibrium model. It is remarkable that, starting from a completely different basis than traditional regional science, we straightforwardly arrive at an indicator which is formally closely related to classical formulae, as has been shown in section 3.3.

What is the advantage of the new approach? Besides its theoretical strength two points are worth mentioning: First, the parametrization is less arbitrary than in the classical approach. One can show (Bröcker 1989) that accessibility patterns calculated by the classical formula dramatically change with a changing parameter in the distance function. There is no direct way of estimating or calibrating this parameter, however, because accessibilities are not directly observable. The parameters of our approach appear in equations describing observables such as trade flows, measured in value terms. Therefore it is possible to check the calibration against the evidence.

Second, and more important, is the advantage in comparative static analysis. If we, for example, want to study effects of economic integration along the lines of Clark et al. (1969), it remains open how to translate changes of the potential measure into changes of economically meaningful variables like factor incomes or welfare. There are no difficulties like that in our approach. We just have to solve a new equilibrium with changed parameters, as explained in Subsection 3.2.5. Income changes directly drop out of the solution. Welfare changes are measured by Hicksian variations defined in Section 3.3. Comparative static analysis of a series of integration scenarios will be our next step.

References

Bröcker, J. (1984), 'How do International Trade Barriers affect Interregional Trade', in Andersson, Å.E., Isard, W. and T. Pu (eds), *Regional and Industrial Development Theories: Models and Empirical Evidence*, North Holland, Amsterdam, pp. 219–39.

Bröcker, J. (1984), *Interregionaler Handel und ökonomische Integration: Empirische Modelle für westeuropäische Länder und Regionen*, V. Florentz, München.

Bröcker, J. (1989), 'How to Eliminate Certain Defects of the Potential Formula', *Environment and Planning A*, vol. 21, pp. 817–30.

Bröcker, J. (1995), 'Chamberlinian Spatial Computable General Equilibrium Modelling: A Theoretical Framework', *Economic Systems Research*, vol. 7, pp. 129–41.

Bröcker, J. and Rohweder, H. (1990), 'Barriers to International Trade: Methods of Measurement and Empirical Evidence', *The Annals of Regional Science*, vol. 4, pp. 289–305.

Clark, C., Wilson, F. and Bradley, J. (1969), 'Industrial Location and Economic Potential in Western Europe', *Regional Studies*, vol. 3, pp. 197–212.

Darroch, J.N. and Ratcliff, D. (1972), 'Generalized Iterative Scaling for Log-Linear Models', *Annals of Mathematical Statistics*, vol. 43, pp. 1470–80.

Dixit, A.K. and Stiglitz, J.E. (1977), 'Monopolistic Competition and Optimum Product Diversity', *American Economic Review*, vol. 67, pp. 297–308.

Ethier, W.J. (1982), 'National and International Returns to Scale in the Modern Theory of International Trade', *American Economic Review*, vol. 72, pp. 389–405.

Fujita, M., Krugman, P. and Mori, T. (1994), 'On the Evolution of Hierarchical Urban Systems', Paper presented at the European Congress of the Regional Science Association, Groningen.

Hayashi, F. (1982), 'Tobin's Marginal q and Average q: a Neoclassical Interpretation', *Econometrica*, vol. 50, pp. 213–24.

Krugman, P. (1991), *Geography and Trade*, MIT Press and Leuven University Press, London.

Krugman, P. (1993), 'On the Number and Location of Cities', *European Economic Review*, vol. 37, pp. 293–98.

Krugman, P. (1994), 'Complex Landscapes in Economic Geography', *American Economic Association Papers and Proceedings*, vol. 84, pp. 412–16.

Krugman, P. and Venables, A.J. (1993), 'Integration, Specialization and Adjustment', NBER Working Paper No. 4559, Cambridge, MA.

Krugman, P. and Venables, A.J. (1994), 'Globalization and the Inequality of Nations', CEPR Discussion Paper No. 1015, London.

Matsuyama, K. (1995), 'Complementarities and Cumulative Processes in Models of Monopolistic Competition', *Journal of Economic Literature*, vol. 33, pp. 701–29.

McCallum, J. (1995), 'National Borders Matter: Canada-U.S. Regional Trade Patterns', *American Economic Review*, vol. 85, pp. 615–23.

McKinnon, A. (1996), 'The Contribution of Road Construction to Economic Development', in *Roads and Economy: State-of-the-Art Report*, T&E Publication 96/1, pp. 19-26, Brussels and Delft. European Federation for Transport and Environment and Centre for Energy Conservation and Environmental Technology.

OECD (1996), *Main Economic Indicators*, Paris, January.

PlanEcon Inc. (1995), *PlanEcon Review and Outlook for Eastern Europe*, August.

PlanEcon Inc. (1995), *PlanEcon Review and Outlook for the Former Soviet Union*, August.

Venables, A.J. (1993), 'Equilibrium Locations of Vertically Linked Industries', CEPR Discussion Paper no. 802, London.
Weber, J. (1987), *Logistikkostenrechnung*, Springer Berlin.

Notes

1. Spatial models with monopolistic competition of this kind have been introduced by Krugman 1993.

2. The formal structure applied in the following to modelling monopolistic competition is due to Dixit and Stiglitz (1977) and has extensively been used in theoretical economic geography by Krugman and co-authors, Krugman 1991, 1993, 1994; Krugman and Venables 1993, 1994; Venables 1993; Fujita et al. 1994. Its use in trade modelling originates from Ethier 1982. The applicability to spatial computable general equilibrium modelling has been shown in Bröcker 1995. For a review of other fields of application see Matsuyama 1995.

3. We have shown elsewhere (Bröcker 1994), that $q_s^{\sigma-1} = b_s$, if the transportation technology has the so called iceberg form. In this paper we refrain from the iceberg assumption, however, as it lacks plausibility. This destroys the direct relationship between the balancing factor b_s and the price q_s.

4. We only know of one other study by McCallum (1995) using intranational and international flows simultaneously.

5. $f_{rs} > 0$ is sufficient, not necessary for existence of a solution.

4 A New Definition of Spatial Accessibility Function in Transportation Networks: Axiomatic Approach

TOSHIHIKO MIYAGI AND TAKAJI SUZUKI

4.1 Introduction

When different configurations of population or employment and resultant activity distributions are assessed relative to one another, some measures of accessibility have traditionally been used in a total benefit criterion (Wilson et al.1981). Especially, in geography accessibility has long been interested in as a fundamental component of the discipline and to some extent as an indicator. Since the seminal work of Reilly (1931), the most common practice has been to relate the concept of accessibility to the basic gravity model or the broader family of spatial interaction models (Wilson 1971). The basic law of gravity model is that movements between two sites are proportional to the products of their characteristics and inversely proportional to a power of the distance separating them. One of the well-known measures of accessibility is a gravity-like formula by Hansen (1959). A number of modified versions of the Hansen-type framework have been proposed so far (for example, Isard 1960; Ingram 1971; Wilson 1967, 1974), however, a more rigorous discussion on the reason why we have to assume a continuous and a decreasing properties of distance function has not been made in the contexts of accessibility. In fact, It is known that the concept of transportation costs generally includes a noncontinuous property (Baumol et al. 1988).

On the other hand, a variety of extensions and alternative frameworks have come after the middle of the 1970s. Studies on the random utility theory introduced by Domencich and McFadden (1975) have flourished in the field of transportation research and those works have affected to the behavioral approach to accessibility measures. In the micro-behavioral approach accessibility is related to the notion of consumer surplus in microeconomic theory (Ben-Akiva and Lerman, 1979; Williams 1976; Williams and Senior, 1978). Weibull (1980) presented a measurement-theoretical framework to clarify a fairly broad range of numerical indicators of accessibility, where accessibility is considered as a property of configuration of opportunities for spatial interaction. Within this framework he discussed a few established indicators of accessibility and introduced notions of separable, additive, and maxitive indicators. While Weibull adopted an axiomatic approach, since the aim of his paper was directed towards the bridging of a gap between the general definitions of the concept and the very specific numerical indicators in current use, he did not discuss about the properties of accessibility functions which may be uniquely derived from the axioms.

The properties of accessibility functions are very important because maximization of accessibility is frequently used as a goal of planning. Some accessibility measures can be easily transformed to the objective functions of the location problem (Hansen et al. 1983). The basic problem of location theory is due to Weber (1909). In geometrical terms, the Weber problem is defined as the minimization of the sum of the weighted distances denoted by $w_i d_i$ (s) where w_i represents the weight of point i and d_i (s) the distance from a point s to be determined, to given points of the plane. A distance between any two points of the plane is usually represented by a particular function, being known as a metric distance like Euclidean, rectilinear (or Manhattan) and l_p - distances. In the network models, a network represents a set of cities connected with transportation systems and points are replaced by the set of nodes connected with the set of links. Hakimi (1965) proved that the set of nodes contains an optimal solution to the Weber problem (or a median) on a network. This may indicate that there is at least one city in a system of cities connected by transportation network which has a maximum accessibility and that the functional form of accessibility is of importance because it must be optimized under some appropriate conditions.

With those issues in mind, the main purpose of this chapter is to provide a general definition of accessibility based on the systems of axiom of accessibility and, then to show the functional form of accessibility compatible with the axiomatic system. In other words, we start with a plain assumption on the definition of accessibility which may be acceptable to anyone, then deduces some properties of the accessibility measure. Unlike Weibull's choice-contexts approach and other demand oriented approaches, we adopt the network transformation (supply oriented) approach where in addition to distances between nodes and weights of nodes, the number of other nodes linked with a node in question is related with the definition of accessibility of the node. This type of approach was first introduced by Kajitani and Maruyama (1976) where centrality in a network was the main concern and characteristics of the function compatible with the axioms of centrality of a node was discussed. Shinoda and Sengoku (1986) generalized the concept of centrality considered by Kajitani and Maruyama. The concept of centrality is very similar with the median in the location problem, however, while in the median problem a center node is found as an optimization problem under the condition of a given and fixed network topology, the main concern in the centrality problem is to characterize the centrality function, which is defined so that a maximum change is observed relative to one another in a certain node when properties of a network have altered by addition or deletion of links and changes in link values or weights of nodes.

The axiomatic derivation of accessibility function in this paper is almost parallel with that of the centrality function undertaken by Shinoda and Sengoku, however, our approach is more general in that the axiomatic system in this paper is consistent with that of Weibull and that the main results in this paper are derived based on the cost complementarity condition. The cost complementarity (we call it a nonincreasing property for additional increment in this chapter) was studied by Panzar and Willig (1977) and accounts for economies of scale and economies of scope in transportation. Furthermore, it has been a well-established evidence in production economics that the cost complementarity provides more general characteristics of production cost (Baumol, Panzar and Willig 1988). This paper may conclude that accessibility function has the property of nonincreasing for marginal increment (i.e. the complementarity condition). In addition, the function must be nonincreasing and nondecreasing with marginal decrement with respect to distances (or transportation costs) and nondecreasing with respect to weights of nodes.

4.2 Notation and Definitions

Consider a network G[V, L, ß] , where V denote a set of nodes, $L \subseteq V x V$ a set of links and ß is a real-valued function defined as:

$$\beta : V \times V \rightarrow R_{+,} \; (R_{+} = [0, \infty]) \tag{4.1}$$

A topological space [V; ß] is called a metric space when ß satisfies the axiom of a metric distance. A distance ß is denoted in terms of ß (r, s) using nodes $r, s \in V$ and represents the degree of interaction of two nodes. Appropriate examples of ß in a transportation network may include transport cost (time), capacity, transport products such as ton-kilometer or passenger-kilometer, so on, however, we restrict our attention to a generalized transport distance (or cost) in the subsequent sections. When there is no room to confuse, we denote a space by V instead of [V; ß].

Following Shinoda and Sengoku (1986), we begin with the concept of *a space transformation* and definitions about sets of nodes associated with the transformation. Let [V; ß '] be a new metric space obtained by changing one or more metric distances defined on a space V, where ß ' also satisfies the definition of a metric function. We refer such changes in a network as a space transformation and denote it as [V;β]→[V;β]. A space is usually transformed , in a transportation network, by addition or deletion of links or by changing link performance functions. Such changes may result in relative changes of interaction between nodes (cities). Of course, the changes in economic activities in nodes also affects interactions between nodes, but we shall wait for discussing the weight of node until Section 4.4.

Next, we define two sets of nodes associated with a space transformation:

$$T(r;\beta)=\{s:\beta'(r,s)\neq\beta(r,s), s\in V\} \tag{4.2}$$

$$I(u;\beta)=\{v:T(v;\beta)\subseteq T(u;\beta),\ T(v;\beta)\neq\phi\} \tag{4.3}$$

The sets of nodes, T and I, are called *a set of changed nodes* and *a set of influenced nodes*, respectively. Each element included in the set of changed nodes represents the node of which relation to r is changed through ß. Now, let us assume that accessibility is defined by all elements included in the set of changed nodes. Since a set of changed nodes of a node v is contained in that of a node u, the degree of influence of v to the change in accessibility may at most equal to the degree of influence of u. In this sense, such a set of nodes is referred to a set of influenced nodes. Whenever no confusion arises, ß in T and I may be omitted.

Definition: Let S be a subset of V. If for p, r and s , it follows that

$$\beta'(p,s)-\beta(p,s)<0 \tag{4.4a}$$

and

$$\beta'(p,s)-\beta(p,s)\leq\beta'(r,s)-\beta(r,s), \tag{4.4b}$$

then such a space transformation is said to be *a reduced transformation* associated with node p on S. In particular, if for all $r\in S$ and $s\in T(p)$, $\beta'(r,s)\leq 0$, then it is said to be *a monotone reduced transformation*. By reversing inequality signs we get the definition of *a expanded transformation* and *a monotone expanded transformation*, respectively.

Consider the network depicted in Figure 4.1. We assume that distances between all pairs of nodes are measured by a shortest-route rule.

Thus, this transformation is a monotone reduced transformation associated with a node 1 on S={1,2, 3, 4} and a node 2 on S'={2, 3, 4} as well. If a new link value from a node 2 to a node 3 is altered from 2 to 4, then this transformation gives a reduced transformation associated with a node 1 on S, but not monotone, and a monotone expanded transformation associated with a node 2 on S'. Likewise, we can consider another example which gives a reduced transformation, but, not monotone. For instance, if routes connecting some node pairs are designated by an alternative rule different from a shortest-path rule, then this space transformation also may provide an example of a reduced transformation, which is not a monotone one.

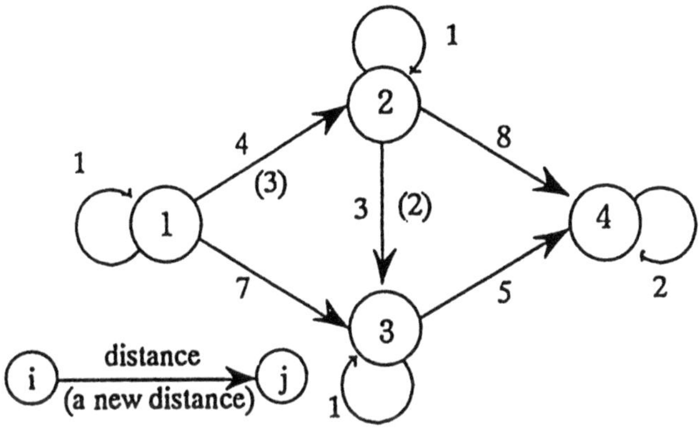

Figure 4.1(a) An example network

$\beta(1,2)=4,\ \beta(1,3)=7,\ \beta(1,4)=12$

$\beta(2,3)=3,\ \beta(2,4)=8,\ \beta(3,4)=5$

$\beta'(1,2)=3,\ \beta'(1,3)=5,\ \beta'(1,4)=10$

$\beta'(2,3)=2,\ \beta'(2,4)=7,\ \beta'(3,4)=5$

Figure 4.1(b) A space transformation

$$B=\begin{array}{cc} & \begin{matrix}1 & 2 & 3 & 4\end{matrix}\\ \begin{matrix}1\\2\\3\\4\end{matrix} & \begin{bmatrix}1&4&7&12\\ \infty&1&3&8\\ \infty&\infty&1&5\\ \infty&\infty&\infty&1\end{bmatrix}\end{array}\quad B'=\begin{array}{cc} & \begin{matrix}1 & 2 & 3 & 4\end{matrix}\\ \begin{matrix}1\\2\\3\\4\end{matrix} & \begin{bmatrix}1&3&5&10\\ \infty&1&2&7\\ \infty&\infty&1&5\\ \infty&\infty&\infty&1\end{bmatrix}\end{array}\quad \delta B=\begin{array}{cc} & \begin{matrix}1 & \overbrace{2\quad 3\quad 4}^{T(1)}\end{matrix}\\ \begin{matrix}1\\ S\ \begin{matrix}2\\3\\4\end{matrix}\end{matrix} & \begin{bmatrix}0&-1&-2&-2\\ 0&0&-1&-1\\ 0&0&0&0\\ 0&0&0&0\end{bmatrix}\end{array}$$

Figure 4.1(c) Distance matrices and its variation

For this network, the set of changing nodes and the set of influenced nodes are as follows:

$T(1) = \{2,3,4\}$, $T(2) = \{3,4)$, $T(3) = \{0\} = T(4)$
$I(1) = \{1,2\}$, $I(2) = \{2\}$

Let F be a continuous, real-valued function and Z be a subset of V. Let us define the following joint function,

$$F_p(\beta) = \sum_{s \in Z} \Phi(\beta(p,s)) \tag{4.5}$$

and the variation of functional values, δF, given by

$$\delta F_p(\beta) = F_p(\beta') - F_p(\beta) \tag{4.6}$$

Based on the above separable function (4.5), Sinoda and Sengoku (1986) proposed axiomatic definition on a centrality function of a node in a network G.

Axioms on Centrality (Accessibility) Function If for $p \in V$ and $s \subset V$, a reduced transformation associated with node p on S satisfies the following conditions:

(I) $\delta F_p(\beta) \geq 0$
(II) for $r \in I(p)$, $\delta F_p(\beta) \geq \delta F_r(\beta)$

then F is a centrality function defined on S or $S \cap I(p)$. If the only condition (I) is satisfied, then F is a semi-centrality function defined on S or $S \cap I(p)$.

Hereafter, we read the above axioms as *the axioms on accessibility function*. Shinoda and Sengoku gives several theorems which characterize the centrality function based on the concept of space transformation. Here we show some of them without proof which will be related with the accessibility function treated in the later part of the chapter.

Theorem 1: Suppose that a reduced transformation on an arbitrary node p on V satisfies the condition (A). Then, the necessary and sufficient condition for F being the centrality (or accessibility) function is (B).

(A) for any node r and s such that $r \in S \cap I(p)$ and $S \in T(r) \cap Z$, it follows that

$$\beta'(p,s) \leq \beta'(r,s)$$

(B) Φ is a nonincreasing, convex function.

It should be noted that a reduced transformation does not always ensure that the condition (A) holds. In the case of $\beta(p,s) \geq \beta(r,s)$,$\Phi$ must be concave. Therefore, the necessary and sufficient condition for a more general case, where the condition (A) is removed, is that Φ is a nonincreasing, affine function.

Let us get back to the previous example shown in Figure 4.1. Suppose that accessibility of each node is measured by the following gravity-type function, where all weights of nodes are assumed to be one.

$$F_p(\beta) = \sum_{s \in Z} \omega_p \exp[-\beta(p,s)]$$

In this case, the variations of functional values for nodes 1 and 2 are δF_1=0.0373368 and δF_2=0.0861246, respectively. For other nodes, the variations of accessibility are all zero. Apparently, a node 1 includes maximum changed-nodes linked with it. Nevertheless, these figures show that the change in accessibility of a node 2 is the greatest. This result may contradict our intuitive feeling. This is due to the reason that the transformation associated with node 1 on S violates the condition (A) in theorem 1. Since $\beta(1,3) \geq \beta(2,3)$ and $\beta(2,4)$, Φ must be a nonincreasing, concave function so that the accessibility function satisfies the axioms. On the other hand, the above function becomes a relevant measure in the case of a monotone reduced transformation associated with a node 2, which is realized when only a link (2-3) is improved. In this case, the set of influenced nodes of node 2 consists of nodes 1 and 2, and the condition (A) is fulfilled. Thus, in order to meet the axioms of accessibility regardless of the condition (A), the function F must be nonincresing and affine (both convex and concave). For instance, consider the following accessibility function:

$$F_p(\beta) = \sum_{s \in Z} [a-\beta(p,s)]$$

where a is a positive constant. The assumption about node-weight is still remained. We have δF_1= 5 and δF_2=2 which satisfy the axioms of accessibility.

In the network depicted in Figure 4.1, link values of two links are simultaneously altered. In such a situation as values of multiple links are altered, the condition (A) is not usually fulfilled because the set of influenced nodes of a specified node p usually includes some nodes of which distances to some destination nodes are shorter than those from the node p. When only a single link's value is reduced, the condition (A) is always satisfied as long as a space transformation is a monotone reduced. The following two lemmas are of a special importance in this respect.

Lemma 1: A space transformation given by the following expression provides a monotone reduced transformation associated with node p:

$$\beta'(p,s) = \min. \{\beta(p,s), \beta(p,q) + \beta(q,s) - \delta\} \quad (4.7)$$

where δ is a positive constant.

Lemma 2: In a monotone reduced transformation demonstrated by (4.7), it follows that for any node r and s,

$$\beta'(p,s) \leq \beta'(r,s) \quad (4.8)$$

Lemma 1 implies that when a reduction of distance, δ, is realized in a single link composed of a route connecting arbitrary two nodes, a minimum-path rule always gives a monotone reduced transformation. Furthermore, it follows from Lemma 2 that such a space transformation as given by (4.7) ensures that the condition (A) in theorem 1 always holds. Therefore, the next theorem holds.

Theorem 2: As long as the space transformation according to the expression (4.7) is demonstrated, the necessary and sufficient condition for F being the accessibility function for an arbitrary metric space is that Φ is a nonincreasing, convex function.

Hereafter, we restrict our attention to a space transformation with change of a single link in a network.

4.3 Cost Complementarity and Related Properties

The real-value function C is said to be nondecreasing if

$$C(x+y) \geq C(x) \quad (4.9)$$

and nonincreasing for marginal increment if it satisfies

$$C(x+z) - C(x) \geq C(x+y+z) - C(x+y) \quad (4.10)$$

whenever x,y,zR^n_+. When C is defined as a cost function, inequality (4.10) is called a cost complementarity condition (Panzar and Willig 1977). If C is twice continuously differentiable, then inequality (4.10) is equivalent to the condition

$$\frac{\partial^2 C(x)}{\partial x_i \partial x_j} \leq 0 \quad (4.11)$$

Inequality (4.9), increasing property of cost, simply states that cost of output or of distance is increasing as output or distance is increasing. As is discussed in Panzar and Willig (1977), cost complementarity expressed by (4.10) requires that marginal or incremental costs of any output of transportation decline when that output or any other output increase. For a single output cost function, cost complementarity implies concavity. When we put x=0 and assume C(0)=0 in (4.10), then we have the following subadditivity condition (Sharkey 1982):

$$C(z) + C(y) \geq C(y+z)$$

Decreasing incremental cost or subadditivity of cost is well known property of transportation cost. For example, the passenger aircraft fuel consumption in gallons per available seat-mile decreases with increasing route segments. Fare of direct travel to a destination using railway or express way may become more cheaper than that of stopover travel where traveler gets off a certain railway station or interchange of expressway and after that goes forwards to his or her destination again. Let us show an example of a cost function which satisfies subadditivity. Let x denote travel time, a,b the distinct levels of railway fare and c the value of time. Consider the travel cost function

$$C(x) = \begin{array}{ll} a+cx & \text{for } 0<x<x^0 \\ a+b+cx & \text{for } x\geq x^0, \text{ where } a,b,c>0 \text{ and } b<0 \end{array} \qquad (4.12)$$

The cost function represents the travel cost of railway users perceived in a way that beyond a certain level of travel time, x_0, an additional fare b is perceived as less costly than a. This cost function is clearly subadditive, because that for z ($<x_0$) , y ($<x_0$) and x=z+y ($>x_0$) we have

$$C(z) + C(y) = 2a+cx \geq 2a+cx \geq a+b+cx = C(y+z).$$

Here we introduce a new joint function, which reverses properties of cost function, by letting

$$\varphi(x) = -C(x)$$

Then the real-valued function φ satisfies a nonincreasing and a nondecreasing for marginal-decrement conditions:

$$\varphi(x) \geq \varphi(x+y) \qquad (4.13)$$

and

$$\varphi(x) - \varphi(x+z) \geq \varphi(x+y) - \varphi(x+y+z) \qquad (4.14)$$

Supperadditivity of φ is straightforward from . If $\varphi(0)=0$ is twice continuously differentiable, then inequality (4.14) is equivalent to the condition

$$\frac{\partial^2 \varphi(x)}{\partial x_i \partial x_j} \geq 0 \tag{4.15}$$

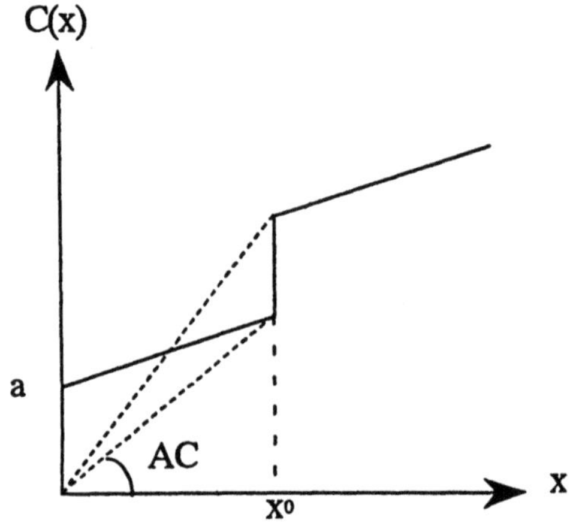

Figure 4.2(a) Subadditive cost function, C(x)

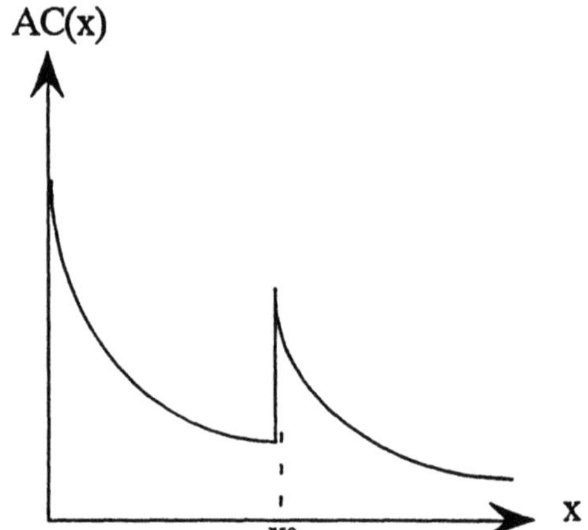

Figure 4.2(b) Average cost of C(x)

Proposition 1: Suppose that a cost function C(ß) is nondecreasing and nonincreasing for marginal increment. Furthermore, we assume that a space transformation is a monotone reduced transformation associated with a node p on S which is obtained by minimum-path operation. Then the accessibility function defined by

$$F_p(\beta) = \sum_{s \in Z} \varphi(\beta(p,s)) \tag{4.16}$$

satisfies the axioms of accessibility (proof see appendix).

Proposition 1 is almost a restatement of theorem 1 or 2, however, supperadditivity is essentially more general than convexity (Sharkey 1982).

4.4 Axiomatic Derivation of Accessibility Function

Up to here, the accessibility function has been defined as a function of only a distance measure. In this section, we shall extend the accessibility function so as to include weights of nodes so that the extended accessibility function can account for the changes in population or activity level of city. The revised space is denoted by [V;ß, ω], where ω represents the weight of node. We refer the change in weight of a node as the incremental transformation and denote it as:

$$\omega'(t) = \omega(t) + \sigma$$

We assume that the extended accessibility function is defined as:

$$F_p(\beta,\omega) = \sum_{s \in Z} \psi(\beta(p,s),\omega(s)) \tag{4.17}$$

A separable function is suitable, and no other type of function is suitable if we admit the system of axioms on separable accessibility which was presented by Weibull (1980). Let us introduce a set of new terminology concerned with the Weibill's axioms. An opportunity α is simply represented as a set of elements concerned with the definition of accessibility: $\alpha = \langle ß,\omega \rangle$. A configuration x is represented as a finite, unordered list of opportunities: $x=\langle \alpha_1,\alpha_2,....,\alpha_n \rangle$. The conjunction of the pair of configuration x and y is described by $x \vee y$. The set of configurations of interest in a particular measurement situation is denoted by M. Weibull proved that there exists a separable accessibility indicator if only if the following three axioms are fulfilled in an appropriate accessibility-measurement situation and that if axiom 3 is satisfied, then every accessibility indicator is separable.

Axiom 1: If x and y belong to M then either yPx or xPy or both.
Axiom 2: If x,y, and z belong to M, yPx, and zPy, then zPx.
Axiom 3: If $x_1 \vee y_1$ and $x_2 \vee y_2$ belong to M, $x_1 I x_2$, and $y_1 I y_2$, then $(x_1 \vee y_1) I (x_2 \vee y_2)$.

We read binary relations 'xPy' and 'xIy' as 'x is at least as good as y' and 'x is indifferent to y', respectively. A binary relation satisfying axioms 1 and 2 is sometimes called a weak order (Fishburn 1968). You should note that a monotone transformation in a network gives a weak order relation, as is seen from its definition. The third axiom expresses a kind of independence of the binary relation vis-å-vis the contents of configurations, namely it essentially excludes considerations of situations where combined trips to several opportunities are important (Weibull 1980). Thus, the separability is a strong assumption, however, since we intend to apply our definition of accessibility function to intercity travel, axiom 3 may be acceptable in our accessibility-measurement situation.

Axiom Systems on Accessibility Function Consider any two points p and t on a space [V;ß, ω]. Suppose a space transformation [V;ß, ω] [V;ß', ω'] be a monotone reduced transformation of ß associated with node p and a incremental transformation of β associated with node t. For such a space transformation , we assume the following conditions:

i) $\delta f_p(\beta) \geq 0$, $\delta f_t(\omega) \geq 0$ and $\delta f_p(\beta) \leq \delta f_p(\beta,\omega)$ or $\delta f_p(\omega) \leq \delta f_p(\beta,\omega)$

ii) for the subset $S \subseteq IP$ of V associated with node p and $r \in S$,

$$\delta F_p(\beta) \geq \delta F_r(\beta)$$

iii) for $\beta(u,t) \leq (v,t)$,

$$\delta F_u(\omega) \geq \delta F_v(\omega)$$

Then, F defined by (4.17) is an accessibility function defined on S.

The condition i) guarantees that tha maximum influenced nodes by this space transformation, p and t, always exhibit nonnegative changes in accessibility and that no configuration provides less accessibility than the empty configuration. These conditions are almost pararell with the following conditions that any accessibility indicator has to satisfy, which were presented by Weibull (1976):

$$\beta > \beta' \Rightarrow F(\beta,\omega(\leq F(\beta',\omega),$$

$$\omega < w' \Rightarrow F(\beta,\omega) \leq F(\beta,\omega)$$

$$F(\beta) \leq F(\beta,\omega) \text{ or } F(\omega) \leq F(\beta,\omega)$$

The second condition ii) implies that since the set of changed nodes associated with a node p has a maximum number of elements in the set of changed nodes, the incremental change of accessibility for a node p is maximum in the change of accessibility. The final condition iii) ensures that if a metric distance from a node u to t is minimum, then the maximum influenced node by the incremental change in a node t is a node u.

The functional form which satisfies these conditions is given by the following proposition.

Proposition 2: F defined by equation (4.17) is an accessibility function on a space [V;ß, ω] if only if ψ is nonincreasing and nondecreasing for marginal decrement with respect to ß, nondecreasing with respect to ω, respectively, and satisfies the condition of nonincreasing for marginal increment :

$$\psi(x_1,y) \geq \psi(x_2,y), \tag{4.18a}$$
$$\psi(x,y_2) \geq \psi(x,y_1), \tag{4.18b}$$
$$\psi(x_1,y) - \psi(x_1+\delta,y) \geq \psi(x_2 y) - \psi(x_2+\delta,y), \tag{4.18c}$$
$$\text{and } \psi(x_1,y_2) - \psi(x_1,y_1) \geq \psi(x_2,y_2) - \psi(x_2,y_1) \tag{4.18d}$$

for $\delta x,y \geq 0$, $x_2 \geq x_1 \geq 0$ and $y_2 \geq y_1 \geq 0$.

(proof) See appendix.

You should note that equation (18d) is equivalent with the property of nonincreasing for marginal increment because that if we put $x=[x_1,y_1]$, $y=[\delta, 0]$, $z=[0,\sigma]$ and $x_2= x_1+\delta$, $y_2= y_1+\sigma$, then (18d) is equal to Equation (4.10). It also means that ψ has the same property as that of utility function.

4.5 Concluding Remarks

Our aim in this chapter lay in the integration of various accessibility functions derived based on different theoretical frameworks. Unlike the conventional approaches, we have defined accessibility in relation with a space transformation and derived functional properties that accessibility functions must possess in the context of the axiom systems of accessibility. The concept of space transformation plays the key role to link the changes in network systems to accessibility function because accessibility function should be defined on that space. The functional properties provided in this chapter is rather general so that most of accessibility functions proposed so far are included and satisfy the axiomatic definition of accessibility presented in this paper. A new definition imposes the property of nondecreasing for marginal decrement on accessibility functions, as is seen in the usual utility function. For, it is easy to see that Hansen's accessibility formula given by

$$A_i = \sum_j H_j \exp(-\theta c_{ij})$$

satisfies the accessibility conditions. Since A_i satisfies axiom systems on accessibility, its monotone increasing transformation also does. Therefore, the following consumer benefit obtained from random utility model (Williams 1977) is also an accessibility measure.

$$CS_i = \frac{1}{\theta} \log \sum_j H_j \exp(-\theta c_{ij})$$

If we replace c_{ij} _ in A_i or CS_i by travel cost function as is expressed by Equation (4.12) or its average cost function, respectively, we have discontinuous accessibility functions.

The problem raised in this chapter is that these asccessibility functions are limited in its application in a case that only a single link is altered in a network. In a case of the changes in mutiple link, the relevant function is affine function. Traditional definitions on accessibility have ignored the second condition (II) in the axioms of accessibility disccussed in this paper. This may be a heighlight of this chapter and shed light on further research on accesibility.

References

Baumol, W.J., Panzar, J.C. and Willig, R.D. (1988), *Contestable Markets and the Theory of Industry Structure*, Harcourt Brace Javanovich Publishers, Orlando, Fl.

Ben-Akiva, M.E. and Lerman, S.R. (1979), 'Disaggregate Travel and Mobility Choice Models, and Measures of Accessibility', in Hensher, D.A. and P.R. Stopher (eds), *Behavioural Travel Modelling*, Croom Helm, London.

Domencich, T. and McFadden, T. (1975), *Urban Travel Demand: a Behavioral Analysis*, North-Holland, Amsterdam.

Fishburn, P.C. (1968), 'Utility Theory', *Management Science*, vol. 14 no. 5, pp. 335–78.

Hansen, P. Peeters, D. and Thisse, J.-F. (1983), 'Public Facility Location Models: A Selected Survey', in Thisse, J.-F. and H.G. Zoller (eds), *Location Analysis of Public Facilities*, North-Holland, Amsterdam, pp. 223–62.

Hakimi, S.L. (1965), 'Optimum Distributions of Switching Centers in a Communication Network and Some Related Graph Theoretical Problems', *Operations Research*, vol. 13, pp. 462–75.

Ingram, D.R. (1971), 'The Concept of Accessibility: A Search for an Operational Form', *Regional Studies*, vol. 5, pp. 101–7.

Isard, W. (1960), *Methods of Regional Analysis: An Introduction to Regional Science*, The MIT Press, Cambridge, Massachusetts.

Kajitani, Y. and Maruyama, T. (1976), 'Functional Expression of Centrality in a Graph: An application to the Assessment of Communication Networks', *Journal of JSEC*, vol. J59-A, no. 7, pp. 531–38.

Panzar, J.C. and Willig, R.D. (1977), 'Free Entry and the Sustainability of Natural Monopoly', *Bell Journal of Economics*, vol. 8, pp. 1–22.

Reilly, W.J. (1931), *The Law of Retail Gravitation*, Putman Ans Sons, New York.

Sharkey, W.W. (1982), *The Theory of Natural Monopoly*, Cambridge University Press, Cambridge.

Shinoda, S. and Sengoku, M. (1986), 'The Concept of Space Modification and a Theory of Function Measuring the Centrality (or Mediality) of a Point in a Network', *Journal of JSEC*, vol. J 69-A, no.1, pp. 42–53.

Weber, A. (1909), *Ueber den Standort der Industrien.Tbingen*, English translation 1929, The Theory of the Location of Industries, Chicago University Press, Chicago.

Weibull, J.W. (1980), 'On the Numerical Measurement of Accessibility', *Environment and Planning A*, vol. 12, pp. 53–67.

Weibull, J.W. (1976), 'An Axiomatic Approach to the Measurement of Accessibility', *Regional Science and Urban Economics*, vol. 6, pp. 357–79.

Williams, H.C.W.L. (1977), 'On the Formation of Travel Demand Models and Economic Evaluation Measures of User Benefit', *Environment and Planning A*, vol. 9, pp. 285–344.

Williams, H.C.W.L. and Senior, M.L. (1978), 'Accessibility, Spatial Interaction and Spatial Benefit: Analysis of Land Use-Transportation Plans', in Karlqvist, A., Lundqvist, L., Snickars, F. and J.W. Weibull (eds), *Spatial Interaction Theory and Planning Models*, North-Holland, Amsterdam, pp. 253–58.

Wilson, A.G. (1967), 'A Statistical Theory of Spatial Distribution Models', *Transportation Research 1*, pp. 253–69.

Wilson, A.G. (1971), 'A Family of Spatial Interaction Models and Associated Developments', *Environment and Planning*, vol. 3, pp. 1–32.

Wilson, A.G. (1974), *Urban and Regional Models in Geography and Planning*, Wiley, London.

Wilson, A.G., Coelho, J.D., Macgill, S.M. and Williams, H.C.W.L. (1981), *Optimization in Location and Transport Analysis*, John Wiley & Sons, New York.

Appendix

This appendix gives the proofs of Propositions 1 and 2.

Proof of Proposition 1

Since C(ß) is a nondecreasing, nonincreasing for marginal increment function, φ(ß) is nonincreasing, nondecreasing for marginal decrement. As long as a distance between any pair of nodes is given by the minimum-path rule, it follows from lemma 1 that for any node r and s such that $r \in S \cap I(p)$ and $s \in T(r) \cap Z$,,

$$\beta'(p,s) \leq \beta'(r,s)$$

Let b_p and b'_p denote vectors with the same dimension defined by $b_p=\{\beta(p,s):p\in V,s\in T(p:\beta)\}$ and $b'_p=\{\beta'(p,s):p\in V,s\in T(p:\beta')\}$, respectively, and δ, δ' vectors with the same dimension as b_p. If we put , then it follows from both the definition of variables, x and y, and the assumption of a monotone reduced transformation that $y \geq x$, $\delta \geq \delta' \geq 0$. From a nonincreasing property, it is straightforward to show that the first condition (I) is fulfilled. Now we let

$$G = \varphi 9x) - \varphi(x+\delta) - \{\varphi(y) - \varphi(y+\delta'\}$$

From a nonincreasing property, we have an inequality condition:

$$\varphi(y) - \varphi(y+\delta') \geq \{\varphi(y) - \varphi(y+\delta)\}$$

Accordingly, the following inequality holds:

$$G \geq \varphi(x) - \varphi(x+\delta) - \{\varphi(y) - \varphi(y+\delta')\} \geq \varphi(x) - \varphi(y) - \varphi(y+\delta)\}$$

Finally, the nondecreasing property for marginal decrement ensures that the last expression is nonnegative. This implies that $\delta F_p(\beta) \geq \delta F_r(\beta)$. QED

Proof of Proposition 2

(Sufficiency). Since ψ is nonincreasing and nondecreasing with respect to ß and ω, respectively, it is straightforward to show that the former part of the condition (i) holds. $\delta F_p(\omega) \leq \delta F_p(\beta,\omega)$ implies that

$$F_p(\beta',\omega') - F_p(\beta,\omega) \geq F_p(\beta',\omega) - F_p(\beta,\omega)$$

That is, variation in accessibility with respect to distance where change in weight is taken into consideration is at least as good as that without change in weight. The above inequality is fulfilled when the next inequality holds:

$$\psi(x_1,y_2) - \psi(x_2,y_1) \geq \psi(x_1,y_1) - \psi(x_2,y_1)$$

Since ψ is nondecreasing with repect to ω, we have , $\psi(x_1,y_2) \geq \psi(x_1,y_1)$, from which the above expression is directly derived. We can show in the same way that nonincreasing property with respect ß leads to $\delta F_p(\beta) \leq \beta F_p(\beta,\omega)$. Thus, the first condition holds. From Proposition 1, the condition (ii) is also satisfied. That is, if we put $x_1=b'_p=b_p-\delta, x_2=b'_r=b_r-\delta'$, then

$$\psi(x_1,y) - \psi(x_1+\delta,y) \geq (x_2 y) - \psi(x_2+\delta,y)$$

Equation (4.18c) implies that

$$\psi(\beta(u,t),\omega'(t)) - \psi(\beta(\upsilon,\tau),\omega(\tau)) \geq \psi(\beta(\varpi,\tau),\omega\ni(\tau)) \angle \psi(\beta(\varpi,\tau),\omega(\tau))$$

Therefore, the condition (iii) holds.

(Necessity). For , we assume that $\beta(p,t)<\beta(r,t)$. Consider a transformation such that for $\delta \geq \delta' \geq 0$

$$\beta'(p,t)=\beta(p,t)-\delta, \beta'(r,t)=\beta(r,t)-\delta', \quad \omega'(t) \geq \omega(t)$$

where we assume without a loss of generality that the interrelationships between other nodes except p, r and t are invariant. This assumption indicates that $r \in I(p)$ and $t \in Z$. Therefore, we get

$$\delta F_p(\beta)=\psi(\beta'(p,t),\omega(t))-\psi(\beta(p,t),\omega(t))=\psi(x_1 y)-\psi(x_1+\delta,y)$$
$$\delta F_r(\beta)=\psi(\beta'(r,t),\omega(t)\_-\psi(\beta(r,t),\omega(t))=\psi(x_2,y)-\psi(x_2+\delta',y)$$
$$\delta F_t(\omega)=\psi\beta(p,t),\omega'(t))-\psi(\beta(p,t),\omega(t))=\psi(x,y_2)-\psi(x,y_1)$$

In order to satisfy the condition (i) , it is necessary that the first and the third expressions are nonnegative, which in turn implies that ψ is nonincreasing with respect to ß and nondecreasing with respect to ω. As for $\delta F_p(\omega) \leq \delta F_p(\beta,\omega)$ the essential point is already described in proof of sufficiency. So omitted here. The conditions (ii) implies that

$$\psi(\beta'(p,t),\omega(t))-\psi(\beta(p,t),\omega(t)) \geq \psi(\beta'(r,t),\omega(t))-\psi(\beta(r,t),\omega(t))$$

From this we have

$$\psi(x_1,y)-\psi(x_1+\delta,y)\geq\psi(x_2,y)-\psi(x_2+\delta',y)\geq\psi(x_2,y)-\psi(x_2+\delta,y)$$

The above inequality imposes ψ be nondecreasing for marginal decrement with respect to ß. Finally, If we let $\beta(u,t)\leq\beta(v,t)$ and

$$\delta F_u(\omega)=\psi(\beta(u,t),\omega'(t))-\psi(\beta(u,t),\omega(t))=\psi(x_1,y_2)-\psi(x_1,y_1)$$
$$\delta F_v(\omega)=\psi(\beta(v,t),\omega'(t)-\psi(\beta(v,t),\omega(t))=\psi(x_2,y_2)-\psi(x_2,y_1)$$

then the condition iii) means that

$$\psi(\beta(u,t),\omega'(t))-\psi(\beta(u,t),\omega(t))\geq\psi(\beta(v,t),\omega'(t))-\psi(\beta(v,t),\omega(t))$$

This requires that ψ satisfies Equation (4.18). QED.

5 Accessibility, Peripherality and Spatial Development: The Question of Choice[1]

ROGER VICKERMAN

5.1 Introduction

This chapter returns to the question of how peripherality affects accessibility and the consequences of this for economic development. It concentrates on the various dimensions of choice inherent in perceptions of accessibility, of mode, route and carrier, and argues the need for a much more disaggregated approach to accessibility measurement for policy purposes. In two previous papers the question of accessibility in peripheral regions has been addressed; first, the concepts of accessibility and the possibility of their measurement (Vickerman 1995a) and, secondly, the relationship of accessibility measures to the potential for regional development (Vickerman et al. 1995). In this chapter we seek to go rather further in considering the problems of accessibility in peripheral regions, arguing that conventional measures fail to identify adequately the real constraints on peripheral regions. This is an important consideration in any discussion of the promotion of cohesion, but also affects attempts to assess the impact on competitiveness of new infrastructure or other improvements to the transport system.

We discuss first various definitions of peripherality to show that peripheral regions in Europe are far from a homogenous group. Secondly, we examine the relationship of these to conventional measures of accessibility. Thirdly, we introduce a number of case studies as an illustration of the issues discussed.

5.2 Peripherality and Accessibility

The first important issue which has to be addressed is the extent to which peripherality is an issue of accessibility. To some extent this will depend on the measure of accessibility adopted. Clearly peripherality is related to accessibility, but there is a danger of circularity in that on conventional measures peripheral regions must have poorer accessibility than central regions, by definition. However much transport is improved, that improvement will typically benefit central regions at least as much as peripheral regions. The problem of peripherality clearly involves more than just a measure of accessibility. The basic premise adopted here is that traditional measures of accessibility suffer from being defined as continuous measures of distance or time. The key problem of peripherality is that it implies discontinuities, either through a lack of connectivity in networks (Rietveld 1995) or the existence of barriers (Ratti 1993, 1995) and these breaks or barriers affect the economic organization and market structures in peripheral regions.

The discontinuities implicit in networks in peripheral regions thus affect more than just the physical transport and telecommunications networks, indeed probably more of the literature has been devoted to assessments of discontinuities in intellectual, innovation, technology transfer networks (e.g. Button and Rossera 1990). Such discontinuities are not unique to peripheral regions, they occur principally as a result of physical or political borders, this incidence of borders is simply more prevalent in more remote regions. For example, a firm in Finland or Portugal exporting to markets in Germany encounters more borders than an equivalent firm in the Netherlands, Belgium or France. However, peripheral regions also tend to suffer from more physical barriers in addition to these political borders. Physical barriers are principally water or mountain barriers. Peripheral countries in the European Union tend to experience one or more of these. Journeys to Finland and Ireland, for example, typically require two sea crossings for the shortest, most usual, routes – alternative routes removing one of these involve either longer sea crossings or poorer road access to the continental port. Traffic to Portugal has to negotiate the Pyrenees and poor road links across Spain.

The further, perhaps least researched, element of peripherality is economic or market peripherality. Lower traffic densities imply less competition in serving markets to and from, and within, peripheral regions. This lower competition applies both between and within modes. Peripheral regions do not have the choice of different modes experienced in core regions. The more remote the region the more likely it is served by only one or two modes (typically road and air). This lack of modal competition will tend to raise prices and reduce quality. The same happens within modes. Remote regions will typically not benefit from the competition between operators increasingly prevalent in and between core regions. This has been seen particularly in air transport where peripheral regions have fewer flights provided by the major flag carrier airlines at high prices.[2]

Even where there is evidence of competition, there may be important technical or technological limits to the market. Roads in sparsely populated regions will be of poorer quality. Except where there are abundant supplies of local hydroelectricity, it may be more difficult to provide electric traction for railways. Small airfields will not permit access to jet aircraft, and will typically not have safety features to allow all weather landing, for example in fog.

This impact is not just on the market structures in the transport sector. The discontinuities in transport and other networks lead to discontinuities in market areas which enable firms in peripheral regions to exploit spatial monopolies, but not scale economies, leading to higher costs and prices. However, factors of production will be less able to exploit this situation and typically we would expect wages, for example, to be lower in peripheral regions than in central regions. The more fragmented the networks the more fragmented will be markets and the less efficient on a world scale.[3]

This discussion leads to a series of propositions about issues in defining peripherality.

- that nothing can be done about geography; peripheral regions are by definition peripheral and no network development can change this. The problem is of the development of networks which is not holistic and which increases the impact of peripherality unnecessarily. Peripheral regions are also more likely to be dependent on a restricted range of, or even a single, mode(s).

- that the growth of the European Union changes the perception and problems of peripherality. The increasing geographical size of the Union emphasizes peripherality, but membership is perceived by new (peripheral) members as making peripheral areas seem to be less peripheral. Changes in the eastern borders of the EU have changed this perception even more.

- increasing peripherality has two dimensions:

  – the increased cost of serving the periphery from the centre, which falls more on the peripheral than on the central regions emphasizing the challenge to cohesion.

  – the interconnection of peripheral regions to each other is made even more difficult. This has the effect of fragmenting the periphery, which has become more diverse and substantial trade flows have not developed between the peripheral countries.

- that networks serving peripheral regions may be required to have a different geometry from those in more central regions. For example, it may be necessary to provide more indirect links through hubs than in core regions, imposing time and cost penalties. Accessibility may thus show greater variation in peripheral regions.

- that a distinction needs to be made between peripheral regions which are 'edge' regions in an absolute sense (e.g. those in the Atlantic Arc and especially those with an island status, such as Ireland), and those whose peripherality is subject to change in economic conditions, trade flows etc. and may change from true peripherality to transit or corridor regions (e.g. those on the eastern or southern fringes of the European Union) (Blum 1991).

- that concern with environmental pressures in central regions imposes costs, including environmental costs, on peripheral regions, leading to rerouting or modal change, to which they are less able to adjust.

- that peripheral regions suffer more from a high variance in access times and costs than just from a high mean in these values: improving reliability could thus be more critical than just increasing speed, especially where changes of mode are enforced by natural barriers or by historical factors such as differing rail gauges.

- that the construction of new infrastructure (e.g. bridges and tunnels) or technological development (e.g. of new transport modes, logistic systems or information technology) to improve accessibility may be less viable in peripheral regions due to lower traffic (especially transit traffic) volumes. Where new infrastructure has been constructed it may impose a serious financial burden on local traffic.

These definitions suggest that there exists a set of differentiable types of peripherality. These differ from each other in critical ways which imply that there is no common solution to the problems of peripheral areas. In an ideal model we would start from the microeconomics of the location of individual activities and the development of their market areas. Models in the tradition of the New Economic Geography following Krugman (1991) provide a basis for this in a theoretical model which offers insights about such factors as the degree of concentration of activity (e.g. Ciccone and Hall 1996) or the extent of vertical integration (e.g. Venables 1996). So far these theoretical models do not have a direct empirical content. They do show, however, the extent to which the outcome is essentially an empirical one in that there is no simple relationship between production function, location and transport. The outcome will depend on a trade off between scale economies, the importance of transport costs, the elasticity of substitution in production, and demand elasticities.

Peripherality is the result of a particular intersection of these factors – identifying the specific intersection is critical in understanding the issue and in defining appropriate policy responses. Table 5.1 provides an overview of the variation in peripherality issues between different types of peripheral region. These are measured in terms of settlement structure, network structure, infrastructure quality and market conditions. These four more easily observed factors represent the underlying economic factors of the microeconomic model outlined above. Settlement structure represents an initial attempt to capture the scale, elasticity and demand factors. Network and infrastructure quality are attempts to improve the rather crude transport cost representation used in the New Economic Geography models, which tend to use a simple Samuelson 'iceberg' approach (Krugman 1991). In this goods are seen to be consumed by transport rather than there being an explicit modelling of the nature of transport costs. The market conditions variable goes rather beyond the New Economic Geography models in that it represents a more explicit modelling of the market structure in the transport sector. These three factors taken together give a fuller representation of the transport sector rather than assuming transport is, in effect, ubiquitous in a region at a given location.

5.3 Measuring Accessibility in Peripheral Regions

It is not proposed to discuss the detail of alternative accessibility indicators here (see Vickerman 1995a, b; Vickerman et al. 1995, for further discussion), but to concentrate on the key issues which need to be taken into account when measuring impacts on peripheral regions. These will affect any conventional measure of accessibility.

Most measures of accessibility typically take an average, distance-based, measure as the basic unit. Where alternative modes are available these are incorporated either by taking the best mode for any particular journey, allowing for the use of different modes for access to the best mode where this is, for example, air or high speed rail, or by a modelling approach using observed mode choice to estimate appropriate weights (Vickerman 1995b). Discontinuities or changes of mode can be allowed for by introducing time penalties. There are three main factors which need to be developed. First, is the question of how to define a 'best' mode in a multimodal environment; secondly, how to measure an average accessibility for region which faces internal variations in accessibility; and thirdly, how to allow for the varying market structures which may be observed within a mode in different regions.

Best modes imply some subjective judgment as this is not necessarily the fastest over any particular distance. Choice of a best mode will need to account for access times, frequencies and the availability of alternatives. Moreover, the concept of a best mode suggests not just the average performance, but also the variance. Road users may prefer the slower but more predictable journey on a conventional road to a potentially faster motorway journey which faces the probability of congestion.

The introduction of fast ferries on some routes has not led to a massive switch from conventional, slower, ferries, given the unreliability of some of the early versions. New modes of transport, such as the Channel Tunnel, have had to prove their reliability in service before they have achieved their forecast market share. Where there have been reliability problems in certain services, such as through railfreight, these shares have still not been achieved.

Table 5.1 Typology and characteristics of peripheral regions

	Location	Settlement structure	Network characteristics	Infrastructure quality	Market characteristics
Edge regions	Coastal fringes	Sparse, but major enclaves, e.g. ports	Sparse, better connections to and between major centres	Generally poor, lack of modern roads, electrified railways, airports with automatic landing equipment	Lack of competition between modes, emphasis on single carriers, substantial state intervention
	Economic fringes	Variable, decline of traditional centres excluded from hinterland	Variable, better networks in areas subject to more recent change in economic relationships	Generally poor, lack of modern roads, electrified railways, airports with automatic landing equipment	Lack of competition between modes, emphasis on single carriers, substantial state intervention
	Mediterranean/Aegean Islands	Sparse, ancient centres lost traditional hinterlands	Very poor internal networks, larger islands have relatively good air links dependent mainly on tourist traffic	Extremely poor, except isolated airports dependent on tourist traffic	No competition between modes, relatively good links for tourist traffic not always available for other activities
Outer peripheral regions	Southern/Mediterranean	Medium density, some major urban settlements	Sparse to medium. Some well connected centres by air	Variable, but below average levels of motorway provision, electrification and airport quality	Lack of competition between modes, emphasis on single carriers, substantial state intervention
	Nordic	Very sparse, large distances between settlements	Very sparse, highly dependent on air, subject to disruption by weather/ require advanced landing systems	Capacity of roads adjusted to needs, quality good, electrified railways, airports better developed	Lack of competition between modes, emphasis on single carriers, substantial state intervention
Inner peripheral regions	Lowland	Medium density, mainly agricultural	Variable, dependent on level of transit traffic, poor provision of airports	Variable, average to below average levels of motorway provision rail electrification, and airport quality	Some competition between land modes, variable competition within modes
	Highland/Alpine	Low to Medium density, some important concentrations of population	Variable, dependent on level of transit traffic, poor provision of airports	Variable, average to low levels of motorway provision and railway electrification (except in certain transit corridors where high)	Some competition between land modes, variable competition within modes
Peripheral core	Edge of core regions	Low to medium density, small settlements, largely rural	Good high level networks, average regional networks, average to poor connectivity, access to airports often poor due to shadow of major centres	Variable, good high level networks, often poorer local networks, lack of airports with international connection	Average to above average competition between and within modes.

Accessibility indicators are typically measured at a regional level, suing some definition of zonal centroid. Distances or times are measured between these centroids. Increasingly it has been recognized that such averaging across a region does not give an adequate measure. Early measures of accessibility and potential such as those used by Keeble et al. (1982, 1988) used such coarse definitions as to be meaningless. More recent refinements (e.g. Lutter et al. 1992) used a finer definition of regions at the NUTS3 level, which in many core regions, based on a local labour markets definition, will give a reasonably accurate picture of accessibility. However in sparsely populated peripheral regions NUTS3 may still involve very large regions. Vickerman et al (1995) show how the use of a raster-based population structure developed by Spiekermann and Wegener (1995, 1996) can produce a much more sensitive accessibility surface. This can allow for differential accessibility to networks within regions. Whilst this highlights the major differences in accessibility between core and peripheral regions, it even more so highlights the differences within both core and peripheral regions justifying the finer gradation within both which is identified in Table 5.1.

Accessibility indicators have, however, never been developed to allow for differences in the market situation in the transport sector which lead to different levels of competition. Modes have generally been defined by the more objective modal characteristics of speed, frequency, comfort etc. Increasingly important, however, as the regulated structure of transport markets has been dismantled, is the increasingly different price structures which can be found for a given mode in different market situations. In air transport for example, fares to peripheral destinations are typically, kilometre for kilometre, substantially higher than those between major cities in the core. Fares between peripheral regions are even more disadvantageous because of the need typically to route through a core airport as a hub and either change carrier or use the carrier based in the core. Both of these can lead to substantial cost penalties. The hub operator often has substantial monopoly power over slots at the hub airport and can use this to offer better connectional facilities, but at a higher price reflecting the monopoly power. Other carriers face increased costs as a result of this, though it is interesting to note how the growth of certain alliances in Europe (e.g. SAS and Swissair) represented an initial attempt by smaller and geographically more peripheral carriers to provide links across core hubs. More recent moves have seen the larger airlines (e.g. Lufthansa) trying to recruit these alliances into their worldwide alliances.

The basic structure of accessibility indicators thus needs modifying, first to allow for continuity in accessibility across space, allowing for access points to networks, and, secondly, to build in a measure of the economic effects of differing transport market structures. Neither of these are fundamental in terms of the basic principles of accessibility indicators, but would provide a set of indicators which are potentially of much greater use, and which, more importantly, could provide a better link with models of location and industry structure. Some refinement is needed to the definition of the above factors before we are in a position to derive a definitive indicator. Towards this end we consider a number of practical issues arising from a series of case studies.

5.3.1 Case Studies

In order to explore the issues raised above in more detail a case study approach is to be used. This approach has been used in an earlier project to explore some of the disaggregation issues (Vickerman 1997). Four case studies have been undertaken, relating to the Nordic countries, Ireland, Portugal and Spain, which raise a number of different issues and deal with a number of the different types of peripheral area identified in Table 5.1. Here we can only present some very preliminary evidence from these studies which are still in progress.

These case studies[4] address the following main questions:

- the main traffic flows, by modes and routes?
- the main origins and destinations within the region, and whether these are principal or secondary nodes?
- the main bottlenecks or missing networks, whether these are outside or within the region, and whether they are related to natural barriers?
- whether the main traffic flows are in competitive industries of many suppliers/purchasers, whether they are handled by specialist logistics firms?
- whether transport is handled in a competitive market, both within and between modes?
- whether there are specific environmental factors affecting transport in this industry?
- whether the flows, route and modes, are likely to be affected by the growth of new markets and/or the possible expansion of the EU?
- whether attempts to overcome bottlenecks have involved the construction of new infrastructures, and how these have been financed?
- the perceived main transport constraints or threats in the region?

Perhaps the first, unsurprising, but nevertheless important to be repeated, finding is the extent to which peripheral regions have adjusted both their structure of production and their trade to suit their locational circumstances.[5] This is a well documented finding from earlier work (e.g. Chisholm 1985, 1987, 1992), but one which is too easily forgotten. This affects both mode choice and destination. For example, eighty per cent of Portuguese exports and over 90 percent of imports (by weight) are transported by sea. Most of this trade involves the import of raw materials (including oil) and the re-export of processed materials. This trade is oriented towards former colonies of Portugal. This is consistent with Portugal's extreme maritime situation. Ireland, however, appeared to specialize less in goods which exploit its location, rather those which can exploit its labour skills and adaptability to international technology (e.g. see Bradley 1995). Portugal's economy is thus less integrated in any real sense into the EU economy than that of Ireland and its transport needs are therefore substantially different. In the Nordic countries, the situation is different again with a heavy emphasis placed on the exploitation of natural resources, including forest products, which have very particular transport needs, and for which the main markets are in the core regions of Europe. However, the Nordic countries are less completely 'edge' economies than Ireland and Portugal with an important though changing transit traffic role with Russia.

All of these countries experience problems of transit traffic with other states. In the case of Portugal this is reduced in importance by the bias of trade away from land transport to the rest of Europe. However, this lack of heavy flows has presented problems in justifying the upgrading of appropriate routes to and through Spain. In addition there are five different frontier crossings which splits the given volume of traffic into even smaller flows.[6] In the case of Ireland the choice is of short sea versus long sea ferry crossing, and given this choice a problem of differential road development in another EU state. Even within the short sea crossing there is a choice between shorter crossing times (via Belfast/Larne-Stranraer/ Cairnryan), but longer land transits and longer sea crossings (via Dublin-Holyhead or Rosslare-Fishguard) but more direct total routes – this being complicated by the inner Irish border which requires the bulk of goods moving via the shortest sea route to pass over the land frontier into Northern Ireland. All UK transit routes also face a further sea crossing, with again a choice between the longer North Sea routes and the shorter Channel routes.[7] The longest sea routes (e.g. Rosslare-Roscoff) can avoid the UK completely but these are only appropriate for certain destinations. This choice of direct but longer sea routes against shorter sea routes, often a combination of such crossings, is particularly relevant to the situation in the Nordic countries. This is further complicated by some of the shortest and most direct routes involving transit of non-EU states with poor infrastructure such as Estonia and Poland.

The development of air transport has been a major factor in improving the accessibility of peripheral regions. However, there is a concentration of both passenger and freight movements in the main airports in each country. In Ireland almost 50 percent of all passenger movements are concentrated in Dublin and almost 85 percent in the main three airports. This is despite a deliberate policy to try and develop regional airports as a potentially more efficient way of improving accessibility than land transport in a sparsely populated region (Reynolds-Feighan 1994). In Spain, Madrid is less dominant with only 20 percent of total traffic and 17 percent of international traffic, given the importance of holiday traffic to the Mediterranean coast and islands. Nevertheless, almost 48 percent of total traffic is concentrated in the three airports of Madrid, Palma de Mallorca and Barcelona and 66 percent of international traffic is carried by the five largest airports, all of which handle more passengers than Dublin. In Portugal only three airports carry any significant international traffic, nearly 50 percent of which is handled by Lisbon.

Despite the rather different geographical and political structure of the Nordic countries the same sort of domination by a single airport occurs. Of the five main Nordic airports (Helsinki, Stockholm, Gothenburg, Oslo and Copenhagen), Copenhagen, the major hub airport for the Nordic countries, handles nearly 40 percent of the total traffic to other EU destinations (outside the Nordic countries) compared to under 30 percent of Nordic traffic. Oslo, by comparison, has only 14 percent of the EU traffic but nearly 22 percent of the inter-Nordic traffic.

The development of infrastructure in peripheral regions also follows rather different paths. Ireland, for example, has seen a major contraction in its once extensive railway system, with recent investment concentrated on improving suburban transport in Dublin and cross-city connections in Belfast. In contrast the road network has remained dense with responsibility falling to local administrations (County Councils) with an interest in improving local access. Road surface per 1000 inhabitants is well over twice the EU average and second only to that in Luxembourg, five time the Spanish provision and almost four times the Portuguese provision. The development of motorway standard roads has, however, fallen well behind that in other European countries and it is this which currently receiving the most attention (European Commission 1994). In Portugal the diversity of possible routes into Spain has led to a multiroute strategy and a deliberate multimodal strategy. This has led to substantial investment in both road and rail over the four major routes. However, effort has been concentrated on the one route which maximizes the investment within Portugal in an attempt to promote internal regional development independently of improved European level accessibility. In the Nordic countries much of the emphasis has been on a series of major new infrastructures across the seaways dividing Scandinavia from continental Europe: the Great Belt and Øresund crossings currently under construction and the proposed direct link across the Fehmarn Bælt. These will have a major impact on the internal accessibility of Denmark and on the ease of access to southern Sweden and the Oslo region as well as creating a major new metropolitan region out of the Copenhagen and Malmo areas. For comparison it can be noted that around 700,000 passengers a year used air services between Copenhagen and Stockholm in 1994/5 and a further 300,000 between Copenhagen and Gothenburg whilst some 23 million passengers travelled between Denmark and Sweden by ferry.

New links between Sweden and Denmark and continental Europe will also have the tendency to accentuate the relative remoteness of Finland which remains accessible only by a relatively long ferry crossing.

Thus a preliminary look at some evidence confirms the diversity of experience in peripheral regions. What this initial review cannot identify is how far the diversity of experience represents deliberate policy choices in the different countries and what the welfare effects of these are. This choice factor, and the balance between choice and constraint emerges as a major feature.

5.4 Choice and Spatial Development

A key theme which has emerged in this paper is that of accessibility as choice. The problem in accessibility disadvantaged regions is the lack of choice. This affects all dimensions of accessibility: destination, mode, route, frequency, reliability. It may affect different parts of a region, and different sectors within them, differentially. Identifying the sources of these differential choice sets, and codifying them, is a key objective in the development of this project.

There is a further issue which requires some discussion. Much of the focus of this chapter has been about the measurement of peripherality in terms of a refinement of the measurement of accessibility. This implies that improving accessibility will reduce peripherality such as to increase economic development and assist in policies of spatial development and cohesion in the European Union. It is suggested that a measure of accessibility which emphasizes aspects of choice will be more likely to represent a genuine measure of economic welfare. However, it remains less clear whether an improvement of accessibility of peripheral regions, however measured, will genuinely lead to a greater cohesion within the EU. This underlines the importance of enhancing such measures if they are to be used as policy indicators.

It is only likely that any progress will be made towards this goal if a better integration of the microeconomics of location and market structure with the economics of transport provision can be achieved. Previously those researching accessibility and location have lacked a consistent theoretical structure for firms in an imperfectly competitive market situation responding to changes in transport provision. This has limited the useful development of disaggregate accessibility models which allow for the competitive structure of the transport market. Now the further development of economic models with an explicitly spatial dimensions is constrained by the need for a better representation of that space than the 'iceberg' model of transport costs.

5.5 Some Conclusions

The main theme of this chapter has been to identify more clearly the link between accessibility and peripherality as operational concepts. The key element in this is one of showing how choice, of destination, mode, timing, reliability etc., is closely linked to the identification of peripherality. It is argued that only by tying these concepts more closely to the specific needs of the regional economies of peripheral regions will it be possible to produce a workable set of accessibility measures.

The preliminary analysis of evidence from four case studies of transport in peripheral regions does confirm the overall typology suggested in Table 5.1. In particular it shows the importance of identifying the differences between the main centres and other centres, especially for international connections. It also shows how strong tourist flows can lead to distortions in the provision of transport from a national perspective. Edge regions are also confirmed as having an economy which is principally directed to links outside the EU, in other words many peripheral regions are able to exploit their relative remoteness to economic advantage (see McKinnon 1997, for further evidence of this point).

A key point on which further work is urgently needed is the effect of poor communications between peripheral regions. Many have improving links to the main cities in the European core, but, as is often the case in urban transport, periphery to periphery links typically need to be routed through the core adding to both the direct cost to the user and to the social cost through congestion in the core. This raises some importunate policy questions as to the appropriateness of evaluation procedures for new links which are based on level of traffic flow. This is increasingly the case where private finance is being sought to enable projects to proceed and larger, more certain, traffic flows become the key factor in determining whether to go ahead. Any project by project assessment may result in an infrastructure network which is less appropriate in the longer term for peripheral regions.

This chapter has only presented the outline of an approach, but it is an approach which is so far proving to be a useful tool in classifying and evaluating transport projects in peripheral regions. The next stage is to move towards more objective and unambiguous measures of accessibility which can be used in evaluation. What is clear is that this will be a set of measures depending on the circumstances of a region, geographical and economic, not a single index.

References

Balassa, B. and Bauwens L. (1988), 'Determinants of intra-European trade in manufactured goods', *European Economic Review*, vol. 32, pp. 1421–37.

Beilinson, L. (1997), *Passenger transport between the Nordic Countries and other EU Countries*, Report to Cost 328, Helsinki.

Blum, U. (1991), 'The New East-West Corridor: An Analysis of Passenger Transport Flows Inside and Through Germany in 2010', in Vickerman, R.W. (ed.) *Infrastructure and Regional Development*, Pion, London.

Bradley, J. (1995), 'Analysing Structural Policies and Growth: Ireland and Portugal', in Armstrong, H.W. and R.W. Vickerman (eds), *Convergence and Divergence Among European Regions*, Pion, London.

Button, K., Rossera, F. (1990), 'Barriers to Communication: A Literature Review', *Annals of Regional Science*, vol. 24, pp. 337–57.

Chisholm, M. (1985), 'Accessibility and Regional Development in Britain: Some Questions Arising from Data on Freight flows', *Environment and Planning A*, vol. 17, pp. 963–80.

Chisholm, M. (1987), 'Regional Variations in Transport Costs in Britain with Special Reference to Scotland', *Transactions of the Institute of British Geographers*, vol. 12, pp. 303–14.

Chisholm, M. (1992), 'Britain, The European Community and The Centralisation of Production: Theory and Evidence, Freight Movements', *Environment and Planning A*, vol. 24, pp. 551–70.

Ciccone, A. and Hall, R.E. (1996), 'Productivity and The Density of Economic Activity', *American Economic Review*,vol. 86, pp. 54-70.

Crowley, J. (1996), *Case Study: Ireland*, Report to COST 328, University College, Dublin.

European Commission (1994), *Competitiveness and Cohesion: Trends in the Regions*, Fifth Periodic Report on the Social and Economic Situation and Development of Regions in the Community, Office for Official Publications, Luxembourg.

Fortunata Dourada, M. (1996), *Acesso de Portugal ao Centro Europa*, Report to COST 328, Junta Autonoma de Estrados, Almada, Portugal.

Hanson, G.H. (1996,) 'Economic Integration, Intraindustry Trade and Frontier Regions', *European Economic Review*, vol. 40, pp. 941–49.

Jacquemin, A. and Sapir, A. (1988), 'International Trade and Integration of The European Community: An Econometric Analysis', *European Economic Review*, vol. 32, pp. 1439–49

Keeble, D., Owens, P.L. and Thompson, C. (1982), 'Regional Accessibility and Economic Potential in The European Community', *Regional Studies*, vol. 16, pp. 419–32.

Keeble, D., Offord, J. and Walker, S. (1988), *Peripheral Regions in a Community of Twelve Member States*; Office for Official Publications, Luxembourg.

Krugman, P.R. (1991), 'Increasing Returns and Economic Geography', *Journal of Political Economy*, vol. 99, pp. 483–99.
Krugman, P.R. and Venables, A. (1990), 'Integration and The Competitiveness of European Industry', in Bliss, C. and J. Braga de Macedo (eds), *Unity with Diversity in the European Community*, CEPR/Cambridge UP, Cambridge.
Lutter, H., Putz, T. and Spangenberg, M. (1992), *Accessibility and Peripherality of Community Regions: the Role of Road, Long Distance Railways and Airport Networks,* Report to DGXVI, European Commission, Bundesforschungsanstalt für Landeskunde und Raumordnung, Bonn.
McKinnon, A. (1997), 'Logistics, Peripherality and Manufacturing Competitiveness', in Fynes, B. and S. Ennis (eds), *Competing from the Periphery*, Dryden Press, London.
Pasi, S. and Himanen, V. (1996), *Transport of Goods between the Nordic Countries and Central Europe*, Report to COST 328, VTT, Helsinki.
Ratti, R. (1993), 'Spatial and Economic Effects of Frontiers. Overview of Traditional and New Approaches and Theories of Border Area Development', in Ratti, R. and S. Reichmann (eds), *Theory and Practice of Transborder Collaboration*, Helbing and Lichtenhahn, Basel.
Ratti, R. (1995), 'How to Overcome Barriers and Border Effects: Theoretical Elements', in Coccossis, H. and P. Nijkamp (eds), *Overcoming Isolation*, Springer, Berlin.
Reynolds-Feighan, A. (1994), 'The Role of Regional Airports in Regional Economic Development in Ireland and The UK', Paper presented at the Regional Science Association International, British and Irish Section, Annual Conference, Trinity College, Dublin.
Rietveld, P. (1995), 'Some Notes on Interconnectivity in Transport Networks', in Coccossis, H. and P. Nijkamp (eds), *Overcoming Isolation*, Springer, Berlin.
Spiekermann, K. and Wegener, M. (1995), 'Microsimulation and GIS: Prospects and First Experience', in Klostermann, R. (ed.), *From Geographical Information Systems to Planning Support Systems*, Center for Urban Policy Research, Rutgers University, Picataway, NJ.
Spiekermann, K. and Wegener, M. (1996), 'Trans-European Networks and Unequal Accessibility in Europe', *EUREG*, no. 4, pp. 35–42.
Venables, A.J. (1996), 'Equilibrium Locations of Vertically Linked Industries', *International Economic Review*, vol. 37, pp. 341–59.
Vickerman, R.W. (1995a), 'Accessibility and Peripheral Regions', in Coccossis, H. and P. Nijkamp (eds), *Overcoming Isolation*, Springer, Berlin.
Vickerman, R.W. (1995b), 'Location, Accessibility and Regional Development: The Appraisal of Trans-European Networks', *Transport Policy*, vol. 2, pp. 225°–34.
Vickerman, R.W. (1997), 'Transport Provision and Regional Development in Europe: Towards a Framework for Appraisal', in Banister, D. (ed.), *Transport Policy and the Environment*, Chapman and Hall, London, forthcoming.

Vickerman, R.W., Spiekermann, K. and Wegener, M. (1995), 'Accessibility and Regional Development in Europe', Paper presented at the NECTAR Conference, Espinho, April.

Zaragoza-Ramirez, A. (1996), *Peripheral Regions and their Access to Networks. Case Study: Spain,* Report to COST 328, Asociacion Espanola de la Carretera, Madrid.

Notes

1. This chapter is based in part on a project 'Transport and Regional Development in Europe' funded by the UK Economic and Social Research Council (Grant No L119251008) and on the work of Working Group 1, Peripheral Regions, in COST328, Integrated Strategic Infrastructure Networks in Europe. An earlier version was presented at the NECTAR Euroconference No 3, FUCAM, Mons, September 1996. I am grateful to members of WG1 for material included in this paper, especially Veli Himanen, Jim Crowley, Kent Bentzen Maria Fortunata Dourado, Aniceto Zaragoza-Ramirez, and to participants in the Mons conference for their comments, but none of these should be held responsible for views expressed here, which are the author's own.

2. Though interestingly some of the most competitive air routes in Europe are those between various major cities in the UK and Ireland. This arises principally because these routes are particularly densely trafficked given the strong labour market ties and other common language and cultural factors, which are seen to increase the degree of trade (Balassa and Bauwens 1988; Jacquemin and Sapir 1988).

3. See for example Krugman (1991); Krugman and Venables (1990); Ciccone and Hall (1996); Venables (1996); Hanson (1996).

4. These case studies have been undertaken as part of the COST328 project.

5. Evidence in this section is drawn mainly from five reports prepared for COST328, Beilinson (1997); Crowley (1996); Pasi and Himanen (1996); Fortunata Dourada (1996) and Zaragoza-Ramirez (1996).

6. Only one exceeded an average of 3500 vehicles per day in 1985.

7. Including now the possibility of using the Channel Tunnel which imposes a break of journey similar to a ferry crossing.

Part B
Methodological Frameworks: Locational Behaviour and Trade

6 Education Intensity and Interregional Location Dynamics

ULLA M. FORSLUND-J.

6.1 Introduction

The purpose of this chapter is to study the dynamic process of industrial location in Swedish and Norwegian regions. This is done by comparing the regional location of economic activities. The process is empirically studied by means of a model which adheres to the tradition of relative urban dynamics (Batten 1985; Johansson and Karlsson 1990). The urban dynamics model is based on two supporting theories. The first is the central place systems model (CPS model) with references to Beckmann (1958, 1996), and Tinbergen (1967). The second theoretical background is a model of spatial product cycles (Hirsch 1967; Andersson and Johansson 1984).

A core region for introduction of new economic activities is identified in a Scandinavian context. Growth and decline paths for each industry in other regions are related to the concentration ratios of the respective industry in the core region. In this exercise we can identify a clear structure of interregional leads and lags in the overall process of structural adjustments. Activities will gradually diffuse between different locations in a hierarchy of urban regions. The chapter also shows, with the help of regression technique, that concentration ratios in the core region can be explained by the education pattern and education intensity of industrial sectors both in the core region and in other regions.

6.1.1 The Process of Economic Restructuring

Structural adjustments in the economy can be characterized in several ways. However, we may extract four elements which are especially important in this process. The first aspect is intersectoral changes due to decomposition of firms into separate establishments. For example, instead of using its own lawyers, a firm may buy the pertinent services from external legal offices. The second aspect relates to standardization and automation in a sector. A consequence of this process is reduced labour input, but also relocation of activities. The third aspect of structural adjustments is growth and decline of output in a sector. Changing demand conditions bring about expanding or shrinking markets for the product. The fourth and last aspect is introduction of new products. In this process new products will compete with old products, and in certain cases squeeze the latter out. Note that the concept of product includes both goods and services.

In general, the four processes described above are initiated in leading urban regions and are followed with lags in the follower regions. There is however one condition which needs to be fulfilled. The structural adjustment consists of both exit and entry events – maturing product vintages leave the region, and new enter. If this process works smoothly, the economy of the region will be renewed. Without sufficient exit, potential entry will be blocked. Since labour, premises and infrastructure are limited resources, economic renewal will be prevented if obsolete activities occupy the existing built environment. The entry/exit process is described in Figure 6.1. It should be emphasized that exit from a leading region may stimulate entry in follower regions. Observe that also in follower regions entry may require that other activities exit.

As mentioned above, infrastructure is one element in the explanation of how economic activities are initiated and spread from one region to another. To explain this process we use both a dynamic CPS model and a dynamic product cycle theory. According to the theory, a region's economic milieu, including size, economic density and infrastructure is one of the key factors which influence economic restructuring (Johansson 1993; Ciccone and Hall 1996). Activities are assumed to move between locations with different economic milieu (location attributes). New economic activities, including new products, demand a different set of infrastructure attributes than established, and mature economic activities. In this process new activities replace old ones in a continuous motion.

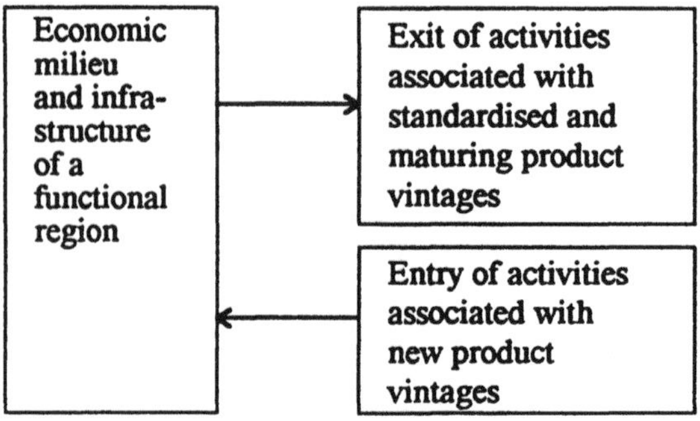

Figure 6.1 Renewal of activity patterns with given urban infrastructure

The concept of infrastructure may be defined in different ways. If we restrict ourselves to built infrastructure, it may be defined as built environment satisfying the following properties (Johansson 1993):

- It is capital with a fixed location and spatial extension.
- It exhibits generality with regard to different categories of actors and types of activities, as well over time.
- It has a public good nature in at least some dimension.
- It has systems functions by providing interaction possibilities and by integrating activities around these possibilities.

Physical capital may be divided into two groups; production specific and production general capital. The production specific capital is heavily fixed and committed to a given production process. As a consequence it will loose its value when production ends. The production general capital, on the other hand, can be used by a number of different activities. This means that there are no, or only small, costs of switching from one type of production to another.

In this context an urban region is infrastructure. It is a built system with components and subsystems with infrastructure properties. This should apply more or less to most urban regions. There are of course exceptions to this. One can identify urban regions which are designed to serve a few specific industrial sectors. As a consequence, other activities which require another type of infrastructure may not find it natural to locate in this region.

From the above discussion it follows that for a region to be leading it is necessary (but not sufficient) to have a rich endowment of production general infrastructure. In such a built environment, maturing activities may migrate away to other regions, while new activities move in. Economic structural adjustment is also influenced by other attributes of the regional milieu. In addition to infrastructure, a region's economic milieu comprises the composition of economic activities located in the region (e.g. Krugman 1991).

Why is it then that some activities move away from one region to another? The answer to that question involves the cost profiles for activities with different stages of standardization. Referring to product cycle theory, after the embryonic and early phase of the product's life – when both the product itself and the production process are developed – the product becomes available to costumers. In this first phase, the cost of producing the product is relatively high. There is a large share of development costs such as knowledge acquisition, information about preferences of customers, R&D and market development. When the product has been established in the market it will be exposed to potential competitive producers. When substitutes are introduced, the cost of producing the product becomes more and more important. Economies of scale in production will be a vital condition for the producer. One important component in the cost of production is the price of land. Compared to small settlements in more peripheral areas, the cost of land is higher in central and larger urban regions (von Thünen 1826). This gives incentives to locate the production process outside the high cost area when the product has reached a more mature stage in its life (Andersson 1985). The same observations can also be used as a means to induce a dynamic relocation process in the CPS model.

Thus, industries which benefit from a certain location more than other activities, can squeeze the latter out from their original premises by offering higher rental payments. In this way the same built infrastructure can be used repeatedly by new economic actors. If this process functions smoothly, an urban region can retain its attractiveness.

Of course, there are other factors influencing location patterns. One factor is the accessibility to labour supply with a broad education profile. Industries that require a specific kind of educated people have to locate where these can be found. In that respect, a large and dense urban region will have an advantage compared with more sparsely populated areas. One may refer to this phenomenon as an infrastructure agglomeration effect, as discussed already by Marshall (1920) and later by e.g. Krugman (1991).

In this chapter we will study the development of a large set of sectors in order to analyse the diffusion process and the leader/follower relationship. Of course, leader and followers cannot unambiguously be classified in a complete and strict way. However, in frequency terms one can order urban regions into a hierarchy which remains invariant during long time intervals.

The spread of sectors from a leading urban region to less central and to peripheral areas cannot be assumed to be valid for all sectors. First, there are sectors which strongly depend on the supply of natural resources. These sectors are restricted to locations close to the relevant primary product. Second, there are sectors that need a critical mass of population. An example of such an activity is an underground transit system. For both these cases the outlined theory does not apply, in the sense that these activities should not be expected to diffuse to a gradually larger number of settlements.

6.1.2 Outline of the Chapter

The chapter starts in Section 6.2 with a description of the underlying theory. Section 6.3 puts forward the hypothesis that the Mälardal region is a leading region in a Scandinavian context. The aim is to trace the spatial diffusion of sectors from the leading region to follower regions. Section 6.4 contains a general study of education profiles for different groups of sectors. In this section, it is shown that the level of education in a sector influences its location pattern in such a way that high education intensity increases the likelihood of a high concentration in the leading regions of a economy. The conclusions of the chapter are presented in Section 6.5.

In the subsequent analysis two classification levels are employed. When the analysis is focused on comparisons between Sweden and Norway, comparability requires that a 90-sector classification is used. In some of the analyses of Sweden and Mälardalen, a 105-sector classification is applied. This is explicitly specified in the pertinent tables.

Irrespective of the level of sectoral subdivision, each sector contains a set of similar but differentiated activities. Moreover, each activity refers to one or several similar but differentiated products. As a consequence, a sector represents a cluster of products. It is assumed that the theoretical framework can be applied to such clusters (product groups) in the same way as to individual products.

6.2 Theoretical Background

6.2.1 Standardized and Non-standardized Activities

An enterprise can develop its business either by adjusting the attributes in response to customer demands and/or improving production and interaction techniques or processes. The first category of renewal is related to non-standardized and the second to standardized activities. An economic activity refers to the production and distribution of both goods and services.

A standardized economic activity may be characterized in the following way: (i) the output is time invariant, standardized and hence the same for many different customers, and (ii) the production method is routinized and often automated. The generic case of development towards increased standardization can be described as follows. We consider a product with given and unchanged attributes. The vintage of the production technique is signified by τ. Following Johansson (1987) the profit per unit output, $\pi(\tau)$, of technique τ can be written as

$$\pi(\tau) = p - c(\tau) \tag{6.1}$$

where p denotes the output price (which is assumed to fall over time) and $c(\tau)$ denotes the unit cost of production, based on vintage τ. The modernity and degree of standardization of a process is described by increasing values of τ = 1, 2,... The different cost levels of various vintages are expressed by the function *c* such that $c(\tau) > c(\tau + v)$ for $v > 0$, where vintage $\tau + v$ has lower costs than τ. New vintages have to be introduced in response to gradual reductions of the output price p.

Let us now distinguish between two categories of inputs. By h-inputs we denote resources which are used for knowledge acquisition, information about preferences of customers, R&D and market development. The share of h-inputs is high for non-standardized activities. On the other hand, b–inputs are basic for automation, standardization and solutions relying on economies of scale. With this specification the cost function becomes

$$c(\tau) = pb(\tau) + \omega h(\tau) \tag{6.2}$$

The improvement of techniques for producing a given category of products follows a systematic path such that the h-resources become successively less important over time as new technical vintages are developed. Hence, $h(\tau)/b(\tau) > h(\tau+ v)/b(\tau+ v)$. All this is a temporal statement. The spatial phenomenon is caused by an uneven distribution of resources of h and b type. The accessibility to h-resources is much larger in certain urban regions than in other less knowledge and R&D intensive regions. Such urban regions are likely to be leaders in the economic development if they also have a high accessibility to alert customers with large purchasing power.

One important difference between the model introduced here and a standard product cycle model is that the distinction in this paper between non–standardized and standardized activities does not necessarily presume that all non-standardized activities develop into maturing, routinized and obsolete activities. In particular, non-standardized activities include customized delivery of goods and services such that each delivery has new and individual attributes. For all such activities we cannot observe cycles at all; renewal is a continuous motion. However, at an aggregate level we can observe how clusters of such activities increase or decrease. In this sense one may still refer to Schumpeter waves of different length and amplitude.

6.2.2 *Two Complementary Explanatory Models*

A central-place systems model (CPS model) classifies all urban regions (cities) such that each city belongs to a rank level k. The market size of cities belonging to category k is denoted by M_k. The system is characterized by its ordering of market sizes such that $M_K > \ldots > M_k, > \ldots > M_1$, where M_K refers to the city with the highest rank and M_1 all regions of the lowest rank. Commodities (goods and services) of the highest rank are supplied only from the city of category K and distributed over the urban system. Commodities of category k+1 are supplied from several centres of rank k+1 to subsystems of centres on lower levels. Some of these features have been studied in detail elsewhere. Here we shall focus on how commodities (or product groups) may shift position over time and thereby reshaping the specialization pattern.

A feasible location for a market oriented firm which supplies a commodity of type j depends on the function which applies at a given point in time for the production of this commodity. To describe this, let F_j denote the fixed costs, including the non-variable part of development costs. Consider also the variable costs which may here be approximated by a proportional cost component c_jQ_j, where c_j is a fixed coefficient and Q_j denotes output or supply. This yields

$$C_j = F_j + c_jQ_j \tag{6.3}$$

It is assumed that supply is always larger or equal to demand such that $f_j(p_j) M_k \leq Q_j$, where $f_j(p_j) M_k$ denotes the demand. Given the cost function in (6.3), a firm supplying commodity j can locate in a central place k, if it can break even. For a given price p_j this is equivalent to the following condition:

$$(p_j - c_j) f_j (p_j) M_k - F_j \geq 0 \tag{6.4}$$

Next, let p_j^* denote the price which maximizes the aggregate profit function

$$\Pi_k(p_j) = (p_j - c_j) f_j (p_j) M_k - F_j \tag{6.5}$$

which describes the maximum profit a single supplier can obtain. With n suppliers, the function changes to $\Pi_k (p_j) = (p_j - c_j) f_j (p_j) M_k / n - F_j$.

In the sequel we shall study the dynamics of this hierarchy by introducing a technical change process. The change of production techniques in an industry *j* is described by technique vintage index τ (based on (6.1)), which is close to 0 for a new process and approaches 1 as the technique matures. Because of this, the cost function in (6.3) has to be respecified to read

$$C_j(\tau) = F_j(\tau) + c_j(\tau)Q_j \tag{6.3'}$$

We assume that $Cj(\tau)$decreases and that $F_j(\tau)$ does not increase as (τ) increases. This implies that an industry which supplies commodity j may initially have a feasible location in central places with k as the lowest rank. As the technique vintage increases, a feasible location can gradually be found in places of lower rank. Hence the location of all supply activities with the described technical change process will filter (or diffuse) down the urban system as a consequence of the following inequality:

$$F_j(\tau + v)/[(p_j^* c_j(\tau + v)) f_j (p_j^*] < F_j(\tau)/[(p_j^* - c_j(\tau)) f_j (p_j^*)] \tag{6.6}$$

where $c_j(\tau + v) < c_j(\tau)$ due to technical change.

The conclusion in (6.6) refers to the dynamic process in relation to (6.1). The product cycle model (PC model) also refers to 6.1. In addition, the specification in (6.2) gives the PC model its characteristic dynamic process. Also in this specification one can observe a decline in the per unit cost as the vintage index τ increases. However, with the PC model one emphasizes that factor prices may differ between different regions. Let us suppose that region r has a high concentration of knowledge resources, h-inputs, and that region k has a low concentration. Then we expect the following price relations:

$$\omega_r < \omega_k \text{ and } \rho_r > \rho_k \qquad (6.7)$$

From (6.7) together with (6.2) one can see that the location advantage of region k will be improved as an economic activity becomes more standardized. For an non-standardized activity we may have $c_r(\tau) = \rho_r b(\tau) + \omega_r h(\tau) < c_k(\tau) = \rho_k b(\tau) + \omega_k h(\tau)$ while a standardized activity may satisfy $c_r(\tau^*) = \rho_r b(\tau^*) + \omega_r h(\tau^*) > c_k(\tau^*) = \rho_k b(\tau^*) + \omega_k h(\tau^*)$, where $\tau^* > \tau$.

It may be concluded that for activities which become standardized in accordance with the CP model, the prediction is that these activities are usually introduced in knowledge oriented regions. Later, less knowledge oriented regions gradually become feasible locations. It is often assumed that large urban regions have a higher knowledge intensity than smaller ones. The extent to which this is correct, the PC model predicts gradual downwards diffusion in the central place system, partly similar to the CPS model.

In summary, the CPS model dynamics which was introduced in (6.3) – (6.6) refers in particular to products for which the h/b-ratio remains fairly invariant, also when the pertinent activities become increasingly standardized. The PC model describes relocation and filtering down for economic activities such that h/b is significantly reduced during the standardization process. Moreover, contrary to the outcome in the CPS model, certain activities may be significantly reduced in or even totally removed from regions in which these activities were initially started. Finally, the leader/follower model which is employed in this study captures the location dynamics of both the CP and the CPS models.

6.2.3 Leaders and Followers

In reference to the analysis in section 6.1 and 6.2, activities can be classified into categories which are expanding as a share of total production and those for which the share is falling. A leader region can be characterized by having an earlier start and initially a faster growth of expanding activities compared with imitating regions. The latter can on the other hand, be expected to achieve a higher expansion rate at a later phase.

A classification of regions into leaders, early and late followers should be interpreted in frequency terms. Innovations and early imitations occur much more often in the leader regions than elsewhere. Moreover, they provide examples to other regions and demonstrate that the new activities are both feasible and profitable. According to the model, novel activities and young, non–standardized product vintages are frequently initiated and promoted in leader regions. In order to leave 'space' for new activities, standardized and maturing product vintages must gradually be removed from the leading region. One important mechanism in this context is the formation of land price differentials of the von Thünen type. In such a model the price-bid functions of different activities vary with the quality of urban infrastructure, designed for synergistic processes of human interaction. This includes the formation of commercial strategies and business alliances, the import of technology and technical equipment as well as scanning the world economy with regard to customer preferences, the emergence of new products, and the introduction of new technical solutions.

The above characterization can be translated into urban infrastructure qualities which are always scarce. A leader region can ascertain the usefulness of the infrastructure by continuously stimulating the exit of standardized, maturing and even obsolete activities to other locations, while simultaneously facilitating the entry of new activities into the same urban environment.

The development of a product i may be described as follows. The employment share of the activity related to product i in region r is defined as:

$$\sigma_i^r = \frac{x_i^r}{\Sigma_j x_j^r} \tag{6.8}$$

where x_i^r denotes the number of persons employed in sector i, in region r, and $x^r = \Sigma_j x_j^r$ For simplicity, x^r is assumed to be constant in the following model exercises. In order to analyse the dynamics of τ_i^r, two extremely simplified models are introduced. Both model variants are assumed to apply to leader, early and late follower regions. As discussed earlier, the dynamics are based on ideas of self-organization, along similar lines as introduced in Arthur (1988), Silverberg (1988) and Metcalfe (1988).

Consider the first model version and introduce the following variables:

A_i^r = resource capacity located in r, which is of critical importance for the possibility of an expansion in sector i, i.e. for $\dot{x}_i^r > 0$. (6.9)

q_j = consumption or use of resource A_i^r per person employed in sector j. (6.10)

D_i^r = demand potential which at a certain point in time is directed towards region r. (6.11)

With these definitions the following adjustment model is formulated:

$$\dot{\sigma}_i^r = \min \begin{cases} a_i^r (A_i^r - \Sigma q_j x_j^r) \sigma_i^r \\ a_i^r (D_i^r - x_i^r) \sigma_i^r \end{cases} \tag{6.12}$$

where a_i^r is a speed of adjustment parameter which for a given sector may differ between leader and follower regions. Stimulation to expansion obtains if

$$A_i^r - \Sigma q_j x_j^r > 0, \text{and}$$
$$D_i^r - x_i^r > 0 \tag{6.13}$$

This means that growth requires both enough critical resources and positive excess demand. Competition from other sectors may make the first equation negative and competition from other regions may make the second negative. In both cases the implication is a falling sectoral share.

Consider now the interpretation of A_i^r. It may, for example, represent the supply of certain categories of labour or producer services, as well as specific infrastructure attributes, including accessibility conditions. Our general assumption is, that leader regions have a richer endowment of resources which are critical for the introduction of new economic activities of products. But also in these regions such resources become scarce when a lot of new activities are introduced, combined with a delayed exit of mature or obsolete activities. Under these conditions, our model implies that new products should be expected to have an opportunity to start also in regions which in other cases would be a typical follower region. To study this, one may as in Arthur (1988) embed the dynamics in a stochastic setting.

In a longer term A_i^r is not a constant itself, but a variable which changes as a consequence of investments. These may be thought of as slow dynamics which respond to capacity tensions.

One may also contemplate the nature of the demand potential represented by D_i^r. Implicitly, we have already assumed that D_i^r with high frequency manifests itself in a leader region. In other words, if r is a typical follower region, one should expect D_i^r to be zero or small at an early stage of activity i's product cycle, while the demand has already become considerable in a leader region. The diffusion from the leader region is then not only a spread of technology information, it is also a diffusion of demand itself. One should also remember that overall demand expands as production costs fall and bring about lower market prices.

The second model version illustrates the importance of intraregional price formation as regards located resources such as infrastructure in general, the supply of premises, producer services and labour. Let us define B_i^r as the budget that firms in sector i have left for the purchase of the local resources which are critical for the expansion of the sector in region *r*. One may think of B_i^r as a kind of gross profit variable, calculated as sales minus costs, except those which are defined as costs of critical resources. Next, let ω_i be the compound price per unit of the critical resources. With these new variables, equation (6.12) may be transformed into the following expression:

$$\dot{\sigma}_i^r = a_i^r \left[B_i^r - \omega_i q_i x_i^r\right] \sigma_i^r \tag{6.14}$$

In equation (6.14) B_i^r will shrink as demand and profits diminish. Moreover, as competition for the critical resources become tight, the price variable ω_i will grow. In this way (6.14) replaces the two different growth conditions in formula (6.12).

Generically, equations (6.12) and (6.14) describe adjustment processes which follow sigmoid paths, either expanding or declining. In this context, one may note that formula (6.12) has two different gap or tension expressions, which both are multiplied by the speed of the adjustment parameter and by σ_i^r. The latter multiplication captures the self-reinforcing of the change process. The same characterization applies to equation (6.14).

Referring back to the discussion in Section 6.2.1, one may observe that activities which enter a phase of standardization in general, also experience that new resources become critical. This is described as a change in relative importance between h- and b-resources in the previous section. At the same time B_i^r may be too small to cover the costs of these new critical resources. Often the demand for production space increases during phases of standardization. This phenomenon represents the relocation incentives in a product cycle development.

6.3 Mälardalen – A Leading Region?

6.3.1 Hypotheses

From the theoretical framework outlined in Section 6.2, several testable hypotheses can be derived. In Forslund and Johansson (1994, 1995) a specific set of hypotheses were examined in order to decide whether the

Mälardal region[1] is a leading region or not. The hypotheses were derived in order to test the leader/follower relationship between the Mälardal region and other regions, including compound regions such as the rest of Sweden and Norway. One of the empirical measures used in the study, is Mälardalen's concentration index, μ_i, for sector i which is defined as:

$$\mu_i = m_i/s_i \tag{6.15}$$

The variable m_i refers to the Mälardal region and denotes the number of persons employed in sector i divided by the total employment in the same region. By s_i we denote the corresponding ratio for Sweden.

First, we make a distinction between expanding and declining sectors. Figure 6.2 illustrates the leader/follower case for expanding sectors. For those sectors the following hypotheses can be derived:

- Sectors with a high concentration index, μ_i, in the Mälardal region, have a fast expansion rate in the follower regions.
- For new activities with a high μ-value but still a rather low m-value, the growth is expected to be high both in the Mälardal region and its follower regions.
- When activities have ended their growth in the Mälardal region (point T in Figure 6.2), the growth may still continue in follower regions.

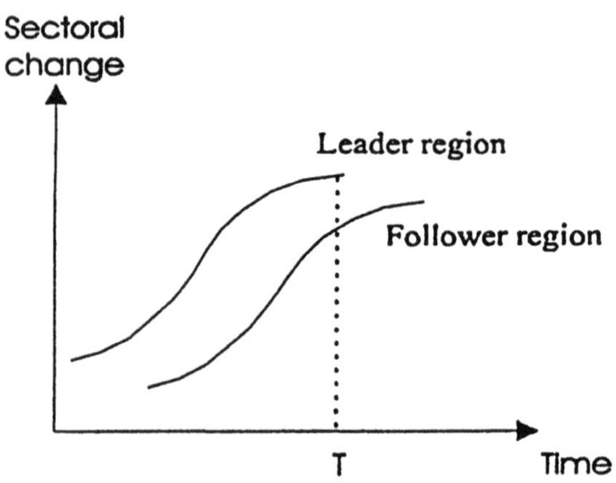

Figure 6.2 Leader and follower regions for expanding sectors

According to the model, sectors with a high concentration in the Mälardal region have been introduced in that region at an early stage of the associated product cycle. As the diffusion process continues, the growth will stagnate in the Mälardal region, but increase in the follower regions.

Sectors with a low concentration in the Mälardal region can be divided into three categories. The first consists of sectors which always have had a low concentration. The second group consists of sectors which have had a high concentration in the Mälardal region in an earlier phase, but are now declining. The third category contains young and recently introduced sectors. For declining sectors the following hypotheses can be formulated:

- Sectors for which μ_i is low in the Mälardal region, will have a negative growth rate in the follower regions.
- For sectors with a low μ-value, the decline is initially slower and later faster in the follower regions than in the Mälardal region.
- When activities have reduced their speed of decline in the Mälardal region, the decline may continue in the follower regions.

In Figure 6.3 the leader/follower relationship for declining sector is illustrated.

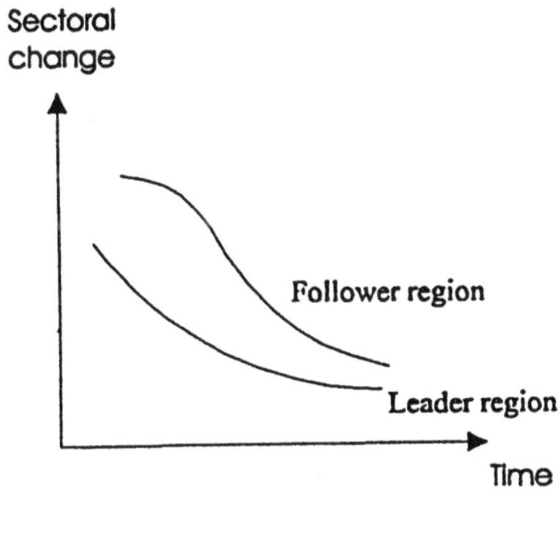

Figure 6.3 Leader and follower regions for declining sectors

In a deterministic sense, one should not expect the hypotheses to be necessarily correct for all sectors at a given point in time. The reason for this is simple: each sector is heterogenous with a different composition in each region. It is easy to specify a set of causes which affect individual sectors and municipalities in such a way that a random deviation patterns is obtained. However, we assume that the hypotheses are acceptable in a statistical sense. For most sectors the statements are expected to be true, in the sense that we cannot reject them. This assessment is presented in the subsequent section.

6.3.2 Preliminary tests

In the first empirical analysis of expanding and declining sectors, the Mälardal region is compared with the rest of Sweden. The economy is divided into 105 sectors and these sectors are grouped according to their different concentration levels and growth rates. In the assessment, we cross–classify the growth rate, G_i, in the follower region against the μ_i-index for each sector in the Mälardal region. Table 6.1 specifies the class limits. The growth rate is given in percent per decade.

Table 6.1 Class limits for the concentration index and growth rate of each sector

High concentration	$\mu_i \geq 1.4$
Medium concentration	$1.4 > \mu_i \geq 0.7$
Low concentration	$0.7 > \mu_i$
Fast growth, %	$G_i \geq 30$
Slow growth, %	$30 > G_i \geq 0$
Negative growth, %	$0 > G_i$

Table 6.2 Sectors with a high concentration index in the Mälardal region, 1990 (105 sector classification)

Fast growth in the rest of Sweden	Slow growth in the rest of Sweden	Negative growth in the rest of Sweden
Financial services	Urban transport	Beer
Computer services	Wine & liquor	Unions & other organizations
R&D services	Instruments	Wholesale of production inputs
Advertisement & marketing	Photo & optical equipment.	Retail trade
Air transports	Printing	
Technology trade	Miscellaneous transp & comm.	
Pharmaceuticals	Other financial institutions	
Restaurants	Insurance services	
Special consulting	Telecomm. products	
Legal services	Computer & office equipment	
	Electr. motors, generators & electr. equipment.	

In Table 6.2 we describe the sectors with a high concentration in the Mälardal region. We also indicate the Swedish growth rate of each sector. We observe that sectors with high concentration in the Mälardal region in general are both R&D and knowledge intensive. The subset of sectors with fast growth in Sweden are to a large extent so called advanced services.

There is a shift when we turn to Table 6.3 which describes sectors with a medium concentration in the Mälardalen region. In this case R&D and knowledge intensity is high only for the subset of sectors with fast growth in Sweden. The pattern is further strengthened in Table 6.4, which contains sectors with a low concentration in the Mälardal region. Most of the sectors exhibit negative growth.

Table 6.3 Sectors with a medium concentration index in the Mälardal region, 1990 (105 sector classification)

Fast growth in the rest of Sweden	Slow growth in the rest of Sweden	Negative growth in the rest of Sweden
Hotel services	Other public & private services	Railroad transport
Cleaning services	Construc. & repair of aircraft	Fertilizers & agrochemicals
Accounting services	Soaps & detergents	Flour products
Rental of machinery	Postal services	Agricultural machinery
Engineering consulting	Construct. & other spec.mach.	Vegetable and animal & fats
	Construction	Ceramics
	Property agencies	Paint products
	Sugar, sweets & chocolates	Lubric., asphalt & coal products
	Other food products	Non-ferrous metals
	Other wholesale trade	
	Bakery products	
	Petroleum products	
	Energy production	
	Electrical engineering	
	Other retail trade	
	Education services	
	Bank services	
	Transportation agencies	
	Recreation services	
	Diary products	

Table 6.4 Sectors with a low concentration index in the Mälardal region, 1990 (105 sector classification)

Fast growth in the rest of Sweden	Slow growth in the rest of Sweden	Negative growth in the rest of Sweden
Other paper products	Motor vehicle	Glassware
Beverages	Fibres & plastics	Wood products
Metal furniture	Road freight transport	Cutlery
Fruit & vegetables	Metal constructions	Preparation of meat
Plastic products	Cycle & motorcycle	Wooden containers
Paper products	Watches and clocks	Other machinery
	Veneer products	Other manufacturing industry
	Other metal products	Fish products
	Consumer electrical products	Clay products
		Chemicals
		Wooden furniture
		Other chemical products
		Tobacco
		Other transport equipment
		Paper & pulp
		Railroad equipment
		Other wood products
		Metal & wood working machinery
		Agricultural products
		Sawnwood
		Mining
		Iron & steel
		Prepared animal feeds
		Turbines
		Textiles
		Clothes
		Waterway transportation
		Leather products
		Rubber products
		Ship building
		Shoes

We may conclude, that the category of fast growing sectors is dominated by various kinds of services and R&D oriented sectors, while stagnation is observed among mature and traditional manufacturing industries. Most of the sectors which are growing with a fast speed in the rest of Sweden have already reached a high concentration rate in the Mälardal region. At the same time the above tables also reveal that activities with a low concentration index in the Mälardal region gradually reduce their relatively importance in the rest of Sweden.

6.3.3 Incidence Matrices

This section presents the result of the analyses of Sweden and Norway as followers to the Mälardal region. The tests were presented in Forslund and Johansson (1994, 1995) and are only repeated here.

The tests were done by contingency table analysis which is a χ^2-test of independence. We cross-classify the concentration rates for the sectors in the Mälardal region with the growth rate for the corresponding sectors in Sweden and Norway, using the class limits reported in Table 6.1. In addition, Table 6.7 cross-classifies the Mälardal region and the rest of Sweden. In this case the result is especially strong.

Table 6.5 Growth of sectors in Sweden for sectors which have a high, medium and low concentration in the Mälardal region (90 sector aggregation; expected values within parentheses)

	Concentration in the Mälardal region, 1990			
Growth in Sweden, 1980-1990	High	Medium	Low	Total
Fast	6 (3.2)	5 (5.8)	7 (9.0)	18
Slow	9 (5.0)	11 (9.0)	8 (14.0)	28
Negative	1 (7.8)	13 (14.2)	30 (22.0)	44
Total	16	29	45	90

Table 6.6 Growth of sectors in Norway for sectors which have a high, medium and low concentration in the Mälardal region (90 sector aggregation; expected values within parentheses)

	Concentration in the Mälardal region, 1990			
Growth in Sweden, 1980-1990	High	Medium	Low	Total
Fast	7 (3.1)	8 (5.5)	2 (8.4)	17
Slow	4 (3.1)	8 (5.5)	5 (8.4)	17
Negative	5 (9.9)	13 (17.9)	37 (27.2)	55
Total	16	29	44	89

Table 6.7 Growth of sectors in the rest of Sweden for sectors which have a high, medium and low concentration in the Mälardal region (90 sector aggregation; expected values within parentheses)

	Concentration in the Mälardal region, 1990			
Growth in Sweden, 1980-1990	High	Medium	Low	Total
Fast	7 (3.2)	4 (5.8)	7 (9.0)	18
Slow	8 (5.7)	16 (10.3)	8 (16.0)	32
Negative	1 (7.1)	9 (12.9)	30 (20.0)	40
Total	16	29	45	90

As we can see from the above tables, the sectors with a high concentration in the Mälardal region tend to be those with fast growth rates across Sweden and Norway, while those with low concentration in the region tend to be contracting nationally. The χ^2-value is significant for all three regions;

$$\chi^2_{\text{Sweden}} = 18.2; \chi^2_{\text{Norway}} = 21.1; \chi^2_{\text{Rest of Sweden}} = 25.0 .$$

The critical value for a 99 per cent level of significance is 13.28, which means that we are able to reject the null hypotheses that the growth rate and the level of concentration are independent of each other.

Norway seems to be more of a follower than Sweden. The sectors are more concentrated along the diagonal. Compared with Sweden, the share of sectors with a high concentration level and a fast growth is somewhat higher in Norway, but above all, there is a large share of sectors which have a low concentration in the Mälardal region, and are declining in Norway.

We may note that the above analyses were carried out using a 90 sectors aggregation. This aggregation was selected due to difficulties in obtaining consistency between Swedish and Norwegian data. However, we also did the same analysis for Sweden and the rest of Sweden with a more disaggregated set of sectors. When using a 105 sector classification, the result is even stronger. It is now particularly clear that a high concentration in the Mälardal region is associated with rapid national growth. The set of activities exhibiting both high regional concentration and rapid national growth is now more biased toward high knowledge intensity sectors and advanced services.

Summarizing this section, one may conclude that the initial tests indicate that the Mälardal region is a leading region, at least compared to Sweden, the rest of Sweden and Norway. It has a large share of employment in expansive sectors, but also a small share – on the average – of declining sectors. In particular, the Tables 6.2-6.4 reveal the following very distinct pattern:

- For sectors with a high μ-value, 21 out of 25 have a positive growth rate.
- For sectors with a medium μ-value, 25 out of 34 have a positive growth rate.
- For sectors with a low μ-value, 31 out of 46 have a negative growth rate – and only 6 have a fast growth rate.

6.4 Education Profiles Across Sectors

6.4.1 Hypotheses

In this chapter we have assumed that sectors with high concentration levels in the Mälardal region mainly consist of knowledge and R&D intensive sectors and that this share for particular products gradually declines as the level of concentration declines. In this section we will study how the level of education differs among sectors. With the preceding sections as background, two hypotheses may be formulated:

- Sectors which have a high concentration in the Mälardal region and are growing fast in the rest of Sweden, have a high share of employment with university education.
- Sectors with a high concentration in the Mälardal region have in general a higher share of university education compared to sectors with a low concentration.

6.4.2 Tests

In Table 6.8 we have grouped the sectors in the same way as earlier in this paper, i.e. according to their (i) concentration levels in the Mälardal region and (ii) growth rates in the rest of Sweden. For each segment we record the (national) average education shares.

According to Table 6.8 there is a strong tendency for sectors with a high concentration to be more education intensive compared to sectors with a low concentration. The same is valid also for fast growing sectors. Especially, sectors which have a high concentration in the Mälardal region and at the same time grow fast in the rest of Sweden is the most knowledge demanding group. Even the sectors which have a negative growth but a high concentration have a larger share of high education than sectors with a low concentration. This result is indeed in line with our hypothesis that the so called h-inputs are more important than b-inputs to fast growing, high concentrated sectors.

The next step in the analysis is to study the relationship between concentration (in the Mälardal region), growth (in the rest of Sweden) and education intensity by means of regression technique. The education variable used here, UNIV, includes both short and long university as well as post graduate education. The education variable is measured on a national basis.

Table 6.8 Education intensity (in percent) for group of sectors, 1992: national average

Concentration in the Mälardal region	Growth of sectors in the rest of Sweden	Post graduate	Long university[1]	Total university[2]
High	Fast	2.2	15.7	33.5
	Slow	0.4	9.4	21.0
	Negative	0.7	14.9	27.0
Medium	Fast	0.4	13.3	26.8
	Slow	0.6	12.9	28.1
	Negative	0.08	3.0	9.8
Low	Fast	0.1	3.1	9.8
	Slow	0.07	2.8	9.0
	Negative	0.2	3.5	10.6

[1] Long university includes three or more years at university.

[2] Total university includes both short and long university as well as post graduate education.

In the first part of the analysis, the relationship between concentration and education intensity is examined. A simple linear regression yields the following result:

$$\underset{}{\text{Concentration}} = \underset{(4.44)}{0.32} + \underset{(8.07)}{3.19}\text{UNIV} \qquad R^2 = 0.39 \tag{6.16}$$

There is a clear association between the two variables. The t-values which are shown within parenthesis are highly significant and the R^2–value is almost 40 percent. How is it then with the subset of sectors which have a high concentration in the Mälardal region and at the same time grow fast in the rest of Sweden? A logit analysis gives:

$$\begin{array}{l}\text{High concentration} \\ \quad \text{and fast growth}\end{array} = \underset{(-5.50)}{-4.67} + \underset{(3.85)}{9.93}\text{UNIV} \qquad \chi^2 = 21.2 \tag{6.17}$$

The connection between concentration, growth and education intensity has also been analysed by multiple regression. Table 6.9 gives the parameter values both for an ordinary linear equation and a Cobb–Douglas function.

Table 6.9 Relationship between concentration, growth and university education

Dep. Variable	Const	Parameter value x_1=UNIV	t-value x_1	Parameter value x_2=Growth	t-value x_2	Adj. R^2	Model
Concen-tration	0.43	2.63	6.80	0.003	4.30	0.47	Linear
Concen-tration	0.92	0.65	4.23	0.04	0.51	21.5	Cobb-Douglas

The results in this section strongly support our hypotheses about the connection between concentration rates and educational level. Education intensity is higher for sectors with a high concentration than for sectors with a low concentration. In particular, education intensity is greatest for those sectors which have experienced the most rapid growth during the period. This applies both to high concentrated as well as low concentrated sectors.

6.5 Conclusions

This chapter studies the spatial diffusion of sectors. A leading region is identified in terms of initiating and developing new activities. Given the economic restructuring process, we may trace the diffusion of categories of sectors from the leading region to follower regions.

The analysis has identified to one important or critical input to expansive, fast growing sectors. They require a larger share of employees with university education than stagnating and declining sectors. If high education is a necessary condition for those sectors, then the diffusion of the sector to other regions will depend on the supply of this input in the relevant region.

The major conclusion is that there is a clear pattern of leads and lags in the joint Sweden-Norway area. Sectors with a high concentration in the Mälardal region are growing fast in Sweden as well as in Norway. In addition, most industries which have a high concentration in the Mälardal region, have a much higher share of employees with university education than industries with a low concentration. Moreover, most of the industries which are knowledge and R&D oriented have a high growth rate and a high concentration in the Mälardal region.

References

Andersson, Å.E. (1985), *Kreativitet, Storstadens Framtid* (Creativity, the Future of the Urban City, in Swedish), Prisma, Stockholm.

Andersson, Å.E. and Johansson, B. (1984), *Knowledge Intensity and Product Cycles in Metropolitan Regions*, Wp-84-13, IIASA, Laxenburg, Austria.

Andersson, Å.E., Batten, D.F. and Karlsson, C. (eds) (1989), *Knowledge and Industrial Organization*, Springer-Verlag, Berlin.

Andersson, Å.E., Batten, D.F., Kobayashi, K. and Yoshikawa, K. (eds) (1993), *The Cosmo-Creative Society*, Springer-Verlag, Berlin.

Anderstig, C. and Karlsson, C. (1989), 'Spatial Diffusion of Information Technology in Sweden', in Andersson, Å.E., Batten, D.F. and C. Karlsson (eds), *Knowledge and Industrial Organization*, Springer-Verlag, Berlin.

Arthur, W.B. (1988), 'Competing Technologies: An Overview', in Dosi, G., Freeman, C., Nelson, R., Silverberg, G. and L. Soete, *Technical Change and Economic Theory*, Pinter Publishers, London.

Batten, D.F. (1985), 'The Changing Economic Structure of Metropolitan Regions', *Scandinavian Housing and Planning Research*, vol. 2, pp. 207–23.

Batten, D.F., Casti, J. and Johansson, B. (eds) (1987), *Economic Evolution and Structural Adjustment*, Springer-Verlag, Berlin.

Beckmann, M.J. (1958), 'City Hierarchies and the Distribution of City Sizes', *Economic Development and Cultural Change*, CI 3, pp. 243–48.

Beckmann, M.J. (1996), 'The Location of Market Oriented Industries in a Growing Economy', Paper presented at the 5th World Congress of the RSAI in Tokyo, May 1996.

Cheshire, P.C. and Gordon, I. (eds) (1995), *Territorial Competition in an Integrating Europe: Local Impact and Public Policy*, Aldershot, Gower.

Ciccone, A. and Hall, R.E. (1996), 'Productivity and the Density of Economic Activity', *American Economic Review*, vol. 86, pp. 54–70.

Dosi, G., Freeman, C., Nelson, R., Silverberg, G. and Soete, L. (1988), *Technical Change and Economic Theory*, Pinter Publishers, London.

Forslund, U.M. and Johansson, B. (1994), 'The Mälardalen: A Leading Region in Scandinavia?', Working paper TRITA-IP AR 94-12, Department of Infrastructure and Planning, Royal Institute of Technology, Stockholm.

Forslund, U.M. and Johansson, B. (1995), 'The Mälardalen: A Leading Region in Scandinavia and Europe?', in Cheshire, P.C. and I. Gordon (eds), *Territorial Competition in an Integrating Europe: Local Impact and Public Policy*, Aldershot, Gower.

Hirsch, S. (1967), *Location of Industry and International Competitiveness*, Oxford University Press, London.

Johansson, B (1993), 'Economic Evolution and Urban Infrastructure Dynamics', in Andersson, Å.E., Batten, D.F, Kobayashi, K. and K. Yoshikawa (eds), *The Cosmo-Creative Society*, Springer-Verlag, Berlin.

Johansson, B. (1987), 'Technological Vintages and Substitution Process', in Batten, D.F., Casti, J. and B. Johansson (eds) (1987), *Economic Evolution and Structural Adjustment*, Springer-Verlag, Berlin.
Johansson, B. and Karlsson, C (1990), 'Stadsregioner i Europa' (Urban Regions in Europe), *SOU 1990:34*, Allmänna Förlaget, Stockholm.
Johansson, B. and Westin, L. (1987), 'Technical Change, Location, and Trade', *Papers of the Regional Science Association*, vol. 62, pp. 13-25.
Krugman, P. (1991), *Geography and Trade*, Leuven University Press, Leuven and the MIT Press, Cambridge, Mass.
Marshall, A. (1920), *Principles of Economics*, Macmillan, London.
Metcalfe, J.S. (1988), 'The Diffusion of Innovation: An Interpretative Survey', in Dosi, G., Freeman, C., Nelson, R., Silverberg, G. and L. Soete, *Technical Change and Economic Theory*, Pinter Publishers, London.
Silverberg, G. (1988), 'Modelling Economic Dynamics and Technical Change: Mathematical Approaches to Self-Organisation and Evolution', in Dosi, G., Freeman, C., Nelson, R., Silverberg, G. and L. Soete, *Technical Change and Economic Theory*, Pinter Publishers, London.
Tinbergen, J. (1967), 'The Hierarchy Model of the Size Distribution of Centres', *Papers of the Regional Science Association*, vol. 20, pp. 65-80.
Von Thunen, J.H. (1826), *Der Isolierte Staat in Beziehung auf Landwirtschaft und Nationalökonomie*, English translation (1966), *The Isolated State*, Pergamon Press, New York.

Note

1. In this study, the Mälardal region includes the county of Stockholm and the municipalities Uppsala, Enköping, Håbo, Västerås, Köping, Arboga, Eskilstuna and Strängnäs.

7 Economic Milieu, Specialization and Location Dynamics

BÖRJE JOHANSSON

7.1 Introduction

This chapter examines how specific combinations of regional attributes offer location advantages for specific categories of economic activities and land use in general. According to the central place model (CPS) a region's most important attribute is its accessibility to demand, and this gives a specialization pattern which tends to reflect the size and density of a region (Beckmann 1958). With reference to the comparative advantage theory (Ohlin 1933), variations in supply attributes of regions give them individual opportunities to specialize in accordance with pertinent advantages. In an LA model (location advantage=LA) every region finds its own specialization, given the located (trapped) resources which constitute the invariant (slowly changing) economic milieu of each particular region. In Beckmann and Puu (1985) milieu differentials are represented by spatial variations in interaction opportunities.

In this study, location attributes of an urban region constitute the region's economic milieu.

A theoretical framework is outlined to explain why such a milieu can be advantageous for sets of economic activities. This framework refers both to the CPS and the LA models and observes that these models define static equilibria of location patterns. In the framework of this chapter, CPS and LA formulations are extended to reflect location dynamics These model exercises are presented as a background for a set of empirical studies referring to Sweden. In these studies the economic milieu is characterized by its density, but also by other location attributes which can reflect location attractiveness in view of CPS and LA models. With regard to different groups of service sectors a location advantage index is estimated. By means of an econometric model it is shown that regions with a high index value are attractors for overall growth of jobs.

7.1.1 *Density, Infrastructure and Accessibility*

Ciccone and Hall (1996) present econometric results indicating that productivity differentials between regions can be attributed to differences in economic density. They employ two models for which spatial density results in aggregate increasing returns. In one of the econometric models this outcome is based on local geographical externalities. A second model refers to the density of local intermediate services (deliveries). The density discussion by Ciccone and Hall can be further illuminated by introducing the concept of economic milieu.

Milieu advantages in urban regions are described by Hägerstrand (1970) by emphasizing that it facilitates considerably the contacts between decision makers, between experts, and between sellers and buyers. This argument is accentuated if it is combined with observations in recent decades of an emerging knowledge economy (Malecki 1980; Noyelle 1983; Andersson 1985). This development implies that the average firm gradually uses an increasing share of knowledge intensive labour inputs. Another and related characteristic of the change is that a growing share of the value added is allocated to R&D investments (Andersson et al. 1989; Anderstig and Hårsman 1986). In this type of economy nearby personal interaction becomes an inherent element of development, production and transaction processes. It can then be argued that under these conditions industries will benefit from urban density with proximity and multiple contact possibilities.

Economic density can be interpreted as intraregional accessibility, where 'region' is defined as a functional region. The latter is characterized by a high frequency of spatial interaction between actors within the region (compare daily commuting region). However, in the model outlined here it is not density per se but accessibility to resources and between economic agents that matters. In other words, a certain level of density needs to be matched by a corresponding capacity and quality of the region's infrastructure. Otherwise congestion phenomena will reduce the accessibility effect which the density in combination with infrastructure (interaction networks) is capable of providing.

The observation above refers back to Marshall (1920) and his discussion of agglomeration economies and to Henderson (1974) who argued that in equilibrium disamenities from agglomeration may offset the corresponding productivity advantages. Another suggestion is the model by Dixit and Stiglitz (1977) which indicates that if non-transportable intermediate inputs are produced with increasing returns, they will generate agglomerations. It has also been argued that agglomeration effects are reinforced by endogenous technology adoption (Johansson and Westin 1987).

According to the analyses and studies presented subsequently, networks for interaction are important for knowledge-handling and development activities of firms, in both service and manufacturing industries. This implies that knowledge intensive and non-standardized activities should be expected to have a high location intensity in dense regions. It remains to make precise which other location attributes, besides density, that provide appropriate conditions for knowledge based and knowledge handling activities (Batten et al. 1989; Kobayashi et al. 1991). In the empirical parts of this paper density dependence is found for knowledge oriented activities both as regards services and goods production.

7.1.2 *Sketching the Theoretical Framework*

Although one can identify a general change process moving towards increasing knowledge intensity across sectors and regions, it is still possible to observe differentiation between two basic types of production, dichotomized into (i) routinized (ii) knowledge-based and non-routinized activities. In addition, it is assumed that routinized production tends to be associated with standardized products (goods and services), while knowledge-based activities are assumed to provide non-standardized products. Following arguments in the previous subsection, activities of type (ii) are attracted by dense, knowledge-intensive urban regions. Routinized activities, on the other hand, favour locations with generous supply and low costs of land, labour and other standardized inputs. This pattern can be assumed to be the result of spatial relocation processes which resemble the established model of spatial product cycles (Hirsch 1967; Norton and Rees 1979; Andersson and Johansson 1984).

Not all products can be assumed to follow a strict spatial product cycle with pertinent relocations. Hence, type (ii) activities may remain in dense and contact friendly environments over extended periods during which firms continuously renew and customize their supply. In such cases there may be very little direct relocation from knowledge intensive regions to other categories of regions.

The distinction between (i) routinized and (ii) knowledge-based activities can be complemented by an additional distinction, separating products with high and low distance sensitivity. High distance sensitivity implies that a dominating fraction of all deliveries will take place within a functional region. When the costs of delivering a product are less distance sensitive, the location of production can to a larger extent be based on where the best input conditions can be found. In view of this one may identify two forms of specialization – demand-based and supply-based specialization. In the first case the CPS model has a role to play, while in the second case LA models are more appropriate. In addition, LA models identify innovative regions as places which combine a concentration of purchasing power and dense supply of knowledge resources. A spatial-price-equilibrium (SPE) model will represent the LA approach. The latter model can also incorporate product cycle phenomena.

In this way the economic milieu of an urban region may provide advantages for demand-based and supply-based locations. The economic milieu is assumed to adjust at a much slower pace than most other economic variables. The regional milieu comprises those location attributes which are regionally trapped and which influence the transaction, production and innovation possibilities. In addition, a dense milieu represents agglomeration economies which implies that it evolves in a self-organizing and self–reinforcing way. Some of the regional attributes are given by nature. Other attributes are created by accumulation and investment processes – including experiences, knowledge and competence of the labour force in the region, assuming that households display a low mobility. Infrastructure and the entire built environment constitute another set of investment-based regional attributes (Biehl 1986; Lakshmanan and Elhance 1985). In the model formulations, the economic milieu is characterized by its accessibility features, i.e. the pattern of accessibility to labour inputs, to intermediate inputs, to competitors, etc.

The CPS and LA models in this paper will be employed to examine how accessibility and other milieu changes influence location conditions. Moreover, when processes of technical change are superimposed, each of the models predict changes in location conditions. These model exercises help to describe how the initiation, expansion and profitability options of economic activities depend on the economic milieu of a region. Given a specification of milieu attributes, the models can be applied to predict location and relocation patterns in frequency or probability terms. The model conclusions are followed by a series of empirical illustrations and indirect tests.

7.1.3 Outline of the Chapter

Section 7.2 presents the theoretical framework of the paper. An initial task is to identify regional characteristics which adjust on slow time scales. A region's economic milieu has to be described by means of these characteristics or attributes. A second task is to formulate models explaining or depicting demand-based and supplied-based specialization of regions, where specialization is identified by observing variations in location intensity.

Section 7.3 classifies regions with respect to population density. It shows with Swedish data how regional density is strongly correlated with location intensities over different categories of industries, such as (i) high and low value manufacturing products, (ii) interaction services, (iii) business services, and (iv) knowledge production services.

Section 7.4 focuses on two aggregates of service production – interaction services and knowledge intensive business and financial services. A set of location attributes are presented and used in regression equations to show how the location intensity of each category of service activity depends on these attributes. Moreover, these regressions generate for each sector a location advantage index (or indicator), with a specific value for each municipality.

In Section 7.5 the location advantage indices are used in a quasi dynamic econometric model which is applied to the aggregate growth and decline of jobs in Swedish municipalities. This exercise shows that the overall change of job location during a decade is strongly correlated with location advantage indices referring to our two categories of service activities. This indicates that location attributes which influence the location of our selected service sectors, also influence the overall growth of private sector jobs. In particular they differentiate the growth rates among municipalities. Section 7.5 ends with conclusions about the relation between the empirical results and the theoretical framework that is introduced in the chapter.

7.2 Economic Milieu and Location Intensity

7.2.1 A Region's Economic Milieu – Time Scales and Indicators

The time scale assumptions in this study are organized as follows. First, production factors of firms such as installed capital and employed labour adjust to market signals in a delayed way, i.e. they adjust slowly compared to the speed of change of market signals themselves, such as prices, current input flows, sales volumes and profits. Second, the economic milieu adjusts on a slower time scale than capital equipment of firms. As a consequence it can affect production possibilities in a fundamental way and influence location dynamics as well. Third, labour supply is assumed to adjust on a time scale which is slow enough to make labour supply a component of the economic milieu. This implies that location attributes will include the production knowledge and experiences of the labour force. Earlier studies inform us that accessibility characteristics of a region represent a basic component of the region's location attributes (Wigren 1984, 1985; Andersson et al. 1990; Forslund and Johansson 1995). In summary: due to its slow pace of adjustment the economic milieu functions as the structure on which the fast game of competition and interaction is played. Because of this time scale difference, one can also assume that the economic milieu of a municipality can attract and repel specific sets of transaction and production activities.

The slowly changing location attributes may be classified as location–specific infrastructure. Other attributes like agglomeration diversity may be somewhat less time invariant but can be assumed to be strongly correlated with slowly changing attributes. In this context we observe that Marshall (1920) identified three specific conditions which explain why firms in a certain sector tend to be localized, i.e. why they can function more efficiently when located near each other. First, an industrial centre – and in particular a diversified urban region with several industrial centres – allows a pooled (and robust) market for workers with specialized skills such that both workers and firms benefit from the robust market. Second, the same urban region can provide non–traded inputs specific to each of its localized industries at lower costs. Third, new and subtle information can spread more easily and accurately in a local environment than in distant networks, and this generates market and technology spillovers. The same three conditions can also be applied to explain why the multiplicity and richness of a specific economic milieu (agglomeration diversity) simultaneously brings benefits to firms in many sectors.

The Marshall inspired arguments above mean that a specialized industrial centre can self-reinforce its location advantages for a specific industry. Moreover, a vital and multifaceted urban region can do even better. It can provide (i) a creative milieu, (ii) a diversified supply of various producer services, (iii) an intraregional network for information flows about new production techniques, products, suppliers and customers, and (iv) a differentiated supply of labour categories (Andersson 1985; Johansson 1993b). This enumeration of location attributes tends to emphasize intraregional accessibility and the associated infrastructure. It also implies that firms mutually may constitute each other's production milieu characteristics. One may simply add the importance of interregional interaction links and pertinent accessibility properties.

In the models employed in the subsequent analysis a distinction is made between intraregional and interregional accessibility to a particular group of contact options. In both cases accessibility is determined by two factors: (i) interaction costs and (ii) the size of contact options. The first component is determined by the capacity and quality of the interaction infrastructure (especially interaction networks). The second component is closely related to the density of contact options in each region (density of economic activities).

Consider a set of zones or nodes ($j = 1,...,m$) within an urban region r. The density of contact options or contact value of each node is denoted by A_j. For a given infrastructure, I_r, the intraregional accessibility increases as the A_j-values are augmented, given that the infrastructure capacity is sufficient. As interaction increases capacity tensions (congestion effects) will start and the accessibility is reduced.

For a given zone the accessibility to the A_j-values can be described as follows

$$a_{rj} = \sum_{k=1}^{m} \exp\{-\lambda_I d_{jk}\} A_k \qquad (7.1)$$

where d_{jk} represents some relevant distance (interaction effort) measure, e.g. time, and where λ_I signifies the distance sensitivity of economic actors. From (7.1) one may calculate an average accessibility value $a_r = [a_{r1} + a_{r2} ... + a_{rm}]/m$ or a compound value $a_r = a_{r1}^{\beta 1} ... a_{rm}^{\beta m}$. These values reflect the 'useful density' of the region. If the density is increased while the infrastructure remains unchanged the product $\lambda_I d_{jk}$ will increase for each link (j,k), and this will reduce accessibility. Hence, in this way accessibility is simultaneously determined by density and infrastructure capacity.

The accessibility between two regions s and r can be described by a formula which resembles (7.1). Using a_r as an indicator of region r's attractiveness, the accessibility from s to r is described by

$$a_{sr} = \exp\{-\lambda_{II} d_{sr}\}\, a_r \tag{7.2}$$

Since formula (7.1) refers to very frequent intraregional interaction and formula (7.2) to much less frequent interregional interaction, consistency requires that $\lambda_I >> \lambda_{II}$. Moreover, one may recognize that $a_{ss} = a_s$. Also in this case, the measure is calculated contingent on the existence of sufficient infrastructure capacity. Congestion on the link (s,r) will increase the value of $\lambda_{II} d_{sr}$.

7.2.2 The Central Place Perspective

In this subsection a hierarchical urban system is introduced, based on the central place theory as formulated in Beckmann (1958, 1996). In this setting, each city has a rank representing its market size, and the rank determines which types of commodities will be supplied from the city itself and which commodities the city has to import. It will be demonstrated that this model generates demand-based specialization, and that location patterns change as a result of both technical development and accessibility alterations.

A CPS model classifies all urban regions (centres) such that each region (city) belongs to a rank level k. The market size of cities belonging to category k is denoted by M_k. The system is characterized by its ordering of market sizes such that $M_K > ... > M_k > ... > M_1$, where M_K refers to the city with the highest rank and all regions of the lowest rank. Commodities (goods and services) of the highest rank are supplied only from the region of rank K and distributed over the urban system. Commodities of category k+1 are supplied from several centres of rank k+1 to subsystems of centres on lower levels.

Beckmann (1996) presents a CPS-model with equilibrium properties, such that the market size of a centre attracts location of activities which in turn attracts population and determines the city size. Moreover, the market size for all ranks of the central place system is determined under complete interdependency (see also Tinbergen 1967). Following Beckmann, a central place of rank k+1 serves its internal market of size $\Psi_{k+1} - \Psi_k + M_k$, where Ψ_i denotes the population size of a city with rank i = k, k+1. In addition the same centre delivers commodities of category k+1 to m_{k+1} central places of rank k. Thus, for a city of rank k+1, the market size can be specified as:

$$M_{k+1} = \Psi_{k+1} - \Psi_k + M_k[1 + m_{k+1} \exp\{-\lambda d_{k+1}\}] \tag{7.3}$$

where d_{k+1} signifies the distance from a city of rank k+1 to its demand associated cities of rank k, λ the friction parameter referring to deliveries from supply sites of rank k+1 to markets of rank k, and where λ may have a specific value for each commodity. It follows directly from (7.3) that accessibility changes which reduce the distance and/or the friction parameter will influence the system of central places and hence the market landscape.

Given the described urban system, how can a feasible location for a market oriented firm which supplies a given type of commodity be determined? Formally, it depends on the production function which applies at a given point in time, and on the technical vintage τ that applies. To describe production when technology τ is employed, let $F(\tau)$ denote the fixed costs, including the non-variable part of development costs. Consider also the variable costs $c(\tau)x$, where $c(\tau)$ is a fixed coefficient for a given τ and where x denotes output or supply. This yields

$$C(\tau) = F(\tau) + c(\tau)x \tag{7.4}$$

Given this cost function a firm can locate in a central place k, if it can break even there. For a given price p this is equivalent to the following condition:

$$\Pi_k (p, \tau) = (p - c(\tau))f(p)M_k - F(\tau) \geq 0 \tag{7.5}$$

where f(p) shows how the demand $f(p)M_k$ depends on the price charged. Next, let p^* denote the price which maximizes the aggregate profit function $\Pi_k (p, \tau)$, which describes the maximum profit a single supplier can obtain. Observe that formula (7.5) applies to a group of n identical suppliers if $F(\tau)$ is replaced by $F(\tau)/n$. Given the profit condition in (2.6) one can specify the set of industries which can locate in a central place of rank k. They include all activities j such that

$$F_j(\tau) / [(p_j^* - c_j(\tau))f_j(p_j^*)] \leq M_k. \tag{7.6}$$

The hierarchy described by (7.3)-(7.6) will be influenced by technical change processes in each industry. The change of production techniques in an industry is described by a technique vintage index τ, which is close to 0 for an initial process and approaches 1 as routinized, low cost (and mature) techniques are introduced. Following vintage production theory (Johansson 1991), one can assume that $c(\tau)$ decreases as τ increases. If $F(\tau)$ also becomes smaller or grows only moderately as τ increases, the vintage dynamics implies that an industry may initially have a feasible location in central places with k as the lowest rank. As the technique vintage increases, a feasible location can gradually be found in places of rank k-1, k-2, etc. Hence, with the described technical change process activities will gradually find feasible locations at lower levels in the hierarchy of the urban system. This location change is induced by the cost reduction $c(\tau + u) < c(\tau)$ which reduces the importance of the fixed cost break-even condition such that

$$F(\tau + u) / [p^* - c(\tau + u))f(p^*)] < F(\tau) / [(p^* - c(\tau))f(p^*)] \quad (7.7)$$

Going back to condition (7.6), one may examine what happens if, for each given commodity, $\lambda = \lambda(\tau)$ decreases as τ increases. This change will augment M_k for each level k. However, at the same time the price level may be stimulated to fall across the regional system. The most significant stimulation to make firms locate at lower levels as the technique develops is that $F(\tau + u) < F(\tau)$. This may reflect reduced set up and development costs.

7.2.3 Location Advantages for Non-Routinized, Expanding Output

Johansson and Westin (1987) present an SPE-model with technical change and location decisions in a temporal setting. The model introduced in this subsection may be seen as a simplified version of its predecessor model. In particular, the following model refers to one specific type of product (possibly differentiated) and to an arbitrary selected supply region, r. In addition, the model assumes that the type of product considered is non–routinized, non-standardized and is meeting an increasing demand (e.g. the early phase of a product cycle). The production in region r is denoted by x_r, the cost by c_r. For each period there is given capacity $\bar{x}_r$, which may be increased by capacity investments, Δx_r, at the periodized cost of δ_r per unit capacity. In addition the model contains two types of accessibility variables, where a_r refers to the intraregional accessibility as defined in (7.1) and a_{rs} to the accessibility between region r and s. The following assumptions are made about cost conditions:

$$c_r = c_r(x_r, a_r), \text{ and } c_r' = \partial c_r / \partial x_r < 0$$

$$\rho_r = \rho(a_r), \text{ and } \partial \rho / \partial a_r > 0 \quad (7.8)$$

where c_r denotes average production cost and ρ_r denotes location cost per unit output. The location cost reflects land values and increase as the intraregional accessibility a_r rises. As specified in (7.8), production costs are characterized by economies of scale on the regional level (localization economies). Moreover, as intraregional accessibility (density) rises, c_r is assumed to fall, which reflects agglomeration economies or economies of density. Agglomeration and localization economies are counteracted by the increase in ρ_r as density increases.

Consider the delivery flow x_{rs} on link (r,s). The customer interaction cost on this link is denoted by $c_{rs}x_{rs}$, where the interregional cost coefficient, c_{rs}, is treated as constant, although one could use the following specification $c_{rs} = c_{rs}(sx_{rs}, a_{rs})$ and $c'_{rs} = \partial c_{rs} / \partial x_{rs} < 0$ which expresses that with given accessibility, a_{rs}, interaction is characterized by economies of scale. Congestion would then be represented by a falling value of a_{rs}, which would cause a rise in c_{rs}.

Next, let the delivery price, p_{rs}, and the average market price across suppliers, p_s, be given each period – possibly updated between periods. Then a demand expression for customer region s, $M_{rs} = M_{rs}(p_{rs}; p_s)$, can be introduced with a market-clearing constraint $x_{rs} = M_{rs}$ for each customer market s, and where $\partial M_{rs} / \partial p_{rs} < 0$. In addition a market-clearing constraint is introduced for the supply region, $x_r = \Sigma_s x_{rs}$, complemented by a capacity constraint $\bar{x}_r + \Delta x_r \geq x_r$. Next, consider the Lagrange function, V_r, in formula (7.9) and assume that the behaviour of profit-maximizing firms in the region correspond to the maximization of (7.9).

$$V_r = \Sigma_s p_{rs} x_{rs} - [c_r + m_r + \rho_r]x_r - \Sigma_s c_{rs} x_{rs} - \delta_r \Delta x_r +$$
$$\mu_r[\bar{x}_r + \Delta x_r - x_r] + \lambda_r[x_r - \Sigma_s x_{rs}] + \Sigma_s \lambda_{rs}[x_{rs} - M_{rs}] \qquad (7.9)$$

where $m_r \geq 0$ is a mark-up factor reflecting a monopoly position of suppliers in region r. Assuming that the total capacity is activated, Kuhn - Tucker conditions yields the following conditions:

$$\lambda_r = p_{rs} + \lambda_{rs} - c_{rs} \qquad (7.10a)$$

$$\lambda_r = \mu_r + c_r + c_r' x_r + m_r + \rho_r \text{, and } \mu_r = \delta_r \qquad (7.10b)$$

where (7.10a) describes the potential mill price and (7.10b) the equality between this price and the marginal cost of output, while observing that $\delta_r = \mu_r$ reflects the net value of additional capacity. Combining the different parts of (7.10) yields

$$p_{rs} = \rho_r + m_r + c_r + c_r' x_r + \delta_r + c_{rs} - \lambda_{rs}; \; c_r' < 0 \qquad (7.11)$$

where $\lambda_{rs} > 0$ indicates how much the price, p_{rs}, should be increased in the subsequent period, and where $\lambda_{rs} < 0$ instead indicates a price reduction. One example is the following myopic price updating process: $p_{rs}(t) = \alpha\lambda_{rs}(t\text{-}1) + p_{rs}(t-1)$, $\alpha<\alpha<1$. Observe also that the link-specific prices satisfy the so called Armington assumption (Armington 1969).

Remark Assume that a firm attempts to locate in region r and sets a price p_{rs} such that $M_{rs} = M_{rs}(p_{rs}; p_s) > 0$, in a given set of markets $S \ni s$. According to the model, such a location, $\Delta x_r = x_r > 0$, is not possible if $\delta_r + c_r'x_r + c_r + m_r + \delta_r > \lambda_r$, where $\lambda_r \geq p_{rs} + \lambda_{rs} - c_{rs}$, and $\lambda_{rs} \geq 0$, for all $s \in S$.

In the implicit dynamics associated with (7.11) demand continues to grow, i.e. $\Delta M_{rs} > 0$ for each new period, and gradual price adjustments direct simultaneous trade flows towards more profitable markets. This process stimulates expansion in location r, so long as the potential mill price does not fall below the marginal cost of output. A crucial factor is the location cost factor ρ_r which increases as economic density rises and may cause the expansion in r to make a halt, a typical von Thünen effect (Andersson and Johansson 1984). On the other hand, the external economies of scale (or increasing-returns effects) stimulates a path–depending expansion in already favourable regions, a typical lock–in effect (Arthur 1988).

The external economies of scale (for regions with initial location advantages) imply that with continued infrastructure investments production may gradually become concentrated in a decreasing number of large urban regions. In the next subsection technological change is introduced as a process which is capable of generating relocation away from initial hosts of non-routinized and non-standardized activities.

As a final remark, one may observe that formula (7.9) may be supplemented by certain multiregional consistency relations. If this is done one may sum across all regions in a multiregional setting. In this way the model generates a sequence of constrained one-period equilibria. These will be imperfect competition equilibria. Moreover, due to increasing returns there will be multiple sequences of equilibria. Hence, in this sense the model generates path-dependent solutions.

7.2.4 Location Advantages with Technological Change

The von Thünen class of location models describe variations in the milieu within an urban region as the consequence of accessibility patterns. An equilibrium solution in this framework is such that contact–intensive and non–routinized activities (with non-standardized outputs) locate in zones or subnodes with high accessibility values, while goods handling, routinized activities (often with standardized outputs) are forced to select less accessible locations. This class of model has been related to spatial product cycle models (Andersson and Johansson 1984).

The previous subsection analyses non-standardized products. Such goods and services comprise young products as well as other types of customized deliveries. According to the model employed in subsection 7.2.3, firms find it advantageous to locate this type of production in urban regions which are characterized by accessibility to a broad set of various customer categories, as well as to R&D resources and suppliers of knowledge services. Other desirable location features are relatively high purchasing power and rich contact opportunities.

When a product gradually matures and a growing market develops it becomes possible to standardize its design and automate and routinize its production process. In this phase the comparative advantages are found in regions which have lower land values and costs of premises, and lower costs of routinized labour inputs. In these environments the supply of knowledge intensive and R&D-oriented labour force is comparatively small.(Andersson and Johansson 1984). In order to illustrate this switch in location requirements the vintage index τ is applied again, with the same interpretation as in subsection 7.2.2. A growing value of τ towards τ_0 reflects a higher degree of standardization and routinization, and a reduced dependency on the economic milieu. These conditions are inserted into the model specified by (7.8)-(7.9).

First, the cost function in (7.8) is respecified in the following way:

$$c_r^\tau = c_r^\tau(x_r,a_r) = \sigma_r^\tau(x_r,a_r) + \hat{\sigma}_r^\tau(x_r,a_r) \qquad (7.12)$$

where $\sigma_r^\tau(x_r,a_r)$ refers to costs of non-routine resources (or inputs) and $\sigma_r^\tau(x_r,a_r)$ to routine inputs. As τ grows towards τ_0 the first component becomes relatively less important such that

$$\sigma_r^{\tau_0} / \hat{\sigma}_r^{\tau_0} < \sigma_r^\tau / \hat{\sigma}_r^\tau, \text{ as } \tau_0 > \tau \qquad (7.13)$$

This means that as the technical change continues, one may disregard the influence of a_r on $\sigma_r^\tau(x_r,a_r)$, as τ approaches τ_0 At the same time we can observe that routine inputs can be expected to have a higher price in a dense economic milieu (with a high a_r-value) than in a less dense milieu. Hence, for any τ

$$\hat{\sigma}_r^\tau(x_r,a_r) < \hat{\sigma}_r^\tau(x_r,\bar{a}_r), \text{ as } \bar{a}_r > a_r \qquad (7.14)$$

Let us also assume that as τ approaches high values (τ_0), the average cost, c_r, ceases to fall any further. Thus, one may set $c_r' \approx 0$. Next, let region r have a high a_r-value and let region k have a low a_k-value. Then our previous assumptions imply that

i $\rho_r > \rho_k$,

ii $\hat{\sigma}_r^{\tau_0} > \hat{\sigma}_k^{\tau_0}$, and

iii $\sigma_r^{\tau_0} = \sigma_K^{\tau_0} = \text{small}$.

Moreover, large τ is usually assumed to correspond to increased price competition, implying that

$$\text{iv} \quad m_r^{\tau_0} = m_k^{\tau_0} = 0 \text{ and}$$

$$\text{v} \quad p_{rs} = p_{ks}.$$

These new conditions can be incorporated in the optimization formulation in (7.9).

Consider the above assumptions and let τ_0 be high and contemplate how the supply has to be reduced in region r and increased in region k. According to the optimum conditions of (7.9), the latter region then manages to attract the location of new capacity by satisfying

$$\lambda_k^{\tau_0} = \hat{\sigma}_k^{\tau_0} + \rho_k + \delta_k = p_{ks} + \lambda_{ks}^{\tau_0} - c_{ks} \qquad (7.15)$$

for a growing number of markets s. For region r, the technical development brings about excess capacity in the region, implying that

$$\Delta x_r = 0 \text{ and } \lambda_{rs}^{\tau_0} = 0 \text{ for all s.}$$

Suppose that there are certain markets, s*, such that

$$\lambda_r^{\tau_0} = \hat{\tau}_r^{\tau_0} + \delta_r = \rho_{rs*} - c_{rs*}$$

Observe next that

$$\lambda_k^{\tau_0} > \lambda_r^{\tau_0} \text{ if } (\hat{\sigma}_r^{\tau_0}) + (\rho_r - \rho_k) > \delta_k \qquad (7.16)$$

From this one can conclude that for all markets $s \neq s^*$, such that $p_{rs} - c_{rs} \approx p_{ks} - c_{ks}$, the mill price $\lambda_r^{\tau_0}$ will be greater than $p_{rs} - c_{rs}$, yielding $x_{rs} = 0$. This illustrates how a previously successful region continues to lose markets as the technique becomes more routinized and the output more standardized.

7.3 Correlation Between Regional Densities and Location Intensities

In general, the population density of a region is not perfectly correlated with the capacity and quality of the region's infrastructure and location attributes. However, there is still a strong relation as will be demonstrated. Given this conclusion we illustrate two phenomena. First, the production of non-standardized, customized and R&D-dependent products are primarily located in dense regions. Second, the production of standardized, routinized, and often natural-resource based products are to a large extent located in less densely populated, peripheral regions. Table 7.1 relates the density and knowledge-intensity of the economic milieu to a region's specialization on activities which are classified in terms of standardization and routinization.

Table 7.1 Degree of production routinization and product standardization

	Non-routinized production	Routinized production
Non-standardized products	(1) Development oriented, knowledge handling activities; both customer relations and production is contact intensive	(2) Contact intensive relations with customer markets, but limited development inputs
Standardized products	(3) Limited development activities, but skill-requiring inputs; price competitive customer relations	(4) Both transaction and production activities require limited contact intensity; price competitive market relations

One basic message from Table 7.1 is that in position (1) economic activities are knowledge and contact intensive, while in position (4) these elements are reduced with the intention to cut down on costs and compete with low prices. The subsequent analysis will focus on these two extreme cases. As a general assumption we expect activities of type (1) to have a high regional concentration in regions with a dense and knowledge-intensive economic milieu. The inverse relation is assumed to hold for activities of type (4) which should have a relatively high location intensity in regions with low knowledge-intensity and low economic density (low intraregional accessibility).

7.3.1 Density Classification of Municipalities

The study presented in this chapter has municipalities as observation units. In certain cases an individual municipality can be characterized as a functional region. For Sweden with more than 280 municipalities, the generic case is that groups of adjacent municipalities constitute integrated functional urban regions. A functional urban region is defined as an area with frequent interaction within the region. In textbook definitions this corresponds to the concept of a daily commuting region. A functional urban region usually has a multinodal structure, although in almost all cases one of its nodes has a definite role as a centre .

The subsequent analysis considers four regional density categories, with the following label: (I) Very sparsely populated municipalities with 2 inhabitants per km^2 on the average, (II) Sparsely populated municipalities with 9 inhabitants per km^2 on the average; (III) Densely populated municipalities with 20 inhabitants per km^2 on the average; (IV) Very densely populated municipalities, forming metropolitan regions with 85 inhabitants per km^2 on the average. In the low-density municipalities (I)-(II), one finds 22 percent of all jobs in Sweden 1985. The corresponding figure for municipalities of category (IV) is 54 percent.

Table 7.2 Regional infrastructure indices of Swedish municipalities, 1985

	I	II	III	IV
Value of the building capital per inhabitant	100	108	112	121
Proportion of the labour force with university education	100	120	138	200
Number of air flight departures per day and inhabitant	100	86	162	281

Source: Statistics Sweden; see also Johansson and Karlsson (1991).

Table 7.2 illustrates the average difference between the four categories as regards building capital, knowledge intensity of the labour force, and air transportation conditions. As regards building capital, one should in particular observe that in a dense region, the amount of public or collective facilities is much larger than elsewhere which accentuates the differences in the table. In regions of type IV (metropolitan) we observe high building capital and education density, as well as an indication of air transport accessibility.

The empirical analysis in this chapter makes use of the notion location intensity, defined as the ratio s_{jr}/s_r, where s_{jr} denotes the size of sector j in region r and s_r the size of the entire economy in the region, and where the measurement can be in value terms or in terms of number of jobs. When nothing else is said the variables s_{jr} and s_r are both specified as number of jobs. The corresponding variables on the country level is s_j and s, respectively. From this, the regional concentration of sector j in region r is defined as follows:

$$\sigma_{rj} = [s_{jr} / s_r] / [s_j / s] \tag{7.17}$$

which can also be recognized as a location quotient.

Table 7.3 illustrates the regional concentration of the manufacturing industry. Regions of type (I)-(II) have the strongest specialization on manufacturing production. In addition, we observe a very high regional concentration of low-value products in the non-dense regions (I)-(II).

In the same regions we also find a high location intensity of firms which operate on price-competition markets, i.e., markets in which products tend to be standardized in such a way that price is the main or sole instrument of competition. Another reason for the high location intensity of low-value products in regions (I)-(II) is that a lot of this production benefits from the accessibility to input resources in these regions, e.g. forestry inputs. One may finally conclude that the location pattern in Table 7.3 is completely congruent with the pattern predicted by product cycle theory as formalized in Section 7.2.4. We note especially that the metropolitan regions have a lower than average location intensity as regards manufacturing in general and a much lower intensity as regards low-value products and price-competing industries.

Table 7.3 Regional concentration in percent for regional groups. Three categories of manufacturing industry, 1987

	Total manu-facturing	Low value products in manufactur-ing*	Price - competing firms with declining employment
(IV) Very dense	82	61	66
(III) Dense	114	116	129
(II) Sparsely (below median)	147	146	161
(I) Very sparsely (lowest quartile)	111	227	133

Source: Johansson and Karlsson (1991); price competition is defined and specified for sectors in Johansson and Westin (1994). * Low value = less than 5 SEK per kilogram.

7.3.2 Distribution of Basic Service Production

Interaction services are performed by sectors as a means to facilitate the transmission and displacement of persons, messages and goods. They enable supply sources to interact with demand sinks in such a way that markets can clear. One can use the employment change between 1977 and 1987 as a way to distinguish stagnating/declining and growing activities. In the 1980s, interaction services with fast growth include (i) property trade brokerage, and (ii) travel agent services, while the slowly growing interaction services comprised (iii) air transportation, (iv) hotel and restaurant, (v) machinery rental services, (vi) mail and telecommunication services.

The largest set of interaction service sectors are those with stagnating or falling employment numbers. They include various forms of trade and transportation sectors as described below:

- Retail trade
- Standard wholesale trade (excluding technology trade with equipment)
- Road transportation by lorries and trucks
- Railway transportation
- Water system transportation

Table 7.4 Regional concentration of interaction services across regional types, 1987

	(IV)	(III)	(I)-(II)
Growing interaction services	118	83	74
Interaction services with stagnating or declining employment	109	93	86

Source: Statistics Sweden; Johansson and Karlsson (1991).

The hypothesis behind the classification in Table 7.4 is that growing interaction services refer to knowledge oriented, differentiated and customized services, and that these have a location advantage in dense regions. At the same time, the stagnating and declining interaction services are assumed to be more standardized and less knowledge dependent and involved in clear price competition. For these activities the advantage from density should be smaller, which is also indicated by Table 7.4. Among the sectors in this group one finds activities for which both employment and production diminishes, while others survive by simultaneously expanding production and reducing the size of the labour force – typical features of price competition in standardized markets. A study by Forslund (1996) supports the hypothesis that growing sectors tend to have a higher knowledge intensity. However, the overall impression from Table 7.4 is that – as regards interaction services – the location intensity varies only moderately, though systematically, between the three density categories.

7.3.3 Business Services with Different Levels of Knowledge Intensity

One should observe that for the period 1980-1990 there are no observations in the Swedish economy of a business service sector that declines. The business services are arranged in two groups. The first group (advanced business services) has a more pronounced knowledge intensity, in the sense that at larger share of its employees has a university education (2 years or longer). In addition, these sectors had a faster employment growth in the 1980s than the second group (Johansson and Karlsson 1991; Forslund 1996).

- *Advanced business services* comprise property management; credit and financial services; computer-processing services; juridical, accounting and word processing services;
- *Ordinary business services* comprise guard-duty services; efficiency improvement services; ordinary bank services; insurance services; cleaning services.

The major conclusion from Table 7.5 is that in comparison with interaction services, business services are extremely much more sensitive with regard to the density of the economic milieu. The revealed location advantage for municipality category (IV) is much higher for the sectors in Table 7.5 than for those in the preceding Table 7.4.

Table 7.5 Regional concentration of business services

	(IV)	(III)	(I)-(II)
Advanced business services (with a fast expansion 1980-1990)	161	35	22
Ordinary business services (with moderate growth 1980-1990)	155	43	27

Source: Statistics Sweden; Johansson and Karlsson (1991).

7.3.4 Concentration of Knowledge-intensive Service Activities

Besides interaction and business services, one may identify two groups of knowledge handling services as specified below. For the period 1980–1990 there is no observation in Sweden of a declining knowledge handling sector.

- *Knowledge handling services with fast growth* comprise R&D services; special consulting; marketing and media services; technology trade (=sales of technical equipment and production methods).
- *Knowledge handling services with slow growth* comprise technical/engineering consulting; organization consulting; architectural services and building consulting.

The major part of all subsectors among the business and capital services have a high knowledge intensity, indicated by a large share of the employment with long education (Forslund 1996). This feature is also emphasized for the knowledge handling and development services (KH services). It will be demonstrated that these services are strongly concentrated on municipalities with high population density. Moreover, this tendency is strongest for the KH-sectors with the fastest growth. In Table 7.6 the Stockholm region is also included, and in that region the concentration of knowledge-handling services is particularly marked.

Let us compare Tables 7.5 and 7.6. It then becomes clear that the revealed location advantage for regions with a dense economic milieu is more pronounced for business services than for KH-services. For the latter, one can expect a location advantage in regions which host universities and other facilities for R&D and higher education – also when such regions are of medium size and lack the density of metropolitan environments.

Table 7.6 Regional concentration of knowledge-handling (KH) service activities 1987. Index in percent of the concentration value for the Stockholm region

	KH-sectors with fast growth	KH-sectors with slow growth
Stockholm region	100	100
(IV) Metropolitan, very densely populated	78	90
(III) Densely populated	32	54
(II) Sparsely populated	23	51
(I) Very sparsely populated	14	27

Source: Statistics Sweden; Johansson and Karlsson (1991). The index in Table 7.6 uses the Stockholm region as a norm.

7.4 Location Advantage Indices for Service Sectors

Section 7.4 presents a set of variables which reflect a municipality's economic milieu in terms of accessibility and density features. The empirical investigation which is presented focuses on two aggregate service sectors. The location intensity of each of these two groups is regressed against location attributes in the complete set of Swedish municipalities. Finally, from the estimated parameters a location advantage index is constructed. It indicates for each sector how strong a municipality's location advantage is with respect to this sector.

7.4.1 Selection of Service Sectors

The objective of Section 7.4 is to investigate how the location intensities of two aggregate service sectors are related to the attributes of the economic milieu in each individual municipality. One of the sectors is wholesale and transportation (WT), representing the interaction service sectors. The second sector is the aggregate of all business services (consulting) and banking activities. In Table 7.7 the WT-sector is described in terms of its subsectors and their national growth 1980–1990.

By comparing Tables 7.7 and 7.8 one observes that the growth rate is considerably higher for the business service activities than for the WT activities. In particular, financial services and computer (processing) services display very high growth figures.

In the econometric analyses presented subsequently, the sectors are organized into the following aggregates:

- WT = Wholesale and transportation
- BC = Bank and business services (including consultancy)
- C = Consultancy services

Table 7.7 Growth of subsectors of wholesale trade and transportation in Sweden

Wholesale trade in	Change in percent 1980–1990	T-sectors	Change in percent 1980–1990
Production inputs	-19.6	Railroad transport	-10.0
Technology (equipment)	+68.0	Waterway transport	-43.9
Other products	+ 5.9	Road freight transport	+20.3
		Urban transport	+22.3
		Transport agencies	+23.5
Total wholesale	+16.5	**Total transportation**	+ 6.7

Source: Statistics Sweden.

Table 7.8 Growth of subsectors of business services in Sweden

Bank services	Change (%) 1980–1990	Other business services	Change (%) 1980–1990
Financial services	+123.2	Computer services	+195.8
Other financial institutions	+ 57.5	Advertisement and marketing	+ 94.7
Bank services	+ 29.8	Accounting services	+ 56.1
		Special consulting	+ 54.6
		Legal services	+ 35.8
		Engineering consulting	+ 31.8
Total banking	+ 30.4	**Total business services**	+ 37.8

Source: Statistics Sweden.

Knowledge intensity may be measured as the share of the labour force in a sector having college or university education. With such measures, the WT sector has a considerably lower knowledge intensity than the BC sector. However, within the WT-sector one finds a high knowledge intensity for technology trade. On the other hand, ordinary bank services have a fairly moderate knowledge intensity and they represent a large share of all jobs in the BC-sector (Forslund 1996; Johansson and Karlsson 1991). However, compared with other sectors of the economy, both WT and BC are expected to have a strong willingness to pay high land rents to stay in urban regions with rich contact opportunities, high purchasing power, accessibility to a broad set of customer categories, to R&D resources, and to suppliers of knowledge services.

7.4.2 Selection of Location Attributes

According to the theoretical framework introduced in this chapter, attributes of the economic milieu should reflect accessibility and density of activities. Moreover, the variables are required to adjust at a slow pace compared with the adjustment speed of normal market transactions and flows of economic resources. In brief, to constitute an economic milieu attribute, a variable must show a certain degree of permanence. Moreover, firms should not be charged specifically for the provision of the attributes of the economic milieu.

Table 7.9 describes the set of milieu variables which were available to the study presented here. Many of these variables satisfy in an obvious way the criteria discussed above and specified earlier in the chapter. However, variables (L1) and (L3), referring to education-specific labour supply, may need some comments. In North America one can observe a much higher labour mobility than in Europe, and models referring to the US economy often exclude accessibility to labour supply from the time-invariant characteristics of the economic milieu. However, one may conclude that in Europe the adjustment of each region's labour supply is a slow process. The accessibility to labour supply from a given municipality (urban node) is a composite variable, and it depends on the location of labour supply and the characteristics of the pertinent commuting networks.

Many of the variables in Table 7.9 have a self-evident interpretation. The accessibility measures in the table have the form specified in formula (7.1) which means that they constitute combined measures of the supply in a municipality and its neighbouring municipalities.

However, attribute variable (L4) needs a detailed specification, especially since it has a central role in the econometric study. It represents the flow capacity of a region's road system. According to our previous discussion one may expect that the flow capacity of the road system, (L4), is a key factor for maintaining a cohesive and robust labour market. The variable is measured in the following way:

$$(L4) = a\,V / A \qquad (7.18)$$

a = width times length of the main road system in a municipality measured in square meters
V = driving speed in meter per second on each segment of the main roads in the municipality
A = total area of the municipality in square meters

The dimension of (L4) is thus meter per second, i.e. a flow characteristic. It describes the relative availability of road capital and its throughput capacity. Statistical analysis shows that L4 is a basic instrument in keeping a compound and robust labour market together (Holmberg and Johansson 1992).

Table 7.9 Variables reflecting attributes of the economic milieu available in the study

LOCAL AND INTRAREGIONAL ATTRIBUTES	INTERREGIONAL ATTRIBUTES
(L1) Labour supply in each municipality specified by education composition	(I1) Frequency of interregional trains
(L2) Number of jobs in each municipality specified by education composition	(I2) Interregional accessibility in the road system
(L3) Accessibility to labour supply of each employment category and the set of job opportunities for each category of job	(I3) Accessibility to airport capacity (number of aeroplane seats departures per day)
(L4) Flow capacity of the road system	(I4) Travel time to the main air traffic hub, nearby Stockholm
(L5) Regional accessibility to population concentrations in the road system	(I5) Accessibility to international harbour terminals for freight flows
(L6) Regional accessibility to population concentration in the railroad system	(I6) Accessibility to universities and research centres
(L7) Frequency of local trains	(I7) Value of all premises in the municipality divided by the total labour supply
(L8) The capacity of intraregional public transport (supply of person kilometres)	
(L9) Capacity, size and value density of built environment (building capital)	
(P) Total wage sum in the public sector, divided by total labour supply	

Source: Johansson et. al. (1991). The correlation between the variables is presented in the appendix.

The variables in Table 7.9 have been used in combinations as variables explaining the location intensity for the three sectoral aggregates WT, BC and C. Only certain combinations are possible, since some pairs of attribute variables are strongly correlated (see Appendix). The major test has been to investigate the robustness of the parameters for the central variables when systematically including and excluding variables belonging to pairs of strongly correlated variables (Johansson et al. 1991). Such a robustness applies to the following set of variables which are included in the regression equations that are presented in Table 7.10 and discussed in the subsequent analysis: (L3), (L4), (I1), (I4) and (I7) together with (P). In addition, variable category (L1) will be used in the analysis of job dynamics in Section 7.5.

Among the variables included in the econometric exercises, we may comment also on variable (I7). Since it reflects the value of premises, it refers to a production factor for which each firm pays a rent, directly or indirectly. However, (I7) does not refer to rental costs paid by individual firms or even by the firms in each sector. Instead (I7) reflects the general or overall density and attractiveness of the region's supply of premises. In this sense it reflects a location attribute, and could be compared with the ρ–variable in formula (7.8).

7.4.3 Location Intensity as Function of Economic-Milieu Attributes

In the econometric study the location intensity is regressed against variables representing the regional milieu. The dependent variable which is called location intensity is based on two observables for each municipality r. The first observable is the wage sum, W_r , of each analysed sector. The second is the potential labour supply across all occupational groups in region r. In this way the location intensity of service sector j in node r is defined as

$$V_{rj} = W_{rj} / H_r \tag{7.19}$$

where H_r represents the potential labour supply in municipality r, which is the sum of all inhabitants in the age interval 16-64 years. For wholesale trade and transportation, the WT sector, the measure in (7.19) ranges between 15 to 1. With regard to the BC sector business and banking services, the variation between regions is even larger. We may finally observe that the wage sum constitutes a large share of the value added in both the WT and BC sector. One may also describe the location intensity measure used in the regressions as the ratio between the number of persons employed in sector j divided by total labour supply and weighted by the wage level of sector j. This means that the intensity between two municipalities differs as a consequence of both the relative size of employment and the relative wage level.

V_{rj} is the dependent variable in the regression equation, and location attributes $a_{rj1}, ..., a_{rjn,}$ referring to region r are the independent variables. The following form of the regression equation was used:

$$V_{rj}(t) = V_j \, a_{rjl}^{\gamma_{j1}} \, a_{rj2}^{\gamma_{j2}} \cdots a_{rjn}^{\gamma_{jn}} \tag{7.20}$$

where V_j denotes the intercept with respect to sector j. This functional form has several advantages in the type of exploratory econometrics carried out in this study. For example, it is easy to add and remove variables while examining the robustness of parameter estimates. Moreover, the multiplicative structure of (7.20) has a capacity to detect synergies, as it is sensitive to small values of any of the a_{rji}–variables. Hence, the composition of the location attributes affects their impact. In Table 7.10 the parameters of four regression equations are presented. It can be seen that the P–variable plays a significant role in the regression.

Table 7.10 Location intensity as a function of economic milieu attributes

Variable	WT sector	BC sector	C sector
(L4) Flow capacity of the road system	0.15 (0.05)	0.09 (0.05)	-
(I7) Value of premises per workplace	0.36 (0.06)	0.50 (0.06)	0.64 (0.06)
(L3) Accessibility to labour force with college education	0.10 (0.05)	0.06 (0.05)	0.19 (0.02)
(I1) Frequency of inter-regional trains	0.06 (0.02)	0.02 (0.01)	0.03 (0.02)
(I4) Travel time to Arlanda	-0.05	-0.10	-
(P) Size of the public sector divided by total labour supply	0.20 (0.10)	0.36 (0.10)	0.45 (0.10)
R-square	0.42	0.49	0.46

Source: Johansson et al (1991). Remark: Standard errors are reported within parentheses.

One may interpret (P) in two different, perhaps complementary, ways. As a first option P_r represents the level of public services in municipality r. One may also consider the public sector intensity as a reflection of the normed size of the public sector's demand for private services from the three sectors.

In a series of alternative regression equations the variable (I7) has a robust parameter value for both the WT and the BC sectors, with an invariantly higher value for the latter case. This difference is also reflected in the selected estimates in Table 7.10. The value of the variable increases as the average attractiveness and usefulness (productivity) of the stock of premises grows. At the same time it should repel activities which cannot afford to pay for the pertinent economic milieu.

Accessibility to labour supply with college education is correlated with the variable (L4) measuring the flow capacity of the road system within the municipality. Experiments show that when this road system variable is removed, the parameter value of (L3) is doubled (Holmberg and Johansson 1992).

The location intensity of the WT, BC and C sectors is regressed against location attribute variables in Table 7.10. One regression equation is selected for each of the three sectors, with regard to the estimation year 1988. Given the estimates in the table, one can calculate an aggregate value of the location attributes for each municipality with regard to the three sectors. The aggregate location attribute value is represented by the a-index in formula (7.21) In each case the a–index is a function of the location attributes so that

$$a_{rj} = a_{rj1}^{\gamma_{j1}} a_{rj2}^{\gamma_{j2}} \dots a_{rjn}^{\gamma_{jn}} \tag{7.21}$$

where j = WT, BC and C. Hence , we may write

$$a_{WT} = a(L4, L3, I1, I4, I7, P)$$

$$a_{BC} = a(L4, L3, I1, I4, I7, P) \text{ and } a_C = a(L3, I1, I7, P). \tag{7.22}$$

The models in Section 7.2 describe how the location pattern across a system of urban regions varies as a consequence of accessibility patterns. An equilibrium solution in this framework is such that contact-intensive and non-standardized activities locate in zones or subnodes with high accessibility values, and where as a consequence land values and the rental price of floorspace is high. This is reflected in the three selected indices by the variable (I7) measuring the overall value of premises per job in private sectors. The influence from this variable is high for WT, higher for BC and highest fro C. The remaining variables reflect intraregional and interregional accessibility of various kinds. As discussed earlier, public sector intensity may be given several different interpretations (cf Hansen 1965).

Consider now the fact that the a-index associated with one of our service sectors is a good predictor of the location intensity of this sector in a static, cross-section perspective. Should we expect the a-index to be an important variable in a dynamic model in which the number of jobs, A_r, in a municipality r adjusts in response to the location attributes in municipality r as well as other municipalities? An answer to this question is provided in Section 7.5.

7.5 Spatial Dynamics of Jobs in Private Sectors

Earlier in this chapter reference was made to a dynamic theory of spatial product cycles (Hirsch 1967; Andersson and Johansson 1984). In this theory a basic distinction is made between the development of new (young) products and the production of mature, standardized products. It is recognized that the early phase of a product cycle benefits from one type of location attributes, while the later phase has other requirements. As a consequence we should expect adjustments towards a location equilibrium to be disturbed when new products are being introduced into the economy from specific regions. Such perturbations may be evenly distributed or may occur in pulses, following temporal cycles of low and high innovation intensity. These observations imply that we should not be satisfied with analyses of static descriptions of equilibrium patterns based on cross-section information. Instead we have to investigate the adjustment process itself and examine the associated speed of change (Wigren 1995).

7.5.1 An Adjustment Model with Endogenous Time Scale

When product innovation refers to service production the activity location spreads primarily in the form of diffusion processes. In a formal model this diffusion looks like an imitation process. In the modern economy such diffusion is related to the WT and BC activities analysed in Section 7.3. In view of this we shall, in the present section, investigate if the dynamic location of all jobs (as an aggregate) is influenced by the same location attributes which can be associated with WT and BC activities, as revealed by the previous analysis.

Swedish studies of the above process of change have been inspired by a study by Mills and Carlino (1989) in which they collect a vector of structural variables from all counties in the US (ca 2500) for the years 1970 and 1980. In a quasi-dynamic econometric model they use these structural characteristics of each region to explain the population change across counties during the decade. The results support the hypothesis that the gradual relocation of households among regions is influenced by the attributes of the regional milieu in the beginning of the period. These attributes comprise infrastructure, the built environment and accessibility properties.

The subsequent analysis refers to a study by Holmberg and Strömqvist (1988) which in turn has been inspired by the approach developed by Mills and Carlino. This type of model is designed to depict the interaction between slowly changing location attributes and changes in location patterns which adjust on a comparatively faster time scale. In the Swedish study the following equilibrium condition is introduced:

$$L_r^* = H(B_r, \hat{B}_r, x_r) \tag{7.23}$$

where L_r^* denotes the equilibrium of jobs and population in municipality r, given the location attributes of the municipality as specified by the vector x_r and the current values of B_r (population in r), and $\bar{B}_r$ (population in adjacent municipalities). According to model assumptions, the system in (7.24) continues to change as long as $L_r^* \neq L_r$, where L_r signifies the current number of jobs in r. The adjustment towards equilibrium is assumed to be gradual and slow. In order to detect this kind of change process with limited data, the econometric analysis is based on observations of B_r, $\bar{B}_r$ and L_r from year t = 1980 and $t+\tau$ = 1988. The model is specified as follows:

$$L_r(t+\tau) = L_r(t) + \lambda(L_r^* - L_r(t)) \tag{7.24}$$

where L_r^* and λ are dependent variables and hence estimated, and where λ denotes the speed at which the gap (L_r^* - $L_r(t)$ is closed, given that the process is allowed to come to rest without further disturbances or incitement. We may first note that the econometric results imply that λ has a low value, corresponding to an adjustment period longer than two decades.

On the basis of the experience reported above a similar type of model is now formulated (cf Holmberg and Johansson 1992). The two observation years are given by t =1980 and $t+\tau$ = 1990:

A_r = Total number of private work-places (jobs) in region r
ΔA_r = $A_r(t+\tau) - A_r(t)$
$H_r(t)$ = Labour supply in region r
$a_{rj}(t)$ = Location advantage index referring to economic sector
j = WT, BC and C.

$$A^*_r(t+\tau)_j = a_{rj}(t)^{\gamma} H_r(t)^{\delta} \tag{7.25}$$

Consider then the following model of job adjustments

$$\Delta A_r = \lambda\, [A_r^*(t+\tau)_j - A_r(t)] \tag{7.26}$$

where λ, δ and γ are endogenously determined by the estimation of (7.26), and where λ denotes the adjustment speed. In the sequel we present results from regressions where three location advantage indices are applied. This means that we will use three different specifications of $A^*_r(t+\tau)_j$ in formula (7.25), i.e. j=WT, BC and C.

7.5.2 *Estimation of the Change Process*

The hypothesis presented in the previous subsection states that one should expect fast growth of private sector jobs in municipalities with a high location advantage index with regard to WT, BC and C. Table 7.11 confirms that such a hypothesis is worthwhile examining. The location advantage index is highly significant in all three estimated equations. Following the size of the F-value one may suggest that the location advantage index of the BC–sector is the strongest predictor of private sector job changes across municipalities.

The size of the F-value indicates that the variables a_r and H_r have a strong influence on the direction of the change process. At the same time, the λ–parameter which reflects the speed of change has a relatively low and robust value - irrespective of which a-index is used. One may interpret the model in (7.25) - (7.26) as a process in which the number of jobs change in response to the size of the gap $A^*_r(t+\tau)_j - A_r(t)_j$. The response is relatively slow which is consistent with the classification of labour supply in municipalities as a slowly adjusting variable.

Table 7.11 Job location change as a function of location advantage index

Parameter	BC sector	WT sector	C sector
a-index (location advantage index; parameter = γ)	0.32 (0.02)	0.31 (0.04)	0.15 (0.02)
Labour supply (parameter = δ)	0.99 (0.006)	0.99 (0.01)	1.01 (0.006)
Adjustment speed (parameter = (λ))	0.17 (0.015)	0.16 (0.015)	0.19 (0.02)
F-value	824	801	762

Source: Holmberg and Johansson (1992). Standard errors are recorded within parenthesis.

7.5.3 *Concluding Remarks*

The observed correlation between regional densities and location intensities in Section 7.3 provides a robust overall support to the interurban location model outlined in this chapter. However, this type of test is indeed coarse. Section 7.4 provides a more elaborate statistical analysis of the location model. In this case one may complain about the lack of alternative observables to represent attributes of the economic milieu. Moreover, it would have been desirable with another sectoral specification. A shadow from these limitations falls also on the quasi-dynamic model in Section 7.5. Hence, all results must be classified as tentative or exploratory. However, the strong model results in Section 7.5 should be a challenge to continue this type of analysis.

The formal model outlined in Section 7.2 emphasizes scale and agglomeration effects as driving forces for location decisions, including decisions to expand and contract already established firms. The existence of such effects implies that at each point in time the future in general contains multiple location equilibria. This means that small perturbations may alter the direction of a change process. Differences in location attributes can influence the selection of competing paths towards alternative equilibria (Andersson and Johansson 1984; Krugman 1991). Only fragments of the associated research issues have yet been touched upon by economists and regional scientists.

References

Andersson, Å.E. (1985), 'Creativity and Regional Development', *Papers of the Regional Science Association*, vol. 56, pp. 5-20.

Andersson, Å.E., Anderstig, C. and Hårsman, B. (1990), 'Knowledge, Communications Infrastructure and Regional Economic Change', *Regional Science and Urban Economics*, vol. 20, pp. 359–76.

Andersson, Å.E., Batten, D.F. and Karlsson, C. (1989), 'From the Industrial Age to the Knowledge Economy', in Andersson, Å.E., Batten, D.F. and C. Karlsson (eds), *Knowledge and Industrial Organization*, Springer-Verlag, Berlin, pp 1-13.

Andersson, Å.E. and Johansson, B. (1984), 'Knowledge Intensity and Product Cycles in Metropolitan Regions', *IIASA WP-84-13*, International Institute for Applied Systems Analysis, Laxenburg, Austria.

Anderstig, C. and Hårsman, B. (1986), 'On Occupation Structure and Location Pattern in the Stockholm Region', *Regional Science and Urban Economics*, vol. 16, pp. 97-122.

Arthur, B. (1988), 'Competing Technologies: An Overview', in Dosi, G., Freeman, C., Nelson, R. Silverberg, G. and L. Soete (eds), *Technical Change and Economic Theory*, Pinter Publishers, London.

Batten, D.F., Kobayashi, K. and Andersson, Å.E. (1989), 'Knowledge, Nodes and Networks: An Analytical Perspective', in Andersson, Å.E., Batten, D.F. and C. Karlsson (eds), *Knowledge and Industrial Organisation*, Springer-Verlag, Berlin, pp 31-46.

Beckmann, M. (1958), 'City Hierarchies and the Distribution of City Sizes', *Economic Development and Cultural Change*, VI, vol. 3, pp. 243–48.

Beckmann, M. (1996), 'The Location of Market Oriented Industries in a Growing Economy', paper presented at the 5th World Congress of the RSAI in Tokyo, May 1996.

Beckmann, M. and Puu, T. (1985), *Spatial Economics: Density, Potential, and Flow*, North-Holland, Amsterdam.

Biehl, D. (1986), 'The Contribution of Infrastructure to Regional Development', Regional Policy Division, EC, Brussels.

Ciccone,, A. and Hall, R.E. (1996), 'Productivity and the Density of Economic Activity', *American Economic Review*, vol. 86, pp. 54-70.

Dixit, A. and Stiglitz, J.E. (1977), 'Monopolistic Competition and Optimum Product Diversity', *American Economic Review*, vol. 67, pp. 297–308.

Forslund, U.M. (1996), 'Industrial Location – Interregional Leads and Lags in Sweden', *Working Paper No 2*, Swedish Institute for Regional Research, Östersund.

Forslund, U.M. and Johansson, B. (1995), 'Assessing Road Investments: Accessibility Changes, Cost Benefit and Production Effects', *Annals of Regional Science*, vol. 29, pp. 155–74.

Hansen, N.M. (1965), 'The Structure and Determinants of Local Public Investment Expenditures', *Review of Economics and Statistics*, vol. 47, pp. 150–62

Henderson, J.V. (1974), 'The Sizes and Types of Cities', *American Economic Review*, vol. 64, pp. 640–56.

Hirsh, S. (1967), *Location of Industry and International Competitiveness*, Oxford University Press, Oxford.

Holmberg, I. and Johansson, B. (1992), 'Growth of Production, Migration of Jobs and Spatial Infrastructure', *Arbetsrapport 1992-6*, Regional Planning, The Royal Institute of Technology, Stockholm.

Holmberg, I. and Strömqvist, U. (1988), 'LOSE – Länstrafik och samhällsekonomi 1', (Public Transport in Counties and Economic Consequences 1), bil 3. Transportforsknings-beredningen, Stockholm.

Hägerstrand, T. (1970), 'Tidsanvändning och omgivningsstruktur', (The Allocation of Time adn Local Environment), *Bilaga 4 i SOU 1970:14*, Allmänna Förlaget, Stockholm.

Johansson, B. (1991), 'Regional Industrial Analysis and Vintage Dynamics', *Annals of Regional Science*, vol. 25, pp. 1-18.

Johansson, B. (1993a), 'Infrastructure, Accessibility and Economic Growth', *International Journal of Transport Economics*, XX, pp. 131–56.

Johansson, B. (1993b), 'Economic Evolution and Urban Infrastructure Dynamics' in Andersson, Å.E., Batten, D.F., Kobayashi, K and K. Yoshikawa (eds), *The Cosmo-Creative Society*, Springer-Verlag, Berlin.

Johansson, B. and Westin, L. (1987), Technical Change, Location,and Trade, *Papers of the Regional Science Association*, vol. 62, pp. 13–25.

Johansson, B., Anderstig, C., Holmberg, I. and Strömqvist, U. (1991), 'Infrastruktur, produktivitet och konkurrenskraft (Infrastructure, Productivity and Competition Power)', in *Infrastruktur och produktivitet*, Expertutredning Nr 9 till Produktivitetsdelegationen, Allmänna förlaget, Stockholm.

Johansson, B. and Karlsson, C. (1991), *Från brukssamhällets exportnät till kunskapssamhällets innovationsnät* (From Export Networks of I-regions to Innovation Networks of C-regions), Högskolan i Karlstad.

Johansson, B. and Westin, L. (1994), 'Revealing Network Properties of Sweden's Trade with Europe', in Cuadrado-Roura, J.R., Nijkamp, P. and P. Salva (eds), *Moving Frontiers: Economic Restructuring, Regional Development and Emerging Networks*, Avebury, Aldershot.

Kobayashi., K., Batten, D.F. and Andersson, Å.E. (1991), 'The Sequential Location of Knowledge-Oriented Firms over Time and Space', *Papers in Regional Science*, vol. 70, pp. 381–97.

Krugman, P. (1991), *Geography and Trade*, Leuven University Press, Leuven.

Lakshmanan, T.R. and Elhance, A. (1985), 'Impacts of Infrastructure on Economic Development', in Snickars, F., Johansson, B. and T.R. Lakshmanan (eds), *Economic Faces of the Building Sector*, Document D20:1985, Swedish Council for Building Research, Stockholm 22-44.

Malecki, E.J. (1980), 'Science and Technology in the American Metropolitan System', in Brunn, S.D. and J.O. Wheeler (eds), *The American Metropolitan System: Present and Future*, New York.

Mills, F.S. and Carlino, G. (1989), 'Dynamics of County Growth', in Andersson, Å.E. et al. (eds), *Advances in Spatial Theory and Dynamics*, North-Holland, Amsterdam, pp. 195-205.

Norton, R. and Rees, J. (1979), 'The Product Cycle and the Spatial Distribution of American Manufacturing', *Regional Studies*, vol. 13, pp. 141–51.

Noyelle, T.J. (1983), 'The Rise of Advanced Services', *Journal of the American Planning Association*, pp. 280–90.

Tinbergen, J. (1967), 'The Hierarchy Model of the Size Distribution of Centres', *Papers of the Regional Science Association*, vol. 20, pp. 65–80.

Wigren. R. (1984) 'Measuring Regional Efficiency – A Method Tested on Fabricated Metal Products in Sweden 1973-75', *Regional Science and Urban Economics*, vol. 14, pp. 363–79.

Wigren, R. (1985) 'Productivity and Infrastructure: An Empirical Study of Swedish Manufacturing Industries and their Dependence on the Regional Production Milieu', in Snickars, F., Johansson, B. and T.R. Lakshmanan (eds), *Economic Faces of the Building Sector*, Document D20:1985, Swedish Council for Building Research, Stockholm, pp. 22-44.

Wigren, R. (1995), 'Trender och trendbrott – Sysselsättningen 1965-2015 i Gävle/Sandvikens A-region', (Trends and Switching Trends – Employment Patterns in the Labour Market Region Gävle/Sandviken), mimeo, Dept of Housing Research, University of Uppsala.

Appendix

The following Table 7.A.1 shows the simple correlation coefficients between economic milieu variables in Table 7.10 and other characteristics of the pertinent municipality regions. Multicollinarity has been examined by means of variance inflationary factors.

Table 7.A.1 Correlation coefficients between the variables under analysis

	L3	L4	I1	I4	I7
L3 College labour access	1.00	0.68	0.04	-0.55	0.61
L4 Flow capacity	0.68	1.00	-0.05	0.39	0.41
I1 Interregional trains	0.04	-0.05	1.00	-0.23	0.29
I4 Arlanda travel time	-0.55	0.39	-0.23	1.00	-0.39
I7 Value of premises	0.37	0.41	0.29	-0.39	1.00
P Size of public sector	0.11	0.03	0.33	-0.02	0.51
L5 Population accessibility-R	0.60	0.44	0.22	-0.72	0.33
L6 Polupation accessibility-T	0.71	0.45	0.25	-0.58	0.27
L8 Public transport capacity	-0.09	0.01	-0.09	0.10	0.19
L9 Building capital	0.68	0.53	0.14	-0.37	0.85
I2 Interregional acessibility	0.60	0.44	0.22	-0.72	0.33
I3 Accessibility to airport	0.61	0.39	0.08	-0.42	0.38
I5 Accessibility to harbours	0.24	0.29	0.10	-0.53	0.04

Source: Johansson et al (1991).

8 Some Simple Macro Economics of Increased Accessibility and Spatial Integration: The Case of a Small Open Region

PETER MCGREGOR, J. KIM SWALES AND YA PING YIN

8.1 Introduction

In this chapter we provide a simple analysis of the macroeconomic impact of increasing 'accessibility' within the context of a small open region. We interpret improving accessibility as implying increasing spatial integration of both commodity and labour markets. Since our context is that of a small, open region the focus of our analysis is quite distinct from most of those dealing with the macroeconomics of European integration in that we start from a position in which the subject economy has no monetary autonomy. The region is treated throughout as a price taker in a spatially integrated national financial market, so that our concern is solely with the effects of greater spatial integration of the real economy within an existing monetary union.

We deal with the macroeconomic consequences of two key aspects of increasing accessibility. First, we consider the impact of the increasing spatial integration of commodity markets. We do not deal directly with the sources of such integration, which could include the removal of trade barriers, the reduction of transport costs and so on, but rather with their indirect consequences for the sensitivity of trade flows to relative price changes. As the degree of spatial integration of commodity markets increases so too does the elasticity of substitution between domestically produced goods and those produced elsewhere. In the limit the location of production of a commodity becomes irrelevant as the elasticity of substitution tends to infinity. In such circumstances commodity markets would be characterized by the 'law of one price': a single common currency price of a commodity would be established. The small open region would become a price taker in such commodity markets. Secondly, increased accessibility in a labour market context implies increased spatial integration through labour mobility. This could be stimulated by a removal of restrictions on mobility, together with reducing psychological and pecuniary costs of net migration.

Again, our concern here is solely with the macroeconomic consequences of increased labour mobility.

The remainder of the chapter is structured as follows. In Section 8.2 we provide a brief theoretical analysis of the impact of increasing integration of commodity and labour markets, using a simple one-sector macroeconomic model of a small open region. While the single sector structure of our theoretical analysis aids intuition and facilitates straightforward results it omits a major feature of regional economies in the real world, namely the presence of a sector which is 'sheltered' from trade (if not wholly non-traded), although explicit incorporation of this feature would unnecessarily complicate our present analysis. The theoretical analysis is also, of course, incapable of indicating the likely orders of magnitude of the effects of increasing accessibility. For both reasons we also provide a numerical simulation analysis employing a computable general equilibrium (CGE) model of a small open region which possesses a substantial sheltered sector. Accordingly, in Section 8.3, we provide an outline of the structure of our regional CGE. In Section 8.4 we present the results of a number of simulation experiments, in an attempt to determine the likely quantitative impact of increasing accessibility on the real effects of both demand and supply disturbances. Section 8.5 is a brief conclusion.

8.2 Theoretical Analysis

8.2.1 An Imperfectly Competitive Macroeconomic Model of a Small, Open Region

For simplicity we develop the theoretical analysis in the context of a one sector model of a small open region. The model is essentially that developed by Layard et al. (LNJ 1991), augmented to accommodate capital stock endogeneity.[1] The intention here is to adopt a non-technical approach which concentrates on the intuition, without providing a formal derivation of the results.

We consider three conceptual time intervals in our analysis: the short run, over which both the population and the capital stock are fixed; the medium run, over which migration ensures an equilibrium distribution of population across space (so that there is zero net migration); the long run, over which the capital stock, as well as population, is optimally adjusted. The distinction between time periods is particularly important for the properties of the aggregate supply (AS) curve in each interval, and the likely impact of increased accessibility on these, but it also matters for the determination of aggregate demand (AD).[2]

Aggregate demand The treatment of aggregate demand in the model is conventional. A simple loglinear approximation suffices for illustrative purposes:

$$y = \sigma_1 x - \sigma_2 p + \sigma_3 l + \sigma_4 k$$

where all parameters are greater than zero. Aggregate demand (y) is positively related to the exogenous components of aggregate demand (x) and to regional competitiveness, defined as the log difference between the domestic currency prices of other regions and the own region price. This latter relationship assumes that the substitution effects of relative price changes dominate the income effects and that the propensity to spend is less than unity. Since the external prices and the nominal exchange rate are assumed here to be fixed, the AD equation simply expresses the relationship in terms of the prices of domestically produced goods (p). The other terms reflect the dependence of aggregate demand on the size of the population/labour force (l), which becomes endogenous in the medium run, and the capital stock (k), the desired value of which is achieved in the long run (and maintained by an appropriate level of replacement investment which impacts on AD). To simplify the illustrative analysis that follows we typically abstract from the longer-term influences on demand (where they are not critical to the argument).

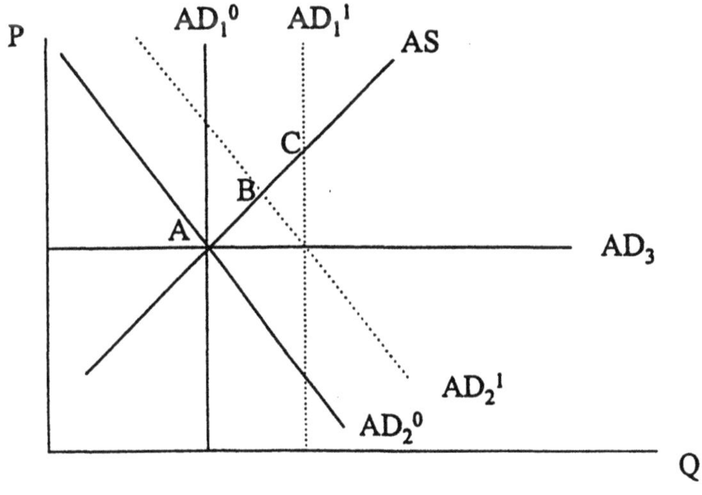

Figure 8.1 Accessibility, commodity market integration and the impact of demand disturbances

Increasing integration of commodity markets raises σ_2, the price elasticity of the aggregate demand curve. In Figure 8.1, AD_1 is drawn under the assumption of zero price elasticity of aggregate demand, such as would be implied by a simple open Leontief system characterization of the regional economy. The curve AD_2 assumes that trade flows are sensitive to relative prices, and this imparts a negative price responsiveness to aggregate demand. AD_3 provides a simple representation of the case where commodity markets become perfectly spatially integrated. Here the 'law of one price' (LOOP) applies in commodity markets, and trade elasticities become infinite. AD_1, AD_2 and AD_3 in Figure 8.1 are therefore indicative of the impact of increasing degrees of accessibility in commodity markets.

Increased labour mobility, as reflected by higher migration elasticities, through its impact on population at any particular period, induces greater AD through σ_3. For simplicity, we ignore this in the diagrammatic exposition, although this effect is embodied in our simulation model.

Aggregate supply - Short run over the short run the AS curve reflects the interaction of firm-union bargaining and the short run production function. The bargained real product wage function[3] (BRW) is of the form:

$$w - p = \gamma_0 - \gamma_1 u - \gamma_2 p + \gamma_3(k-l) + \gamma_4 z$$

where all parameters are greater than zero; all variables are in natural logarithms and: w is the nominal wage; p is the price of domestically produced goods; u is the unemployment rate; (k-l) is the capital- labour force ratio (to pick up trend productivity effects); z is a measure of union militancy. We assume that the short run interval is of sufficient duration to ensure an absence of all forms of nominal inertia, in contrast to most traditional regional macroeconomic analyses. Workers bargaining power is taken to be inversely related to the unemployment rate, and this is the source of the negative sign of the u coefficient in the BRW equation.

The regional price determined real wage (PRW) curve (which becomes the labour demand curve when commodity markets are perfectly competitive) is given by:

$$p - w = \beta_0 - \beta_1 u - \gamma_3(k - l)$$

where all parameters are greater than zero. Here the main idea is that the markup of prices over wages decreases with an increase in unemployment since demand is less likely to be buoyant in such circumstances. In fact a competitiveness wedge may also enter here through a variety of routes, but this has little effect on our analysis here, so we simplify by abstracting from it (see e.g. Harrigan et al. 1993).

For short run equilibrium the PRW and BRW must be equal. Solving the PRW and BRW curves for the equilibrium rate of unemployment, and using the definition of unemployment and the short run production function yields a positively sloped short run aggregate supply curve (SRAS, see Figure 8.3 below). The SRAS curve is positively sloped, despite the absence of price or wage surprises or any source of nominal inertia, because of the competitiveness wedge effect, reflected here in γ_2. As the prices of domestically produced goods increase, a less than proportionate increase in the nominal wage is required to restore the value of a given real consumption wage, so that the real product wage falls and stimulates supply. Increasing accessibility in the commodity market will make SRAS more elastic. Increased labour mobility, however, has no effect here since migration elasticities do not enter the SRAS curve.

Medium run In the medium run aggregate supply reflects the fact that net migration flows adjust so as to ensure an optimal distribution of population across regions. The zero net migration (ZNM) condition implied by the LNJ (1991) net migration function, which relates net inmigration positively to the real wage differential in favour of the own economy and negatively to the unemployment differential as in Harris and Todaro (1970), is as follows:

$$w - p = -\alpha_0 + \alpha_1 u - \gamma_2 p$$

where all parameters are greater than zero and we have included the terms in the other region's real wage and unemployment rate, which are exogenous, in the intercept for simplicity. Notice that the competitiveness wedge enters both the BRW and ZNM conditions symmetrically, because both behavioural functions assume households are governed by the real consumption wage. Accordingly, both can be reparameterized with the real product wage on the left hand side of the BRW and ZNM equations and the competitiveness wedge on the right hand side. Here, as for the BRW, we include the exogenous components of competitiveness in the intercept. The parameter α_1 reflects the ratio of the net migration elasticities with respect to unemployment and wage differentials (and so is unity in the pure Harris–Todaro case).

Over the medium run the behaviour of w-p and u is entirely determined by the BRW and ZNM conditions. It is straightforward to show that the resultant equilibrium unemployment rate is now unrelated to the prices of domestically produced goods. This reflects the natural rate or NAIRU properties of the model across medium run equilibria. Demand has no impact on the rate of unemployment across such zero net migration equilibria: indeed the unemployment rate depends only on the supply side shift variables that are arguments of the BRW and ZNM functions (such as bargaining power and amenity values, where the latter are reflected in α_0).[4]

However, the medium run AS curve (MRAS) retains its positive price elasticity. Indeed, it can be shown that MRAS is more price elastic than the SRAS (as illustrated in Figure 8.3). The intuition is straightforward: in the medium run the constraint of the available labour supply is relaxed through net migration, and this imparts a greater price elasticity to the MRAS. The effect of increasing accessibility in the commodity market is similar to the short run: the AS curve will be more elastic.

It is important to recognize, however, that *increasing* accessibility reflected in *higher* migration elasticities has no direct impact on the elasticity of the MRAS curve per se given the LNJ model of net migration. The nature of the net migration function (combined with our exogeneity assumptions) is that net migration continues until a zero-net migration equilibrium is established at the original wage and unemployment rate: the wage and unemployment elasticities simply govern the speed of adjustment to that equilibrium for all demand and many supply side disturbances. Nevertheless, the impact of increases in union militancy and changes in amenity differentials for example, does depend on migration elasticities, although even here it is only the *ratio* of these elasticities (α_1) that matters; (see the equation for ZNM above).

Long run If full adjustment of capital stocks is combined with the zero net migration equilibrium condition, or put another way, if both labour and capital markets are perfectly integrated in the long run, the long run aggregate supply (LRAS) curve becomes infinitely elastic, as in Figure 8.3. This reflects the fact that ultimately both labour and capital are in infinitely elastic supply. Thus our assumption that the small, open region is a price taker in national financial markets ties down the interest rate. Since the real consumption wage is ultimately fixed by the zero-net migration condition, the model conforms to Samuleson's (dynamic) non-substitution theorem. An aggregate demand disturbance has no effect on prices (relative to the numeraire, namely external prices). In a multisectoral context the system will emulate the behaviour of an I-O system with respect to demand disturbances (McGregor et al. 1996b). In this case, since there is no change in relative prices, accessibility in the commodity market does not matter in the AS curve.

Note the asymmetry of our analysis of the impact of increasing accessibility in the commodity and labour markets for the AD and AS curves. Increasing commodity market integration has an impact on both AD (for all time intervals) and AS (for the short to medium run). In contrast increasing labour mobility has no direct impact on aggregate supply curves given the LNJ (1991) net migration function, although it has an impact on aggregate demand in the medium run.

8.2.2 *Increasing Accessibility and the Spatial Integration of Commodity Markets: Impact on the Real Effects of Demand and Supply Disturbances*

As we have seen, increasing spatial integration of commodity markets increases the price elasticity of the region's aggregate demand and aggregate supply curves, and this in turn has implications for the impact of both aggregate demand and aggregate supply disturbances including, of course, those that are regional-policy-induced.

Consider first, the effects of increased spatial integration of commodity markets on the impact of a disturbance to aggregate demand. In order to avoid unnecessary cluttering, we initially ignore the implications of increased spatial integration of commodity markets for the AS curve. Figure 8.1 illustrates the impact of a stimulus to regional aggregate demand (AD) under alternative assumptions about the price elasticity of the AD curve. An exogenous stimulus to aggregate demand, such as an increase in export demand, causes equal (horizontal) outward shifts in aggregate demand in the presence of zero or intermediate trade elasticities in Figure 8.1, to $AD_1{}^1$ and $AD_2{}^1$ respectively. In the LOOP case the aggregate demand curve is unaffected: since the economy could sell all it wishes at the prevailing (national/world) price at the initial equilibrium, the disturbance makes no sense in this case. Export demand simply replaces domestic demand on a one-for-one basis. Accordingly, given a conventional AS, the new equilibria are established at points C, B and A for the zero, intermediate and infinite price elasticities of AD respectively. The output effects are greatest with the vertical AD curve and are smallest – and precisely zero – in the LOOP case.

It is clear that increases in accessibility which result in more closely integrated commodity markets will reduce the impact of demand disturbances on the real economy and on prices. The intuition of this result is straightforward: demand stimuli tend to increase prices, and this leads to a degree of crowding out of foreign trade which is dependent on the responsiveness of trade flows to such changes. As this responsiveness increases, the degree of crowding out increases, until it becomes complete under LOOP assumptions.

The above analysis ignores possible supply side effects as a result of the increased integration of the commodity markets. Since the AS curve now becomes more elastic, the ultimate equilibrium associated with intermediate trade elasticities will move to the southeast of B in Figure 8.1. Therefore, the demand side and supply side responses to the demand disturbance will tend to offset each other. However, the demand side response dominates and so the net effect of increased integration of the commodity markets is to reduce the impact of demand disturbances on the real economy and on prices.

We now consider the impact of an increase in the spatial integration of commodity markets on the real effects of supply disturbances. Figure 8.2 illustrates the impact of a positive supply disturbance. To make things more concrete we consider the impact of introducing a regional labour subsidy that reduces the costs and therefore the price, of supplying a given output level[5]. In the simple Input-Output (I-O) case of a completely inelastic AD schedule the new equilibrium is established at B. In this case the supply stimulus simply reduces prices, with no impact on output. In the case of intermediate trade elasticities output does increase as prices fall (through the stimulating effect on trade flows), and equilibrium is re-established at point C. The LOOP case maximizes the output effects of the supply disturbance: the increase in domestic supply can all be sold at the original price in world markets. Accordingly, the greater the price elasticity of the AD curve the more effective supply disturbances become in terms of their impact on the real economy. Moreover, as the AS curve becomes more elastic, and the vertical shift of AS will be the same as above following the introduction of the supply disturbance, the ultimate equilibrium associated with the intermediate case of AD (AD_2^0 in Figure 8.2) will move further to the southeast of C. Hence the supply side response will now reinforce the demand side response and the impact on the real economy will be even greater.

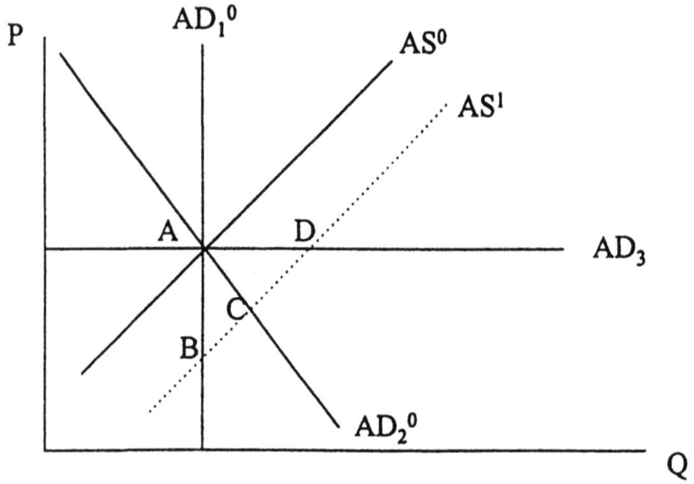

Figure 8.2 Accessibility, commodity market integration and the impact of supply disturbances

Increasing accessibility which is reflected in increasing absolute values of trade price elasticities therefore limits the price effects of demand and supply disturbances. However, this has *opposite* effects on the real impact of both types of disturbances: the impact of the former diminishes (to zero in the limit), while that of the latter increases. Moreover, increased commodity market accessibility will lead to demand side and supply side responses offsetting each other in the presence of demand disturbances and reinforcing each other in the presence of supply disturbances.

8.2.3 Accessibility and the Degree of Spatial Integration of Labour Markets: Impact on the Real Effects of Demand and Supply Disturbances

As noted above, we take one dimension of increasing accessibility to be the degree of labour mobility, here reflected in the scale of the elasticities on the net migration function of LNJ (1991). We know from the preceding analysis that the nature of this function is such that medium and long run price–elasticities of aggregate supply are quite independent of the migration parameters: variations in these parameters do not change the equilibrium levels of output and employment.

Although comparative statics of the kind conducted for the integration of commodity markets is not as obviously applicable in the present case, it is still capable of providing some intuition. In particular, the greater the migration elasticities then the more elastic will be the AS curve at any arbitrarily selected point during the adjustment process to the medium and long run equilibrium. Accordingly, if we focus on the present value of the real impact throughout the adjustment period (rather than simply its medium run or long run equilibrium level), this will be sensitive to the migration parameters. Furthermore, for alternative specifications of the net migration functions the medium and long run equilibria can become sensitive to the migration parameters, with increases in the latter actually increasing the price–elasticities of the medium and long run AS curves. However, once adjustment is complete the elasticity of the medium and long run aggregate supply curves is independent of migration responses.

Again, to avoid unnecessary cluttering in the diagrams, we initially ignore the implications of increased labour mobility for the AD curve and concentrate on the AS curve. Figure 8.3 illustrates the impact of a demand disturbance under different assumptions about the price elasticity of the AS curve. Not surprisingly, the real impact of a stimulus to aggregate demand varies directly with the price elasticity of aggregate supply. In the short run, with fixed capital and population stocks, the AS curve is comparatively inelastic. Once migration flows have reestablished zero net migration equilibria in the medium run, the effect is to increase the elasticity of the AS curve. For a given demand stimulus this implies a new equilibrium at a point like C, where output is higher and prices lower than at B, the short run equilibrium. In fact, migration also stimulates AD further, but for simplicity here we abstract from this effect. It is fully accommodated in the simulations that we report below.

Finally, in the long run, when physical capital and labour are optimally adjusted, the AS curve becomes infinitely elastic and equilibrium is established at D. Again, in general, AD expands with population and the equilibrium capital stock. These effects are captured in our simulations, but ignored in Figure 8.3 for simplicity. The greater are the migration elasticities the more rapidly does the system converge on C and D, and the greater the present value of the real impact associated with any adjustment path.

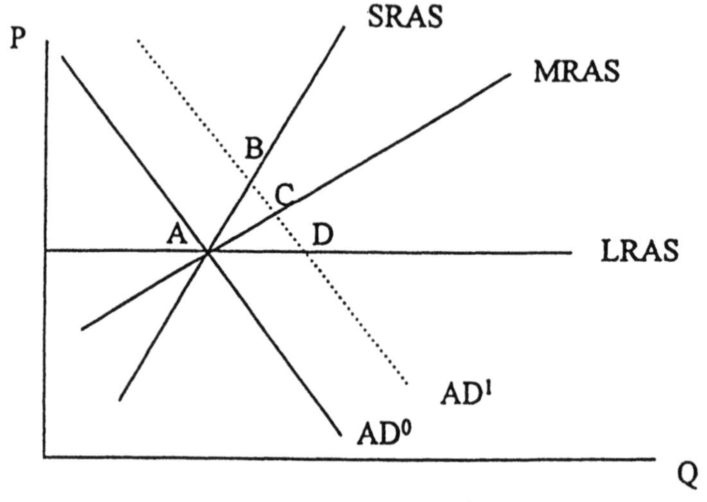

Figure 8.3 Accessibility, labour market integration and the impact of demand disturbances

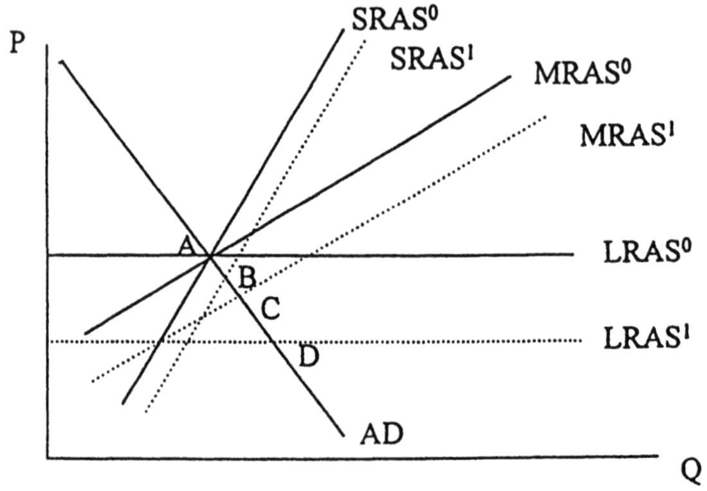

Figure 8.4 Accessibility, labour market integration and the impact of supply disturbances

In Figure 8.4 we illustrate the sensitivity of the real effects of a labour subsidy to the elasticity of the AS curve. The subsidy reduces the price at which any output will be supplied, so that it generates a common (vertical) downward shift in the SRAS and MRAS curves in Figure 8.4. However, in the long run capital variability implies that optimal adjustment to the change in relative factor prices is possible, so that the vertical shift in the LRAS is greater than that in SRAS and MRAS. In the short run equilibrium prices fall and output expands to point B. In the medium and longer runs the expansionary effect on the real economy is even greater as output and price effects are further reinforced. The long run impact is greater than that in the medium run both because the shift in the AS curve is greater and the AS curve is more elastic over this interval. Again the increase in the migration elasticities has no impact on the equilibria B, C or D. However, this change does increase the speed of adjustment from B to C and D and thereby increase the present value of the real impact generated by the labour subsidy.

Once the implications of increased labour mobility for the AD curve are also considered (the AD curve will become more elastic in Figures 8.3 and 8.4), it is again straightforward to illustrate that increased *labour* market accessibility, like increased *commodity* market accessibility, will lead to demand side and supply side responses offsetting each other in the presence of demand disturbances and reinforcing each other in the presence of supply disturbances.

8.3 AMOS: A Regional CGE

AMOS is a CGE modelling framework parameterised on data from a UK region, Scotland[6]. A very brief description is presented in this section[7]. AMOS has three domestic transactor groups, namely households, corporations and government[8]; and three commodities and activities: manufactures, non-manufacturing traded and sheltered[9]. In the simulations we report below commodity markets are, for simplicity, taken to be competitive, in which circumstances the PRW function is indistinguishable from the demand for labour function. We do not explicitly model financial flows, our assumption being that Scotland is a price taker in competitive UK financial markets.

The AMOS framework allows a high degree of flexibility in the choice of key parameter values and model closures. However, a crucial characteristic of the model is that no matter how it is configured, we impose cost minimization in production with multi-level production functions, generally of a CES form but with Leontief and Cobb-Douglas being available as special cases. There are four major components of final demand: consumption, investment, government expenditure and exports. Of these, real government expenditure is exogenous. Consumption is a linear homogeneous function of real disposable income. Exports (and imports) are determined via an Armington link (Armington 1969) and are therefore relative-price sensitive. Investment is a little more complex as we discuss below, depending on whether the system is being run in multiperiod mode or solved directly for the new long run equilibrium.

In each period of the multi-period simulations we report here, both the total capital stock and its sectoral composition are fixed, and commodity markets clear continuously. Each sector's capital stock is updated between periods via a simple capital stock adjustment procedure, according to which investment equals depreciation plus some fraction of the gap between the desired level of the capital stock and its actual level. This process of capital accumulation is compatible with a simple theory of optimal firm behaviour given the assumption of quadratic adjustment costs. Desired capital stocks are determined on cost-minimization criteria and actual stocks reflect last period's stocks adjusted for depreciation and gross investment. In long run equilibrium, desired and actual capital stocks become equal. Accordingly, in the long run simulations which solve directly for such equilibria, capital stocks are endogenous, and determined on cost-minimization criteria, with investment equal to depreciation at the optimal capital stock[10].

In all the simulations in this paper we impose a single Scottish labour market characterised by perfect sectoral mobility. We eschew the traditional approach of regional analysis which is associated with persistent sources of nominal inertia (that takes the form of a fixed nominal wage in the limiting case). Instead we follow a number of authors who have recently argued in favour of a regional bargained real wage function (BRW) in which the regional real consumption wage is directly related to workers bargaining power, and therefore inversely to the regional unemployment rate (see, for example, Layard et al. (1991) and Blanchflower and Oswald (1994)). Here we take the BRW function from the regional econometric work reported by Layard, Nickell and Jackman (LNJ 1991):

$$w_{s,t} = \alpha - 0.113u_s$$

where w_s and u_s are the natural logarithms of the Scottish real consumption wage and the unemployment rate respectively.

We investigate two alternative characterizations of labour mobility in the simulations. The first case assumes that labour is geographically immobile, an assumption often implicit in past UK regional policy analyses. Alternatively, we take net migration to be positively related to the real wage differential and negatively to the unemployment rate differential in accordance with the estimated model reported in LNJ (1991, chpt. 6). This model is based on that in Harris and Todaro (1970), and is commonly employed in studies of US migration (e.g. Greenwood et al. (1991) and Treyz et al. (1993)). The net migration equation we employ is:

$$m = \beta - 0.08(u_s - u_r) + 0.06(w_s - w_r)$$

where m is the net in-migration rate – as a proportion of the indigenous population; w_r and u_r are the natural logarithms of the real consumption wage and unemployment rates, respectively, in the rest of the UK. In the multi-period simulations reported below the net migration flows in any period are used to update population stocks at the beginning of the next period, in a manner analogous to the updating of the capital stocks. Ultimately, net migration flows reestablish a zero net migration equilibrium. This 'medium run' equilibrium may also be solved for directly through imposition of the zero-net-migration condition on the model.

Unless otherwise specified, all sectors use a CES technology with 'best guess' elasticities of substitution of 0.3 (Harris 1989) and Armington trade substitution elasticities of 2.0 (Gibson 1990). The capital stock adjustment parameter (λ) is taken to be 0.5 in each sector[11]. Throughout, we typically discuss results by interpreting the conceptual 'periods' of our model as 'years'. We believe this to be reasonable in that all of the data we have employed in the calibration (and, where applicable, estimation) of the model are annual. However, since the model is not (and cannot be) entirely econometrically estimated on annual data, this interpretation is suggestive, rather than definitive.

8.4 The Simulations

In this section we report the results of simulating AMOS to examine the impact of increased accessibility, as reflected in increased spatial integration of both commodity and labour markets, on the real effects of demand and supply disturbances. The demand disturbance that we consider is a 20 percent stimulus to manufacturing exports, and the supply shock takes the form of the introduction of an across-the-board labour subsidy of 5 percent of the gross wage. We interpret 'real effects' simply in terms of the induced changes in GDP relative to its initial equilibrium level. However, since we emphasize the importance, in practice, of the sectoral dimension for regional economies (in particular the presence of a sheltered sector), we also focus on sectoral value-added changes.

We simulate the impact of changes in the degree of spatial integration of the commodity market by varying the absolute value of all the Armington (1969) elasticities in the model. This implies changing the elasticity of substitution between Scottish, the rest of the UK (RUK) and the rest of the world (ROW) commodities in intermediate demand, consumption, investment, and export demand. As these elasticities vary from zero to infinity we move from the I-O to the LOOP model of aggregate demand (for traded goods). In fact, we find that varying these substitution elasticities between 0.2 and 9.9 is sufficient to convey the essential points since price changes quickly approach zero as the absolute value of all of the Armington elasticities is increased. Finally, we simulate the impact of increasing spatial integration of labour markets by increasing the absolute values of the elasticities of the net migration function. Here we also consider a comparatively limited range of migration elasticities, from {0.01 – 0.03} to {0.15 – 0.17} for the logarithmic wage and unemployment rate differentials. However, we do not actually deal directly with all of the limiting cases. For example, the LOOP characterization of AD would generate indeterminacy if combined with the LRAS (in the presence of labour mobility). The range of key parameter values selected here does not generate any problems for our (Levenburg-Marquardt) solution algorithm, but allows sufficient variation to allow us to communicate all the essential points.

We begin by presenting the simulation results for demand and supply disturbances using the default values for all key parameters, including those for the degree of commodity market integration and of labour mobility. We then examine the impact of changes in accessibility on the simulation results under the assumption of zero labour mobility, in which context only the commodity market impact is relevant. We then allow for labour mobility and investigate the impact of this dimension of accessibility on the real effects of demand and supply disturbances. Finally, we examine different combinations of the degrees of accessibility in the product and labour markets.

8.4.1 The Impact of Demand and Supply Disturbances under Default Assumptions about Accessibility

Prior to introducing variations in the degree of accessibility, it is useful to present, and briefly discuss, the impact of the demand and supply disturbances with default values for all key parameters, including trade and net migration elasticities. (The default values are 2.00 for all Armington trade elasticities, 0.06 for the response of net in-migration to the real wage differential and -0.08 for the response to the unemployment rate differential.) In Table 8.1 we present the percentage changes in selected key variables as a result of the introduction of the 20 percent manufacturing export demand stimulus and the 5 percent (externally financed) labour subsidy respectively.

The results for the export stimulus confirm our earlier theoretical analysis. First, the presence of the competitiveness wedge effect ensures a price responsive SRAS (fixed capital and population), so that the export demand stimulus increases GDP (by 1.0 percent) and total employment (by more, 1.3 percent, given the fixity of the capital stock). The concentration of the expansion in the manufacturing sector is apparent from the simulation results, and the increase in the real consumption wage necessary to increase employment given the BRW pushes up wages and prices, so that there is some crowding out. In the non–manufacturing sectors this generates a contraction in value added and employment.

Secondly, as the time horizon extends the impact of the demand stimulus on output and employment increases. In the short run real consumption wages rise and the unemployment rate declines, creating an incentive for inmigration. Accordingly, when population reallocation is complete, over the medium run, the stimulus to GDP increases to 2.3 percent and that to employment increases to 3.0 percent. Furthermore, the results over this interval exhibit natural rate or NAIRU results, with the real consumption wage and the unemployment rate being restored to their initial equilibrium values. Over the medium run net inmigration offsets the short run rise in the wage, and so limits price rises in all sectors, reducing the degree of crowding out. Furthermore, the stimulus to consumption demand more than outweighs the contraction in the exports of the non-manufacturing sectors, so that all sectors expand over this interval.

Table 8.1 Impact of the export stimulus and the labour subsidy under different time horizons (percentage changes from base-year values)

	Export stimulus			Labour subsidy		
	short-run	medium-run	long-run	short-run	medium-run	long-run
GDP (@ income measure)	1.0	2.3	8.1	1.7	3.4	9.2
Consumption	2.8	3.7	8.1	2.3	3.0	7.5
Nominal take home wage	2.5	0.8	0.0	2.3	-0.9	-2.5
Real take-home consumption wage	1.5	0.0	0.0	2.6	0.0	0.0
Value-added:						
Manu	6.4	8.1	17.6	1.8	3.8	8.8
N Manu Tr	-0.4	0.9	6.9	1.7	3.5	11.3
N Manu N Tr	-0.8	0.4	3.8	1.6	3.2	7.7
Total Employment (000's):	1.3	3.0	8.2	2.1	4.3	9.7
Manu:	7.9	10.1	17.6	2.1	4.6	9.1
Non-Manu tr:	-0.6	1.2	6.9	2.3	4.8	11.8
Non-Manuf N tr:	-0.9	0.4	3.8	1.8	3.7	7.9
Unemployment rate	-12.6	0.0	0.0	-20.6	0.0	0.0
Population	0.0	3.0	8.2	0.0	4.3	9.7
Price of value added:						
Manu	7.4	7.0	0.0	-1.1	-2.8	-6.1
Non-Manu tr	2.0	1.8	0.0	-0.3	-1.3	-5.7
Non-Manuf N tr	2.1	1.0	0.0	-1.5	-3.8	-6.3
Capital rental rates:						
Manu	32.0	38.8	0.0	4.8	10.0	-2.1
Non-Manu tr	0.5	4.7	0.0	5.5	10.5	-2.1
Non-Manuf N tr	-0.4	2.2	0.0	3.7	6.7	-2.1
Capital stocks:						
Manu	0.0	0.0	17.6	0.0	0.0	7.5
N Manu Tr	0.0	0.0	6.9	0.0	0.0	10.1
N Manu N Tr	0.0	0.0	3.8	0.0	0.0	6.3
Exports to ROW:						
Manu	10.4	12.0	20.0	1.3	3.0	6.6
N Manu Tr	-3.3	-2.7	0.0	0.5	2.0	9.0
N Manu N Tr	-4.4	-1.8	0.0	3.3	7.4	12.6
Real income (CPI deflator):						
Households disposable	2.8	3.7	8.1	2.3	3.0	7.5
Firms disposable	5.0	8.3	8.2	24.6	28.1	29.4

In the long run (with labour mobility) the effectively infinitely elastic supplies of labour and capital constrain all price rises to zero, and the system operates as an I-O model, with equiproportionate expansions in employment, capital and value-added within each sector, exactly as our theoretical analysis implies. Thus the manufacturing sector experiences the full 20 percent hike in export demand, and all sectors expand significantly, generating an 8.1 percent rise in GDP and a similar stimulus to total employment.

The impact of the labour subsidy also confirms our earlier theoretical analysis. However, we should note that, for simplicity, we consider an externally-financed subsidy in the model simulations, so that the change simultaneously involves a stimulus to aggregate demand. We provide a full analysis of this case in Harrigan et al (1996), and so keep the discussion to a minimum here. In the short run the unemployment rate falls and the real consumption wage rises. Over the medium run net inmigration increases the impact of the labour subsidy, and NAIRU results are established. The long run impact (with labour mobility) maximizes the impact of the labour subsidy but, in contrast to the demand shock case, the impact on prices is also maximized over this interval.

8.4.2 Accessibility in the Presence of Immobile Labour: Spatial Integration of Commodity Markets

In this section, in order to focus on the effects of increasing spatial integration of commodity markets, we assume that labour is immobile. As mentioned above, changing the degree of accessibility in the product market involves changing the Armington elasticities. We examine the effects of varying all of these elasticities between 0.2 and 9.9, since, as we shall see, the latter provides a good approximation to the LOOP case. (Recall that the default value for all of these elasticities is 2.0.) Figures 8.5 and 8.6 present the effects of varying the degree of spatial integration of commodity markets on the regional GDP and sectoral value added changes generated by the manufacturing export demand stimulus, for fixed and optimally adjusted capital stocks, respectively. Figures 8.7 and 8.8 record the corresponding effects on the real impact of the regional labour subsidy.

We begin by examining the effects on the impact of the demand shock (Figures 8.5 and 8.6). As we approach the limiting case of zero trade substitution elasticities, we have a regional economy which can be characterized by a simple, open economy Leontief system. In this case, the demand shock exerts the strongest impact on GDP. As the values of the trade elasticities increase, aggregate demand becomes more and more price sensitive and the impact on the real economy of the demand shock becomes less and less significant because of crowding out. As trade elasticities are increased we approach the other limiting case associated with the 'law of one price' (LOOP), under which the impact on employment of the demand shock disappears completely (although GDP may still exhibit moderate change). Although the largest absolute value we employ for trade elasticities is only 9.9, the approximation to the 'law of one price' is almost complete, as is confirmed by the movement of the manufacturing commodity price.

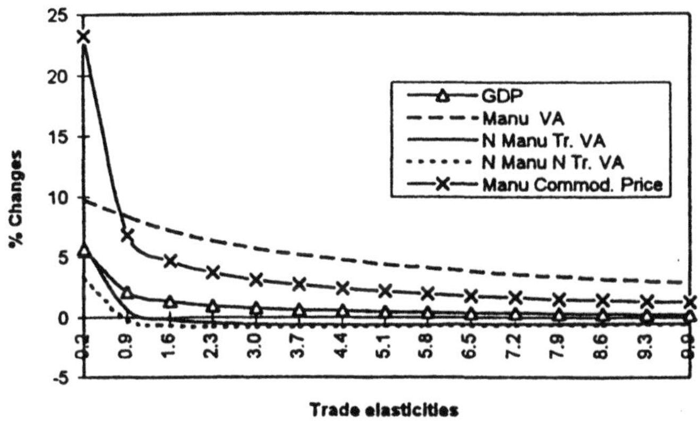

Figure 8.5 Sensitivity of impacts of the demand stimulus wrt variations in trade elasticities (fixed capital)

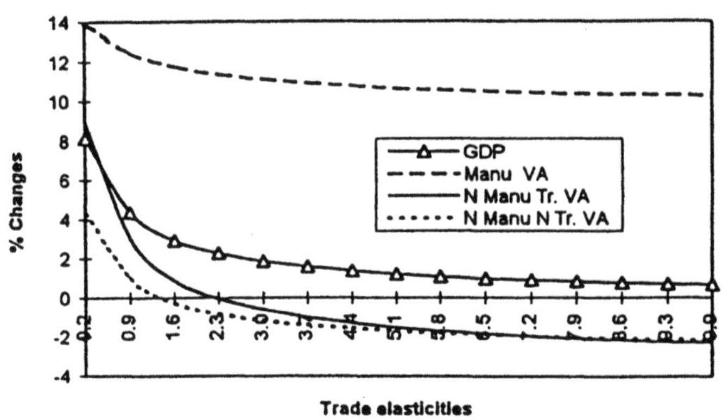

Figure 8.6 Sensitivity of impacts of the demand stimulus wrt variations in trade elasticities (endogenous capital)

Figure 8.5 clearly shows that the manufacturing commodity price increases dramatically in response to the export stimulus with low values of trade elasticities, but is close to zero when the trade elasticities are 9.9. In such circumstances the stimulus to manufacturing export demand simply displaces activity in the other two sectors, reflecting the complete crowding out that occurs in this case (at least for employment).

The effects of varying trade elasticities on the impacts of the demand shock are qualitatively similar for the cases of fixed capital (Figure 8.5) and endogenous, optimally adjusted capital (Figure 8.6). Nevertheless, with endogenous capital, the impact on GDP is much greater than with fixed capital (although this would not be so for GDP changes in the LOOP case), confirming the greater price elasticity of aggregate supply in these circumstances. Further, the rate of decline of GDP effects with respect to trade elasticities decreases rapidly. For example, in the short run (with fixed capital) as elasticities increase from 0.2 to 1.6 the GDP stimulus falls from 5.72 percent to 1.34 percent, whereas increases from 7.2 to 8.6 limit the stimulus from 0.37 percent to 0.32 percent. In the long run the rate of decline is less marked and here the corresponding figures are 8.15 percent and 2.92 percent for the change from 0.2 to 1.6, and 0.91 percent and 0.77 percent for the change from 7.2 to 8.6.

We now turn to the impact of the supply shock. Our theoretical analysis suggests that the impact of the supply shock increases with the value of the trade elasticities.

8.4.3 Accessibility and the Spatial Integration of the Labour Market

Figures 8.7 and 8.8 broadly confirm our earlier theoretical analysis. Again, the impacts under optimally adjusted capital are greater than under fixed capital (except for the zero elasticity case where the labour subsidy has no effect in either case). The distinctive behaviour of non-manufacturing traded in Figure 8.7 reflects its relative capital intensity. As the price elasticities increase there comes a point where the price of this commodity actually rises as the impact of increasing rental rates and upward pressure on wages begins to offset the direct impact of the labour subsidy. Beyond this point further increases in price elasticities increase the real effects of the price rise, and value-added in this sector falls further. The effect is, of course, not apparent in Figure 8.8 since here capital is optimally adjusted.

Here we proxy changes in accessibility, as reflected in the spatial integration of labour markets, by variations in the magnitudes of the parameters indicating the responsiveness of net inmigration with respect to the real wage and unemployment rate differentials: the larger these magnitudes, the more accessible the labour market is taken to be. In Figures 8.9 through 8.12, we plot the percentage changes in GDP generated by the export demand and labour subsidy disturbances against the elasticities of the net migration equation. It should be noted that all of our analysis in this section of the paper relates to what we have termed either medium run (population optimally adjusted with capital stocks fixed) or long run equilibria (optimal adjustment of capital stocks as well as population).

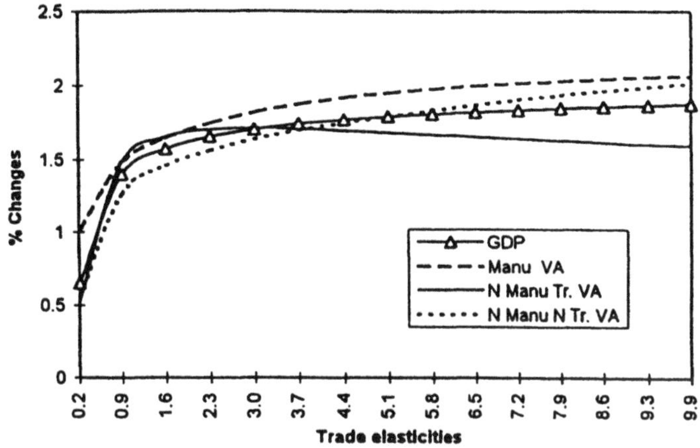

Figure 8.7 Sensitivity of impacts of the labour subsidy wrt variations in trade elasticities (fixed capital)

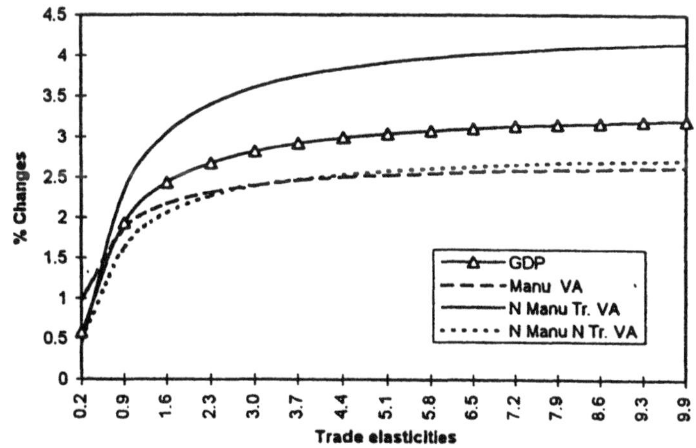

Figure 8.8 Sensitivity of impacts of the labour subsidy wrt variations in trade elasticities (endogenous capital)

Consider first the effects on impact of the export demand stimulus which are plotted in Figures 8.9 and 8.10. In accordance with our earlier theoretical analysis, changes in the degree of labour mobility have no effects on the ultimate equilibrium level of GDP. However, the more accessible the labour market is in terms of the migration elasticities, the larger are the *short run* impacts and the faster is the adjustment process to the ultimate equilibrium position. Accordingly, we would expect the elasticities to be positively related to the discounted present value of GDP associated with any disturbance. As already noted, relaxation of the constraint of fixed capital stocks (Figure 8.10) implies that the export stimulus generates a much greater impact on GDP than under the fixed capital stocks case (Figure 8.9). Not surprisingly, allowance for gradual adjustment of capital stocks extends the duration of the adjustment period.

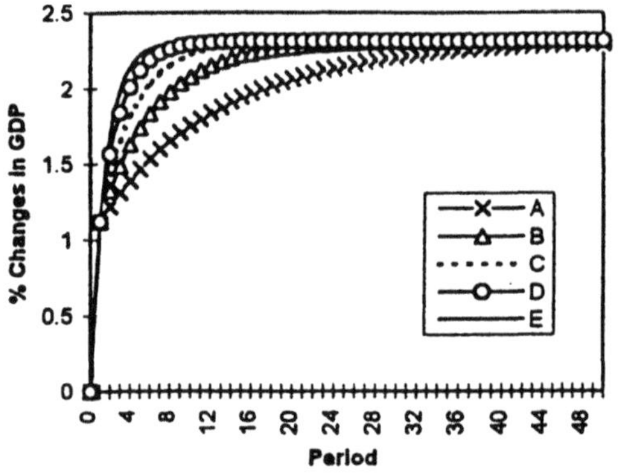

Figure 8.9 Sensitivity of impacts of the demand stimulus wrt variations in NMG parameters (fixed capital)

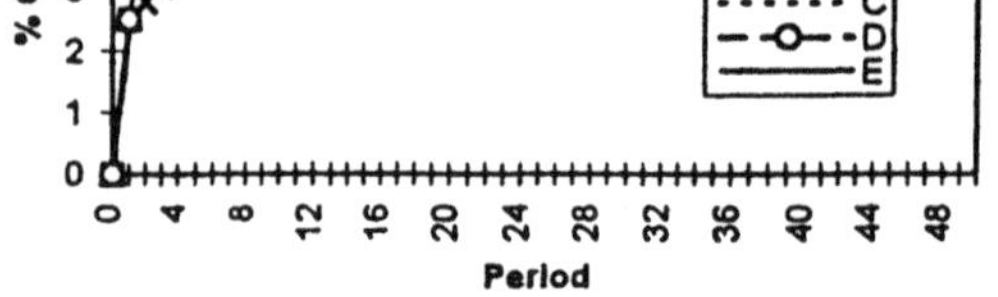

Figure 8.10 Sensitivity of impacts of the demand stimulus wrt variations in NMG parameters (endogenous capital)

Inspection of Figures 8.11 and 8.12 reveals qualitatively similar impacts of the supply shock, with increases in labour mobility again having no impact on the equilibrium levels of GDP, but increasing the speed of adjustment. Notice that the labour market ramifications of accessibility are the same for both demand and supply disturbances: the speed at which equilibria are attained is increased in both cases, thereby increasing the present value of real effects. This contrasts with the asymmetrical impact of increased commodity market integration on the real effects of demand and supply disturbances.

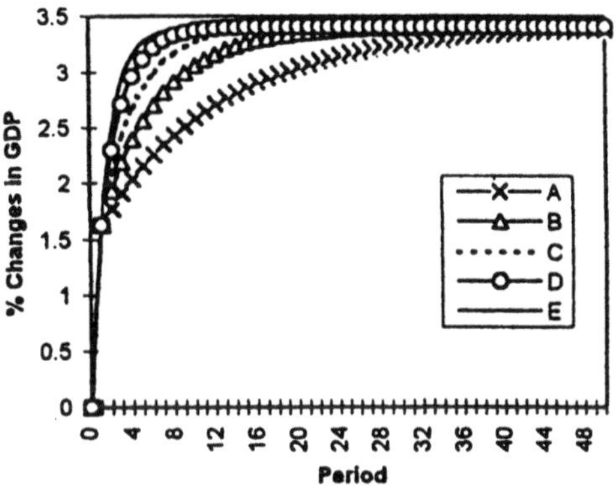

Figure 8.11 Sensitivity of impacts of the labour subsidy wrt variations in NMG parameters (fixed capital)

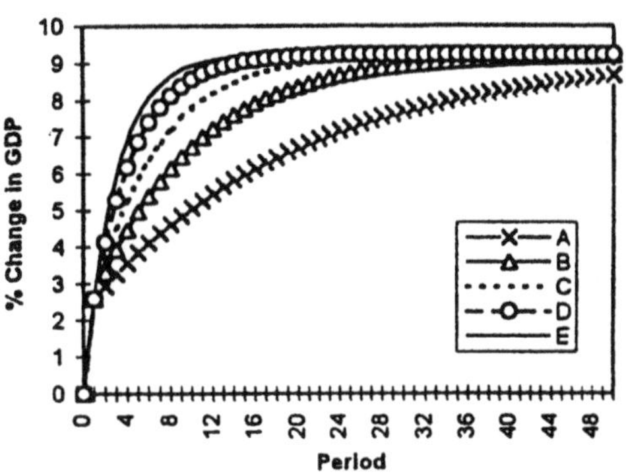

Figure 8.12 Sensitivity of impacts of the labour subsidy wrt variations in NMG parameters (endogenous capital)

8.4.4 Accessibility and the Spatial Integration of Commodity and Labour Markets under Labour Mobility

Here we take a more systematic approach to examining the consequences of variations in the degree of spatial accessibility. We combine varying degrees of accessibility in both commodity and labour markets and examine their impact on the effect on GDP of the export demand stimulus and labour subsidy. For each combination of trade elasticities and migration parameters, we run the model for 50 periods and obtain the equilibrium level of GDP in each of these periods. We then calculate the present values of these changes, PVGDP (using the 6 percent discount rate currently recommended by the UK Treasury (HM Treasury 1991)) and report the results in Tables 8.2 to 8.5 in the form of a grid of trade and migration elasticities. Moving from left to right in a row reflects greater accessibility in the labour market, and moving from top to bottom in a column indicates greater accessibility in the product market. Tables 8.2 and 8.4 report the impact of changes in accessibility on medium run equilibria, that is for equilibria across which the zero net migration condition is satisfied. Tables 8.3 and 8.5 relate to the sensitivity of long run equilibria to accessibility, and so allow optimal adjustment of capital stocks as well as population.

Tables 8.2 and 8.3 report the results for the demand stimulus with fixed and optimally adjusted capital respectively. Moving down the columns, the demand impacts decrease with the (absolute) values of the trade elasticities, and across the rows, the impacts increase with the values of the migration parameters, in line with our earlier analysis (though note that labour is mobile in all the simulations in this sub-section). However, the PVGDP is clearly much more sensitive to variations in trade elasticities than to migration elasticities. This result is hardly surprising since variations in trade elasticities impact on the equilibrium levels of GDP whereas the migration elasticities only affect the system's speed of adjustment. Increases in commodity market integration have a very marked impact on the real effects of the demand stimulus, with the GDP change associated with price elasticities of 3.0 being less than half that for demand elasticities of 0.9 given a fixed capital stock and the lowest set of migration elasticities.

Table 8.2 NPV of percentage changes in GDP in all the simulation periods as a result of the demand stimulus (fixed capital)

Trade elasticities	Migration parameters				
	0.02	0.05	0.08	0.12	0.15
	-0.04	-0.07	-0.14	-0.14	-0.17
0.9	53.51	56.34	57.68	58.67	59.12
3.0	21.67	23.64	24.63	25.38	25.73
5.1	14.17	15.62	16.36	16.92	17.20
7.9	9.83	10.91	11.48	11.91	12.12
9.9	8.11	9.03	9.51	9.88	10.06

Table 8.3 NPV of percentage changes in GDP in all the simulation periods as a result of the demand stimulus (endogenous capital)

Trade elasticities	Migration parameters				
	0.02	0.05	0.08	0.12	0.15
	-0.04	-0.07	-0.14	-0.14	-0.17
0.9	105.8	113.2	116.8	119.4	120.6
3.0	71.2	85.8	94.4	101.6	105.2
5.1	53.5	68.9	79.1	88.2	93.1
7.9	40.1	54.3	64.7	74.9	80.6
9.9	33.9	47.1	57.2	70.0	73.4

Table 8.4 NPV of percentage changes in GDP in all the simulation periods as a result of the labour subsidy (fixed capital)

Trade elasticities	Migration parameters				
	0.02	0.05	0.08	0.12	0.15
	-0.04	-0.07	-0.14	-0.14	-0.17
0.9	31.0	32.6	33.3	33.9	34.2
3.0	47.7	52.0	54.2	55.9	56.6
5.1	52.6	58.0	60.7	62.7	63.7
7.9	56.0	62.1	65.3	67.7	68.8
9.9	57.6	64.1	67.4	70.0	71.2

Table 8.5 NPV of percentage changes in GDP in all the simulation periods as a result of the labour subsidy (endogenous capital)

Trade elasticities	Migration parameters				
	0.02	0.05	0.08	0.12	0.15
	-0.04	-0.07	-0.14	-0.14	-0.17
0.9	49.3	52.8	54.6	55.9	56.5
3.0	121.7	149.8	166.7	180.8	188.0
5.1	158.9	213.2	251.0	286.3	305.6
7.9	186.4	267.9	332.8	400.7	441.3
9.9	198.7	294.7	376.2	466.8	524.0

The optimal adjustment of capital naturally significantly magnifies the impact of the export stimulus for all parameter values, but the same qualitative relationships continue to hold. However, it is clear from Table 8.3 that the sensitivity of the PVGDP to trade elasticities is much less when capital is optimally adjusted than when it is fixed. In contrast, the sensitivity to migration parameters is increased, reflecting the longer intervals required for the completion of capital stock adjustments.

The results for the labour subsidy with fixed and optimally-adjusted capital are reported in Tables 8.4 and 8.5. The impacts of the supply shock increase with the absolute values of the trade elasticities (migration parameters) when moving down the columns (across the rows). Here, increasing product market accessibility and increasing labour market accessibility both work in the same direction in accentuating the real impact of the supply shock. As with the demand shock, the PVGDP is also much more sensitive to variations in trade elasticities than to migration elasticities. Moreover, capital endogeneity significantly enhances the real impact of the supply shock. For example, when the labour market accessibility is low (the migration parameters are 0.02 and –0.04), increasing the trade elasticities from 0.9 to 9.9 will increase the real impact of the supply shock by 86 percent in the fixed capital case, and by 303 percent in the endogenous capital case. When the labour market is highly accessible, these effects are even more marked. When the migration parameters are 0.15 and –0.17, increasing the trade elasticities from 0.9 to 9.9 will increase the real impact of the supply shock by 108 percent in the fixed capital case, and by 827 percent in the endogenous capital case. In contrast, when the trade elasticities are low (0.9), increasing labour market accessibility from the least accessible case to the most accessible case in our selected range will increase the real impact of the supply shock by only 10 percent with fixed capital. Even with capital endogenous, such an increase is only slightly higher at 15 percent. However, when the trade elasticities are high (9.9), increasing labour market accessibility from the least accessible case to the most accessible case will increase the real impact of the supply shock by 24 percent with fixed capital. Now capital endogeneity does have a much greater impact, and increasing labour market accessibility from the least accessible case to the most accessible case will increase the real impact of the supply shock by 164 percent.

8.5 Conclusions

In this chapter we examine the macroeconomic impact of increasing accessibility, interpreted as implying increasing spatial integration of commodity and labour markets, in a small, open economy context. Our theoretical analysis, based upon an illustrative, one sector model, establishes a number of important points. First the spatial integration of commodity markets impacts directly on the price elasticity of aggregate demand and aggregate supply. If the degree of spatial integration is zero, then we obtain the I-O case of a completely price inelastic aggregate demand curve, whereas under perfect spatial integration the 'law-of-one-price' prevails. Secondly, increases in the degree of spatial integration of commodity markets *reduces* the real effects of demand changes, but *increases* the real effects of supply disturbances.

Thirdly, the degree of spatial integration of labour markets, as reflected in the absolute values of the elasticities of the net migration function, does not exert an analogous impact on aggregate supply given the LNJ (1991) migration function that is employed here (and widely elsewhere). The price elasticity of aggregate supply does vary directly with the time interval under consideration: it is positive, but finite, in the short run; is greater in the medium run as migration relaxes the labour supply constraint; is infinite in the long run if labour is mobile. Increases in migration elasticities have no impact on equilibria, but they do increase the system's speed of adjustment to equilibria. Fourthly, while an increase in labour mobility ultimately has no impact on the real effects of either demand or supply disturbances when comparison is restricted to equilibria, it does increase the present value of GDP effects associated with *both* types of change, since it increases the speed of adjustment.

The theoretical analysis is limited both by its one-sector structure and because it is incapable of indicating the likely scale of the various effects. We simulate the impact of changes in accessibility on the real effects of a manufacturing export demand stimulus and a general labour subsidy using AMOS, a regional CGE model, in an attempt to overcome these limitations. The simulation results confirm the broad implications of the theoretical analysis. Increases in the degree of spatial integration of commodity markets reduce the real effects of the demand stimulus quickly, so that the 'law of one price' case is closely approximated by elasticity values less than ten in absolute value, at least when capital stocks are fixed. The sensitivity to the degree of spatial integration is reduced the greater the elasticity of the aggregate supply curve, although the real effects of the demand disturbance does vary directly with the latter. Increases in the absolute value of the migration elasticities are demonstrated to have no impact on equilibria in the short, medium or long runs, but to increase the speed of adjustment of the system, thereby increasing the present value of the GDP effects associated with both demand and supply disturbances.

Overall it is clear that increases in the degree of commodity market integration may have quite dramatic consequences for the small open region, substantially reducing the real effects of aggregate demand disturbances and raising that of supply disturbances. The impact of increasing labour market integration is much less dramatic, affecting only the speed of adjustment of the system to both demand and supply disturbances. However, even this may exert non-trivial effects on the present value of GDP associated with changes in both aggregate demand and supply.

Acknowledgement

The authors gratefully acknowledge the research assistance of Ayèle Gelana and the comments of an anonymous referee. We also benefitted from the comments, on a related paper, of participants in the Regional Science Association's World Congress, Tokyo 1996. Funding from the

Economic and Social Research Council for initial model development is gratefully acknowledged, as is funding from Scottish Enterprise National for recent modifications, including the updating of the model's data base.

References

Armington, P. (1969), 'A Theory of Demand for Products Distinguished by Place of Production', *IMF Papers*, vol. 16, pp. 157–78.

Blanchflower, D.G. and Oswald, A. (1994), *The Wage Curve*, MIT Press, Cambridge, Mass.

Gibson, H. (1990), 'Export Competitiveness and UK Sales of Scottish Manufactures', Paper delivered to the Scottish Economists Conference, The Burn.

Greenwood, M.J., Hunt, G.L., Rickman, D.S. and Treyz, G. (1991), 'Migration, Regional Equilibrium and the Estimation of Compensating Differentials', *American Economic Review*, vol. 81, pp. 1382–90.

Harringan, F., McGregor, P.G., Dournmashkin, N., Perman, R., Swales, J.K. and Yin, Ya Ping (1991), 'AMOS: a Macro-Micro Model of Scotland', *Economic Modelling*, vol. 8, pp. 424–79.

Harrigan, F., McGregor, P.G. and Swales, J.K. (1996), 'The System-wide Impact on the Recipient Region of a Regional Labour Subsidy', *Oxford Economic Papers*, vol. 48, pp. 105–133.

Harrigan, F., McGregor, P.G. and Swales, J.K. and Yin, Ya Ping (1993), 'Openness, Imperfect Competition and the NAIRU', *Journal of Economic Studies*, vol. 20 (1/2), pp. 52–72.

Harris, J.R. and Todaro, M. (1970), 'Migration, Unemployment and Development: A Two-Sector Analysis', *American Economic Review*, vol. 60, no. 1, pp. 126–42.

Harris, R.I.D. (1989), *The Growth and Structure of the UK Regional Economy (1963–85)*, Avebury, Aldershot.

HM Treasury (1991), *Economic Appraisal of the Central Government Departments*, HMSO, London.

Layard, R., Nickell, S. and Jackman, R. (1991), *Unemployment, Macroeconomic Performance and the Labour Market*, Oxford University Press, Oxford.

McGregor, P.G., Swales, J.K. and Yin, Ya Ping (1995a), 'Regional NAIRU's', University of Strathclyde, mimeo.

McGregor, P.G., Swales, J.K. and Yin, Ya Ping (1995b), 'Migration, Equilibria/Disequilibria and the Natural Rate of Unemployment in a Regional Context', *International Journal of Manpower*, vol. 16, pp. 66–72.

McGregor, P.G., Swales, J.K. and Yin, Ya Ping (1996a), 'Migration Equilibria in Regional Economies: A Multi-Period CGE Analysis of an Improvement in Local Amenities', in Van den Bergh, J.C.J.M., Nijkamp, P. and P. Rietveld (eds), *Recent Advances in Spatial Economic Modelling: Methodology and Applications*, Springer, Berlin.

McGregor, P.G., Swales, J.K. and Yin, Ya Ping (1996b), 'A Long-Run Interpretation of Regional Input-Output Analyses', *Journal of Regional Science*, vol. 36, no. 3, pp. 479–501.
Treyz, G.I., Rickman, D.S., Hunt, G.L. and Greenwood, M.J. (1993), 'The Dynamics of US Internal Migration', *Review of Economics and Statistics*, vol. 75, pp. 209–14.

Notes

1. Harrigan et al. (1993) deal with the macroeconomic model; McGregor et al. (1995 a,b) develop the analytics of the regional variant.

2. Although commonly employed, aggregate demand (AD) and supply (AS) representations of macroeconomies which treat these functions as independent must strictly be incorrect: domestic incomes, and so demand, are dependent on suppliers' decisions. Nonetheless, we adopt the conventional approach here since it simplifies the exposition but has no significant bearing on our results. Furthermore, our simulation model fully captures the interdependence of aggregate supply and demand.

3. This real product wage equation is obtained by a re-parameterisation of a real consumption wage equation, which results in a 'competitiveness' wedge appearing as a right-hand-side variable. Since external prices and the nominal exchange rate are fixed, the only endogenous component of competitiveness is the price of domestically produced goods.

4. See McGregor et al. (1996a) for an analysis of the impact of a change in amenities).

5. We assume throughout that the subsidy is not fully captured by union bargaining.

6. AMOS is an acronym for a macro-micro model of Scotland.

7. A full listing of the model is provided in Harrigan et al. (1991), although the social accounting matrix data base of the model has since been updated.

8. In AMOS, Scotland is treated as a self-governing economy, in the sense that there is only one consolidated government sector. Central government activity is partitioned to Scotland and combined with local government activity.

9. Manufacturing comprises sectors 12-89, non-manufacturing traded sectors 1-10, 91-97, 99-102 and 109-111 and sheltered sectors 11, 90 and 98, 103-108 and 112 - 114 in the 1989 Scottish Input-Output Tables.

10. Our treatment is wholly consistent with sectoral investment being determined by the relationship between the capital rental rate and the user cost of capital. The capital rental rate is the rental that would have to be paid in a competitive market

capital rental rate is the rental that would have to be paid in a competitive market for the (sector specific) physical capital: the user cost is the total cost to the firm of employing a unit of capital. Given that we take the interest, capital depreciation and tax rates to be exogenous, the capital price index is the only endogenous component of the user cost. If the rental rate exceeds the user cost, desired capital stock is greater than the actual capital stock and there is therefore an incentive to increase capital stock. The resultant capital accumulation puts downward pressure on rental rates and so tends to restore equilibrium. In the long-run, the capital rental rate equals the user cost in each sector, and the risk-adjusted rate of return is equalised between sectors.

11. This default value of the adjustment parameters is based on investment equations estimated for the Scottish manufacturing sector. This is, in fact, the only sector in AMOS for which a time series of investment data exists. For other sectors information is available only for the years in which a Scottish I–O table has been constructed.

9 A Prototype Computable General Equilibrium Model of Trade between Two Countries

HIDEO HASHIMOTO

9.1 Introduction

This chapter presents a prototype computable general equilibrium (CGE) model of trade between two countries, developed as a non-linear complementarity programming (NLCP) problem.[1] The chapter is motivated partly for pedagogical purposes and partly as a basis for actual trade models to be developed later.[2]

The present model is developed as an extension of the Negishi model (1960) and the Takayama-Judge model (1961). The model consists of two countries, two products and two production factors. The model solves each country's demand and supply quantities of products, trade flows of products between the countries, and quantities of factors demanded by each industry in each country. In addition, the model solves demand and supply prices of products, and prices of factors.

All the prices in the model are expressed in terms of each country's currency to facilitate comparison of solved prices with actual prices. It is assumed that the authority of each country determines the exchange rate in such a way that it is equated to the marginal utility of income.

To demonstrate how the model works, we conduct comparative static studies analysing the impact of trade policies, such as import tariffs, export taxes, export subsidies, import quotas and grants, as well as transportation costs. The number of countries, products and factors can be increased easily.

NLCP, instead of nonlinear programming (NLP) or a system of simultaneous equations, is used to develop this model, because it contains foreign exchange constraints, ad-valorem import tariffs and export taxes/subsidies, and spatial equilibrium conditions.

9.2 Model

9.2.1 Characteristics of The Model

The model consists of two countries, say Japan and the USA, which are spatially separated and connected with trade. Each country has two economic agents: households and firms. There is no government as a consuming or producing agent.

Each country has two factors, say capital and labour, whose endowments in each country are given exogenously. The factors are assumed to be immobile beyond the national boundary. Households own the factors and gain the remuneration for their uses. Households in each country are assumed to have the same preferences and to maximize their utility, given a utility function.

There are two products, say steel and wheat.[3] Both of these products are tradeable. There is no non-tradeable good in either country. It is assumed that incomplete specialization always holds. Under given technology of production of each product, firms of each industry in each country maximize their profit. The utility and production functions are assumed to be Cobb-Douglas functions. Prices of products and factors in each country are expressed in terms of its own currency.

The present model is a static one, assumes full employment and does not include money. Except for savings to finance grants in Case 7 explained later, neither households nor firms make savings. The income constraint of households and firms combined in each country is supposed to be satisfied. Similarly, the foreign exchange constraint in each country must be satisfied.

The exchange rate in each country is expressed in the amount of the local currency per unit of a neutral currency, say, SDR. It is assumed that the authority of each country determines the exchange rate in such a way that it is equated to the marginal utility of income. The exchange rate of the US dollar vis-à-vis SDR is treated as the numeraire.

Firms in each country are equipped with an infinite amount of transportation facilities for trade. We assume only one route and one mode of transportation between two countries. In Case 6 explained later, transportation costs in each route are institutionally set at positive levels, expressed in SDRs per unit of a given product. Exporting countries use their own transportation facilities for their exports, and claim the transportation costs from importing countries. In this treatment, transportation costs are, in fact, equivalent to ad-quantum export taxes imposed by exporting countries.

Within a country, perfect competition is assumed to prevail. Regarding conditions in international markets, we make seven distinct assumptions on trade. First, free trade is assumed (Case 1). Second, Japan is assumed to impose an ad-valorem tariff on its imports of wheat (Case 2). Third, Japan is assumed to impose an export tax on its steel exports (Case 3). Fourth, Japan is assumed to give a subsidy to its steel exports (Case 4). Fifth, Japan imposes a quota on its imports of wheat (Case 5). Sixth, it is assumed that an importing country of a given product pays a positive transportation costs to its exporting country (Case 6). Lastly, no trade restrictions are assumed, but a given amount expressed in SDRs is assumed to be granted from Japan to the USA (Case 7). The assumptions of these sample problems do not give any hint at Japan's or the USA's actual trade practices whatsoever.

The revenues from import tariffs and export taxes, and the expenditures for export subsidies are treated as lump-sum transfers between households and the government within a country. Except for Case 7, trade (including net transportation receipts in Case 6) of each country is balanced. The model allows us to combine these cases, if necessary.

Complete substitution between domestically produced and imported goods is assumed. Therefore, for example, a country that exports steel imports no steel at all. Equivalently, if a given product is traded from a country to the other country, trade of the same product in the opposite direction is zero.[4] In other words, our model does not include a composite good à la Armington (1969). This is because we intend to preserve the spatial equilibrium conditions à la the Takayama-Judge model.[5]

The spatial equilibrium conditions are as follows. If there is no transportation cost, the supply price of a given product in an exporting country is equal to the importing country's demand price, both expressed in SDRs, as long as trade of that product takes place from the former country to the latter. The supply price may be strictly greater than the demand price, when no trade takes place. In Case 6, the supply price in the sentences above must be replaced by the sum of the supply price and the given transportation cost. The spatial equilibrium conditions with import tariffs and export subsidies, etc. are explained in detail later.

The model is developed as a NLCP problem. The reason why NLCP is used for this model will be explained in detail later.

9.2.2 Description of The Model

Notation

a Subscripts

i	Production factor.
j	Product.
m, n	Country.

b Endogenous variables inside the model

QD_{jm}	Demand for product j in country m.
QT_{jmn}	Trade of product j from country m to country n.
QS_{jm}	Supply of product j in country m.
FD_{ijm}	Demand for factor i in production of product j in country m.

PF_{im} Price of factor i in country m, expressed in country m's currency.

PSF_{jm} Supply price (at factory gates) of product j in country m, expressed in country m's currency.

PSR_{jm} Supply price (at retailers) of product j in country m, expressed in country m's currency, before an export tax is imposed or an export subsidy is given if product j is an export good.

PD_{jm} Demand price for product j in country m, expressed in country m's currency, after an import tariff is imposed and/or the rent generated by an import quota is added if product j is an import good.

RQ_{jm} Rent generated by an import quota of product j in country m, expressed in country m's currency.

XR_m Exchange rate of country m's currency with respect to SDRs, expressed in terms of the amount of country m's currency per unit of SDRS.

MI_m Marginal utility of income in country m.

c Endogenous variables outside the model

UTL_m Utility of households in country m.

SWF Social welfare function defined as the weighted sum of each country's utility.

ω_m Social importance of the m-th individual.

PD'_{jm} Demand price for product j in country m, expressed in Sdrs.

XR'_m Exchange rate of country m's currency with respect to Sdrs, measured in terms of the amount of Sdrs per unit of country m's currency.

d Inequalities

EQD_{jm} The relationship between the demand price for product j and its marginal utility in country m.

EQT_{jmn} The relationship between the supply price of product j in an exporting country m and the demand price in an importing country n.

EQS_{jm} The relationship between the factory gate supply price and the retailers' supply price of product j in country m.

EFD_{ijm} The relationship between the price of factor i and the value of its marginal product in production of product j in country m.

EPF_{im} The relationship between the endowment of factor i and its demand in country m.

$EPSF_{jm}$ The relationship between the production of product j and its supply in country m.

$EPSR_{jm}$ The relationship between supply of product j and the sum of all the outflows of that product in country m.

EPD_{jm} The relationship between the sum of all the outflows of product j and its demand in country m.

ERQ_{jm} The relationship between the quota imposed on imports of product j and its imports in country m.

EMI_{m} Foreign exchange constraint in country m, expressed in SDRs.

e Exogenous variables and parameters

$\overline{FE}_{im}$ Endowment of factor i in country m.

$\overline{TC}_{jmn}$ Transportation cost in SDRs per unit of product j from country m to country n.

$\overline{CT}_{mn}$ Net grant in SDRs from country m to country n.

$\overline{AT}_{jmn}$ Ad-valorem tariff, imposed by country n on its imports of product j from country m, expressed in terms of a ratio of the import price.

$\overline{EX}_{jmn}$ If $\overline{EX}_{jmn} > 0$, export tax, imposed by country m, on its exports of product j to country n; if $\overline{EX}_{jmn} < 0$, export subsidy, given by country m to country n, both expressed in terms of a ratio of the supply price at retailers.

$\overline{IQ}_{jm}$ Import quota on product j in country m.

a_{jm} Share parameter for product j in the utility function in country m.

b_{ijm} Share parameter for factor i in production of product j in country m.

Utility and production functions and market-clearing conditions Households as consumers in country m are assumed to have the following utility function:

$$UTL_m = \prod_j QD_{jm}^{\alpha_{jm}}, \quad \forall\, m \tag{9.1}$$

It is also assumed that households in each country maximize their utility, given their income constraint.

The production function of product j in country m is as follows:

$$\prod_i FD_{ijm}^{b_{ijm}} \geq QS_{jm}, \quad \forall\, j, m \tag{9.2}$$

It is assumed that firms in production of each product in each country maximize their profit, given the production function stated above.

Each country is endowed with factors $\overline{FE}_{im}$'s. The market-clearing condition of factor i in country m is as follows:

$$\overline{FE}_{im} \geq \sum_j FD_{ijm}, \quad \forall\, i, m \tag{9.3}$$

If there is no trade, the market-clearing condition for product j in country m is as follows:

$$QS_{jm} \geq QD_{jm}, \quad \forall\, j, m \tag{9.4}$$

A closed economy model as a utility maximization problem The closed economy model for country m, which describes the pre-trade situations, can be formulated as the following utility maximization problem:

maximize UTL_m

subject to (9.2), (9.3), (9.4) and

$$QD_{jm} \geq 0,\ QS_{jm} \geq 0, \quad \forall\, j$$

$$FD_{ijm} \geq 0, \quad \forall\, i, j$$

The Langrangean multipliers of constraints (9.2), (9.3) and (9.4) can be interpreted as supply price of product j, price of factor i and demand price of product j in country m respectively.

Equilibrium conditions of an open economy model The equilibrium conditions of an open economy model with two countries, two products and two factors can be written below:

a Demand price and marginal utility

$$EQD_{jm} = PD_{jm} - a_{jm}\left(\prod_{j} QD_{jm}^{a_{jm}}\right) / QD_{jm} \geq 0,$$

$$QD_{jm} \geq 0 \text{ and } EQD_{jm} \cdot QD_{jm} = 0, \qquad \forall \text{ j, m} \tag{9.5}$$

This equilibrium condition assumes the following:

$$XR_m = MI_m$$

This means that the authority of country m determines the exchange rate by equating it to the marginal utility of income. Under this assumption, the demand price of product j, expressed in country m's currency, is equal to its marginal utility, if the demand quantity is positive; and the former may be strictly greater than the latter, if the demand quantity is zero. See (9.18).

b Supply price and demand price

$$EQT_{jmn} = (1 + \overline{AT}_{jmn}) \cdot XR_n \cdot \{1/XR_m \cdot PSR_{jm} \cdot (1 + \overline{EX}_{jmn}) + \overline{TC}_{jmn}\}$$

$$+ RQ_{jn} - PD_{jn} \geq 0,$$

$$QT_{jmn} \geq 0 \text{ and } EQT_{jmn} \cdot QT_{jmn} = 0, \quad \forall \text{ j, m, n if m} \neq \text{n} \tag{9.6}$$

This stipulates the spatial equilibrium conditions of prices and quantities. The supply price in an exporting country is equal to the demand price in the importing country (both measured in the currency of importing country n), if trade takes place from the former country to the latter country; and the former price may be strictly greater than the latter price if no trade takes place. If an ad-valorem import tariff is imposed, the supply price should be multiplied by unity plus the tariff rate. In the case of an export tax (or an export subsidy), the supply price should be multiplied by unity plus (minus) the export tax rate (or the subsidy rate). If an import quota is imposed, the rent generated by the quota should be added to the supply price. If the transportation cost is positive, the sum of the supply price in an exporting country and the transportation cost is greater than or equal to the demand price in the importing country. Equality holds when trade takes place.

Within country m, the demand price is equal to the supply price at retailers,[6] as long as a positive amount of product j is demanded.

$$EQT_{jmm} = PSR_{jn} - PD_{jm} \geq 0,$$
$$QT_{jmm} \geq 0 \text{ and } EQT_{jmm} \cdot QT_{jmm} = 0, \quad \forall\, j, m \qquad (9.6')$$

c Factory gate supply price and retailers' supply price

$$EQS_{jm} = PSF_{jm} - PSR_{jm} \geq 0, \;\; QS_{jm} \geq 0 \;\; \text{and}$$
$$EQS_{jm} \cdot QS_{jm} = 0, \quad \forall\, j, m \qquad (9.7)$$

In this model, factory gate supply price PSF_{jm} and retailers' supply price PSR_{jm} are distinguished. Both supply prices are equal as long as a positive amount of product j is supplied within country m.[7]

d Factor price and the value of the marginal product

$$EFD_{ijm} = PF_{im} - b_{ijm} \cdot PSF_{jm} \cdot \left(\prod_{j} FD_{ijm}^{b_{ijm}} \right) / FD_{ijm} \geq 0,$$
$$FD_{ijm} \geq 0 \;\; \text{and} \;\; EFD_{ijm} \cdot FD_{ijm} = 0, \quad \forall\, i, j, m \qquad (9.8)$$

The price of factor i is equal to the value of its marginal product in production of product j in country m, as long as the factor is used in production of that product. The price may be strictly greater than the value of the marginal product, if factor i is not used in production of product j.

e Factor endowment and its demand

$$EPF_{im} = \overline{FE}_{im} - \sum_{j} FD_{ijm} \geq 0, \;\; PF_{im} \geq 0 \;\; \text{and}$$

$$EPF_{im} \cdot PF_{im} = 0, \quad \forall\, i, m \qquad (9.9)$$

The endowment of factor i must be greater than or equal to its demand. The price of factor i must be zero, if some amount of the factor is not used.

f Production and supply

$$EPSF_{jm} = \prod_{i} FD_{ijm}^{b_{ijm}} - QS_{jm} \geq 0,$$

$$PSF_{jm} \geq 0 \text{ and } EPSF_{jn} \cdot PSF_{jm} = 0, \quad \forall\, j, m \qquad (9.10)$$

Production of product j must be greater than or equal to its supply. If the production is strictly greater than the supply, the factory gate supply price must be zero.

g Supply and the sum of all the outflows

$$EPSR_{jm} = QS_{jm} - \sum_{n} QT_{jmn} \geq 0,$$

$$PSR_{jm} \geq 0 \text{ and } EPSR_{jm} \cdot PSR_{jm} = 0, \quad \forall\, j, m \qquad (9.11)$$

Supply of product j in country m must be greater than or equal to all the outflows from that country including those for its self consumption; and if the former is strictly greater than the latter, the retailers' supply price must be zero.

h The sum of all the inflows and demand

$$EPD_{jm} = \sum_{n} QT_{jnm} - QD_{jm} \geq 0,$$

$$PD_{jm} \geq 0 \text{ and } EPD_{jm} \cdot PD_{jm} = 0, \quad \forall\, j, m \qquad (9.12)$$

All the inflows of product j to country m including its own supply must be greater than or equal to the demand for that product in that country; and if the former is strictly greater than the latter, the demand price must be zero. If the transportation cost is set at zero, re-exports are suppressed. In other words, the following condition is added:

$$QT_{jnm} = 0 \text{ if } QT_{jmn} > 0, \quad \forall\, j, m, n$$

This condition affects none of the other variables.

i Import quota and total imports

$$ERQ_{jm} = \overline{IQ}_{jm} - \left(\sum_n QT_{jnm} - QT_{jmm}\right) \geq 0,$$

$$RQ_{jm} \geq 0 \quad \text{and} \quad ERQ_{jm} \cdot RQ_{jm} = 0, \quad \forall\, j, m \qquad (9.13)$$

Country m's total imports of product j must be less than or equal to a given import quota; and if the quota is filled, a positive rent may be generated.

j Foreign exchange constraint

$$EMI_m = \sum_j \sum_n \left\{ 1/XR_m \cdot PSR_{jm} \cdot \left(1 + \overline{EX}_{jmn}\right) + \overline{TC}_{jmn} \right\} \cdot QT_{jmn} - \sum_n \overline{CT}_{mn}$$

$$- \sum_j \sum_n \left\{ 1/XR_n \cdot PSR_{jn} \cdot \left(1 + \overline{EX}_{jmn}\right) + \overline{TC}_{jmn} \right\} \cdot QT_{jnm} \geq 0,$$

$$XR_m \geq 0 \text{ and } EMI_m \cdot XR_m = 0, \quad \forall\, m \qquad (9.14)$$

This expresses the foreign exchange constraint of country m, measured in SDRs. The counterpart variable of the foreign exchange constraint is the marginal utility of foreign exchanges, or equivalently the marginal utility of income, explained later. As stated before, it is assumed that $MI_m = XR_m$; thus MI_m is replaced by XR_m in (9.14). The export revenue (including revenues from transportation) must be greater than or equal to the sum of the net grants plus the import payment (including payments to transportation), adjusted by export taxes/subsidies. Therefore, if the export revenue is strictly greater than the sum of the net grants plus the import payment, i.e. there is redundancy in foreign exchanges in country m, XR_m becomes zero; in other words, that country's currency appreciates infinitely.

9.2.3 Some Remarks

Income constraint and exchange rate The model does not explicitly include each country's income constraint. The income constraint of country m, expressed in country m's currency, can be written as follows:

$$\sum_i PF_{im} \cdot \overline{\overline{FE}}_{im}$$

$$+ \sum_j \sum_n \left\{ PSR_{jm} \cdot \overline{EX}_{jmn} + XR_m \cdot \overline{TC}_{jmn} \right\} \cdot QT_{jmn} - XR_m \cdot \sum_n \overline{CT}_{mn}$$

$$- \sum_j \sum_n XR_m \cdot \left\{ 1/XR_m \cdot PSR_{jn} \cdot \left(1 + \overline{EX}_{jmn} \right) + \overline{TX}_{jmn} \right\} \cdot QT_{jnm} \geq 0, \ \forall\, m \tag{9.15}$$

Because the production functions in (9.2) are linear homogeneous, it holds that:

$$\sum_j \sum_n PSR_{jm} \cdot QT_{jmn} = \sum_i PF_{im} \cdot \overline{\overline{FE}}_{im}, \quad \forall\, m \tag{9.16}$$

Thus, the income constraint above (9.15) is always satisfied if the foreign exchange constraint (9.14) is satisfied.

Next, recall the Negishi model of a perfectly competitive market, which maximizes the following social welfare:

$$SWF = \sum_m \omega_m \left(\prod_j QD_{jm}^{a_{jm}} \right) \tag{9.17}$$

where ω_m is the social importance of the m-th individual subject to a given set of production technology, institutional assumptions and each individual's income constraint. In equilibrium, the marginal utility of product j is equal to its price multiplied by the marginal utility of income of the m–th individual MI_m, which is the inverse of the social importance of the m–th individual ω_m. This relation can be expressed as follows:

$$MI_m \cdot PD'_{jm} - a_{jm} \left(\prod_j QD_{jm}^{a_{jm}} \right) / QD_{jm} = 0, \quad \forall\, j, m \tag{9.18}$$

as long as QD_{jm} is positive. (PD_{jm}' stands for a price, expressed in terms of SDR's.) With the assumption that $XR_m = MI_m$, equilibrium condition (9.18) turns out to be (9.5).

Numeraire of the model Like other standard CGE models, the present model can solve only relative prices. In the following sample problems, XR_m of the USA, i.e. the exchange rate of the US dollar with respect to SDRs (expressed in terms of US dollars per unit of SDR) is set at unity as the numeraire of the model. Under this treatment, unit transportation costs and grants, given in terms of SDRs, are in fact fixed in US dollar terms.

An NLCP model The equilibrium conditions described in (9.5) through (9.14) correspond to the general form of the NLCP problem, namely,

Find the vectors w and z that satisfy;

$$w = F(z),\ w^{T}z = 0;\ \text{and}\ \ w \geq 0, z \geq 0 \tag{9.19}$$

There are three reasons why we use NLCP to develop this model. First, the foreign exchange constraints make it impossible to use NLP. Consider the Negishi model, where ω_m is not a constant parameter, which must be solved endogenously. By the same token, in our model is endogenous. Thus, the model cannot be developed as a NLP problem. Second, ad-valorem import tariffs and export taxes/subsidies cannot be fitted into NLP.[8] If our model were a NLP problem with price variables as primal variables, QT_{jmn}, which is the counterpart variable of PSR_{jm}, must be multiplied by $(1 + \overline{AT}_{jmn})$ in (9.11). However, if that were the case, the quantity balance of (9 11) would not hold. The same is the case for $(1 + \overline{EX}_{jmn})$. Third, the spatial equilibrium conditions cannot be accommodated within a system of simultaneous equations. In other words, if QT_{jmn} is strictly positive, trade in the opposite direction QT_{jnm} must be zero; thus, $EQT_{jnm} = 0$ may not hold. This makes it impossible to use a system of simultaneous equations. All the three problems can be solved by use of NLCP.

Currently, two solvers for NLCP are available. One is called MILES developed by T. Rutherford (1995), and the other is PATH by M. Ferris. Both are written in GAMS.[9]

9.3 Sample Problems

9.3.1 Summary of Seven Cases

To analyse the impact of import tariffs, export taxes, export subsidies, import quotas, transportation costs and grants on the whole economy of each country and trade flows, seven cases are considered. Specific assumptions of each case are summarized in the table below. The parameters of the model commonly used in all the cases are as follows:

Share parameters of the Cobb-Douglas utility function a_{jm}

	Japan	USA
Steel	0.5	0.6
Wheat	0.5	0.4

Coefficients in the Cobb-Douglas production function b_{ijm}

	Capital		Labour	
	Japan	USA	Japan	USA
Steel	0.2	0.4	0.8	0.6
Wheat	0.8	0.6	0.2	0.4

Note that technology of production of both products differs in the two countries.

Factor endowments $\overline{FE}_{im}$

	Japan	USA
Capital	20	50
Labour	50	70

9.3.2 *Simulation Results*

Case 1 (base case) This base case, which assumes free trade, is made for comparison with the other cases.

In the pre-trade situation, the relative price of steel to wheat is lower in Japan (0.58) than in the USA (0.95). The opening of trade is expected to lead to Japan's exports of steel and the USA's exports of wheat. This actually occurs in the base case model. When trade is allowed, both countries decrease their demands for potential export goods (i.e. steel in Japan and wheat in the USA) and increase their demands for potential import goods (i.e. wheat in Japan and steel in the USA). Both countries increase their supply of potential export goods and decrease supply of potential import goods. As a result, Japan exports steel to the USA, while the USA exports wheat to Japan. The relative price of steel to wheat becomes 0.92.

As for income distribution within the countries, the relative price of capital to labour in Japan in the pre-trade situation is 2.50 and the same relative price in the USA is 1.29. When trade takes place, the former becomes 1.15 and the latter 1.53. With trade, labour is better off in Japan and capital is better off in the USA.[10]

Table 9.1 Changes from Case 1 (solutions in percent)

Case	*1* *Free trade*	2 Japan's 3% ad-valorem *import tariff* on wheat	3 Japan's 3% ad-valorem *export tax* on steel	4 Japan's *3% export subsidy* on steel	5 Japan's *import quota* of 5 units on wheat	6 Positive *transportation cost* in all trade	7 *Grant* of 2 SDRs from Japan to the USA
Terms of trade(1)	0	+0.208	+0.208	-0.215	+2.013	-2.224	+0.096
Japan							
Relative price(2)	0	-2.711	-2.711	+2.872	-23.640	-5.070	+0.096
Welfare	0	+0.034	+0.034	-0.098	-2.191	-0.704	-9.393
Exchange rate(3)	0	+1.468	-1.487	+1.556	+15.353	-0.192	-0.009
Steel: Quantity							
Supply	0	-1.517	-1.517	+1.554	-15.353	-2.879	+0.053
Demand	0	+1.418	+1.418	-1.502	+11.930	+1.913	-9.436
Exports	0	-6.287	-6.287	+6.522	-59.703	-10.667	+15.478
Wheat: Quantity							
Supply	0	+6.279	+6.279	-6.615	+56.385	+11.773	-0.221
Demand	0	-1.331	-1.331	+1.326	-14.530	-3.254	-9.350
USA							
Relative price(2)	0	+0.208	+0.208	-0.215	+2.013	+0.400	+0.096
Welfare	0	-0.042	-0.042	+0.047	-0.295	+0.412	+6.413
Steel: Quantity							
Supply	0	+3.193	+3.193	-3.309	+30.484	+6.133	+1.469
Demand	0	-0.125	-0.125	+0.133	-1.086	+2.522	+6.373
Wheat: Quantity							
Supply	0	-2.043	-2.043	+2.113	-19.683	-3.929	-0.940
Demand	0	+0.082	+0.082	-0.082	+0.905	+0.653	+6.474
Exports	0	-6.092	-6.092	+6.293	-58.892	-12.655	15.060

Notes: (1) The terms of trade of steel to wheat.
(2) Relative price of steel to wheat.
(3) US dollars per yen. Positive numbers mean appreciation of the Japanese yen vis-à-vis US dollars.

Case 2 (import tariff) In Case 2, Japan imposes a 3 percent ad-valorem tariff on its import good, wheat. The relative price of steel to wheat for both Japan's consumers and producers becomes 2.9 percent lower than the USA's relative price.[11] In comparison with Case 1 solutions, Japan and the USA both increase their demands for export goods, while they decrease their demands for import goods. The opposite is the case for supply. As a result, trade of both products decreases by similar rates (by 6.3 percent for steel and by 6.1 percent for wheat). The terms of trade for Japan[12] improve by 0.2 percent. Japan's welfare increases by 0.034 percent, while the USA's decreases by 0.042 percent. The Japanese yen appreciates by 1.5 percent.

By changing the tariff rate parametrically, we can derive the optimum tariff rate, which maximizes Japan's welfare with an assumption that the USA does not retaliate to Japan's move. Such a rate is 3.2 percent.

Beyond this optimum rate, Japan's welfare decreases as the import tariff rate increases. At the tariff rate of 6.5 percent, Japan's welfare becomes equal to the one in Case 1, where no import tariff is imposed. The USA's welfare is lower by 0.086 percent. The relative price of steel to wheat in Japan becomes 6.1 percent lower than in the USA. Trade of both products is lower by 13.3 percent for steel and 12.9 percent for wheat than in Case 1. The terms of trade for Japan improve by 0.44 percent. The Japanese yen appreciates by 3.1 percent.

If both countries simultaneously impose 3 percent ad-valorem tariffs on their imports, the relative price of steel to wheat in Japan becomes 5.7 percent lower than the USA's. The terms of trade for Japan deteriorate by 2.5 percent, compared with Case 1. Both countries decrease supply of export goods and increase supply of import goods. The impact on demand is more complicated. Because the income effect resulting from the improved terms of trade for the USA exceeds the substitution effect, its demand for steel increases, although the relative price of steel to wheat increases in the USA. However, the increase in the USA's demand for steel is relatively small, trade of both products decrease. Compared with Case 1, Japan's welfare deteriorates by 0.79 percent and the USA's improves by 0.46 percent. The Japanese yen depreciates by 0.042 percent.

Case 3 (export tax) In this case, Japan imposes a 3 percent ad-valorem export tax on its export good, steel. Both countries' relative prices, quantities of supply, demand and trade flows, and welfare are exactly the same as those in Case 2, where Japan imposes a 3 percent ad-valorem import tariff on its import good, wheat. This confirms the validity of Lerner's symmetry theorem.

If both countries simultaneously imposes 3 percent ad-valorem export taxes on their export goods, the results are exactly the same as those in a variation of Case 2, where 3 percent import tariffs are simultaneously imposed by Japan and the USA.

Case 4 (export subsidy) In Case 4, Japan subsidizes its steel exports with a rate of 3 percent of the domestic supply price. The relative price of steel to wheat in Japan is higher by 3.1 percent than the USA's relative price. Both countries decrease their demands for their export goods, while they increase their demands for import goods. The opposite is the case for supply. Both steel and wheat trade increases. The terms of trade for Japan deteriorate by 0.22 percent. Japan's welfare decreases while the USA's increases. The Japanese yen appreciates by 1.6 percent.

Case 5 (import quota) In this case, a quota on Japan's wheat imports is set at 5 units, compared with its imports of 12.2 units in Case 1 solutions. Japan's wheat quota is filled, and the rent of 1.78 SDR per unit generated by the quota is added to the demand price of wheat in Japan. As a result, the relative price of steel to wheat in Japan becomes 25.1 percent lower than the USA's relative price. Steel trade decreases by 59.7 percent and wheat trade by 58.9 percent. The terms of trade for Japan improve by 2.0 percent. Both Japan's and the USA's welfare decrease. The Japanese yen appreciates by 15.4 percent.

The model can solve the ad-valorem import tariff rate which is equivalent to this import quota. Such a tariff rate on Japan's wheat imports would be 33.6 percent.

Case 6 (transportation cost) In our model, transportation costs are claimed by exporters and borne by importers. This is equivalent to exporters' marking-up of their price tags with as much as transportation costs, paid by importers. Therefore, transportation costs can be considered as ad-quantum export taxes that are simultaneously imposed by Japan and the USA.

So far we have dealt with cases where transportation costs are assumed to be zero. In this case, it is assumed that Japan and the USA claim 0.014375 SDR per unit[13] on their exports. As a result, both countries' exports decrease. Japan's welfare decreases while the USA's increases.

If only Japan claimed the transportation cost on its exports of steel to the USA, the results would be exactly the same as those of Case 3, where Japan imposes a 3 percent ad-valorem tax on its steel exports.

Case 7 (grant) In this case, with a grant of 2 SDRs from Japan,[14] the USA is allowed to have a trade deficit of the same amount, which is exactly matched by Japan's trade surplus. In comparison with Case 1 solutions, the USA's demand for both steel and wheat increases in sacrifice of Japan's demand for both products.

In the present model, where the ratio of the marginal propensity to expend for the export good to the marginal propensity to expend for the import good in the USA (1.5) is higher than the ratio in Japan (1.0), the terms of trade for Japan improve by 0.10 percent. That means, the transfer paradox does occur. Both of Japan's export quantity and value increase, while both of the USA's decrease. Welfare in Japan decreases by 9.4 percent, while the USA's increases by 6.4 percent. The impact on the exchange rate is minimal. The Japanese yen depreciates by 0.093 percent.

If both countries impose 3 percent ad-valorem tariffs while keeping a grant of 2 SDRs from Japan to the USA, the terms of trade for Japan deteriorate by 2.4 percent, compared with Case 1. The imposition of tariffs causes the transfer paradox to disappear. Japan's welfare decreases by 10.3 percent, while the USA's increases by 7.0 percent.

Furthermore, if the share parameters of the utility function in the USA are revised so as to make the ratio of the marginal propensities in the USA (0.43) lower than the ratio in Japan (1.0), the terms of trade for Japan would deteriorate by 0.19 percent, compared with those in a variation of Case 1, where the USA's ratio of the marginal propensities are set at 0.43 and no grant is assumed. In this case, the transfer paradox does not occur. Japan's welfare would decrease by 9.3 percent, while the USA's would increase by 6.2 percent.

9.4 Concluding Remarks

In this chapter, we presented a simple CGE model of trade between two countries, developed as a NLCP problem. Then, we demonstrated how it worked to analyse the impact of various trade policies and transportation costs. The simulation results of the seven cases seem reasonable. In addition to trade policies, the model can be used to simulate changes in factor endowments, preferences, technology and others. Although the present model is developed primarily for pedagogical purposes, it can be used to solve real world trade problems by increasing the numbers of countries and products.

Acknowledgement

The author wishes to acknowledge the financial support of the International Cooperation (Osaka Gas) Fund, Faculty of Economics, Osaka University. An early version of this paper was presented at the session on 'Accessibility, Trade and Location Behavior' in the 5th World Congress of the RSAI held in Tokyo on May 2–6, 1996. The author thanks for valuable comments given at the Conference, by Kenzo Abe and Nobuhiro Hosoe of Osaka University, and by an anonymous referee. However, the remaining errors are entirely the author's.

References

Armington, P. (1969), 'A Theory of Demand for Products Distinguished by Place of Production', *IMF Staff Papers*, vol.16, pp. 159–78.

Ethier, W.J. (1984), 'Higher Dimensional Issues in Trade Theory' in Jones, R.W. and P.B. Kenen (eds), *Handbook of International Economics*, vol. 1, pp. 131–84.

Hosoe, N. (1995), 'Kanzen Kyoso Ippan Kinko no Suchi-kai no Doshutsu – NLP Mondai Kara NLCP Mondai e-no Tenkan' – (Computation of the General

Equilibrium Solution of a Perfectly Competitive Market – from an NLP Approach to an NLCP Approach), Mimeo, Osaka University: Osaka.

Negishi, T. (1960), 'Welfare Economics and Existence of an Equilibrium for a Competitive Economy', *Metroeconomica*, vol.12, pp. 92–7.

Rutherford, T.F. (1995), 'Existence of GAMS for Complementarity Problems Arising in Applied Economic Analysis', *Journal of Economic Dynamics and Control*, vol.19, pp. 1299–324.

Samuelson, P.A. (1954), 'The Transfer Problem and Transport Costs, II: Analysis of Effects of Trade Impediments', *Economic Journal*, vol. LXIV, pp. 264–89.

Shoven, J.B., and Whalley, J. (1984) 'Applied General-Equilibrium Models of Taxation and International Trade: An Introduction and Survey', *Journal of Economic Literature*, vol. XXII, pp. 1007–51.

Takayama, T. and Judge, G.G. (1971), *Spatial and Temporal Price and Allocation Models*, North-Holland, Amsterdam.

Notes

1. A NLCP formulation of a general equilibrium model with more than two consumers in one country is in Hosoe (1995).

2. There are many trade CGE models that are based on actual data. They are formulated as a NLP problem or a system of simultaneous equations, not as a NLCP problem. See, for example, Shoven and Whalley (1984).

3. Equality of the numbers of products and factors is assumed to avoid complete specialization. See Ethier (1984).

4. When transportation costs are set at zero as in the cases other than Case 6, reexports are forced to be non-existent.

5. In real world, 'cross hauling' may be a common phenomenon, which can be conveniently dealt with by the Armington assumption. However, if goods are subdivided sufficiently, 'cross-hauling' may not occur. Or at least, the occurrence of 'cross-hauling' cannot be assumed on an a priori basis.

6. If necessary, a marketing margin can be added to the supply price.

7. Neither transportation costs within a country nor marketing margins are assumed.

8. See Takayama and Judge (1971 Chapter 13).

9. GAMS (General Algebraic Modelling System) is a computer language, developed by GAMS Development Corporation.

10. Because the production technology of each product is assumed to differ between the two countries, as shown by different coefficients of the assumed production functions, the factor prices are not equalized even though trade takes place. If the production technology were assumed to be identical in both countries, the factor prices would be equalized.

11. The relative price of wheat to steel in Japan is exactly 3 percent higher than in the USA.

12. The terms of trade for Japan, defined as the ratio of prices of steel to wheat realized on the ocean between Japan and the USA, are between Japan's and the USA's relative prices. In this case, the terms of trade for Japan are 3 percent higher than Japan's relative price, while they are equal to the USA's relative price. See the intermediate terms of trade in Samuelson (1954, p. 270).

13. This transportation cost corresponds to the price differential between Japan and the USA under the 3 percent ad-valorem export tax, assumed in Case 3.

14. This amount is equivalent to 30.6 percent of Japan's export value in Case 1.

10 Proximity in Networks: The Role of Transport Infrastructure

ANTJE BURMEISTER AND KRISTIAN COLLETIS-WAHL

10.1 Introduction

This chapter attempts to contribute to the recurring debate on the determinants of regional development and the particular role of transport systems. In a context of decreasing transport costs, quasi-ubiquity of quality infrastructure and the increasing importance of non material flows, transport infrastructure appears to be less important as a location factor for industry. However, the globalization of markets and the restructuring of production systems (just-in-time, lean production etc.) lead to an increased role of transportation in industrial strategies. The traditional framework dealing with transportation mainly as a cost thus becomes less relevant for understanding the spatial dynamics of industry.

The framework developed in this chapter divides production into transformation and circulation activities. Interactions between the transformation process and its environment of resources, suppliers, customers, and other producers form a system of circulation of goods, information and knowledge and go far beyond market transactions. Transportation here becomes a particular set of techniques of interacting in the space-time grid.

The spatial dimension is introduced, not through the idea of mere spatial propinquity or accessibility as a determinant of production networks, but through the concept of organizational proximity and its spatial and circulatory dimensions. The circulatory dimension of proximity describes rapid, reliable and well adapted circulation of goods and information as well as the efficient mobilization of external resources, especially of non-traded, specific resources. This dimension of proximity thus includes more than geographical accessibility. Its determinants are as much the infrastructure as a generic resource for circulation as the organization and the degree of control of flows of goods, information and people.

The first section will look into the difficulties of some of the main approaches of the role of transportation investment in regional development to establish a clearcut and robust correlation. We will then introduce a new framework drawing on the network approach of production systems. By introducing space into this network framework, we demonstrate that these interactions rely on combinations of several forms of proximity, derived from the central concept of 'organizational proximity'. The circulatory dimension of proximity will be analysed in a more detailed manner in order to conceptualize the role of the transport system as a factor of proximity.

10.2 Transport Systems, Production Systems and Space: Beyond Accessibility to Generic Resources

The standard analytical framework of transportation economics deals with transportation investments and their impacts on the economic system, in terms of growth, productivity and regional development. This framework leads to a structural determinism of regional development through transport infrastructure investments. However, the results of empirical research do not allow to establish a clear-cut correlation of transport infrastructure investment and regional growth. We will go back to the implicit theoretical framework of production as a combination of generic resources. Space is, in this framework, viewed as neutral, and transportation has the role of allowing access to generic production factors.

10.2.1 Does Transport Infrastructure 'Create' Regional Development? – Limitations of the Causal model

The major part of socioeconomic research on transportation infrastructure represents the relationship between these investments and the economic system in terms of 'impacts' of investments on regional development (see, for instance, Blum 1982; Botham 1983; Martin et al. 1995; Rietveld and Nijkamp 1993). In classical location theory, transportation is considered as the main factor in the organization of space. Models concerning the role of transportation in interregional trade, gravitation models, accessibility analyses and, more recently, models of endogenous growth taking into account the stock of public capital tend to develop a causal relationship between improvements of the transport system and regional growth. However, it is well known that the results of empirical work remain heterogeneous, if not contradictory. As far as the production function approach is concerned, the review articles of Munnell (1992) and Gramlich (1994) highlight some of the theoretical and empirical difficulties of the approach.

In another family of research work using the concept of accessibility as a determinant of regional growth, Vickerman et al. (1995) demonstrate the limitations of this concept. The *level* of regional development (GDP) in European regions appears to be clearly correlated the different levels of accessibility. However, the direction of the causal relationship remains ambiguous here, since infrastructure endowment can be interpreted as well as a cause as a consequence of regional development. Moreover, the dynamics of regional development and their relationship to infrastructure investment remain difficult to explain. As a matter of fact, the authors demonstrate that *variations* in regional GDP over time cannot be clearly correlated to variations of accessibility. Their conclusions throw serious doubts on the theoretical foundations of policies using transport investments as a tool for regional development. What is more, the automatic nature of infrastructure effects in some of these theories leads to a dangerous vision of infrastructure investment as a universal tool of regional development strategies, as well as of European policies towards economic cohesion.

Thus, it appears to be problematic to establish a clear causal relationship between transportation and the performance of production systems within the traditional conceptual framework of transportation analysis. Three main difficulties can be highlighted in this respect:

- Analysing the effects of infrastructure investments on the equilibrium of the economic system leads to a representation of a transport system exogenous to the system that is being analysed. In fact, the causality from transportation to development can not be considered as established once for all (Biehl 1991; Plassard 1977; Offner 1993).
  An alternative approach would be to consider that there is no deterministic relationship going from the configuration and the possibilities offered by a transport system to the performance of production systems. The goal of understanding the interactions should be to render transportation development an endogenous variable in the development process.

- Isolating transportation as a factor of regional development leads to overrating the flows of goods in an economic system that appears to be more and more influenced by flows of information and knowledge. In transportation research, some results of research are available on the simultaneous development of telecommunications, new information technologies and their use in order to overcome distance (see, for instance, Salomon and Tsairi 1995). Nevertheless, most research in the field of transportation seems to ignore the fundamental role of knowledge and innovation in development and fails to offer a comprehensive framework of the role of transfer of goods, information and knowledge in space.

- The implicit conceptual representation behind most models refers to the standard neoclassical framework of production. In this framework, the improvement of technologies meant to overcome space in interacting (i.e. transportation and telecommunication techniques) will lead to the abolition of spatial friction. This is based on two essential assumptions:

  - production is a combination of generic production factors, exclusively procured through market transactions;

- space is a reservoir of generic resources that can be transferred (or are accessible) at a certain cost.

Recent theoretical developments on the theory of production and in regional science can be useful to develop alternative assumptions. The evolutionist theories of production and innovation, for instance, adopt an approach in terms of resource creation (as opposed to resource allocation). Production is here based on specific resources created through organizational learning. The paradigm of neutral space, on the other hand, has been contested by a long tradition of heterodox research from industrial districts and growth poles to local systems of innovation (milieu) and production and, more recently, the concept of proximity related to organizational learning and innovation (Bellet et al. 1993).

Examining the limitations of the traditional models of the role of transport investments leads to the following conclusion: The relationship between transport infrastructure (accessibility, public capital endowment) and regional development is weak, because other factors are more influent in the determination of regional differentiation and regional development trajectories. The question thus becomes: What are the main determinants of the spatial dynamics of development, and what can be the (limited) role of transport infrastructure?

10.2.2 Beyond Generic Resources for Production and Neutral Space: Elements of an Alternative Framework

An alternative approach can draw on the heterodox approaches in regional science of socially constructed space, as well as on the Swedish network approach of innovation. The creation of products uses specific resources, such as knowledge, which can be tacit and non standardized and embedded in actors, organizations and collective learning processes. We will thus consider that the location and circulation of actors and resources continue to matter in the spatial dynamics of production systems.

Storper (1995) develops the idea of the 'region as a nexus of untraded interdependencies'. These interdependencies are not transferable on a market and generate region-specific assets in production. According to this author, these assets are the central form of scarcity in contemporary capitalism, and not the availability of generic resources, as it is assumed in most location analyses.

Colletis and Pecqueur (1993) develop a similar approach by making the assumption that the main factor of differentiation of space does not lie in relative prices of production factors nor in transport costs, but in the supply of specific assets and resources, which do not compete directly on the market. They make a distinction between *assets* and *resources*: resources are potential production factors, whereas assets are production factors that are in use in a production process. A second distinction is made between *generic* and *specific* resources and assets.

Generic production factors exist independently from their participation in a production process and can thus be transferred from one production to another. Specific assets are related to a specific production process and cannot be transferred to another without sunk costs. Specific resources are virtual and can thus not be transferred. These specific resources are critical factors in the process of technology creation.

Traditional location analysis refers only to generic resources and assets, which can be transferred in space. In the alternative framework, regional development trajectories are mostly related to specific resources, which cannot be transferred and which are constructed by the actors of a territory in a path-dependent, cumulative process.

These alternative analyses of regional development can be translated into the following assumptions:

- Regional development is mainly related to the path-dependent process of creation of specific resources.
- Transport infrastructure is, in most cases, a generic resource which can be used in different production processes.

The conjunction of these two assumptions would imply that regional development is less and less directly related to the endowment in terms of generic infrastructure. We will now turn to a more detailed development of this framework.

10.3 The Interactions Between Production and Transportation: A Network Framework

10.3.1 A Different Approach to Production: Coordination of Transformation and Circulation in Economic Networks

The concept of economic networks will here be referred to in order to acknowledge the complexity of interactions in production systems that go far beyond market transactions. The network concept will also allow us to take into account the decreasing importance of geographical territories as determinants of accessibility, which is not equivalent to the disappearance of space, location and embeddedness of resources, actors and activities (Johansson et al. 1994).

For a better understanding of the role of transportation in the creation of value, we will go back to the Swedish network approach (Håkansson ed. 1987) and divide production into two distinct categories of activities contributing to the creation of value: *transformation* activities and *circulation* activities. This definition is quite similar to the distinction made by Håkansson (1987) between transformation and transaction, or by Lakshmanan and Okomura (1995) between transformation (altering the physical characteristics of the product) and transfer (altering the location of products in space and/or time). However, we suggest replacing the idea of transfer/transaction by circulation. In fact, we do not agree with the vision of immaterial resources and products travelling in space in a disembodied way. We assume that knowledge has tacit, non standardized aspects and can thus not be transferred if it is not embodied in persons or organizations.

Transformation is at the core of the production process. This set of activities can be defined as the combination of resources in order to create a product. The coordination of transformation activities differs according to the nature of resources (generic versus specific), the scale and the scope of production, and the characteristics of demand (differentiation, variety, customization). In a functional approach, transformation concerns the concept of products and processes, the process of production itself (components, assembly, physical alteration etc.), the concept of strategies as well as managing and accounting activities.

Circulation activities will be defined as the set of activities that are meant to establish the links between transformation and its environment of resources, suppliers, customers and other producers. Circulation activities can be vertical (procurement, sales and transportation) as well as horizontal (cooperation). Circulation thus materializes in the form of flows, incoming or outgoing: flows of goods, information and knowledge.

In this framework, transportation becomes one possible vector for flows: transportation of goods. Passenger transportation is a vector of circulation of information and knowledge. Another possible vector for circulation is telecommunication using the various technologies of information and communication.

10.3.2 Transportation as a Particular Set of Techniques of Interacting in the Production of Value

We now further develop a representation of production systems through the linkages between firms and groups of firms. Such conceptual representations are well known in the area of material inter-industry linkages, such as in the Leontief input-output matrix.

However, the conceptual representation that has to be developed brings up a departure from the standard model of the production function linking generic resources to outputs in the form of material goods. The traditional representation of production systems does not take into account the rising importance of immaterial linkages (other than the purchase and sale of material goods). More recent frameworks, such as the new institutional economics, the evolutionist approach of innovation and the economics of networks acknowledge the non material and non market forms of interactions in production. The network approach emphasizes the non material linkages between manufacturing establishments that go together with the development of new information technology. We suggest adding to this representation non market linkages in the form of knowledge flows (e.g. learning through interacting).

Interactions between actors in the production systems (individuals and organizations) encompass a variety of forms. The transaction cost approach (Williamson 1975) distinguishes short term market transactions, repeated transactions, and long term interactions. The scope of interactions thus goes from sales and procurement on a spot basis to vertical integration, cooperation and stable subcontracting and distribution systems. In the Swedish network school, on the other hand, only durable links (such as subcontracting, cooperation and alliances) are taken into consideration.

All these interactions and links form a system of circulation of goods, information and knowledge. They materialize in the form of flows of goods, people and information. Flows of goods are related to procurement of intermediate products, sales and inventories. Flows of information are related to procurement and sales management, among others in the form of electronic data interchange (EDI). Knowledge circulates in the production system mainly through the circulation of people, for motives such as interplant coordination, management, marketing, research, quality control, selection of subcontractors etc. The media that support these flows in space are transportation of goods and people, and communication technologies.

Transportation can thus be described as a set of generic techniques of transaction in the space-time grid (Storper and Scott 1995). We suggest replacing transaction by interaction, in order to account for non market linkages. Transportation techniques allow the transfer goods and people in space, whereas communication technologies transfer information.

Such a representation of production suggests the emergence of a circulation paradigm, instead of a post-industrial (service production) paradigm. This representation considers that circulation becomes more and more important in a global network economy, characterized by a contraction of space and time. The improvement of transport and communication technologies can induce better performance of circulation in the production system. In the context of globalization, circulation activities have a growing share in the production of value, whereas the relative cost of circulation in space is falling. We will now turn to the question of how to introduce space into this framework.

10.4 Interactions and Space: the Different Forms of Proximity

10.4.1 From Spatial Propinquity to a Socioeconomic Concept of Proximity: Different Dimensions of Proximity in Networks

We will here introduce the spatial dimension into the network representation of coordination between actors, activities and resources through the concept of 'proximity'. Recent research emphasizes the necessary distinction between mere spatial propinquity and other dimensions of proximity in the explanation of the emergence and development of local systems of production and innovation (see the contributions in Bellet et al. 1993).

Spatial proximity can be derived from Perroux' definition of geonomic space (Perroux 1950). Propinquity in space only creates a potential of interacting, making interactions possible, without necessarily creating them, as would suggest a superficial interpretation of the 'milieu' literature. The role of spatial proximity in local production systems is related to the greater probability of encounter between actors of the system. Spatial proximity can be partly substituted by improved transport accessibility.

Recent literature introduces a different concept of proximity, which can be related to Perroux' concept of 'economic space' and is based on organizational analysis.

Organizational proximity is here of an immaterial and non market nature. It draws on the existence of common knowledge and shared representations. This form of proximity generates a capacity of putting together fragmented information, tacit knowledge and other immaterial and non standardized resources through interactions in inter–industry relations, cooperation and collective learning processes. Organizational proximity between actors improves the quality of reception of signals coming from the outside of an organization. This form of proximity is thus a prerequisite for collective learning processes, cooperation between different organizations for the creation of new resources and innovation.

The construction of organizational proximity is a path-dependent process to which various dimensions of proximity contribute. The *relational* dimension of organizational proximity refers to the existence, the frequency and the quality of interactions between the actors. Proximity also encompasses an *interpersonal* dimension, deriving from interactions between individuals that are simultaneous and parallel to the process of resource creation, without necessarily being directly related to it.

Another field of literature analyses the conditions of innovation and learning in their *institutional* context. The existence of rules and standards accepted by a community of actors is an important factor in theorizing national systems of innovation. The collective institutional framework can mean language, culture, as well as a legislative framework. This institutional dimension has been emphasized as a factor of efficiency of territorialized systems of innovation and public policies in this field (National Systems of Innovation).

Reading the spatial dynamics of industry through the conceptual framework of proximity leads to putting organizational proximity at the centre of the process of resource creation in a learning economy. Organizational proximity is simultaneously necessary for, and a result of the interactions between actors (individuals and organizations) participating in a particular process of resource creation.

From a purely conceptual point of view, organizational proximity can be considered as non spatial. It connects agents participating in a particular activity, inside a specific structure (Kirat and Lung 1995). Nevertheless, since space exists as a physical constraint, or, to use a metaphor suggested by Storper and Scott (1995), unless 'magic carpets' exist, organizational proximity requires spatial mediation that can take different forms: spatial proximity, whether it is permanent or temporary, and/or circulation. Nevertheless, the possibility to transfer goods, information and knowledge in space is far from unlimited.

This analysis leads to a different concept of proximity and of its role in economic networks. Economic networks are not necessarily territorialized (they are even less and less so). However, such networks are always defined by some forms of proximity between actors. The different dimensions of proximity defined above can thus be understood as a support of network linkages. Through this socioeconomic definition, proximity ceases to be a factor of (Euclidean) distance. Subsequently, the performance of circulation (i.e. overcoming of distance) will be measured by other indicators than transportation costs.

10.4.2 The Circulatory Dimension in the Coordination of Production

After introducing different concepts of proximity, we will now take a look at how the different levels of proximity relate to space and circulation, and to the transformations of the socioeconomic space-time grid that are labelled through the term of globalization.

It seems quite clear that organizational proximity, without being synonymous to spatial propinquity, can be supported and reinforced by the absence of spatial distance between the actors. It also necessitates an institutional dimension to become efficient.

Spatial propinquity appears to be more and more replaced by the organization of circulation between economic actors. Thus, better performance of circulation media and technologies can extend the geographic scale of feasible interactions. We will here add a new circulatory dimension to our conceptual framework of proximity. 'Circulatory proximity' is a particular aspect of organizational proximity and can be defined as the degree to which it is possible to overcome distance in the circulation activities. It describes the access to the various types of resources combined in transformation as well as the access to demand. This aspect of proximity is, of course, not isomorphic to spatial distance. Research on the effects of transport system's improvements shows that space-time accessibility can be transformed through the introduction of high speed trains and highways.

However, accessibility in terms of travel times is only one aspect of this circulatory dimension. Network characteristics such as interconnection and frequency further transform space and circulation. Moreover, less studied factors such as reliability, punctuality, and the management of circulation have to be included.

The circulatory dimension of proximity thus appears to be a hybrid category. It possesses a *spatial* dimension in the sense that it concerns the overcoming of distance in the space-time grid. Above all, it has an *organizational* dimension, being involved in the coordination between actors and activities and the quality of this coordination (time, reliability, punctuality etc.). Moreover, circulation activities being supported by collective equipment (infrastructure), also have an *institutional* dimension.

Organizational proximity necessarily relies on circulation to a certain degree. Unlike the confusion of spatial and organizational proximity in 'innovative milieu' analyses, recent research emphasizes the existence of networks of innovators that allow collective learning through various spatial scales. The real time circulation of information in various forms made possible by new technologies of information and communication can even create totally global networks, where actors interact efficiently without being spatially close. The circulation of people can complement the interactions through information channels by allowing necessary face-to-face contacts. For instance, fast long distance transportation by air or high speed trains allow more frequent meetings.

At first glance, our analysis of the circulatory dimension of organizational proximity appears to be similar to the well-known concept of accessibility. However, the definition of accessibility differs in a network economy. Accessibility loses its strong correlation with geographic distance together with the changing nature of economic networks.

Furthermore, in our framework, transport cost and geographical accessibility appear to be only some of the many factors that define this circulatory dimension. It contains, of course, a structural component through the state and performance of infrastructure. Beyond this dimension of geographical accessibility, however, circulatory proximity is determined by the organization of flows of goods, information and knowledge. Its central dimension is the capacity of the network of actors to coordinate the access to *specific* resources.

10.5 The Role of Circulatory Proximity in the Coordination of Production

10.5.1 The Differentiated Role of Circulation in Production

The same level of 'physical' accessibility can have very different meanings according to the organization of production. Our idea is here to introduce the modes of circulation and the effective use of transportation and communication means, depending on the needs of the actors according to the intrinsic nature of the production process.

Salais and Storper (1992) analyse the differentiation of development trajectories through the concept of 'worlds of production', which express abstract types of coordination in production. They distinguish four worlds of production according to two dimensions: the coordination with demand and coordination with resources.

The first dimension concerns the construction of the market and opposes generic products (defined independently from the identity of the buyer), to dedicated products, for which each individual demand is specified in a unique manner.

The second dimension concerns the construction of the production process and opposes specialized products, produced from specific production factors, to standard products, which are not dependent on specific production factors.

The combination of these two dimensions leads to the distinction between four worlds of production: industrial, merchant, immaterial, interpersonal. We will use this framework in order to differentiate the role of transport systems in various forms of coordination of production and circulation.

The *industrial* world of production is composed of standard generic products, i.e. products that are produced from generic labour and technologies for undifferentiated demand. This world is represented by mass production, based on economies of scale and price competition. Transportation is here a mere cost of distance. Its role is to assure the availability of the product in space at minimum cost. The strategic dimension of logistics is weak. Space is neutral towards production activities, since it is only a reservoir of generic transferable resources.

The *merchant* world of production is represented by standard products that respond to a differentiated demand. Coordination of production is narrowly dependent on demand, its variations and its segmentation. Competition is based on price, quality an timeliness. The role of transportation becomes strategic, since it has to assure rapid and reliable circulation of products in a just-in-time organization. As in the previous case, space introduces only a cost of distance. Transportation, however, is integrated in logistic strategies, allowing to relate supply to a differentiated demand. The goal is to adapt the flow of products to variations and segmentation of demand at a minimum cost.

The *immaterial* world concerns the production from specialized resources for a generic demand. This world emphasizes the creation of new products through a process of innovation and learning. Information flows become strategic, whereas material transport has only a secondary role. The main factor is organizational proximity among the actors of the production process, which allows to put together fragmented knowledge and to reveal it in the creation of a new product. Spatial propinquity can improve the construction of organizational proximity. The location of production can become stable, since spatial dynamics can contribute to the creation of specific resources through localized learning.

The *interpersonal* world of production is represented by products for a differentiated demand, produced from specific production factors. As in the previous case, production is based on specialized and spatially embedded knowledge. The organizational proximity between the actors of the production process is crucial in this case, allowing for frequent contacts and circulation of knowledge. Transportation (in the sense of material flows) is not strategic here. Circulation concerns mainly information and people instead of products.

This taxonomy demonstrates the multiplicity of forms of coordination in production processes. Moreover, it throws an interesting light on the role of accessibility in production systems. In fact, accessibility to generic resources and generic demand is a determinant only in the case of the 'industrial world', the importance of which, according to Salais and Storper, is declining in real worlds of production. The much cited and often analysed case of just in time production and integrated logistic systems play an important role in the merchant world.

The immaterial and interpersonal worlds are based mainly on circulation of information and knowledge, related to organizational proximity. Transportation of material goods is not a strategic aspect here. The interesting aspect here is that these two worlds of production are more and more recognized as being particularly dynamic in regard to regional development.

On the whole, recent transformations in the organization of production appear to come with very different spatial forms, where 'circulatory proximity' may explain the differentiation. It is important to understand that this circulatory dimension includes much more than geographical accessibility.

10.5.2 Criteria of Evaluation of the Circulatory Dimension of Proximity

The circulatory dimension of organizational proximity, as defined above, has to do with overcoming space in interactions between actors, activities, and resources. Evaluating the performance of circulation is much more complex than the mere comparison of transport costs between different locations and/or different modes of transportation. Even more, unlike recent analyses of just in time (JIT) and lean production systems emphasizing the role of time and speed, circulatory proximity cannot be summarized by time distance (accessibility). The most important factor of competitive circulation systems is not so much the shortest time of transfer of a good from one place to another, but the reliability of the transfer, i.e. the ability to guarantee arrival times of shipments for JIT production. Thus, unlike the emphasis given to high speed transportation means in most analyses, even low speed transport modes such as waterways can be compatible with JIT production, as long as the process of transfer in space is highly reliable.

We thus suggest that the circulatory aspects of organizational proximity contain more than low cost and short transportation times: punctuality, reliability, safety, frequency, flexibility, and, above all, the ability to control the whole process of production and circulation (including innovation). Thus, this definition is highly differentiated according to product characteristics, the nature of the production process, and demand characteristics. Transport modes that can easily adapt to specific constraints such as product characteristics, emergency, fragmentation and handling problems offer therefore superior circulation performance.

As the most important feature, the control of the production and circulation process refers back to issues of market structure and power. In fact, the reorganization of circulation processes to just-in-time systems is closely linked to market power between the firms at the different stages of production (probably much more than to the mere technical possibilities of transport infrastructure for establishing just in time circulation).

Up till now, we have only dealt with circulation of *goods*. We wish to give a broader sense to circulatory dimension as a factor of spatial strategies: it is a way of reducing the friction of space by different means:

- rapid, reliable and well adapted circulation of goods,
  and, moreover,
- rapid, reliable and controllable circulation of *information*
- efficient mobilization of *external resources*, especially of non traded, specific resources through cooperation and organizational learning.

As far as the efficiency of information flows is concerned, we stress the growing importance of simultaneous flows of goods and information that characterize JIT procurement and distribution systems. EDI systems, logistics and quality management are facilitated and improved by the constant development of new technologies of information and communication (NTIC) and by the adoption and adaptation of NTIC to the new production methods.

Nevertheless, it is important to understand that efficient circulation of information inside the organization (for example between production plants and headquarters) and between firms (e.g. real time transmission of data from suppliers and subcontractors) is as much associated with the technical capacities of communication infrastructure as with power and control of the production process.

As for the efficient mobilization of specific resources, the non–traded and tacit character of knowledge and its prevailing importance in the creation of new technologies have been emphasized in recent literature as the main argument for the performance of local production systems theorized as milieus and districts. We basically agree with the argument that technological development is rooted in communities that are highly localized. However, spatial proximity is not the primary feature of innovative networks. Moreover, spatial proximity can be permanent or temporary, depending on the trajectory of the network. In fact, efficient passenger transportation and new communication tools (such as videoconferencing) can make face-to-face contact temporarily possible, or even partly replace it. We hereby want to suggest, that, since circulation also concerns people, embedded knowledge and information, innovation and creation of specific resources is not necessarily limited to localized systems of production.

10.6 Some Concluding Ideas on Transport Infrastructure as a Generic Resource for Circulation

We will finally go back to the initial question addressed in this chapter: the role of transport infrastructure in regional development. The starting point of our analysis was a critique of the traditional framework viewing transport infrastructure as a location factor for production facilities, and transport accessibility as a direct determinant of regional development. We then introduced a new conceptual representation of production derived from the network framework. Infrastructure, in this framework, has the role of a generic resource for interacting within networks. This point of view shifts attention to the question how firms use different modes of circulation for their needs of interaction.

First of all, this question leads to distinguish transport and communication *infrastructure* from the *services* that they allow to produce. The evaluation of circulatory capacities is as much related to ubiquitous generic infrastructure as to highly differentiated organizational aspects of circulation. For instance, the contemporary superiority of trucks for goods transportation is highly sensitive to regulation, the pricing of external costs and congestion.

The determinants of circulatory capacity are as much the infrastructure as a generic resource for transportation and communication, as the organization and management of flows of goods, information and people.

Secondly, it is crucial to distinguish between *infrastructure* and *modes of circulation*. The relationship between infrastructure and its utilization in the production process is not deterministic. Forecasting the effects of adding a new mode of circulation (e.g. Internet) or the improvement of an existing mode (e.g. high speed trains) must be based on more than mere traffic history. For instance, the history of the French Minitel shows that the utilization of a new communication tool can be far from the use of existing tools or from the forecasts.

The analysis developed in this chapter finally leads us to the assumption that the role of transport infrastructure in a network economy cannot be anything more than a generic resource for circulation. Particular modes of circulation and their impacts are derived from the strategies of actors and the nature of resources engaged in a particular production system. The crucial distinction here is between generic and specific resources. When regional development is analysed as a process based on the creation and mobilization of specific resources (instead of access to generic resources), the limited role of transport infrastructure in the process of development becomes evident.

Our initial question of the role of transport infrastructure investments in regional development has thus to be analysed in a different manner.

The main focus shifts to the issue of the conditions under which this type of infrastructure can play the role of an instrumental factor in the creation and mobilization of specific resources for production.

Acknowledgements

A previous version of this paper was presented at the 5th RSAI Congress in Tokyo in May 1996. Some parts of the material used in this paper were published in the review *European Urban and Regional Studies*, vol. 4, no. 3 (July 1997).

The empirical study is cofinanced by the French Ministry of Public Equipment, Housing, Transportation and Tourism (DRAST, Direction of Research and Scientific and Technical Action).

References

Amin, A. and Thrift, N. (1993), 'Globalisation, Institutional Thickness and Local Prospects', *Revue d'Economie Régionale et Urbaine* 3, pp. 405–26.

Bayliss, B. (1993), 'Industry, Industrial Location and the Role of Transport in a Single European Market', in Polak, J. and A. Heertje (eds), *European Transport Economics*, Blackwell, Oxford , pp. 266–86.

Bellet, M., Colletis, G. and Lung, Y. (eds) (1993), 'Economie de proximités', *Revue d'Economie Régionale et Urbaine* , vol. 3, pp. 357–402.

Biehl, D. (1991), 'The Role of Infrastructure in Regional Development', in Vickerman, R.W. and P.W.J. Batey (eds), *Infrastructure and Regional Development*, pp. 9-35.

Biencourt, O., Favereau, O. and Eymard-Duvernay, F. (1994), *Concurrence par la qualité et viabilité d'un marché. Le cas du transport routier de marchandises.* Research Report, Commissariat Général au Plan, FORUM, Nanterre.

Blum, U. (1982), 'Effects of Transportation Investments on Regional Growth', *Papers of the Regional Science Association*, no. 49, pp. 169–84.

Botham, (1983), 'The Road Programme and Regional Development: The Problem of the Counterfactual', in Button, K. and D. Gillingwater (eds), *Transport Location and Spatial Policy*, Gower, Aldershot.

Bruinsma, F. and Rietveld, P. (1996), 'The Accessibility of European Cities. Theoretical Framework and Comparison of Approaches', Paper presented at the NECTAR Euroconferences 3, Mons, Belgium.

Cabaret, K. (1995) *La logistique: Interface entre les dynamiques industrielles et let dynamiques spatiales. Etudes de cas: Sollac Biache, Sevelnord, IBM.* Postgraduate Dissertation, INRETS-TRACES and University Lille I, September.

Cuadrado, J.R., Nijkamp, P. and P. Salva (eds) (1994) *Moving Frontiers: Economic Restructuring, Regional Development and Emerging Networks,* Avebury, Aldershot.

Congressional Budget Office (1991), *How Federal Spending for Infrastructure and Other Public Investments Affects the Economy*, Congress of the United States, Washington, July.

Eymard-Duvernay, F. (1989) 'Conventions de Qualité et Formes de Coordination', *Revue Economique* 40, no.2, pp. 329–60.

Gifford, J.L. (1994), 'Non-Incremental Infrastructure Improvements and Uncertainty: Insights from Increasing Return Economics', Communication presented at the AEA Congress 'The Econometrics of Transportation', Calais (France), January.

Gramlich, E.M. (1994), 'Infrastructure Investment: A Review Essay', *Journal of Economic Literature* , vol. 23, pp. 1176–96.

Granovetter, M. (1985), 'Economic Action and Social Structure. The Problem of Embeddedness', *American Journal of Sociology*, vol. 91, no. 3, pp. 481-510.

Håkansson, H. (ed.) (1987), *Industrial Technological Development. A Network Approach*, Routledge, London.

Janssen, B., Machielse, K. and De Ruyter, P. (1989), *Logistics, Flexibility and the Control of Production Processes. The Rise of a New Industrial Landscape in The Netherlands?*, TNO Institute of Spatial Organisation, INRO-TNO, Delft, Netherlands.

Johansson, B., Karlsson, C. and L. Westin (eds) (1994), *Patterns of a Network Economy*, Springer-Verlag, Berlin.

Kalsaas, B.T. (1995), *Transport in Industry and Locational Implications: 'Just-in-time' Principles in Manufacturing, Generation of Transport and the Relative Impact on Location. Scandinavian and Japanese Experiences*, PhD Thesis, University of Trondheim, Norway.

Krugman, P. (1991), *Geography and Trade*, MIT Press, Cambridge, Mass.

Langlois R.N. (ed.) (1986), *Economics as a Process. Essays in the New Institutional Economics*, Cambridge University Press, Cambridge.

Lakshmanan, T.R. and Okomura, M. (1995), 'The Nature and Evolution of Knowledge Networks in Japanese Manufacturing', *Papers in Regional Science - The Journal of the RSAI*, vol. 74, no. 1, pp. 63–86.

Lung, Y., Rallet, A. and Torre, A. (1996), 'Innovative Activity and Geographical Proximity', Paper presented at the 36th Congress of the European Regional Science Association, Zurich.

Marengo, L. (1994), *Learning, Competencies and Co-ordination in Organisations'*, Proceedings of the Interdisciplinary Seminary 'Technology, Learning, Space and Time', Université de Technologie de Compiègne, January, pp. 18-37.

Martellato, D. and Nijkamp, P. (1996), 'The Concept of Accessibility Revisited', Paper presented at the 5th World Congress of the RSAI, Tokyo.

Martin, F., Dagenais, M. and Bolduc, D. (1995), 'The Interregional Allocation of The Economic Integration Effects from The Building of a High Speed Rail Link in The Quebec-Windsor Corridor', Communication at the International Symposium 'Large-Scale Transport Infrastructure and the Regions', INRETS, Lille (France).

Moati, P. and Mouhoud, E.M. (1992), *Les transports et les télécommunications dans l'arbitrage entre modes d'organisation de la production*, Research for the PREDIT and France Telecom, Paris: CREDOC, December.

Moulaert, F., Swyngedouw, E. and Wilson, P. (1988), 'Spatial Responses to Fordist and Post-Fordist Accumulation and Regulation', *Papers of the Regional Science Association*, vol. 64, pp. 11-23.

Munnell, A.H. (1992), 'Infrastructure Investment and Economic Growth', *Journal of Economic Perspectives*, vol. 6, no. 4, pp. 189–98.

Nijkamp, P., Perrels, A. and Schippers, L. (1995), 'The Strategic Role of New Infrastructure Networks in Europe', in Batten, D., Casti, J. and R. Thord (eds), *Networks in Action. Communication, Economics and Human Knowledge*, Springer Verlag, Berlin, pp. 229–50.

Nijkamp, P. and Reggiani, A. (1996), 'Modelling Network Synergy in a Sustainable Perspective: Approaches and Experiments', Paper presented at the 5th World Congress of the RSAI, Tokyo, May.

Plassard, F. (1977), *Les autoroutes et le développement régional*, Economica/Presses Universitaires de Lyon.

Perroux, F. (1950), 'Les Espaces Économiques', *Economie Appliquée*, no. 1, pp. 224–5.

Rallet, A. (1993), 'Choix de Proximité et Processus d'Innovation Technologique', *Revue d'Economie Régionale et Urbaine* 3, pp. 365–86.

Rietveld, P. and Nijkamp , P. (1993), 'Transport and Regional Development', in Polak, J. and A. Heertje (eds), *European Transport Economics*, Blackwell, Oxford, pp. 130–51.

Salais, R. and Storper, M. (1992), 'The Four Worlds of Contemporary Industry', *The Cambridge Journal of Economics*, vol. 16, pp. 169–93.

Salomon, I. and Tsairi, I. (1995), 'Global Production, Transport and Telecommunications: A Case Study of Coping with Barriers in Japanese–Israeli Collaboration, *Journal of Transport Geography,* vol. 3, no. 1, pp. 15–27.

Storper, M. (1995), 'The Resurgence of Regional Economies, Ten Years Later: The Region as a Nexus of Untraded Interdependencies', *European Urban and Regional Studies,* vol. 2, no. 3, pp. 191–221.

Storper, M. and Scott, A.J. (1995), 'The Wealth of Regions. Market Forces and Policy Imperatives in Local and Global Context', *Futures,* vol. 27, no. 5, pp. 505–26.

Veltz, P. (1993), 'D'une Géographie des Coûts à une Géographie de l'Organisation. Quelques Thèses sur l'Évolution des Rapports Entreprises – Territoires', *Revue Economique* , vol. 44, no. 4, pp. 671–84.

Vickerman, R., Spiekermann, K. and Wegener, M. (1995), 'Accessibility and Economic Development in Europe', paper presented at the ESF/EC Euroconference 'European Transport and Communication Networks: Policies on European Networks', Espinho, Portugal.

Williamson, O.E. (1975), *Markets and Hierarchies. Analysis and Antitrust Implications*, Macmillan Free Press.

Zuscovitch, E. and Justman, M. (1995), 'Networks, Sustainable Differentiation, and Economic Development', in Batten, D., Casti, J. and R. Thord (eds), *Networks in Action. Communication, Economics and Human Knowledge*, Springer Verlag, Berlin, pp. 269–86.

11 Regional Active Space: A Regional Scientist's Paradigmatic Answer to the Local-Global Debate

REMIGIO RATTI

11.1 Introduction

The 'World Economy', according to the concepts of Wallerstein (1974) and Braudel (1985), obviously does not carry today's date; however, if the debate on reciprocal relationships between 'local' and 'global' has taken centre stage today, this is not only because of the nature and broadness of the globalization process acting on the economy and society, but above all, in our opinion, because the preponderant direction of relations seems to be inverse (Reich 1993): if in the past the process was seen as 'local' moving towards 'global', today the predominant orientation is rather 'global' towards 'local'.

The latter aspect is particularly important for regional sciences, considering that the predominance of the 'global' tends to obscure the 'territorial'; so the territorial aspect could be seen and experienced even more as a 'simple support space' of phenomena whose explanation lies elsewhere. The territorial space will be characterized, then, only by the product of functional logic of economic activity.

Indeed, following Vidal de la Blanche, the geographers taught the value of the concept of living space, and the scientific debate on the relationship between territory and innovation has allowed – based particularly on the work of economists and regionalists (on industrial areas, innovative milieux and the flexible economy), but also on the work of sociologists (Granovetter 1985; Grabher 1993) and institutional economists (Williamson 1985) – the discovery of a 'territorial space as actor of development', according to Rallet (1988). In this light, space, far from being a simple passive support, becomes an active element in the explanation of territorial development processes. We thus speak of 'regional active space', attributing to this concept the role of a true paradigm.

In this chapter we want first of all to enter into the fundamental problem areas of 'regional active space', interpreted as a useful instrument for the understanding of possible solutions to the debate, still very open, on the dichotomous relations between 'global' and 'local'.

We will subsequently present a simplified model that describes the logic of an active space in a process of territorial economic development.

11.2 The 'Regional Active Space': A Proposal for a Paradigmatic Approach

The nation state has represented – as long as the great majority of exchanges of goods and services took place in the classic framework of international trade among companies belonging to different domestic production systems – the leading territorial level in the mediation between local and global. Today, it is clear how this is increasingly less possible; on the contrary, new emerging spatial configurations are actively influencing the productive organization and the strategies of individual actors and companies: this is the emergence of the regional level and territorial logic, which take on the role of complements to macroeconomic approaches. So for the minority of economists who integrate the spatial aspect in their reasoning, numerous are the supporters (with Perrin 1983, 1992) of a formalization of the meso analytical spatial level in the general theory. The concept of 'regional active space' can be a valid instrument for achieving this aim.

11.2.1 The Concepts of 'Regional Active Space' as a 'Force Field Space'

As mentioned, economists, geographers and sociologists - belonging to different schools of thought, but all of them aiming to understand what takes place in the spatial reality - by now consider that, contrary to what takes place according to the conception of a passive space, the development trajectory of a region interacts with the technological development trajectories. In particular, the region becomes integrated in a process of creation/destruction, diffusion, or concentration of technological innovation. This is the view of active space (Ratti 1992) that takes on the role of a paradigm; i.e. of research orientation starting with a series of hypotheses that can not yet be consolidated.

We prefer to talk explicitly about *active space* rather than use other notions such as 'space as actor', 'factor of development', because, irrefutably, this active role is not taken on by the region intended as a pole space and therefore characterized by the existence of a sole and sovereign decision-making centre, but rather this active role of the region is the fruit of a '*force field*' (Ratti 1980), i.e., a coherent game of initiatives and responses that the actors of a given territorial space are together able to produce within the space and towards the outside.

Each region is potentially an active space, but what counts in reality is the *degree* to which it is that. It is precisely here that one can find the main conceptual novelty for those who have up to now considered the cases of industrial districts or innovative milieux as exceptions in a context where space remains a simple support for the sectoral functional logic.

As already pointed out in an article co-authored with M. Van Geenhuizen (1995), active regional space is situated in a force field characterized by three aspects: openness, concern, and the creative ability of a specific territorial system.

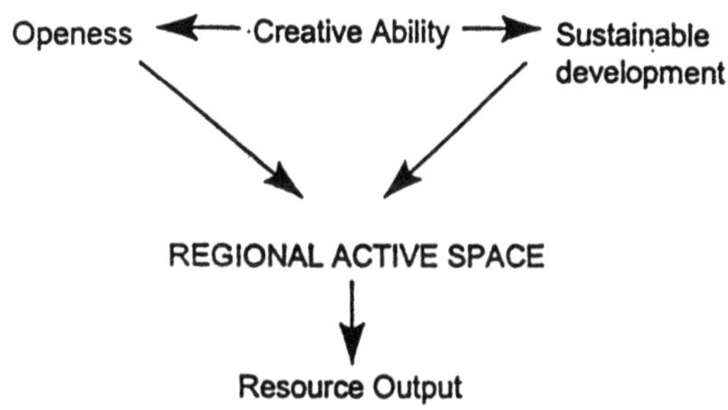

Figure 11.1 Regional active space as a force field (model applicable to different spatial scales)

Source: Van Geenhuizen and Ratti 1995.

Openness is intended as the *entering into communication* between the different components of a system (regional or city) and between the components and the system centres. It implies the ability to take advantage of economies of scale and 'scope', in particular to overcome physical, socioeconomic, cultural or political trade barriers and impediments.

'*Sustainability*' here refers not only to the territorial system's capacity to sustain environmental development, but also its *sociocultural content*. If in reality openness potentially enriches the local culture, an overly strong external influence could be perceived as a danger to society because of the loss of cultural cohesion (integration) and social stability (Mlinar 1993). Sustainability thus sets a limit to this danger.

Finally, the *creative ability* or 'territoriality' represents the aspect determining the local system's ability to *respond to internal and external challenges with objectives, norms and strategic behaviour*. It is based on knowledge capital and on regional collective learning processes that also must find an equilibrium between cohesion and openness, between internal and external networks (Storper and Scott 1993).

Altogether, regional active space is the result of a force field whose degree of output depends on its ability to generate an adequate and complex response to system dynamics; this response is expressed by the strategic behaviour capable of innovation related to openness as well as internal cohesion in order to gain economic benefits from the potential for sustainable development of a territorial space.

The degree or value of the active component of space will therefore depend on the combination of factors worth studying and modelling. This matches the conclusions of various regional approaches according to which numerous local models, through very differentiated, coexist in a single global area (Benko 1995).

11.2.2 The Axes on Which The Active Regional Space Lies

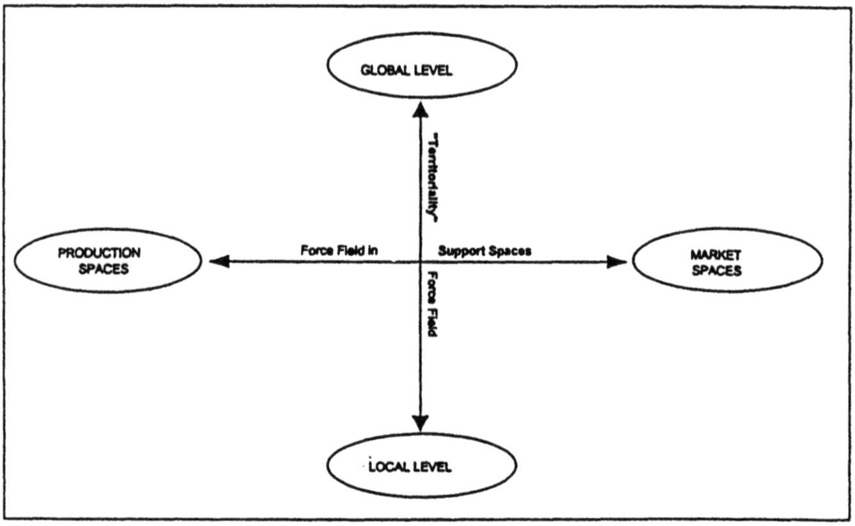

Figure 11.2 The regional active space (RAS) viewed as a meso economic force field

Source: Ratti 1995.

The meso economic force field represented by the *regional active space* can be viewed in a spatial-economic approach on two axes: a vertical axis where the tensions between different spatial levels (global–local; micro–macro) are situated and a horizontal axis on which the force field of companies' functional spaces is situated – between production spaces and market spaces.

The *vertical axis* – between global and local – is the axis of the force field that may be described in terms of '*territoriality*' (see for example,

Raffestin 1986). In human sciences, territoriality is a paradigm that expresses a complex and dynamic relation between a group of people and its environment. It is characterized by a body of principles, rules and strategic behaviour aimed, in general, at the search for dynamic coherence able to give a society and a specific territory the capacity to define their sustainable development trajectory.

The territoriality of a Country or a Region therefore represents a construction, a socio-cultural, economic and political product, and also a complex process through which a society develops its ability to respond – internally and externally – to changes.

The *horizontal axis* is the axis of companies' functional spaces, which we consider a composition of not only classic production and market spaces, but also a third category of relations, namely, support space.

Support space (Ratti 1995) is defined as a whole body of relations outside the market or preceding it. More precisely, it comprises three types of qualified relations: those connected to factors of production (labour, capital, technologies) and in particular researchers and educators (trainers); those determined by alliances and informal agreements with suppliers and customers; and those deriving from relationships that firms maintain with institutions and government (and thus correlated with 'territoriality'). A part of this space can be territorialized; the other, instead, has network-like characteristics and concerns discontinuous space.

The *support space* plays the role of a connection - beside and beyond the price system - *between the production space and the market space*; it characterizes the development trajectory of a specific territorial reality (region, city).

In conclusion, regional active space is - as a result of the entrepreneurial and territorial strategic behaviour of a region's actors - the mirror of a specific society's culture of development.

11.2.3 The Factors and Instruments for Determining and Managing Regional Active Space

Regional active space – defined in terms of territoriality and support spaces – can be analyzed by adopting four methodological frameworks (see Figure 11.3):

- the new institutional economy
- decision-making and governance models
- the logic of network cooperation/competition
- the economy of strategic resources

The interrelation between institutions and organizations is at the centre of active space interests Although the *new institutional economics* is not yet able to provide a well-established methodological corpus (Parri 1995), the interrelation between 'institutions' and 'actions' is the centre of interest today. In effect, the processes of economic liberalization or deregulation tend to modify the rules of the game and the strategic behaviour of a region's individual and collective actors. In particular, it is necessary to pay attention to complementarities, as well as substitution games, between the role of institutions and the role of organizations.

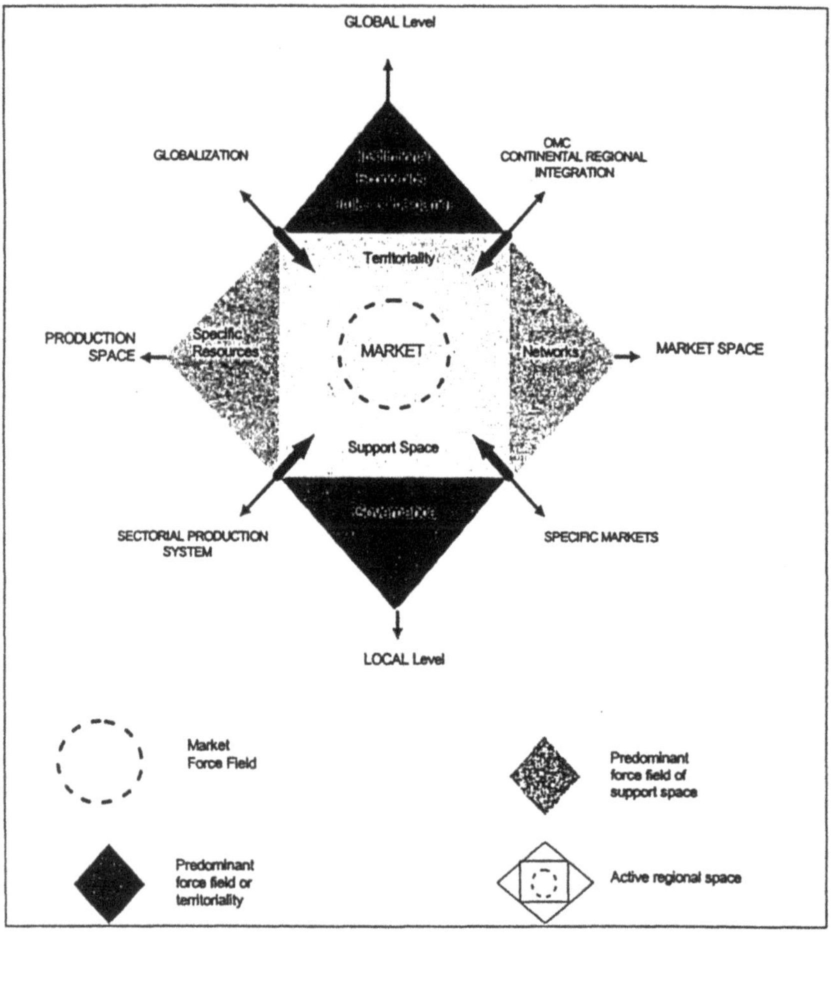

Figure 11.3 Regional active space – 'market + support space + territoriality' and its essential elements

Source: Ratti 1997.

Institutions are identified or characterized by the formal rules of the game (constitutions, legislation, regulations) or informal ones (implicit social pacts, procedures/applications leading to a sort of unwritten law (Williamson 1991); organizations refer instead to actors (political parties, representatives of the state, groups of businesses, unions and entrepreneurs). The latter will be treated further on, under the heading 'governance'.

The institutions may represent both limitations and opportunities for regional active space (North 1990), and their function, by setting the rules of the game, is to reduce uncertainty. Examples of this can be found in the definition of property rights and contracts, antitrust legislation or temporary receivership.

The analytical instruments applicable to this area of interrelations between institutions and actors are those of risk and uncertainty reduction, as well as those of the distribution and negotiation of duties between different institutional levels through game theory. So, in a phase of deregulation and privatization and of debate over the competencies among the various political-institutional hierarchies (Anderson 1992), and thanks to North's works, the influence of institutional factors no longer seems to be contested. All the same, the optimal quality of institutions does not seem to be guaranteed by rational choice processes (despite Williamson) nor even by spontaneous evolutionary or historical processes such as those described by Hayek or North (Parri 1995). In our view, this is how we consider the institutional factors in the inventory model of the force field, which make a regional space active.

The importance of 'governance' in the active space The other emerging approach is undoubtedly that of '*governance*' and the analysis of its structure (Amin and Thrift 1993). First of all – if we accept the debate on the social construction of the market (Bagnasco 1988) and the postulates of Coase (1937) on organizational forms – we discover that cooperation is the third mode along with the firm and the market. According to Williamson (1975), we find ourselves in the realm of transaction costs, due to imperfect information, entrance barriers, opportunism and control costs. The regional active space can be significantly influenced by these factors and by the ability or not to translate into a coherent management system these governance relations, which by their nature are part of the field of companies' functional spaces and which are not necessarily in line with the needs of a territorial logic.

According to Storper and Harrison (1992), the structures of 'governance' involve different typologies (presence/absence of a leader; central-peripheral relations; cooperative or non-cooperative relations), which again are key to establishing the degree and intensity of logic that make a territorial space active. In particular (Bramanti and Senn 1995), governance structures seem to be able to orient the movement law of innovative regions, with above all a 'core ring with coordinating firms' type of structure. The object of this first element of governance is thus represented by the *structure of companies' relations*; it plays a considerable role in defining the dynamics of the territorialized productive system.

The second element is represented by *organizations*. From a political and economic viewpoint, the typology of relations between social partners must also be analyzed. In effect, in connection with the institutional rules of the game, it determines the fundamental strategic behaviour at the actor level (sectoral corporatism, pluralism). An excellent historical example that is still timely is given by consensual practices and democratic corporatism, which constituted a significant part of Switzerland's development (Ratti 1995).

The object of this second field of governance concerning organizations will be based, for example, on the framework of labour contract conditions and wage negotiation rules and will be manifested in the participatory process leading to the formation of a socio-political consensus.

This point can thus be concluded with Lipietz (1983, p. 53), who affirms that governance comprises 'all forms of regulation that are neither commercial nor state'. Governance 'is civil society, minus the market, plus the local political society, the prominent, the municipalities'.

Functional relations within active space At the level of economic actors, a first category of 'off-market' relations concerns the search for openness by constructing networks of qualified functional relations, upstream (suppliers) or downstream (customers). The network is in effect (Maillat et al. 1993), 'a whole, composed of selected and explicit ties, with preferential partners, included in a perspective of a company's market relations and its search for complementary resources, having as a main objective the reduction of uncertainty'. We will immediately underline how the creation of a support space, through a similar strategy of creating a network, concerns the search for *complementary resources* that accompanies the gain in economic benefits from specific resources. The network thus becomes a channel (Camagni 1990) to

- reach sufficient economies of scale, through links in R&D and in the structures of marketing or production systems;
- control certain key components of the market, so that the ability to adapt/react quickly is ensured;
- verify the development trajectory of crucial components, so that a continuous process of adaptive innovation is ensured.

The contribution of support spaces thus created consists of the structuring of a network economy whose value lies in its flexible and interconnected architecture, allowing overall management of individual relations.

Gaining economic benefits from specific resources in the active space
Another area of relations in which the definition of support spaces acts is that of gaining economic benefits from a region's *specific resources.* These are characterized by a considerably more strategic feature than *generic resources* (low or unskilled labour reserves, availability of buildings and land, fiscal benefits, etc.). Among the specific resources for which it seems particularly interesting to develop 'off-market' strategic relations and that possess a strong stimulating impact on innovative behaviour, we cite (Perriard 1994):

- the competence of labour (which obviously represents the basic value of specific resources);
- the presence of universities and research centres, above all as far as their indirect effects on human capital and regional culture are concerned, as well as the support given to technological transfers;
- access to valid transport and communication networks;
- the possibility to turn to consultants and information services and the existence of a diversified urban base;
- access to financing (capital and risk);
- regional amenities, such as the natural and manmade environment, and cultural and educational offerings.

Finally, another category of relations that contribute to the definition of a support space – those that come into play along with collective, public or private actors of the territorial environment – brings us to a particular aspect of governance approaches, and in particular of institutional economics (Granovetter 1985). The instruments for analysing strategic behaviour of actors towards institutions also depend on important methodological approaches that go from the classical analysis in terms of imperfect competition, to game theory, up to theories of nonprofit organizations (Bluemle and Schauer 1995).

Ultimately, in the context of an active space, the new deployment of sectoral support spaces allows a regional system to gain economic benefits from the region's specific resources as a content space (labour, capital, technology) and to add complementary resources, which represent the fruit of the region as a relations space.

The *regional active space* – and, in particular, its *degree of activity* – will therefore be the result of a force field; that is, of numerous regulatory processes that interact among themselves, such as the *market*, company *support spaces*, the rules of the game and of the governance of territoriality. We point out, finally, that each region is potentially active, although to different degrees.

11.3 The Logic and Dynamics of Regional Active Space: A Draft of a Model of Theoretical Analysis

In the first part of this chapter, we presented the foundation of the concept of active space as an element of the paradigm of analysis and political action for regional development in the current context of the globalization of the economy and society. Market, companies' support space, and the ability to develop regional 'territoriality' together constitute the regulatory factors of a complex system of relations between society's territorialized spaces and the companies' functional spaces. We then saw how some new approaches, in particular multidisciplinary ones (networks, governance, new institutional economy), support the onward progression of the RAS, from an empirical as well as theoretical model point of view. As far as its empirical value is concerned, it can be pointed out how the application of the new concepts has turned out to be particularly fruitful on a number of specific occasions: the application of support space to the study of innovative milieux (Ratti and D'Ambrogio 1992; Ratti and Alberton 1997), that of territoriality to the Swiss reality (Ratti 1995) as well as the more recent and complex application in the study of transportation (Van Geenhuizen and Ratti 1995).

In this second part, we would like to stay at this theoretical level, well aware of the extreme broadness of the field of study and of the possibilities to model; that is, in conformity with the paradigmatic nature of the concept of active space.

11.3.1 The Trajectory of Regional Active Space Development

We define the variation in degree of an RAS by three aspects: 'openness', 'concern', and 'creative ability'. We start with a simplified model based on the relation between 'openness' and 'sustainability' (Figure 11.4).

We may assume a nonlinear relation between openness and sustainability. Indeed, an excessively high level of openness could turn out to be unsustainable for a region's development, while at overly low levels its development could be blocked by autarchy. In general, however, openness represents the possibility to turn to complementary resources and to gain greater economic benefits from specific resources.

But now we wonder: with which logic will a change in the degree of regional openness translate into a greater or lesser degree of RAS?

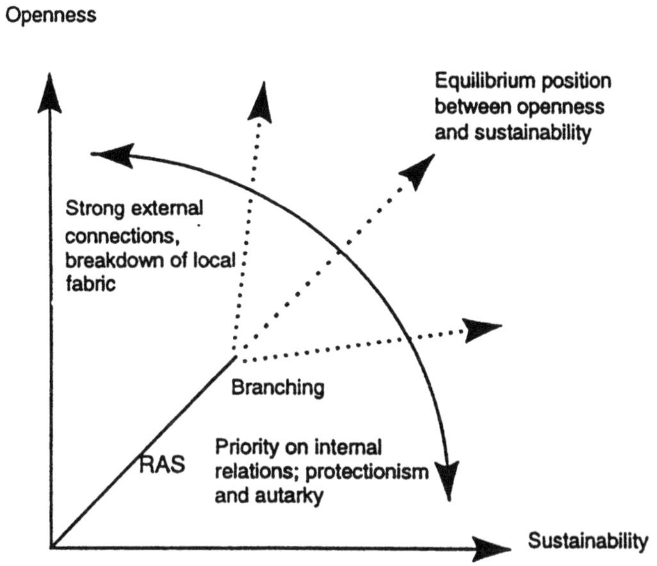

Figure 11.4 The trajectory of regional active space development

Source: Ratti on Bramanti et Miglierina (1995).

11.3.2 The Logical Process of Active Space

Figure 11.5 develops our reasoning from a simplified situation, recognizing the fact that a typology of cases is possible starting with the different curves shown in the quadrants of the figure.

Box 1 The market economy is strongly dependent on its degree of openness. Transaction costs represent an instrument for measuring market access. The form and slope of the curve, which here represent the relation between the 'degree of openness' of a region and 'transaction costs', normally show decreasing transaction costs. For the sake of simplify, we will not consider other cases here.

Let's suppose that there is a variation in the degree of openness, which goes from t_0 to t_1. The consequences of this openness can above all be interpreted in terms of transaction costs. Normally, a higher degree of openness generates lower transaction costs. Box 1 is the 'market' box.

Box 2 A decrease or increase in transaction costs signifies – according to the concepts of the new industrial economy – a benefit (or loss) measured in terms of a different form of regulation of the market/hierarchy/alliance triad, and, definitively, in terms of a different degree of integration (Box 2). In this quadrant, the ability of companies to adapt their support space to the new situation can be read in the curve. In the case shown in the figure, this ability to adapt and hence the sectoral development trajectory are positive.

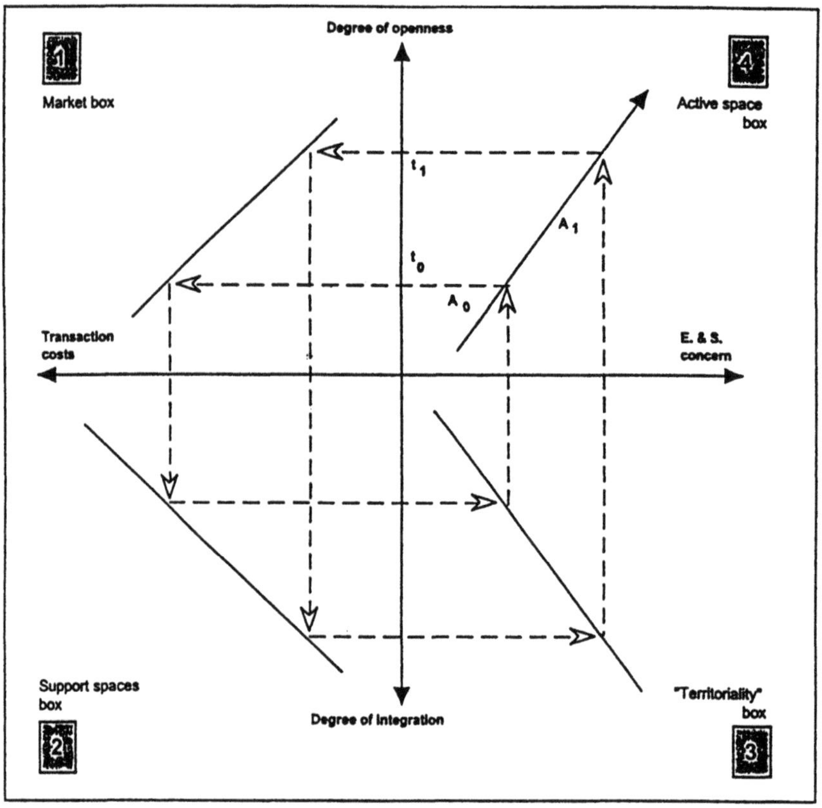

Figure 11.5 The logic of the active space (simplified case)

Source: Ratti 1997.

Box 3 The variation in transaction (market) costs and the degree of companies' integration (whose success is linked in particular to the specificity of support spaces) have repercussions on regional development (in terms of RAS grade reached) as a function of 'territoriality', in other words, the ability of governance and also of institutions to face change. Box 3 indicates, depending on the curve, the trajectory of territorial development. Again, the case carried over to the figure is an example of positive trajectory (an innovative milieu). In many cases, however, the curve could be very different (with a greater slope and therefore less sensitive to external changes, or with an inverse slope, in the case of declining regions).

Box 4 Box 4 indicates the result, i.e. the arrival point in the development trajectory in terms of the degree of RAS. In the specific case shown in Figure 11.5, an increase in the region's openness is translated into an increase in regional sustainability and as a repercussion, the degree of active space.

11.3.3 Empirical Application

The framework analysed in the prior point is suitable for an empirical application on the condition that the configuration possible in the relations indicated in each box be constructed, or at least be drafted and described.

An initial application took into consideration research conducted over several decades on the development dynamic of a border region (Ratti 1971, 1982, 1995) and was formalized in a recent paper on new European logistics (Van Geenhuizen and Ratti 1996).

It concerned the empirical case of the Chiasso area, a very important border point about fifty kilometres north of Milan between Switzerland and Italy, a region situated along the European rail route and the north–south motorway across St. Gotthard.

- The starting point (t_0) corresponds to the 1950s, the eve of the establishment of the European Common Market (Figure 11.6). The border between Switzerland and Italy is still a barrier-line, a point where all goods must halt for customs procedures and that often entails a shipping interruption, with a restructuring of the shipment and/or reshipment of goods. In this situation a region's degree of openness is therefore very limited, and because of the border, transaction costs are high (box 1) because market integration is weak (box 2). However, at the regional level this situation constitutes an advantage for agents in specific markets (customs shippers and international service activities) to be concentrated in one point. In Chiasso a network of specific relations is organized and exists (the bridge function indicated in Curve 1 in box 3) with relatively high entrance costs. The degree of support and coherence of regional economic activities with respect to external dynamics (active space) is good.

- The progressive realization and success obtained in the first phase of the integration process of the European industrial economy (t_1 in Figure 11.6) has as a consequence the significant increase in trading within the European Community and the continent. However, the transportation infrastructures, customs procedures and international trade (including financial transfers connected to import/export) are not yet changing radically. Even if the procedures are softened, the position of Chiasso remains strong in Italy, and local operators gain further economic benefits from their know-how, putting themselves in an almost monopolistic position or in an innovative mileau (Ratti 1995).

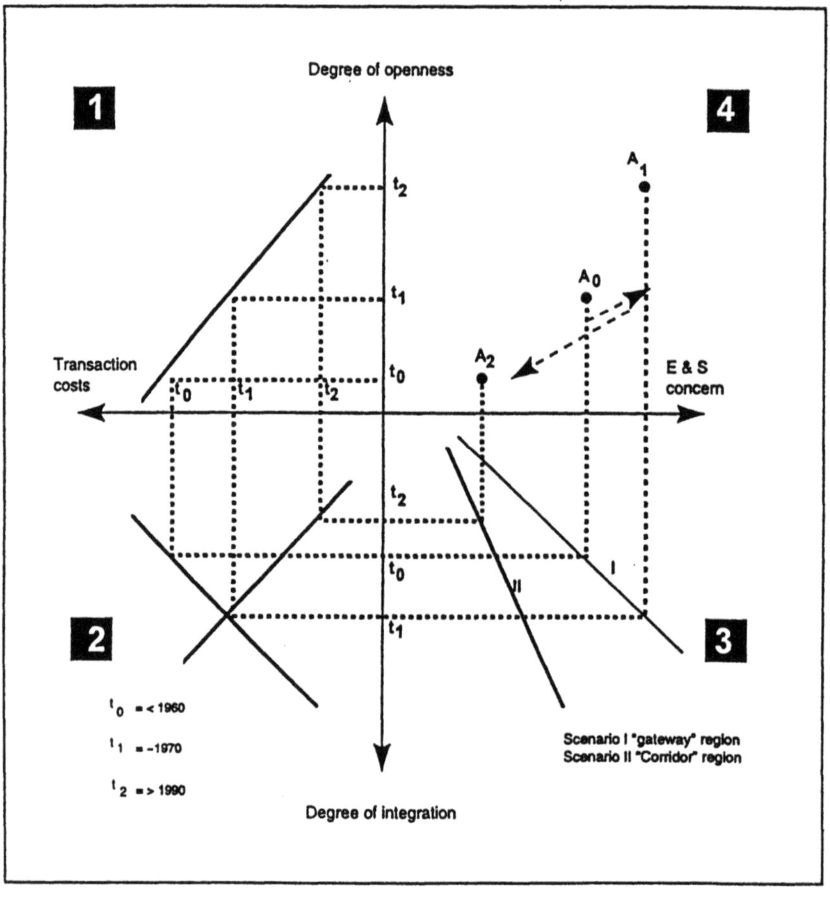

Figure 11.6 Example of an active space trajectory: the case of the Swiss-Italian border region

Source: Van Geenhuizen and Ratti 1995.

During the Seventies, the situation of the Chiasso region was that of a region giving an active type of response to changes in the external scenario: openness causes transaction costs to decline (box 1); economic integration processes began (box 2), followed by import/export service operators and transit traffic across the Alps. The Chiasso region therefore develops and affirms its own ability to manage these flows through strategic alliances and, as a transit area, brings out the value of its economic culture, particularly open to the needs of international trade. The result is also a certain enrichment of the region that reinforces, with the creation and the development of other banking and asset management activities, its position as a gateway region (box 3). This result can be seen in the improvement of the situation in the scale of appreciation of active space (box 4).

The third period of analysis (t_2) relates to the Eighties, in which economic processes – openness – are increasingly influenced by the creation of the single European space. Transaction costs fall thanks to new communication technology, to computerization, to EU directives (box 1), along with the ability of sector actors, above all Italian, to operate outside domestic conditions and without feeling the need for intermediaries. What is changing is definitely the nature of integration processes that shift from commercial trading processes between domestic economies to a globalization process of logistic activities. These processes can lead to breakdowns in relation to traditional territorial structures (for this reason there is a branching in box 2). In the new scenario of integrated logistics a location along a border point is in principle reduced to the role of a passage point.

Within Europe, true logistic regions are coming into existence, which are in turn linked to some bridge heads. In the context of the empirical example in question, the logistic region is that of northern Lombardy with the Milan actors fundamentally taking on the role of leader (Creti 1994). Transit across the border is increasingly devalued and takes on the characteristics of a transit corridor (box 3).

The resulting viewpoint of the specific Chiasso region's ability to respond in terms of active space logic can be read in box 4. This box shows a substantial loss in the region's ability to manage in relation to the external context, with a break in the milieu effect. The region progressively loses the collective capacity to create specific factors and complementary resources connected to the network strategies. What results therefore is the realization of a smaller degree of appreciation of the regional active space (box 4).

It should be emphasized in any case how a premature policy for evaluating changes in trends could have allowed the region to remain on a positive trajectory and to maintain its gateway functions, in particular through an innovative strategy aiming at rendering functional services to the new needs of integrated logistics. The goal of this operation would have been that of finding other niche products and of substituting specific factors due at the border: for example modifying and developing the potentialities connected to the capacity to manage of the communications/transport/distribution networks.

11.4 General Conclusions

Fundamentally, the concept of regional active space – created above all as a reaction to the concept of support space – proves to involve a degree of pertinence and generalities decidedly greater than what was imagined up to now. Indeed, the contribution of the active space concept appears, under various aspects, to be scientifically rich and promising:

- for its ability to explain an open and dynamic regional reality; in particular thanks to the consideration of a 'force field' space;
- for its applicability to each region (and not only to textbook cases of industrial districts or innovative milieu), in the sense that each region has at its disposal, actually or potentially, a degree of 'active space', be it small or large;
- for its federating role; that is, for its tendency to gain economic benefits and its inclusion of diverse disciplinary contributions in a common orientation, which is what makes it a research paradigm;
- for its theoretical and empirical operative possibilities. In this manner, on a theoretical level the active space tends to put the market, the socioeconomic actors and the agencies of regional territoriality in a logical circuit; on a practical level it presents itself as an effective connecting thread for regional development analysis and policies.

In any case, efforts are already underway to measure the degree of openness or to reach representative indicators of the quality of (eco)systems and their sustainability in environmental and socioeconomic terms (Camagni et al. 1995).

Subsequently, the analytical construction of a model and of trajectory curves regarding the measure of the degree of integration of firms (support space box) or of the degree of 'sustainability' ('territoriality' box) calls for further research.

In the first case we have, however, already proposed a theoretical framework (and one which has revealed itself to be very useful in empirical studies within the study of the border-barrier; Ratti 1995).

The problem is posed concerning preference for support strategies (alliances, agreements) in terms of transaction costs, control costs and creativity (technological innovation and preference for integration).

Finally, it is precisely the formalization of territoriality – with numerous non-economic variables – that poses the greatest problems in view of the construction of a curve indicating a territory's development trajectory. However, despite the liberty in the construction of these curves, it is easy to demonstrate the interest in the logical formalization applied to empirical cases (Van Geenhuizen and Ratti 1995).

To conclude, the RAS seems to offer a new and promising approach in the analysis and policy of regional dynamics. In addition, it integrates numerous partial concepts – such of those of functional support space and territoriality – and presents itself as a possible answer of regionalists to the local-global debate.

References

Amin, A. (1993), 'The Globalisation of the Economy: An Erosion of Regional Networks?' in Grabher, G. (ed.), *The Embedded Firm. On the Socioeconomics of Industrial Networks*, Routledge, London, pp. 278–95.

Amin, A. and Robins, K. (1990), 'Le Retour des Économies Régionales? La Géographie Mythique de l'Accumulation Flexible', in Benko, G. and A. Lipietz (eds), A., *Les Régions qui Gagnent*, P.U.F, Paris, pp. 123–61.

Amin, A. and Thrift, N. (1993), 'Globalization, Institutional Thickness and Local Prospects', *Revue d'Economie Régionale et Urbaine*, no. 3.

Anderson, J. (1992), *The Territorial Imperative – Pluralism, Corporativism and Economic Crisis*, Cambridge University Press, Cambridge, pp. 34–5.

Bagnasco, A. (1988), *La Costruzione Sociale del Mercato*, Il Mulino, Bologna.

Benko, G. (1995), 'Les Théories du Développement Local', *Sciences Humaines, Numéro spécial Régions et mondialisation*, Paris, Février/Mars.

Benko, B. and Lipietz, A. (eds) (1992), *Les Régions qui Gagnent*, PUF, Paris.

Blümle, E. and Schauer, R. (1995), *Non Profit-Organisationen - Dritte Kraft zwischen Markt und Staat*, Universitätsverlag, Linz.

Boyer, R. (1992), *Les Alternatives au Fordisme. Des années 1980 au XXI Siècle.*

Bramanti, A. and Senn, L. (1997), 'Understanding Structural Changes and Laws of Motion of Milieux: A Study on North-Western Italy', in Ratti R., Bramanti A. and R. Gordon (eds), *The Dynamics of Innovative Regions*, GREMI, Ashgate, Aldershot, pp. 47–75.

Braudel (1985), *La Dynamique du Capitalisme*, Arthaud, Paris.

Camagni, R., Capello, R. and Nijkamp, P. (1995), 'Sustainable City Policy: Economic, Environmental, Technological', Paper presented at the International Urban Habitat Conference, Delft.

Christaller, W. (1933) *Die Zentrale Orte in Süddeutschland, Wissenschaftliche Buchgesellschaft*, Darmstadt, reprinted 1980.

Coase, R.H. (1937), 'The Nature of Firms', *Economica*, no. 4, pp. 386–405.

Gaudard, G. (1987), 'Regional Economic Development and the Future of Environment', in Pillet G. and T. Murota (eds), *Environmental Economics*, Genève.

Grabher, G. (ed.) (1993), *The Embedded Firm. On the Socio-economics of Industrial Networks*, Routledge, London.

Granovetter, M. (1985), 'Economic Action and Social Structure: the Problem of Embeddedness', *American Journal of Sociology*, no. 3, pp. 481–510.

Joskow, P. (1995), 'The New Institutional Economics: Alternative Approaches', *Journal of Institutional and Theoretical Economics*, pp. 248–59.

Knight, J. (1992), *Institution and Social Conflicts*, Cambridge University Press, Cambridge.

Lipietz, A. (1992), 'Le Local et le Global: Personnalité Régionale ou Interrégionalité?', in *IREPD Actes du Colloque Industrie et Territoire*, Grenoble.

Loesch, A. (1940), *Die Räumliche Ordnung der Wirtschaft*, G. Fischer, Jena.

Maillat, D., Quévit, M. and Senn, L. (1993), *Réseaux d'Innovation et Milieux Innovateurs: Un Pari pour le Développement Régional*, GREMI/EDES, Neuchâtel.

Mlinar, Z. (1992), *Globalisation and Territorial Identities*, Avebury, Aldershot, pp. 15–35.

North, D.C. (1990), *Institutions, Institutional Change and Economic Performance*, Cambridge University Press, Cambridge.

Paelinck, J. and Sallez, A. (eds) (1983), *Espace et Localisation, Economica*, Paris.

Parri, L. (1995), 'Le Istituzioni nelle Scienze Economico-sociali: Una Torre di Babele Concettuale', Working Paper DSS Papers SOL 3–95, Brescia.

Pecqueur, B. (1993), 'Territoire, Territorialité et Développement', in *IREPD Actes du Colloqie Industrie et Territoire*, Grenoble.

Perriard, M. (1994), *Infomotion et Dynamique Spatialisée de l'Économie*, Editions Universitaires Fribourg, Fribourg, Switzerland.

Perriard, M. (1995), 'Toward a Measure of Globalisation', UCSA/CRESUF, Santa Cruz/Fribourg, Working paper.

Perrin, J.P. (1983), 'Economie Spatiale et Mésoanalyse', in Paelinck, J. and A. Sallez (eds), *Espace et Localisation, Economica*, Paris, pp. 201–30.

Perrin, J.P. (1992), 'Pour une Révision de la Science Régionale. L'Approche par les Milieux', *Revue Canadienne des Sciences Régionales*, vol. XV, no. 2.

Piore, M. and Sabel, C. (1984), *The Second Industrial Divide: Possibilities for Prosperity*, Basic Books, New York.

Raffestin, C. (1986), 'Territorialité: Concept ou Paradigme de la Géographie Sociale?', *Geographica Helvetica*, vol. 2, no. 1, pp. 91–6.

Rallet, A. (1988), 'La Région et l'Analyse Économique Contemporaine', *Revue d'Économie Régionale et Urbaine*, no. 3, pp. 365–80.

Ratti, R. (1980), *Investimento Pubblico ed Effetti Economico-spaziali*, Editions Universitaires, Fribourg.

Ratti, R., (1991), 'Small and Medium-size Enterprises, Local Synergies and Spatial Cycles of Innovation', in Camagni, R. (ed.), *Innovation Networks*, Belhaven Press, London and NewYork, pp. 71–89.

Ratti, R. (1992), *Innovation Technologique et Développement Régional*, IRE–Méta Editions, Bellinzona, Switzerland.

Ratti, R. (1995), *Leggere la Svizzera. Saggio Politico Economico sul Divenire del Modello Elvetico*, ISPI/Casagrande Editore, Milano/Lugano.

Ratti, R. (1997), 'Lo Spazio Attivo', in Bramanti, A. and M.A. Maggioni (eds), *La Dinamica dei Sistemi Produttivi Territoriali*, F. Angeli, Milan, pp. 134–56.

Ratti, R. and Alberton, S. (1997), 'Crises, Mutations des Espaces Fonctionnels des Entreprises et Mutations des Réseaux/Milieux Innovateurs', in Ratti R., Bramanti A. and R. Gordon (eds), ^*The Dynamics of Innovative Regions*, GREMI, Ashgate, Aldershot, pp. 75–107.

Ratti, R. and D'Ambrogio, F. (1992), 'Processus d'Innovation et Intégration Locale dans une Zone Périphérique', in Maillat D. and J.C. Perrin (eds), *Entreprises Innovatrices et Développement Territorial*, GREMI/EDES, Neuchâtel, pp. 167–95.

Reich, R. (1993), *L'Économie Mondialisée*, Dunod, Paris, English translation 'The Work of Nations', 1991.

Rostow, W. (1963), *Les Étapes de la Croissance Économique*, Seuil, Paris.

Scott, A.J. (1992), 'L'Économie Métropolitaine: Organisation Industrielle et Croissance Urbaine', in Benko, B. and A.Lipietz (eds), *Les Régions qui Gagnent*, PUF, Paris, pp. 103–20.

Stöhr, W. and Taylor, D.R. (eds) (1981), *Development from Above or Below*, Wiley, Chichester.

Storper, M. and Harrison, B. (1992), 'Flexibilité, Hiérarchie et Développement Régional: les Changements de Structure des Systèmes Productifs Industriels et leurs Nouveaux Modes de Gouvernance dans les Années 1990', in Benko, B. and A.Lipietz (eds), *Les Régions qui Gagnent*, PUF, Paris, pp. 265–91.

Storper, M. and Scott, A.J. (1993), 'The Wealth of Regions: Market Forces and Policy Imperatives in Local and Global Context', UCLA, Lewis Center for Regional Policy Studies, Working Paper Series.

Storper, M. and Walker, R. (1989), *The Capitalist Imperative. Territory, Technology and Industrial Growth*, Blackwell, Oxford.

Van Geenhuizen M. and Ratti, R. (1995), 'New Network Use and Technologies in Freight Transport. An Active Space Approach', Paper presented at the ESF/EC Euroconference on European Transport and Communication Networks, Espinho, Portugal, April.

Wallerstein, I. (1974), *The Modern World-System. Capitalist Agriculture and the Origin of the European World-Economy in the Sixteenth Century*, Academic Press, New York.

Williamson, O.E. (1985), *Economic Institutions of Capitalism:Firm, Market, Regional Contracting*, Free Press, New York; Collie Macmillan, London.

Williamson, O.E. (1991), 'Economic Institutions: Spontaneous and Intentional Governance', *Journal of Law, Economics and Organisation*, vol. 7, no. 2, pp. 159–87). French translation (1994), *Les Institutions de l'Économie*, Interéditions, Paris.

Part C
Empirical Frameworks: European Freight Transport Networks

12 What Port for the Future? From 'Mainports' to Ports as Nodes of Logistic Networks

PAUL DREWE AND BEN JANSSEN

12.1 To Set the Stage

Recently, the Dutch government has decided to build a new rail connection for the transport of goods, the Betuwe line. This is to link Rotterdam, Europe's premier seaporty to its (German) hinterland. A critical evaluation of the planning and decision making process (Drewe and Janssen 1996) has revealed a major flaw of a strategic nature. Why is there a need for the Betuwe line has not been sufficiently explained. Referring to the seaport of Rotterdam needing the new rail connection to connection to secure its posirtion as 'mainport', evidently has rather tended to clinch any fundamental debate. 'Mainport' has been used as a slogan. The danger with slogans is that they keep us from penetrating to the heart and essence of the problem. Of course, expertise has been provided, even a large amount. It boils down to assumingf that the predicted growth of containers, cargo and bulk – to be transported along the East-West axis – meets with infrastructure bottlenecks and therefore asks for additional capacity. This turns out to be rail capacity, in order to strengthen the multimodality of the port (also anticipating the possible political pressure for rail transport of goods). The future mainport function of Rotterdam seems to imply continued growth of flows of goods along the axis at a rate of 93 percent over a period of 25 years (see Table 12.1). Not all the goods transport along the East-West axis originatre from or arrive at the port of Rotterdam. although the position of this seaport is a dominant one. The table also shows that container flows are expected to be the fastest growing category of goods. Bulk will *only* grow by 57 percent until 2014 according to the experts, but will still remain the *bulk* of the goods transported.

Container transport is not only expected to be the fastest growing category of goods, Rotterdam is also Europe's number one container port compared with, e.g. Hamburg, Antwerp, Bremen and Le Havre (some 45 million tons of containers in 1993). It is the fourth container handling port in the world, after Hong Kong, Singapore and Kaohsiung. According to the Rotterdam Port Authorities, the number of containers is expected to grow by 232 percent between 1989 and 2010 (see Figures 12.1a and 12.1b). The modal split shows that the roads to and from the seaport have to cope with a growth of 182 percent.

Table 12.1 Total flows of goods East-West axis by category (in million tons)

	1990	2015	percent change
Containers	10	32	+220
Cargo	66	177	+168
Bulk	174	274	+ 57
Total	**250**	**483**	**+ 93**

Source: Commissie Betuweroute 1995.

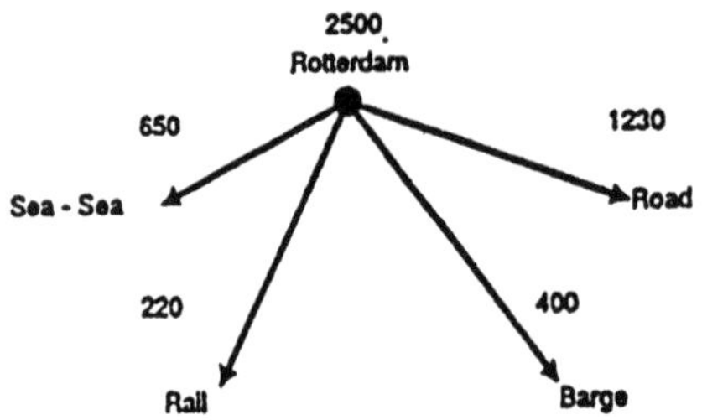

Figure 12.1a. Modal split containers, Rotterdam 1989 (x 100 TEU)

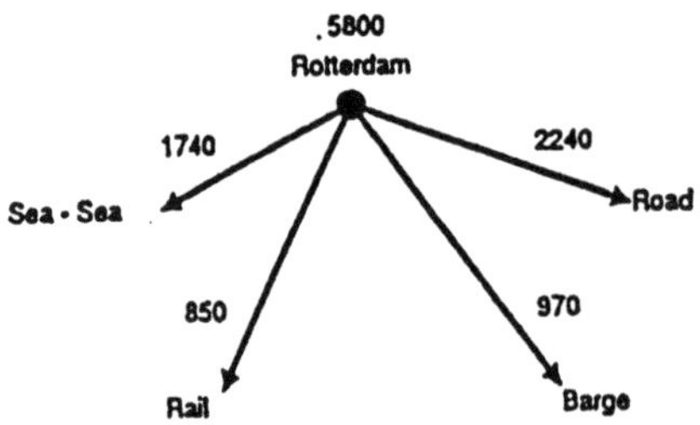

Figure 12.1b. Modal split containers, Rotterdam, 2010 (x 100 TEU)

Source: Gemeente Rotterdam 1990.

So there are shifts ahead both with regard to the mix of goods to be handled and transported, and the modal split. However, the underlying model of extrapolated growth remains unaltered. The answer to the question 'What future for the port?' is further growth, measured in terms of tonnage. To simplify a problem in this manner may lead to a wrong solution as the mainport slogan might distract from the alternative question of 'What port for the future?'. Is it not heroic to assume that the world will not undergo substantial changes till the year 2015, that we are not living in an uncertain world? What about new ways of coping with supply and distribution of raw materials and goods called product channel logistics? And does not the port for the future therefore appear as a node of logistic networks? The interest in these developments is not purely academic, but rather dictated by both socioeconomic and environmental reasons.

12.1.1 The Socioeconomic Perspective

The origin of the growth model, referred to above, can be traced to the late 1960s when a plan was set up for the Greater Rotterdam area aimed at maximizing the volume of tons shipped. Some critics at the time pointed out that the authors of the plan had glossed over the production of value added in the area requiring a different use of land. Amazingly, it took decision makers in Rotterdam more than 20 years to recognize this fallacy. The development plan for the port of Rotterdam in the year 2010 stresses the urgency of creating more space in the port area for activities that generate value added. But critics have pointed out that there may not be enough space left for locating these activities which, moreover, tend to further increase the existing congestion (Van Klink 1993). The Greater Rotterdam economy needs a new impulse. Its overall vitality in the years 1986-93 has been relatively low (vitality being measured in terms of turnover, investment and net profit) (Louter and De Ruyter 1995). The province of South Holland, to which Greater Rotterdam belongs, has a Gross Domestic Product per inhabitant just above the average of the European Union: 106.3 percent in the period 1989–91 as against 109.3 percent in the years 1986–88. The GDP per person employed has dropped from 126.2 percent in the period 1986–88 to 105.7 percent in the more recent period (European Commission 1994a; Commissie van de Europese Gemeenschappen 1991).

12.1.2 The Environmental Perspective

The second reason for dealing with an alternative future for the port of Rotterdam is environmental. The area is already highly congested which causes delays in the journey-to-work, as well as in the transport of goods. In order to transport 800 TUEs, about 580 (automatic guided) vehicles are needed with a total length of 6.8 kilometres. Can the Greater Rotterdam area really handle an increase in the road transport of containers of 182 percent between 1989 and 2010? 'Traffic jams are not only exasperating, they also cost Europe dearly in terms of productivity' – according to the White Paper of the European Commission. Indeed, in 1994 the economic damage caused by congestion in the Netherlands has been estimated at 1.4 billion guilders. But will investment in transport infrastructure automatically bring relief (even when combined with improving alternatives for cars and a better utilization of the existing infrastructure by traffic management)? Does the Netherlands need a Betuweline? In the final analysis, the success of the line largely depends on limitations to be imposed on road transport which, in turn, depend on measures to be put into effect at the European level. Without these limitations, however, i.e. with an unchanged policy in the Netherlands, emissions (NO_x, CO_2, VOS, SO_2), and energy consumption will augment markedly. Various hazards should be added to pollution, linked to the transportation of dangerous goods as well as to industrial hazards in the port area which has a high concentration of petrochemical complexes. Even without a nuclear power plant (as in the Antwerp port region), the Greater Rotterdam area, densely populated with some 1000 inhabitants per km2, qualifies as a potential environmental disaster area. The environmental problems tend to worsen under a continued growth regime. This is not only detrimental to the quality of life in the area, but may also thwart attempts to create a new impulse for the Greater Rotterdam economy. Note that the European Commission has warned against 'the rising costs of congestion in the central areas of the Community-delays, pollution, etc. – likely to act as an increasingly powerful deterrent to new investment in these areas' (Commission of the European Communities 1991).

To set the scene, we so far have used Europe's premier seaport as an example. The question 'What port for the future?', as a matter of course, also applies to other ports, both in and outside Europe, though the ports of the Hamburg-Le Havre type are our primary concern. In Section 12.2, product channel logistics will be explained in a nutshell. With the rise of this kind of logistics, the positioning of ports is about to change. Section 12.3 deals with the transition from a competitive world of ports to a strategic cooperation of ports. If this is to be more than just a wild goose chase, one has to search for complementarities. The future of ports, however, is embedded in an uncertain world. Hence the necessity of managing uncertainties. 'The art of the long view' will be handled in the final section.

12.2 Product Channel Logistics and Port Development

We witness today some important, interdependent, trends in freight transport (Ruijgrok et al. 1991):

- globalization: the market produced for and transported to is becoming more diversified, covering a growing geographic scale (alongside a globally networked production)
- the rise of buyers' markets: the development of a less standardized production entails smaller, varied product series and hence smaller batches in transportation (economies of scope tend to become as important as economies of scale)
- flexibility: the flexibility of production and labour processes is increased in order to cope better and faster with market changes
- dematerialization: less traditional bulk goods and more lighter and smaller products (with a high value density) requiring flexible and varied means of transport
- integration: transport is increasingly integrated with production chains and networks
- computerization: the rise of farreaching management and control of production and transport flows, using computer techniques and information engineering.

12.2.1 *Product Channel Logistics in a Nutshell*

Logistics is basically concerned with the movement and storage of goods in the supply chains to customers. In the past decade we have been witnessing a transformation in the ways the movement and storage have been managed by companies. In the 1970s, companies began to implement the concept of 'integrated distribution' which brought together transport, warehousing and inventory management. As the benefits became evident, this approach was extended to become 'channel integration' in which there was coordination of the management of materials and finished goods, from the sourcing of raw materials through to the point of final consumption of finished products: integrated supply chain management or product channel logistics (NEA and Cranfield 1994).

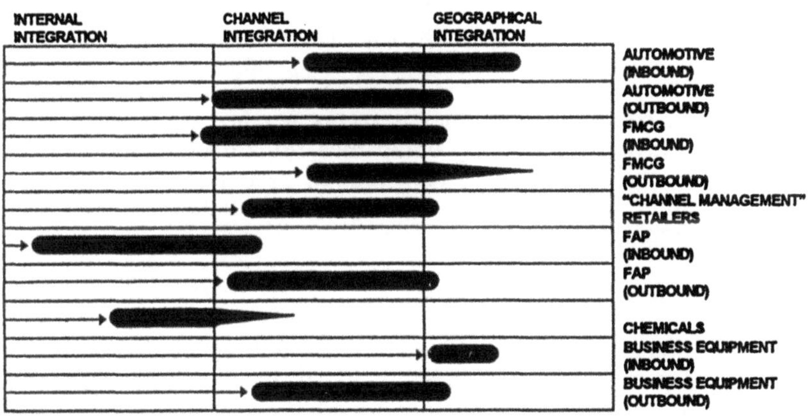

Figure 12.2 Logistics integration by industry sector

Source: NEA and Cranfield 1994.

Product channel logistics provides a means to cope with the trends referred to above by evaluating cross-functional trade offs to maximize overall (chain) profitability, rather than managing supply, production or distribution activities individually (Anderson 1989). Product channel logistics differ from traditional approaches to logistics. There is a shift from managing assets (such as warehouses, trucks, inventories) towards managing processes (product systems, transport systems, product flows and information flows). This requires a new way of handling linkages between a firm and its suppliers and distribution channels by new intracompany and, above all, inter-company transport and information systems. Inbound and outbound traffic is no longer 'just transportation', based on minimum cost or similar 'hard' criteria. Shippers and transport firms must redefine transport as a critical factor in product channel and value chain management. The chain's critical linkages involve transportation companies as well as suppliers, distributors and customers – seen from the vantage point of a production company. By using new communications and information technologies, firms are able to rearrange activities in physical space in such a way that the time involved in production and distribution is drastically reduced.

A study dealing with the development of product channel logistics in six industry sectors relevant to the Dutch economy, has shown that companies in the automotive and business equipment industries are most advanced in the logistics integration process – especially with regard to inbound logistics. Food and agriculture production companies are still at the stage of linking (internally) their separate logistic activities. Most companies, however, are engaged in restructuring their logistic systems in order to reap the significant benefits accruing from economies of scale in purchasing, manufacturing, warehousing and distribution. They are not yet in a position to integrate their operations geographically, simply because they have not reached a European span of activities. Nevertheless, many companies remain committed to the transformation and integration of their logistic systems because they are anxious to capture the potential advantages, both in terms of cost and service. See Figure 12.2.

12.2.2 A New Positioning of Ports

What implications does the rise of product channel logistics have for the positioning of ports? First of all, a rethinking of the 'tonnage approach' is called for. The conventional positioning approach can be summarized by the following equation:

$$M.Ce = Co.Q \qquad (12.1)$$

where:

M = mass of goods to be transported per port
Ce = centrality index of port
Co = transhipment/transit costs in port in relation to competing ports
Q = quantity of goods transhipped in port

The central index measures the infrastructural access of ports to their hinterland by rail, road and inland waterway. Another way of positioning ports in terms of accessibility is by calculating the so-called market distance (Roodenburg 1989). The higher a port's multimodal physical accessibility, the higher the mass of goods it attracts and the higher the transit of goods – provided the costs can be kept relatively low. The left-hand side of the equation 'explains' why port authorities today fixate on multimodal, physical infrastructure expansion: seaside, in port and landside. The impact of product channel logistics on this kind of reasoning is twofold. On the right-hand side of the above equation, 'tonnage thinking' is replaced by 'chain and value-adding thinking'. And, as far as the left-hand side is concerned, the emphasis is shifting from physical accessibility to controlled and dedicated logistic accessibility and hence to facilities and services.

From tonnage to chains and value adding Let us first take a closer look at chains and value adding. As a first step, freight volumes are to be divided into segments and the (gross) value added per segment per ton is to be calculated.

A rule of thumb (Winkelmans 1991) can be applied to illustrate that it is possible to create the same amount of value added or even more value added by shipping lesser volumes of goods:

$$1 \text{ ton CC} = 3 \text{ tons UL} = 6 \text{ tons DB} = 15 \text{ tons LB} \qquad (12.2)$$

In the year 2015, one expects 274 million tons of bulk to be transported along the East-West axis of the Netherlands (see table 1). Assuming that the goods are transhipped in the port of Rotterdam and that the bulk is dry (DB), then the same amount of value added can be earned by transporting 46 million tons of conventional cargo (CC). In the case of liquid bulk (LB), the equivalent volumes of conventional cargo amount to 18 million tons. Similarly, equivalent volumes of containers or unit load (UL) can be calculated. As far as containers are concerned, it is also important to distinguish between 'Full Container Load' (FCL) and 'Less than Full Container Load' (LCL). The latter can generate a value added about five times as high as the former (either in the port or elsewhere, dependent on where the regrouping takes place). And, as a large part of continental container flows in Europe consists of 'empty boxes', this has to be deducted from the gross value added – unless better ways are found to handle the logistics of empty containers. CC, UL, DB and LB or similar segments are still transhipment categories. It is preferable to use a classification more apt to deal with product channel logistics (Janssen 1991). First, a distinction can be made between producing activities, referring to the production of goods in an industrial process, and service providing activities. The latter include other goods handling activities (storage, transportation, distribution and trading of goods) and other producer services, in especial knowledge intensive services essential to the strategic design, planning and execution of the entire production process. Next, the producing activities group is subdivided into four types of activities: continuous processes:

- the production of large series of standardized products, in general the processing of raw materials;

- discontinuous processes: medium sized series of different standardized products (semifinished products, components, consumer products);
- product groups: small to medium sized series of heterogeneous products such as fashion-sensitive, ready-to-wear clothing or consumer electronics;
- project situations (single and multiple): small series or 'series of just one product', manufactured by the piece following consumer specifications (e.g. buildings, ships, airplanes etc.).

This typology is two dimensional. Variety in products relates to the ever increasing market (consumer) demand for a broad range of products, stressing the importance of economies of scope or flexibility of the production process. Standardization of production, on the other hand, refers to the way in which a variety of products can be produced as efficiently as possible, building on one or more standardized modules – a matter of economies of scale. Different products or markets imply different lead times, the time intervals between the placing of an order and delivery. This brings us to the topic of controlled and dedicated logistic accessibility.

From physical to logistic accessibility With the rise of product channel logistics, either centrality or market distance changes into:

$$\text{closeness in lead time} = \frac{\text{density of population}}{\text{quantities/times}} \qquad (12.3)$$

Population density and quantities of goods, should preferably be weighted according to the wealth of the population and the values of goods respectively. Logistic accessibility involves networks and platforms. In the channels connecting units of production to points of sale or final destinations, platforms (terminals) intervene in different ways. Logistic platforms are not only material platforms for the consolidation as well as the deconsolidation of flows of goods, but increasingly turn into platforms in data-flow networks. They are also hierarchically positioned, ranging from international main logistic centres down to city/local distribution centres. Where do the ports come in? They are mainly cast as inter(national) nodes of logistic networks. Seaports are just one type of node among others (airports, border nodes of infrastructure, inland terminals). Seen from a different perspective, the port is the focus of two divergent types of logistics: 'product logistics' and 'transport logistics'. 'Product logistics' focuses on the individual product moving through a logistic chain, along which a range of activities is performed adding value and tailoring the product to consumer needs. 'Transport logistics', on the other hand, refers to efforts of transport firms to optimize the utilization of their equipment and networks while maintaining the required level of service.

With regard to ports, the latter implies a strategy of standardization and massing of flows and services. Parallelling this strategy often is a move toward 'mainporting'. The aim is to establish (global) transport pipelines in which the port no longer constitutes a breakpoint in the transportation of goods. Ports consequently become 'ship-oriented', with increasing economies of scale. Returns measured in terms of value added and employment per ton of goods handled in the port, however, tend to diminish. The strategy of product logistics, on the other hand, requires a broad spectrum of logistic services and facilities. This type of logistics calls for a 'cargo-oriented port', marked by more value adding and customization of activities and less technology driven port development. Today, it is still an open question whether ports like Rotterdam, Antwerp or Hamburg will develop according to both types of logistics or just one, the mainport strategy which is, essentially, a strategy of transport logistics. With the emphasis shifting from physical to logistic accessibility, the provision of logistic services becomes of vital importance:

'The choice of a port is less determined by the facilities of a port, but more and more by the logistics facilities offered. Hinterland connections and telematics facilities of a port have become essential elements of these logistics facilities' (Haven van Rotterdam 1986).

Logistic service providers may be companies that, in relation with a shipper, offer services concerning the control and operation of goods flow processes in order to achieve an optimal exchange between consignor and receiver. They may also be physical distribution companies that provide, at the request of shippers, transport plus warehousing and distribution services. In both cases, the services provided may either be shared by many different customers or tailored to the needs of one specific customer. Within the European Union, complementary logistic organizations and networks of producers and their suppliers, wholesale and retail companies, and logistic service providers are, emerging. They tend to internationalize ('europeanize') as well as to concentrate spatially.

The integration of shippers and logistic service providers can take different forms. They depend on the choices and management approaches of shippers and the degree of logistics integration they have achieved (which, in turn, differs from one industrial sector to another and may even very within the same sector).

Apart from shippers' logistics, logistic service providers have their own strategies geared to the logistics of transport. Strategies can be developed in four directions:

- the geographic scale of own networks (ranging from local to pan–European presence, potentially);
- the complexity of own transport networks (referring to the modality in networks);
- the number of activities in own networks (ranging from general haulage to high value-adding logistic services, i.e. assembly);

- the number of specialisms (focusing on type of products, conditioning, size of shipment, volume of transport).

Hence, as far as possible future developments are concerned, there are different options for the actors of logistic service provision as shown in Figure 12.3. Every logistic service has to combine successfully the two concepts of product and transport logistics. The same holds for the ports of the future. As a node, it represents the physical and functional link between logistic and transport networks. The degree to which the ports are prepared for the future is an empirical question. Compare the requirements to be met in the case of an international main logistic centre (see Table 12.2 in Section 12.3.2). They can serve as a checklist.

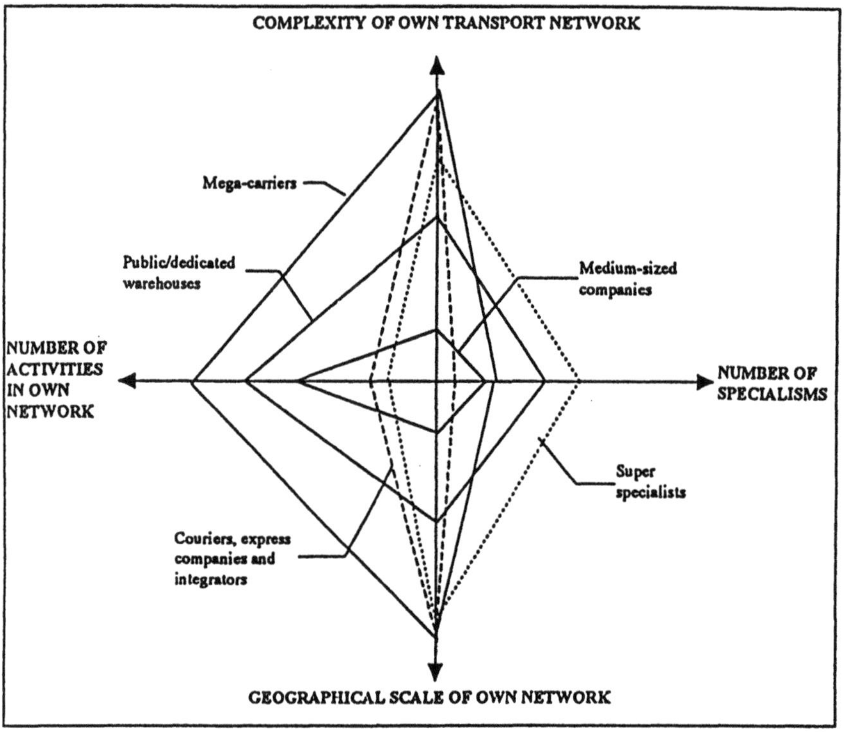

Figure 12.3 Possible future developments/actors in the market of logistics service provision

Source: Janssen 1994.

12.3 Ports: From Competition to Cooperation

The rise of product channel logistics, combined with transport logistics, implies a new way of structuring transeuropean networks (TENs). A guiding principle is that of corridors. Once the corridor principle has been adopted, different modes of transport and types of infrastructure will be approached in an integrated manner, not separately as in the present practice of planning transeuropean networks. Apart from road, rail and inland waterways, one also has to look at pipelines, airports and telematics. Infrastructure planning in cross-border regions calls for special attention. Insufficient coordination creates problems as in the case of the Betuwe line where the decision of the Dutch government regarding the cross-border link does not concord with the decision of the government of Nordrhein–Westfalen. The new way of organizing TENs leads to the planning of inland terminals, logistic platforms, distribution centres and the like at appropriate locations along the corridor, both in the country of origin and abroad (asking for an efficient coordination of both transport and spatial planning). This kind of developments can lead to a deconcentration of port-related activities. This trend can hardly be expected to stop at the border. But problems may arise if the policy stances of different member countries of the EU are not compatible. Take for example the Dutch-German case of the provinces of Limburg and Noord-Brabant, favouring locations of logistic activities, which meets the opposition of Nordrhein-Westfalen and of certain municipalities in particular. Among the con arguments are a low value added and environmental risks. But how about links between corridors originating in different ports, say, Rotterdam, Antwerp or other ports of the Hamburg-Le Havre type? One may consider sea-sea links, in especial short sea. More important, however, seem strategies of cooperation.

12.3.1 The Competitive World of Ports

Seen from a distance, the Rhine-Scheldt Delta may appear as one coherent port region. In reality, however, there is a lot of competition among its constituent ports. Even recent strategic alliances like those between Rotterdam and Flushing (the latter is not shown on the map), Antwerp and Zeebrugge or Ghent-Terneuzen are rather intended to strengthen the competitive position of the larger ports of each couple vis-à-vis the rest. Only recently the Association of Flemish ports has launched a plan that aims at a farreaching cooperation among the Flemish ports of Antwerp, Zeebrugge, Ghent and Oostende – against 'the rest', including the Dutch ports.

Especially Rotterdam and Antwerp see themselves as competitors rather than as partners. There are firms operating in or from both ports, but the port authorities and municipalities in question do not seem to be inclined to cooperate. Despite the fact that both seaports possess certain complementarities and that the two cities might even constitute potential intercity network (Drewe 1994).

The problems rising from the competitive attitudes can be illustrated by the recent plan to build the Betuwe line. Each of the two ports, located at a distance of some 100 kilometres from each other, favours its own rail connection for the transport of goods to the German hinterland. In the case of Antwerp the link, the so-called IJzeren Rijn, already exists, but needs upgrading. The existing rail line for freight that could connect both port areas stops at the former Dutch-Belgian border (not too far from Antwerp). The case of the Betuwe line demonstrates that a transeuropean network – between the Netherlands and Germany – may foster competition instead of cohesion – between the ports of Rotterdam and Antwerp. Competition is not limited to infrastructure projects, witness e.g. the concern about terms of employment, recently expressed by transport unions from Belgium, Germany and the Netherlands. See also the frequent complaints about 'unfair competition' caused by different national regimes of subsidization. Considering the amount of capital investment needed to equip a port region and its related infrastructural hinterland networks in line with the latest technology, competition may be a costly strategy. How about, for example, Le Havre's 'Port-2000' plan, a mega-container project aiming at strengthening Le Havre's competitive position especially vis-à-vis Hamburg and Rotterdam? What is at stake here is the causal linkage between public investment in seaports (transport infrastructure) and long term employment as well as value added (Debisschop et al. 1995).

12.3.2 In Search of Complementarities

The socioeconomic cohesion of the Community may be served by a strategic cooperation of ports rather than by unchecked competition. This, in turn, could help to improve the competitive position of Community ports vis-a-vis the 'rest of the world'. It asks for further study which, in the first place, could cover the ports of the Hamburg-Le Havre range.

Lessons from cross-border cooperation or inter-city networks for that matter, teach us that complementarity is a key factor in cooperation. In search of complementarities, it is important to position potential partners. How to position the ports of the Hamburg-Le Havre range?

Let us first take a look at recent research focusing on flows of goods between four seaport regions and their hinterland (NEA 1995a). The four regions selected for study are:

- Netherlands (Zuid-Holland, Noord-Holland);
- Belgium (Antwerp);
- Northwest-Germany (Hamburg, Bremen);
- Northwest-France (Nord-Pas de Calais, Haute-Normandie, Basse-Normandie).

Their distribution function has been analysed per mode of transport, i.e. road, rail and inland waterways. The main results are that the Dutch ports excel in inland-waterway distribution of basic, agricultural and oil products (covering the river basin of the Rhine, Main and Moselle, among others). The German and Belgian ports have a strong international position as far as sea-road transport is concerned. In Germany there is a strong North-South orientation whereas Belgium has considerable influence in Eastern Europe, especially in Poland. And, finally, sea-rail distribution is a speciality of the German ports, mainly oriented towards Central and Eastern Europe. See Maps 12.1a through 12.1c for details. The exploratory study also deals with the cost - efficiency (least costs) of different modes of transport, measured in guilders per ton-kilometre. The main reason for commissioning the study has been to identify both opportunities and threats with respect to the present position of Dutch ports as a European distribution centre. It has been shown clearly that the function of the Netherlands in Europe is far from unique.

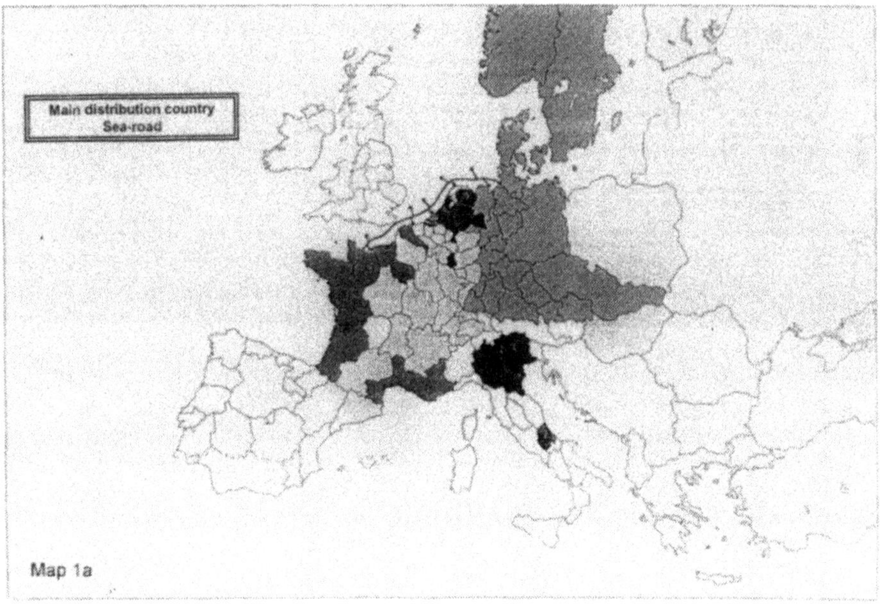

Maps 12.1a, 12.1b, 12.1c: Most important North-European country in the distribution from/to regions of the hinterland by road in 1990 (more than 20,000 tons)

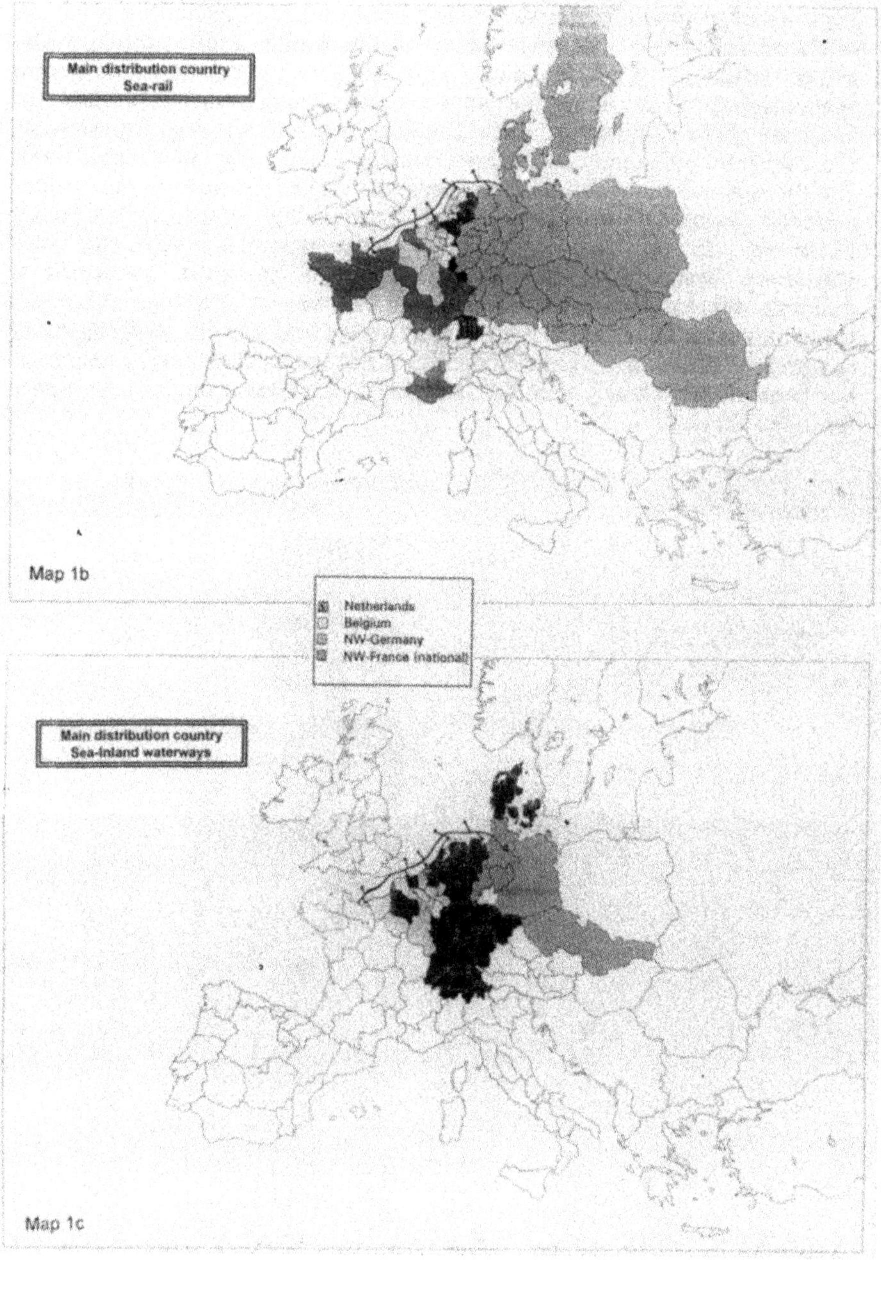
Main distribution country
Sea-rail
Map 1b
Netherlands
Belgium
NW-Germany
NW-France (national)
Main distribution country
Sea-inland waterways
Map 1c

Once again, the larger ports in Northwest-Europe are revealed as competitors. But it has also been indicated that they are, to some extent, complementary to one another: as to modes of transport and their cost efficiency. Even if the method applied is still a classic one that does not yet take into account the impact product channel and transport logistics might have on the positioning of ports. The study results also lend credence to the Hamburg-Le Havre range as a multiport system notwithstanding the dominant position of the Dutch ports distributing more than 149 million tons of goods as against some 140 million towns of the Belgian, Northwest German and Northwest French ports taken together.

Trends in (international) freight transport, however, seem to favour mainport development: a concentration of flows of goods in one port only; trends like economies of scale in shipping, 'global transport', regrouping of flows, specialization of carriers and door-to-door integration of transport services. Only the increase in the number of small consignments seems to work in favour of multiport (provided that a regrouping in the port is not possible). But these trends do not alter the fact that mainport development is still an empirical question. Empirical evidence (Knaapen 1993) suggests that a multiport system should at least no be discarded hastily. A large majority of US shippers of forest and food products, e.g., reaches their European destinations via a number of European ports and does not intend to change this pattern. This is also related to the fact that their European clients (producers and importers) are dispersed over Europe and prefer the port nearest to their country (which determines the choice of the shipping company to be contracted). Multiport-shipping companies include several ports in their regular service in order to reach the largest possible hinterland in accordance with their clients' preferences. Moreover, choosing a mainport strategy causes feeder costs that exceed the costs of calling at an additional port (nevertheless, the number of European ports of call is expected to be reduced to three or four as far as regular services are concerned). What about complementarities in the light of product channel and transport logistics? It is generally expected that platforms or terminals will be hierarchically positioned. This also holds in essence for future ports as nodes of logistic networks. See Table 12.2 for a new hierarchy of distribution centres.

Is not the main problem today that all ports of the Hamburg-Le Havre range (or elsewhere) more or less aspire to the level of an international main logistic centre? Many ports may be called, but only few will most probably be chosen, because not all ports are able to meet the requirements. Unchecked competition only causes excessive costs. Finally, the maritime main centres are likely to the take the form of a multiport system.

Table 12.2 New hierarchy of distribution centres

Type of Node	Characteristics
International main logistic centre (mainport)	· Located at main economic development and transport axes · directly linked to intercontinental flows · technically advanced combined loading/unloading facilities for road and rail · intermodal facilities for road/rail and water transport · sophisticated information exchange facilities (EDI) capacity and space to handle/store large quantities of different types of goods for different customers to different quality levels · availability of vacant space for logistic platforms of all different kinds of logistic/producers services
International logistic centre	· located at main European transport axes · active on various international networks and flows · functions as logistic platform for consolidation/de-consolidation of nearly all types of products · various logistic and producer services · dominant mode is truck, but also accessible by rail and combined rail/road transport
International transport and distribution centre	· located at important international transport axes to and from the mainports · function primarily as favoured locations for transfer, transhipment, storage and/or distribution activities of international operating carriers and shippers · dominant mode is truck. Many are also linked by another mode of transport, rail or water
Regional transport & distribution centre	· located at junctions and others platforms in infrastructural networks and/or platforms for the distribution of goods within about 50 km · predominant location factor is size of the market (population), degree of competition for space · spatial clusters of transport companies

Source: Janssen 1993.

The 'Gateway to Europe' can hardly be monopolized by one mainport. But a multiport system, consisting of a limited number of mainports, implies that a number of existing ports will have to settle for a lower rank in the hierarchy of international, national or even regional and local reach (the 'maritime' equivalents of the 'terrestrial' hierarchy of distribution centres still need to be defined preferably as constituent parts of logistic networks). From a container-port point of view, a reshaped market may be divided into three major categories: major deep-sea hub terminals, secondary feeder locations and smaller ports where limited container handling was a function of a broader multipurpose facility. To implement such a new hierarchy of ports is another way of achieving complementarity.

As we said before (in Section 12.2.2), there are two ways in which the conventional approach to the positioning of ports is changing under the impact of product channel logistics. On the one hand, 'tonnage thinking' needs to be replaced by 'chain and value-added thinking' and on the other emphasis must shift from physical accessibility to controlled and dedicated logistic accessibility and hence to the complimentary relationships between services and facilities. Searching for complementarities and – subsequently – cooperation, both sides are to be delved.

But the search should go beyond the economics of port development. Advocates of product channel (transport) logistics may claim that the very essence of this kind of economic-technical innovation is to foster sustainable development as it provides an alternative to the dominant tonnage-growth model. Big, today, may be bad when it comes to the environmental costs of port activities. Among the priorities are: dangerous goods, water pollution, problems related to dredging operations, port-city relations and restructuring of derelict areas, air pollution, wastes, land/soil contamination, industrial plant regulations, visual contamination, stench and noise. Note that these 11 priorities, listed in decreasing order of importance, are a result of research carried out among 218 ports/port organizations' terminal operators covering 51 maritime nations worldwide. See also the checklist of port-related environmental impacts, developed by the World Bank as an aide-memoire both for port planners and developers and World Bank staff engaged in the appraisal of lending operations related to port development (Dankfort 1995).

Hence it is essential to also consider the specific environmental and spatial setting of ports in the search for complementarities. This should be viewed in relation to key indicators such as population density. The Hamburg-Le Havre range of port regions covers a variety of population densities. Among the most urgent environmental problems are those emanating from the present modal split relating to the transport of goods. In the period 1970–1990 road transport has increased by almost 100 percent whereas rail has lost about 15 percent (transport by inland waterways has roughly remained constant and pipeline transport has grown by more than 10 percent). Hence road transport obviously presents the biggest problem. In searching for solutions, four avenues can be distinguished (Verhage 1994):

- reduction of total number of ton-kilometres: through changes in the spatial structure and internalization of external costs;
- technical improvements of vehicles ('green technology'): improvement of existing modes and of driving and sailing habits, using the potentials of telecommunication technologies;
- optimalization of transport logistics ('green logistic'): telecommunication technologies, trip planning techniques ('fuller', 'less empty', 'bigger'), introduction of sophisticated logistic transport concepts, improvement of the use of intermodal transport;
- shift to more environmentally sound modes of transport ('green transport'): sophisticated logistic transport concepts, intermodal transport, change of modal split.

Each avenue is not only described in terms of types of intervention, but comprises physical and regulative measures, too. It should be noted that internalizing the environmental costs of transport should not be limited to road transport, but rather cover all modes of transport.

12.4 Future Ports or 'The Art of the Long View'

Cooperation still appears to be far cry from the way port authorities view their business. Research has shown that the authorities of seaports in Western Europe are mainly interested in increasing their market share at the expense of range competitors, as well as in diversifying their activities. Growth rates remain the foremost indicator of port efficiency which unfortunately implies a very limited concept of efficiency. Any attempt to develop a strategy of cooperation must take this into account (even if the prisoners' dilemma suggests that cooperation pays off). Port authorities are business firms sui generis. May be there are lessons to be learned from the experience of 'ordinary' firms with strategic cooperation, preferably firms operating in or from ports. In sectors like sea transport, road transport and distribution, some firms have already embarked on a cooperation course. In general, strategic cooperation often is only sought when other strategies are not feasible, say, mergers, take-overs or go-it-alone strategies. Of course, there are both advantages and disadvantages involved in cooperation. The advantages include cost sharing, risk reduction, gain of time, synergy and economies of scope, opportunities for specialization, increase in flexibility, access to markets and the like. Some disadvantages are inherent: cultural differences, a lesser degree of freedom, opportunism, instability and so forth. Other disadvantages (control, undesired dependence etc.) can be met. In an uncertain world it does not suffice to simply extrapolate present (growth) trends into the future as they are most likely to break in the next 25 years. Scenarios may help to scan alternative futures (Schwartz

1991). In a recent study in the Netherlands, three scenarios have been elaborated dealing with structural change in world-trade flows:

- 'global village' (the worldwide liberalization makes it easier to export from one location to the rest of the world);
- 'global crisis' (an economic crisis leads to a regionalized production, but may also cause its centralization in the most productive locations);
- 'greening of business' (a stronger emphasis on the environment will probably lead to less transport and hence 'globalization'; some production processes, however from a global environmental policy point of view, might also be served by worldwide centralization) (Junne et al. 1993).

These scenarios have different impacts on the transport, trade and distribution function of the Netherlands (in which the port of Rotterdam holds a pivotal position). If one measures the impact in volume of goods, different estimates emerge (see Table 12.3).

Table 12.3 The transport, trade and distribution function of the Netherlands, three scenarios: 1990-2015 (a synthesis of 10 groups of goods at world level)

	1990 (x1 million tons)	Global village (1990=100)	Global recession (1990=100)	Greening of business (1990=100)
Transport	130.2	125	99	69
Trade	146.5	122	105	72
Distribution	71.3	129	108	67
Total	**348.2**	**124**	**103**	**70**

The Netherlands loses most in the greening of business-scenario, more or less maintains its position in the case of the global recession-scenario and only wins in the case of the global village scenario. It can be concluded from this that the 'mainport' ambition stands or falls with the global village scenario. In fact, the Port of Rotterdam (1995) has also developed four scenarios only one of which pictures the future of the port as 'mainport'. As the future, alternatively, may have in store: a 'controlport' (subject to farreaching European regulations), a 'leanport' (optimizing the existing facilities with a minimum amount of new investment) or – finally – a 'serviceport' (focusing on logistic services and environmental innovation).

Moving up the Hamburg-Le Havre range, one also runs into scenarios for the (port) region of Hamburg (Läpple et al. 1994). This time only two alternative futures have been elaborated: a competitive location scenario ('Standortkonkurrenz') as opposed to a 'milieu policy' led scenario ('Milieupolitik'). The former mirrors the traditional growth-oriented regional policy, dominated by 'economics of scale' thinking (combined with lean production and global sourcing) and marked by an 'Eurogate' ambition for the region. The 'Milieupolitik' scenario, contrastingly, stresses the use of endogenous development potentials and a strengthening of regional production and innovative milieus or environments. In order to assess the regional impact of the two scenarios the Hamburg economy has been split up into eleven clusters of economic activities ranging from 'port, storage, transport' to the public sector.

Two kinds of impacts have been singled out for analysis: employment and land use. The overall results in terms of employment are rather negative, except for producer services and urban (public) consumer services. Only the milieu policy led scenario offers possibilities for extenuating employment losses in the urban industrial cluster and for stabilizing the employment situation of city-district and neighborhood firms. The competitive location scenario, in general, demands more space, especially the 'port, storage, transport' cluster (but with the exception of seaport industries, the urban industrial cluster, the insurance cluster, city-district and neighborhood firms, and the public sector.

A lesser growth of land use overall is to be expected in the case of the 'Milieupolitik' scenario. The demand for space mostly only slightly increases, remains constant or even decreases (except for trade, producer and urban services).

The port region of Hamburg, in the period 1989–1991, has been the most prosperous region of the EC out of 179 NUTS 2 regions, according to its level of GDP per head. The scenarios, however, teach us that even Hamburg has to arm itself against an uncertain world.

Scenario planning is a tool that can help to understand the implications of alternative futures. Whenever scenarios are developed, this is a sure sign of uncertainty related to processes, objectives and means. But how to manage these uncertainties (Drewe and Janssen 1996)? They might be reduced in several ways:

- further research (as far as processes or the operating environment is concerned);
- clearer objectives (particularly in the case of conflicting interests);
- more or different means (in order to achieve the objectives);
- a more coordinated approach (involving relevant parties or even competitors).

A more coordinated approach – this is where a strategy of cooperation among ports comes in, as an antidote to unchecked competition. Cooperation may go a long way towards reducing uncertainty, but unlikely the whole way. So it may also be necessary to accept uncertainties to some extent. Then one can only resort to flexibility to be achieved by an intelligent phasing of the implementation of plans;

distinguishing immediate actions, delayed actions and contingency plans. Of course, one can also opt for a risky laisser-faire.

The different ways of coping with uncertainty all belong to the strategic planner's tool box. In recent years another way has emerged, referred to as innovative environment (milieu) and/or knowledge infrastructure. It is closely related to technology and know-how which – according to UNCTAD (1991) – are decisive factors to third-generation or value-adding ports whereas first generation traditional ports and second-generation industrial ports depended on respectively labour/capital and capital. In other words, the port of the future must be continuously innovative.

The port of Rotterdam, for example, has created a foundation charged with the mainport-knowledge infrastructure (Stichting Kennis-infrastructuur 1995). Three spearheads have been selected, i.e. mainport strategy, transport and logistics, (petro)chemical industry.

The foundation's activities cover interrelated projects such as:

- a round table (with two pilot studies, one dealing with value-added dry bulk logistics, the other with a simulation model for logistic chains);
- a centre for simulation and training;
- a regional college dedicated to vocational training in the field of process industry;
- an educational electronic highway.

A knowledge infrastructure has a supply and demand side. In order to turn into an innovative environment for the port and its region, it is vital that supply and demand become tuned to each other. Do the foundation's organizational structure and functioning provide sufficient guaranty for that? As a matter of fact, the demand side often has to set up its own research projects because it either does not know whom to turn to or does not expect to receive adequate answers to its questions. Suppliers of knowledge, on the other hand, are willing to work for the firms in question, but often formulate the topics themselves before 'the market' has had its say. This conclusion is drawn from research with regard to the transport and distribution sectors' knowledge infrastructure in the Netherlands as a whole (NEA 1993b). See also the related research topic of innovation in the transport sector (NEA 1995b).

A milieu – as assumed in the case of Hamburg's milieu policy-led scenario – is characterized by:

- a collective of actors (entrepreneurs, research and training institutions, local authorities and so forth) that are relatively independent in their decision making and in their formulation of strategic choices;
- material elements such as firms and infrastructures as well as immaterial (know-how) and institutional elements (different forms of local authorities and decision making organizations);

- a synergetic interaction and cooperation between actors: the whole of the know-how of the actors being more than the sum of their individual knowhow;
- a learning process ('apprenticeship') in which the actors in the course of time develop the capability of modifying their behaviour and of implementing new solutions reacting to a changing environment (Maillat 1994).

A milieu qualifies as an innovative environment if it fosters innovations such as new or improved products, processes and services that are commercially successful or non-market goods and services that are socially accepted. The European Research Group on Innovative Enviroments (GREMI), from 1987 onward, has provided ample empirical evidence on this kind of milieus. Its current research program focuses on urban innovative environments. The Regional Technology Plan, a pilot action of the European Commission (1994b), looks as if it has been modelled upon the GREMI research experience or as if it has at least been inspired by it (especially after having been rebaptized recently as 'Regional Innovation Strategy'). The final question, however, is whether ports will be able to practice the art of the long view and, in doing so, will cope successfully with uncertainty. According to a Dutch writer, 'tomorrow was written yesterday'. As the example of Rotterdam has shown, the growth model was written in the late 1960s. There are good reasons for rewriting tomorrow today.

References

Anderson, D., (1989), *Product Channel Management. The Next Revolution in Logistics*, Temple, Barker & Sloane, Lexington, Mass.

Commissie Betuweroute, (1995), *Rapport*, Den Haag, no. 29.

Commissie van de Europese Gemeenschappen, (1991), *De Regio's in de Jaren Negentig*, Brussel and Luxemburg.

Commission of the European Communities, (1991), *Europe 2000, Outlook for the Development of the Community's Territory*, Brussels and Luxembourg, 14.

Dankfort, J.M.M., (1995), 'Chain Analysis as a Tool for Value-Adding Port Planning, with Special Reference to Brazil', *OPB*, Bouwkunde, Delft University of Technology.

Debisschop, K. et al., (1995), 'Problematiek van de Causaliteit tussen Overheidsinvesteringen in Infrastructuur en Duurzame Toegevoegde Waarde', *Tijdschrift Vervoerswetenschap*, vol. 3, pp. 253–77.

Drewe, P., (1994), 'The Towns of Benelux Faced with the Challenge of Transborder Cooperation', *Regions of Europe*, no. 9, pp. 29–33.

Drewe, P. and Janssen, B., (1996), 'The Betuwe Line: an Evaluation', EUREG, *European Journal of Regional Development*, vol. 3, pp. 44–9.

European Commission (1994a), *Competitiveness and Cohesion: Trends in the Regions*, Brussels and Luxembourg.
European Commission, (1994b), *Regional Technology Plan Guide Book*, CM International, Vlizy-Villacoublay.
Gemeente Rotterdam, (1990), 'Delta 2000-8, Naar een Grootschalig Containeroverslag- en Goederendistributiecentrum op de Maasvlakte', Rotterdam.
Haven van Rotterdam, (1986), Spoorweghaven Rotterdam, Rotterdam, 7.
Janssen, B.J.P., (1991), 'Product Channel Logistics Networks and a Changing Spatial Organization, Conceptual Issues and Empirical Results', in Savy, M. and P. Veltz (eds), *Flux Logistiques et Organisation du Territoire*, CERTES-ENPC, Paris.
Janssen, B.J.P., (1993), 'Product Channel Logistics and Logistic Platforms', in Nijkamp, P. (ed.), *Europe on the Move, Recent Developments in European Communications and Transport Activity Research*, pp. 173–85.
Janssen, B.J.P., (1994), 'The Spatial Behaviour of Logistic Service Providers', NEA, Zuid, Tilburg.
Junne, G. et al., (1993), Eindrapport structuurverandering in wereldhandelsstromen, Faculteit Politieke en Sociaal-culturele Wetenschappen, Universiteit van Amsterdam.
Knaapen, M., (1993), *Mainport versus Multiport, een Onderzoek naar de Trend tot het Concentreren van Goederenstromen in één Haven*, Buck Consultants International, Nijmegen.
Läpple, D. et al., (1994), *Strukturentwicklung und Zukunftperspektiven der Hamburger Wirtschaft unter rumlichen Gesichtpunkten, Clusterstruktur und Szenarien*, second revised edition, Technische Universitat Hamburg-Harburg.
Louter, P.J. and De Ruyter, P.A., (1995), *Ruimtelijk-Economische Ontwikkelingspatronen in Nederland*, INRO/TNO, Delft.
Maillat, D., (1994), 'Comportements Spatiaux et Milieux Innovateurs', in Auray, J.-P et al. (eds), *Encyclopdie d'Économie Spatiale, Concepts-Comportements-Organisations*, Economica, Paris, 255–62.
NEA Transportonderzoek en -opleiding, (1993a), De Transport-, Handels- en Distributiefunctie van Nederland, Tilburg.
NEA Transportonderzoek en -opleiding, (1993b), Voorverkenning Kennisinfrastructuur in de Transport & Distributiesector, Tilburg.
NEA, Transportonderzoek en -opleiding, (1995a), Verkenningsstudie ter Bepaling Internationale Transportketens; Kansen en Bedreigingen voor de Nederlandse Distributiefunctie, Rijswijk.
NEA Transportonderzoek en -opleiding, (1995b), Innovatie in de Transportsector: Rijswijk.
NEA Transport Research & Training and Cranfield School of Management, CLT, (1994), Future Logistics Structures, the Development of Integrated Supply Chain Management across 6 Industry Sectors, Synthesis Report, Tilburg/Cranfield, pp. 11–2.

Port of Rotterdam, (1995), Rotterdam dàn... een Scenario-Verkenning; Mainport, Controlport, Leanport & Serviceport, Directie Haveninnovatie, Rotterdam.
Roodenburg, H.J., (1989), 'Central Locations in the European Common Market', Research Memorandum, no. 59, Centraal Planbureau, The Hague.
Ruijgrok, C.J. et al., (1991), 'Sustainable Development and Infrastructure', INRO/TNO, Delft.
Schwartz, P., (1991), *The Art of the Long View, Scenario Planning – Protecting your Company Against an Uncertain Future*, Century Business, London.
Stichting Kennisinfrastructuur Mainport Rotterdam, (1995), Jaarplan 1995, Begroting en Meerjarenraming, Concept, Rotterdam.
UNCTAD Secretariat, (1991), 'Port Marketing and the Challenge of the Third Generation Port', United Nations, Geneva.
Van Klink, H.A., (1993), 'De Rotterdamse Haven als Schakel in Transportketens', *Economisch Statistische Berichten*, vol. 78, pp. 268–71.
Verhage, R., (1994), 'Goederenvervoer, Ruimtelijke Ordening en Milieu, naar een Ruimtelijk Inrichtingsconcept voor een Minder Milieubelastend Goederenvervoer', Rijksplanologische Dienst, Den Haag.
Winkelmans, W., (1991), Een Strategische Positionering van de Zeehavens in het Scheldebekken, Zomer Universiteit Zeeland, Vlissingen/Middelburg.

13 Transport of Goods Between the Nordic Countries and the European Mainland

SIMO PASI AND VELI HIMANEN

13.1 Introduction

Fundamental political changes have led and are leading to internationalization of trade, deregulation of economic activities, and the elimination of frontiers between the European countries. In addition to the political and organizational changes, the development of the transportation infrastructure and the general technological advancement – not least in telematics – have impact on the future of the transport sector in Europe. Higher train speeds and the introduction of fast ships will also have impact on the European goods transportation. Further on, the attention to environment is getting more and more importance besides the changes in infrastructure and technology. In the near future, the most significant change in the transportation network of the Nordic countries will be the construction of a fixed land link between Sweden and Germany via Denmark.

This chapter aims at identifying the main actors involved in the transport of goods between the Nordic countries and the European mainland. Finland, Sweden, Norway and Denmark are dealt with, but Iceland is left outside the sphere of this study. In addition to the identification of the main actors, their objectives and strategies are studied, as well as the synergies and conflicts between them.

In broad terms, the actors can be divided into two main categories: logistics service consumers (consignors and consignees) on one hand and logistics service providers on the other. The emphasis of this paper is on the consumption of logistics services. In addition to these actor groups, the public sector plays an important role in the transport of goods. Regulation of other actors' behaviour, financing of the transport infrastructure and taxation of transport activities are the principle actions of the public sector.

What are the policies of the different actors and what strategies do they follow in order to fulfil their missions? This question will be treated in Section 13.2 of this paper besides the typology of actors. The analysis of policies and strategies is a basis for the identification of synergies and conflicts of the actors in Section 13.3. Synergy means the positive results of combining actors' special knowhow. Conflicts are divided into two categories for further treatment: the conflicts of benefit and the conflicts of value. Finally, the needs for further research are dealt with in Section 13.4.

This chapter forms a part of the Finnish contribution to the 'COST Action 328 – Integrated Strategic Infrastructure Networks in Europe' of the Commission of the European Community and it has been financed by the Ministry of Transport and Communications in Finland.

13.2 Actors Involved in Logistics and their Strategies

As stated in the Section Two of this chapter, the actors involved in the transport of goods can be divided roughly into demand and supply sides of logistics services. Additionally, the public administration is a very influential actor and its activities have impact on both the demand and supply sides of the goods transport. The demand for logistics services stems from those actors who produce, distribute, or consume the goods. The providers of logistics services do not normally work up the goods that they transport, handle and stock. Of course, in many cases there are no strict limits between the users and providers of the logistics services. However, this division is fundamental when we analyse the strategies of the different actors.

13.2.1 Demand for Logistics Services

Raw materials are refined by the artisans or the industrial enterprises, distributed by the traders, consumed by the households or the public sector, and finally treated by waste handling organizations. The majority of goods flows start and end in the premises of these actors. It is, first of all, the geographic distribution of raw materials, production, and consumption that generates commodity flows across the continent. Another important factor affecting foreign trade is the purchasing power of private and public consumers.

In an investigation of the goods transport between the Nordic countries and the European mainland, the following actor groups affecting the goods flows have to be taken into account:

- sources of raw materials and raw material suppliers (production),
- manufacturing and power generation companies (production and consumption),
- trade enterprises (distribution),
- households (consumption),
- public sector (consumption), and
- waste handling organizations (recycling and destruction).

These actor groups are presented in the paragraphs below. The following aspects of each group will be treated: the most important branches of activity, number of actors, and the policies and tendencies behind the behaviour of these actors.

Raw Material Suppliers and Industrial Companies Mining and quarrying, oil drilling, agriculture, forestry, and fishing are the most important sources of raw materials for manufacturing, trade, and consumption. Moreover, these activities create large amounts of waste, even more than ten times the amount of municipal waste in several European countries (EiF 1995). European countries have large natural resources, although there are great differences between the different countries and regions as regards the quantity and the utilization of these resources. Mining, quarrying, and oil drilling have concentrated around the deposits of these resources. On the contrary, agriculture, forestry and fishing are distributed over a wide area in every country. The structure and technology of these activities, of course, vary considerably from one country to another.

The volume of the raw material flows between the Nordic countries and the European mainland can be estimated on the basis of the foreign trade statistics. Even though the foreign trade statistics only deal with monetary value of the trade, they still give a valuable source of information as regards the commodity flows. It is obvious that the production of energy is the key factor to explain the raw material flows of the Nordic countries (Tables 13.1 and 13.2). Norway is the most important oil exporting country in Europe and the other Nordic countries import oil in great quantities because of the climatic conditions, lack of crude oil, and the high density of motor vehicles.

Fishing is an important industry in those Nordic countries that neighbour the Atlantic Ocean. Exporting of fish and related products is a natural source of income in these countries where the population is very small with respect to the amount of fishing ground.

Denmark is the only Nordic country in which the export of farming products plays an important role. In 1993, this trade was almost entirely directed to the countries of the European Union. Other Nordic countries neither exported nor imported farming products in considerable quantities.

Due to the appropriate climate and low population density, forestry has attained an important role in the economy of Sweden and Finland. For example, the transport of wood alone made up 14 percent of the total transport performance on Finnish roads in 1993 (FINRA 1994) and 25 percent of the total transport performance on Finnish railroads in 1991 (Statistics Finland 1992).

The organizational structure in exploiting natural resources varies between the industrial branches in the Nordic countries. In 1990 there were 16 establishments in Norway dealing with extraction of petroleum and natural gas, and 6 of them employed more than 500 persons. (EiE vol. II 1994). The same kind of industrial structure applies to the import of crude oil in Sweden, Denmark and Finland; there are only 9 petroleum refineries in Sweden, 3 in Denmark and 4 in Finland. In average, petroleum refineries employ more than 1000 employees (YNS 1995). Thus both the import and export of crude oil is very centralized in the Nordic countries which probably is a natural consequence of the production technology.

Table 13.1 Export of raw materials and manufactured goods from the Nordic countries to the European Union in 1993. Trade between the Nordic countries is included

Export flow	Value (million ECU)	Primary origins in the Nordic countries
Petroleum, petroleum products and related material	12 600	Norway
Paper, paperboard and articles thereof	8 100	Finland and Sweden
General industrial machinery and equipment	4 200	Sweden, Denmark and Finland
Road vehicles	3 900	Sweden
Fish, crustaceans and molluscs, and preparations thereof	3 600	Norway, Denmark
Iron and steel	3 500	Sweden and Finland
Miscellaneous manufactured articles	3200	Denmark and Sweden
Electrical machinery, apparatus and appliances	2 800	Sweden and Denmark
Non-ferrous metals	2 800	Norway
Telecommunications and audio - visual equipment	2 500	Sweden and Finland
Wood	2 400	Sweden and Finland
Machinery specialized for particular industries	2 400	Sweden, Denmark and Finland
Medical and pharmaceutical products	2 300	Sweden and Denmark
Manufactures of metal	2 300	Sweden and Denmark
Gas, natural and manufactured	2 100	Norway
Furniture and parts thereof	2 000	Denmark, Sweden
Meat and meat preparations	1 800	Denmark

Source: YNS 1995.

Table 13.2 Import of raw materials and manufactured goods to the Nordic countries from the European Union in 1993. Trade between the Nordic countries is included

Import flow	Value (million ECU)	Primary destinations in the Nordic countries
Road vehicles	4 600	Sweden, Denmark and Norway
Petroleum, petroleum products and related material	4 500	Sweden, Finland and Denmark
Electrical machinery, apparatus and appliances	4 400	Sweden, Finland and Denmark
General industrial machinery and equipment	4 200	Sweden, Denmark and Norway
Iron and steel	3 100	Sweden, Norway and Denmark
Manufactures of metal	2 400	Sweden and Denmark
Office machines and automatic data processing machines	2 400	Sweden, Denmark and Norway
Machinery specialized for particular industries	2 400	Sweden and Norway
Paper, paperboard, and articles thereof	2 200	Denmark
Articles of apparel and clothing accessories	2 100	Sweden, Denmark and Norway

Source: YNS 1995.

Fisheries and farming are much less concentrated than the production of petroleum products, and there are many actors dealing with the exploitation of flora and fauna. For example, in 1993 there were 74 000 agricultural holdings in Denmark and 31 000 of them raised cattle (see YNS 1995).

In summary, raw materials cause relatively few important commodity flows in the foreign trade of the Nordic countries and the most important single flow is the export of Norwegian petroleum and this flow is controlled by a low number of actors.

The location of manufacturing enterprises is mainly influenced by the location of markets, the sources of energy, and the availability of raw materials. Additionally, there are several other elements that guide the spatial distribution of manufacturing capacity: They are the prices for energy and raw materials, the labour costs and the qualification and adequacy of work force, subsidies and taxation, the local competition and traditions, and the environmental standards, for example.

Nevertheless, the availability of raw materials and energy is crucial for many industries that generate voluminous commodity flows. The Finnish forest industry is a good example of an industrial branch that is located close to the raw material sources. Consequently, the existence of a large industry generates extensive goods flows: In 1991, nearly 20 percent of the goods transport performance of the Finnish State Railways and 6 percent of the total road transport performance dealt with the transport of forest industry's products (FinRA 1994; Statistics Finland 1992).

In addition to the transport of energy and raw materials, the transport of manufactured goods is a key factor in explaining the type and amount of freight between the Nordic countries and Western Europe. There are seventeen commodity groups that make up over 50 percent of that intra-European trade where the Nordic countries are involved (see Tables 13.1 and 13.2).

It seems that the trade between the Nordic countries and the other areas of the European Union has concentrated on such commodities that can be used by manufacturing enterprises as raw materials (export and import of metals and products of the forest industry) or as production machinery (import and export of machinery for industry). There are few important products which are destined to the consumer market (road vehicles, electrical appliances and pharmaceutical products). Therefore the dynamics of the foreign trade can be explained by the dynamics and strategies of the industry rather than by demographical patterns.

In the last two decades many managers and consultants have recognized that logistics has strategic importance for the competitiveness of industrial companies. There are two principal ways to compete with logistics: the reduction of costs and the improvement of customer service.

There are several names for the new principles guiding the location of companies and the transport frequencies of raw materials, semi-finished parts and final products. The philosophy of these techniques have often been adopted from the Japanese manufactures. Just-in-time, zero inventories, and lean production have all similar characteristics. One key characteristic of the modern operations management is the elimination of stocks and redundant materials handling operations (Schonberger 1982). The increase of transport frequency and the simplification of handling operations can reduce capital tied up in stocks and thus improve the financial performance of the company. Another tendency is to improve customer service by cutting the throughput time of the total production and distribution process. The reduction of stocks and the speeding up of the delivery chain are simultaneous efforts.

Logistics connects different companies with each other. Operational alliances are groups of companies that join together in order to benefit from co-operation. Andersson (1995) has found three major groups of driving forces that influence the set-up of an operational alliance in logistics: reduction of costs, improved strategic flexibility, and need for structural change.

The modern production technologies also set requirements for the transport system. Deliveries should be frequent and reliable. Lot sizes go down because of the need to react quickly to the customers' requirements and because of the tendency to avoid obsolete stocks. The road haulage fits better than rail transport to the requirements of the fast production cycle.

In the Nordic countries the manufacturing industry has been very active in promoting the fixed link between Sweden, Denmark and Germany (Scandinavian Link 1987). Their interest can be explained by the establishment of international subcontracting networks and the growing requirements for flexibility and fast deliveries.

Wholesale distribution A large share of international trade is managed by the wholesale distributors. It is not possible to keep the different branches of wholesaling apart because of the generalizing statistical sources. Therefore the characteristics of the consumer products and the technical trading can not be distinguished in this overview.

However, it is interesting to pay attention to the concentration of wholesale distribution in the different Nordic countries. In this overview, the level of concentration is assessed on the basis of the percentage of turnover generated by companies of different size. The size of companies is measured by the number of employees. When the share of turnover generated by large companies is greater in one country than in another, the following reserved conclusion can be made: The business is more concentrated in those countries where the large companies' share of the total turnover is higher than in other countries (see Figure 13.1).

Figure 13.1 Concentration of wholesale distribution in four Nordic countries

Source: EiE vol. II 1995.

As regards the comparison between the different Nordic countries, it seems that the wholesale distribution is the most concentrated in Finland, where less than 50 percent of the turnover is generated by companies smaller than 200 employees. There are no data on the distribution of the other half of the turnover. On the contrary, in Norway and Denmark 75 percent of the turnover in wholesaling is generated by companies smaller than 200 employees. Wholesaling in Sweden is a bit more concentrated than that in Norway and Denmark, but less concentrated than wholesaling in Finland (EiE 1994, vol. II).

What conclusions can be drawn on the basis of the concentration in wholesaling? First, if the observed concentration applies to foreign trade, it can be concluded that especially in Finland and in Sweden a large amount of incoming commodity flows are controlled by fewer companies than in Denmark and Norway. Further on, concentration of wholesaling may give better possibilities for the large companies to optimize distribution activities, which gives a cost advantage to them. However, concentration may also decrease competition and lead to inefficiency in the wholesaling business.

Households It is obvious that households do not transport large quantities of commodities from one country to another. It is also clear that the amount of commodities exported directly by households is unimportant with respect to those quantities exported by industrial enterprises. However, private consumption still plays a vital role in explaining what goods and how much of them are exchanged between different countries.

There are two major factors that determine the influence of private consumption on foreign trade: demography and purchasing power of private citizens. Additionally, cultural differences, natural resources, and trade policies affect private consumption as well, but the number of consumers and their abilities of financing the consumption set clear limits to the amount of imports that can be consumed by households. In general, the Nordic countries are not densely populated, but the inhabitants of these countries have a relatively high standard of living. The high taxation and income transfers guarantee the basic standard of living in all social classes, but, on the other hand, decrease the purchasing power of the upper class.

Since 1950, the total population of the Nordic countries has passed 20 million inhabitants (see Figure 13.2). Population is growing rather slowly: In 1993, the excess of births with respect to deaths ranged from 0,9 (DK) to 3,0 (NOR) and the net immigration from 1,7 (FIN) to 3,7 (SWE) per 1000 of the mean population (YNS 1995).

Purchasing power can be evaluated on the basis of average income and taxation. There are no major differences in average net income between the four Nordic countries. The average yearly net income was almost 10000 ECU per inhabitant in 1992.

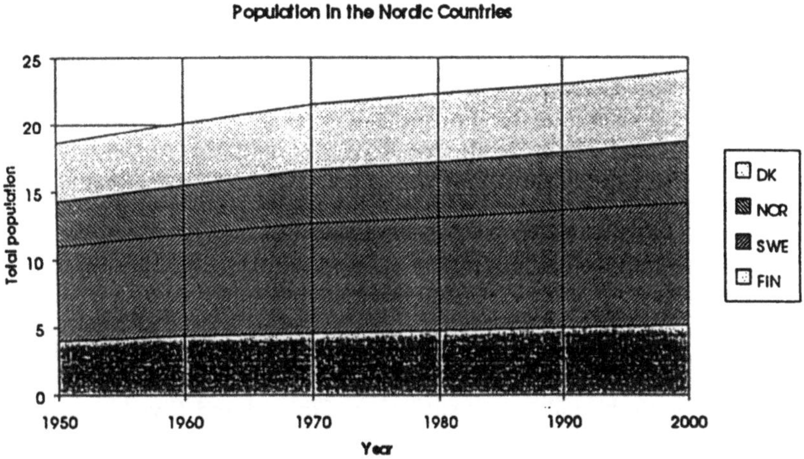

Figure 13.2 There are less than 25 million inhabitants in the Nordic countries

Source: YNS 1995.

What kind of commodities and services do the inhabitants of the Nordic countries purchase then? There are three groups that form up to 60 per cent of the households' expenditure: housing and heating, food and non alcoholic beverages, and transportation and communication (see Table 13.3).

Table 13.3 Households' expenditure in the Nordic countries in 1990

Expenditure group	Finland	Sweden	Norway	Denmark
Housing and heating (%)	17,0	25,5	26,6	34,5
Food and beverages (%)	18,6	18,4	15,6	14,4
Transport and communication (%)	18,0	17,6	19,3	15,7
Recreation, culture and education (%)	10,1	8,9	11,4	8,8
Clothes and footwear (%)	7,1	6,1	6,5	5,2
Other expenditure (%)	29,2	23,5	20,6	21,4

Source: YNS 1995.

The exports of the Nordic countries, as stated before, are very much concentrated on industrial commodities. There are, however, some consumer sectors that also are significant in the imports to these countries. The import of petroleum, petroleum products and related material, of road vehicles, and of vegetables and fruit mainly come to the consumer markets of the Nordic countries. These commodities are first of all daily necessities: houses have to be heated, people need nutrition and they move from one place to another in private cars. Because of the daily use, those commodity flows that come to the consumer market of basic necessities do not vary much in time. However, the development of employment, the level of salaries and exchange rate fluctuations naturally have some effect on the amount of consumer products imported to the Nordic countries.

Public sector The public consumption is rather important in the Nordic countries. There is, however, no information of the share of foreign trade that goes to the public consumption. Finland and Sweden struggle to reduce the growth of foreign debt and this struggle decelerates also the consumption of the national and the local administrations. The role of the public administration in logistics is many-sided, and the maintenance and development of the transport infrastructure is an activity which requires large amounts of funding from the public sector. Construction of infrastructure requires a lot of earth moving and related transports, but this activity does not affect the international commodity flows.

Waste handling organizations Waste handling is mainly carried out locally. Especially because the Nordic countries are not densely populated, the capacity of the environment does not yet limit the dumping of waste. However, there is a growing concern as regards environment and waste handling. The Nordic countries have a very high production of municipal waste per inhabitant: 624 kg per inhabitant of municipal waste was produced in Finland, 374 kg in Sweden, 472 kg in Norway (EiF 1995). In any case, waste flows are minor in the international traffic and can here be left without further treatment. The only important goods flow related to waste handling in the Nordic countries could be the import of used packaging material and paper from the European mainland. At the moment, this material flow does not yet appear in the trade flow statistics.

13.2.2 Logistics Service Providers

There is a wide range of different companies involved in the production of logistics services. A fundamental division can be made between the organization and execution of material flow on one hand and information flow on the other. Before the industrial revolution both passenger, goods, and information moved from one place to another using the same infrastructure (roads, rivers, and seas) and the same means of communication, but today this status quo has changed completely. There are two sets of infrastructure: one for physical communication and another for information exchange. Additionally, new technologies have been developed and they increase the gap between material and immaterial communication. Sometimes the two communication technologies compete with each other, but in the most cases their relation is complementary. Hence, for example, freight documents traditionally followed the load in a vehicle, but today they can be transferred between the consignor and the consignee using electronic data interchange.

Transport business has been strictly controlled by the public administration during the last decades. However, because free competition is one of the principal policies of the European Union, the liberalization of the transport sector has progressed very quickly since the Single European Act and the Maastricht Treaty. In order to accept cabotage, the factors affecting competition must be harmonized in the single market. The following acts are examples of the harmonization in the road transport sector:

- harmonization of excise duties on mineral oil,
- harmonization of the taxation of heavy goods vehicles,
- equal requirements in starting haulage business, and
- standardization of maximum weights and dimensions of lorries and road trains.

One of the results of this political development is the internationalization of road haulage. According to Kähäri (1993), there are four current phenomena in the market of logistics services: bundling of logistics services, specialization, internationalization, and concentration. In the most extreme cases, the bundling of logistics services means that the logistics service provider takes the responsibility of the total logistics chain of the customer company. A specialized logistics service provider focuses on a specific customer or a group of customers. In the European market, the internationalization of logistics service providers takes place via takeovers or co-operation between companies of different countries. The struggle for the economies of scale is the reason for the concentration in the logistics sector.

In 1992 there were five Nordic road transport companies among the 50 largest road transport companies in Europe. These companies were Bilspedition, Inter Forward, ASG, DFDS, and Frigoscandia. Four of them were Swedish – only DFDS was a Danish company. The merchant fleet of Norway is the biggest in the Nordic countries and it amounts to 20 million gross register tonnes. The Danish merchant fleet is the next biggest, about a quarter of the size of the Norwegian fleet. There are several large shipping companies, but only four national rail companies in the Nordic countries (Kähäri 1993; YNS 1995).

The public sector provides the logistics service companies with the transport infrastructure in the Nordic countries. The road infrastructure is the most important part of the national goods transport network, even though the dimensioning of the road network is determined by the requirements of the passenger transport. The goals of the different road administrations in the Nordic countries are much alike (see Table 13.4).

Table 13.4 The goals of the road administrations in the four Nordic countries

	Finland	Sweden	Denmark	Norway
Road safety	- road safety shall be improved	- the number of traffic accidents shall be reduced	- traffic accidents shall be reduced	- traffic accidents shall be reduced
Sustainability	- environment shall be taken into account	- energy consumption, damage to environment shall be reduced and conflicts with the neighbourhood avoided	- environmental problems shall be reduced - visual environment shall be taken care of	- environmental damage shall be reduced and environment shall be improved
Efficiency	- transport costs and efficiency shall be optimal for the society	- efficiency of the transport system shall be increased	- transports shall be carried out efficiently - the development of traffic shall be optimal	
Accessibility	- possibilities to carry out necessary passenger and goods transport shall be guaranteed - service shall be equal in all parts of the country	- road administration shall contribute to regional balance	- feasible accessibility shall be maintained	- accessibility shall be guaranteed in all parts of the country - road administration shall contribute to regional development
Other goals	- the capital value of the road network shall be maintained		- the passengers' needs regarded as a positive, experience of the trip shall be pursued	

Source: Data is based on the material collected by Asplan Viak (1995) and classified by the authors of this chapter.

Many of these goals are general and deal with both passenger and goods transport. However, the goals dealing with efficiency and accessibility have a lot of importance to private enterprises and the transport of commodities. Of course, there is a strong political influence on the goals of road administration and thus, for example, the report of the second parliamentary committee (1991) includes many of the Finnish road administration's goals.

13.2.3 Commodity Flow Statistics

The results of the different actors' strategies as regards international goods transportation can be seen in the realization of the commodity flows. If we look at the international commodity flow statistics of the Nordic countries (Tables 13.5 and 13.6), a plain conclusion can be drawn: From the foreign trade point of view, the four Nordic countries can be regarded as islands.

Table 13.5 Export of goods from the Nordic countries by mode of transport in 1993 (1000 tons)

Export	Ship	Car ferry	Rail ferry	Road	Rail	Air	Pipe-line	Other	Onboard	Total
Finland	22687	2455	871	1238	523	13	..	3	26013	27790
Sweden	31449	7548	4348	2343	14890	43	..	1	43345	60622
Norway	108268	1221	..	2193	551	20	45032	2	109489	157287
Denmark	19970	..	..	6906	703	38	..	845	19970	28462
TOTAL	182374	11224	5219	12680	16667	114	45032	851	198817	274161

Source: YNS 1995.

Table 13.6 Import of goods to the Nordic countries by mode of transport in 1993 (1000 tons)

Export	Ship	Car ferry	Rail ferry	Road	Rail	Air	Pipe-line	Other	Onboard	Total
Finland	28882	2014	315	1060	6956	18	..	2182	31211	41427
Sweden	42672	6635	1657	2561	370	69	..	2	50964	53966
Norway	18929	1056	..	3025	727	22	..	8	19985	23767
Denmark	35964	..	..	5832	577	43	..	34	35964	42450
TOTAL	126447	9705	1972	12478	8630	152	..	2226	138124	161610

Source: YNS 1995.

Approximately three quarters of the international commodity flows starting or ending in the Nordic countries cross the border on board. This is due to the geographical situation of the Nordic countries in relation to their principal trade partners. The modal split, of course, has profound importance on the analysis of the actors and their strategies on the supply side of logistics services. Yet, even if the borders are crossed by maritime transport, the commodity flows of foreign trade burden other transport modes in one or several Nordic countries before and after the maritime transport.

Statistics on trade and commodity flows draw attention to the following aspects: From environmental point of view, maritime transport is desirable. However, maritime transport requires more time than land transport modes and therefore does not fit well with the needs of the modern trade and industry.

13.2.4 Background of The Actors' Strategies

In order to understand the actors motives that affect their strategies, a profit and loss account -approach is adopted. Hence each actor group is treated as a business unit and the effects of other actor groups' behaviour are analysed on the basis of their influence on the profitability of this business unit. It is commonly known that a business unit can increase its profits in four different ways:

- by increasing sales prices,
- by increasing sales volumes,
- by reducing costs, and
- by increasing efficiency.

The actor groups are as follows: the consumers of logistics services (industrial and trade enterprises), the providers of logistics services, the households, and the public sector. The consumers and providers of logistics services are commercial enterprises, so no further characterization of costs and income are needed. For the households and the public sector, a definition of costs and prices is shown in Table 13.7.

However, the treatment of the households and the public sector as business units needs some clarifications. The income of households comprises in this context of only the income from the labour market and the social welfare. This means that the return on capital investments is ruled out of this framework. The direct and indirect taxes belong to the costs of households, like the purchase of goods and services. As mentioned in paragraph 13.2.1.3, the households spend 15–20 percent of their (net) income on transportation and communications (Table 13.3).

On the other hand, the income of the public sector consists nearly completely of the direct and indirect taxes paid by the households. A large share of the tax income comes from the taxation of road traffic. The public sector spends its income on social assistance, retirement allowances, housing subsidies, supplements on child maintenance, on labour and capital costs and on the purchase of goods and services. Public sector is a very important employer in the Nordic countries:

33–40 percent of the work force in the Nordic countries is employed in 'community, social and personal services' (YNS 1995).

Table 13.7 The actors' possibilities to increase their profits in the logistics system

	Sales price	Sales volume	Costs	Efficiency
Consumers of logistics services	sales prices of goods and services	number of products sold	labour, capital, and purchase of intermediate products, taxes	profit per invested capital at different levels of the company
Providers of logistics services	sales price of logistics services	amount of services	labour, capital, and purchase of intermediate products, taxes	profit per invested capital at different levels of the company
Households	salaries and social security	number of working hours	prices of products and services (incl. costs of transportation), capital costs, and taxes	not defined
Public sector	tax income	tax base	labour, capital, and purchase of goods and services, income transfers	budget surplus per public assets(?)

It is obvious that the logistics service consumers and providers aim at increasing their profits: that is the *raison d'être* of the business units. For the consumers and providers of logistics services, the liberalization of the European market should lead to the reduction of sales prices. If this happens, the companies can react by increasing sales, cutting costs and improving efficiency. This applies to those market segments where the products are homogenous. In the heterogeneous markets it is also possible to increase sales prices due to superior quality of the products. The increase of the sales volume can be based on the increase of the market share or the extension of the markets. The single market provides the companies with good possibilities to conquer markets all over the continent. Takeovers of local companies have been used by several Scandinavian companies both in the manufacturing and in the logistics sector. Cooperation between companies of different countries is a milder form of internationalization.

However, the goals of the households and the public sector are less obvious. The households do not act on the basis of economic abundance only – free time has also more and more importance. The Nordic countries are not densely populated and therefore the total purchasing power of these countries is low, even though the average income per inhabitant is quite high. That part of the private consumption which generates foreign trade is usually rather stable.

However, for example, the import of motor vehicles to Finland has dropped down during the last economic recession. Still, it is probable that the sales of motor vehicles will increase again when the private consumers start feeling that the future is getting more secure.

It can be assumed that the public sector does not aim only to maximize the tax income, but it is a fact that the taxation of physical persons is rather high in the Nordic countries. However, the taxation of vehicles and mineral oil is also high in comparison with most countries of the European union. The political parties present far reaching goals for the public administration, and the fulfilment of these goals guides the decisions made by authorities. In any case, the insufficiency of funding is one of the driving forces in the public administration of the Nordic countries in this decade. Therefore the economic aspects have gained more importance in the public administration too. The European legislation on public procurement will possibly increase competition and the share of imports in the public sector's acquisitions. Moreover, if the tax burden of the households were lowered, this would probably result in growing imports of private cars and fuel.

13.3 Synergies and Conflicts of the Actors

There is a wide range of actors involved in the transport of goods, as noted in the previous chapter. These actors depend on each other, and this interdependence has been analysed in literature with the aid of industrial network approach. Network approach, in general, is the study of the connected exchange relationships between actors. According to Cook[1] (1982), 'exchange relations are defined as connected if exchange in one relation is contingent upon exchange in the other relation'.

In broad terms, relations can be classified into complementarity and competition. Complementarity deals with the combination of the different actors' efforts to gain synergy for one or several partners. On the contrary, competition leads to conflicts between the actors, when the economic actors compete for the scarce resources. This kind of conflict will be called the conflict of benefits in this paper. There is, however, another type of conflict, which takes into account other aspects than the quantitative benefits of actors. This type of conflict will be called the conflict of values. In this chapter, we study the nature of synergy and conflicts related to complementarity and competition in the transport of goods between the Nordic countries and the European mainland.

13.3.1 Synergy and Complementarity

Cooperation of various factors or organs with a common goal or performance is called synergy (Capineri and Kamann 1995). This concept is often referred to as 'the 1+1=3 -rule'. The basic idea behind the concept of synergy is that the different actors can increase their benefits by joining their efforts.

Synergy can be divided into two main categories: vertical and horizontal synergy.

Vertical synergy can be acquired by specializing and outsourcing the components and services that fall outside the key knowhow. This type of synergy deals with the complementarity of actors and their activities and it is closely related to the economies of scope.

Positive effects can be attained, however, by combining the activities of similar actors as well. This kind of benefits are often referred to as the economies of scale.

The concept of synergy can be clarified by thinking of a division of a cake. One powerful actor can increase his share by decreasing that of the others. This kind of behaviour coincides with the traditional view of competition and it has nothing to do with synergy. However, if the actors join together to increase the size of the cake so that every one of them can get a bigger slice, the effect of the behaviour can be called synergy. In some occasions, synergy is also called 'win–win' situation. The power relations of the different actors play a fundamental role in determining whether only the powerful or all actors can increase their share of the bigger cake.

As far as the transport of goods is concerned, the following examples of synergetic conduct can be listed (based on Capineri and Kamann 1995):

- improvement of infrastructure layout (straighter lines),
- introduction of safety controls,
- changes in the traditional role of (railroad) stations,
- revitalization and functional redefinition of waterfronts,
- introduction of logistic chains,
- bypasses in metropolitan areas,
- development of multimodal transport,
- new heavy infrastructure (Great Belt, Chunnel),
- new policy co-ordination at different levels (master plans and regional plans), and
- creation of new hubs.

There have been several attempts by the actors in the transport sector to increase synergy in the transport of goods between the Nordic countries and the European mainland. In brief, the following actions can be listed as tendencies to increase synergy of different actors:

- The European Union: The Nordic triangle as part of the Trans European Networks.
- Nation states (Sweden and Denmark): Fixed link between Malmoe and Copenhagen
- Scandinavian industry: Support to Scandinavian link

- Transport companies (Bilspedition, ASG, Inter Forward, DFDS, Frigoscandia, Maersk, SAS etc.): Internationalization by cooperation and mergers.

13.3.2 Conflicts and Competition

Interdependence, scarcity of resources, and trade-offs between members are, according to Stern and El Ansary (1988), the primary causes of potential and actual conflicts of benefit in distribution channels. Palamountain (1955) has divided conflicts in physical distribution into three different forms: horizontal competition, intertype competition, and vertical conflict. 'The horizontal competition is defined as competition between middlemen of the same type in the channel while intertype competition is competition between middlemen of different types in the same channel sector. Vertical conflict is a conflict between channel members at different levels.' (Hertz 1993)

'Heide and Miner concluded that trust, communication, high frequency of deliveries, lack of ambiguity, and expectations for future meetings increase the likelihood of cooperation... The amount of conflicts in a channel depends to a large extent on goal incompatibility, domain consensus, and differing perceptions of reality, which only seem possible to solve through communication and a certain amount of mutual trust. All methods to solve conflicts seem to involve increased communication in different forms.' (Hertz 1993)

Studies on conflicts, quoted by Hertz (1993), merely concentrate on those conflicts that can be discovered in distribution channels. Goods transport system naturally forms part of the distribution system and hence the conflicts that lurk in the distribution system are also relevant for the goods transport sector. However, goods transport has a very far - reaching role in the society and conflicts are not limited to the transactions in the distribution channel. Therefore other aspects than pure economic benefits have to be dealt with. These aspects include also quality of life. Quality of life consists of, for example, security, rich natural resources, control over the use of time – and the traditional standard of living.

Both the construction of infrastructure and the operation of vehicles cause external effects (externalities). According to Rothengatter (1992) 'externalities occur if variables are introduced into the utility function of a consumer or the production function of a producer and these variables are not controlled by the decision maker himself rather than by other actors of the economic and social system. Externalities can be exchanged between agents within one sector, as in the case of congestion costs, but they can also occur as an activity's byproduct and affect agents who have nothing to do with the activity in question, as with air pollution in agglomerations which can devastate forests and produce erosion damages in remote mountain regions'.

External effects, especially when affecting outside actors, can lead to conflicts. In some cases conflicts are related to the actors' objectives, which are not commensurate with the objectives of those who cause the effects. This type of conflicts will be called conflicts of values.

Kasanen and Svento (1989) carried out an analysis on the nature of the conflicts of values. In their paper, economic theory was used as a framework in analysing conflicts in the policy on energy. The starting point of this analysis fulfils the following prerequisites:

- there are at least two parties which have different interests,
- negotiation of the parties deals with at least one public, obligatory and indivisible commodity, and
- one of the parties may find some of the possible negotiation results unacceptable.

In the following example, utility functions are used to describe a simplified example of a conflict of values. This example is analogous with the example presented by Kasanen and Svento (1989). The utility functions used in the analysis describe the proportional value of different commodities for different actors. In our example, the following assumptions are made:

- there are two actors in the economy: the Entrepreneur and the Conservationist,
- the Entrepreneur is negotiating with the Conservationist on the extension of the motorway network,
- the extension of the network would increase the wealth of the society but at the same time it would decrease the biodiversity of the nature, and
- there is a minimum of biodiversity acceptable to the Conservationist and a minimum of wealth acceptable to the Entrepreneur.

This kind of situation can be clarified by using the functions of equal utility for the two utilities and actors (Figure 13.3). A conflict situation arises, for example, when the Entrepreneur wants to build a motorway which reduces biodiversity to such an extent that the Conservationist can not accept it (conflict area 1). A similar situation emerges if the ban on building a motorway reduces wealth under the acceptable limit set by the Entrepreneur (conflict area 2). This kind of conflict positions always include beliefs and facts on the on the impacts of different actions on the utility of the different actors. For example, the Conservationist knows (or believes) that building a motorway indeed affects biodiversity.

In order to cause a conflict of values, it is necessary that at least one of the commodities is public, obligatory, and indivisible. In this example, biodiversity can be assumed to fulfil these requirements: the Conservationist can not go to the market and buy extinct species, neither can he alone require legislation which sets biodiversity at a minimum level.

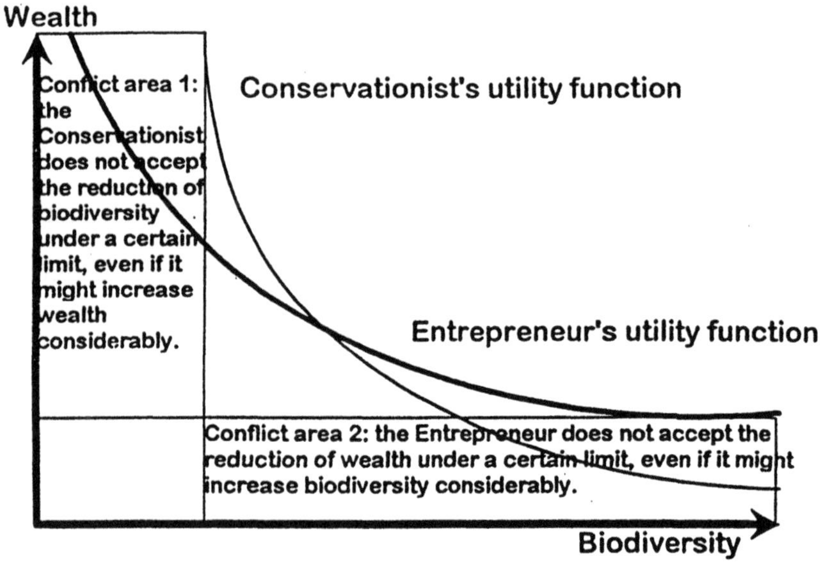

Figure 13.3 An economic analysis of conflicts

Kasanen and Svento (1989) present different cases where the division of property, regions of economic rationality, and utility functions vary. The possibilities to avoid the conflict depend on these variables, and the following possible situations can be listed:

- there is no rational solution to the conflict,
- despite the existence of economic irrationality, no conflict occurs,
- conflicts can be solved by transfers of property between the actors, and
- actors cannot solve the conflict because of the lack of property.

13.3.3 A Framework for the Analyses

Relationships between the different actors in the transport system of goods can be complementary or competitive. Complementary relations aim at creating more value either by horizontal or vertical cooperation. Horizontal cooperation deals with the joint use of scarce resources. In vertical cooperation the different actors create more value by combining their special knowhow (see Figure 13.4)

In our opinion, the most important aspect that this framework brings along is the insertion of intangible aspects to the analysis of relations between actors. There are several phenomena in the present day public life that require people's and organizations' different values to be taken into account. This applies especially to the conflicts in the transport sector. However, this descriptive model of the relations between the actors does not directly help to solve the conflicts but it does provide us with a tool which may allow a rational discussion between contrasting actors.

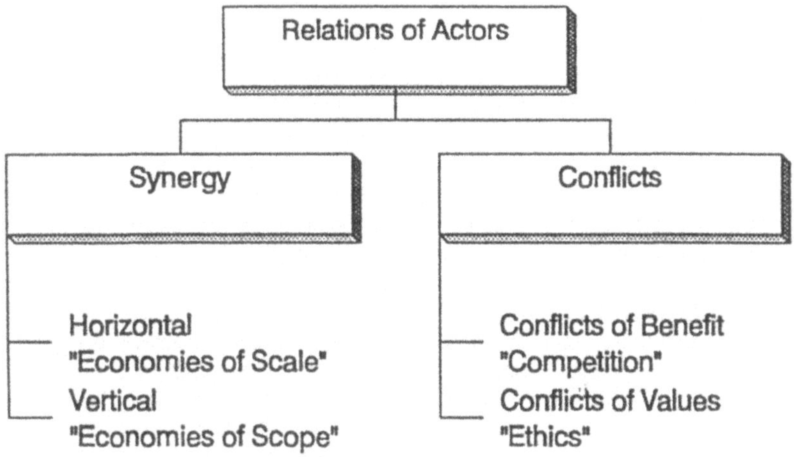

Figure 13.4 A framework for the analysis of the relations between different actors

13.4 Discussion

In this section, the results of the overview of actors, their strategies and the typology of synergies and conflicts will be considered in one. Moreover, conclusions are drawn on the basis of the study – and themes for further research are suggested.

13.4.1 Synergies and Conflicts

In the theoretical framework of synergies and conflicts we concluded that there are four types of them in the transport of commodities: horizontal synergies, vertical synergies, conflicts of benefits, and conflicts of values.

Horizontal synergies may occur between different enterprises at the same level of the industrial structure. In the case of goods transport, the costs for logistics providers can be decreased, for example, if the public sector improves the infrastructure. For this reason, it is reasonable for logistics providers to join together and tend to affect the decisions of the public sector in order to increase the amount of money invested in the infrastructure. Especially if the total costs of using the infrastructure are not paid by the users, there is a very strong incentive to demand for a better service and infrastructure.

The relation between passenger and goods transportation offers excellent possibilities for the search of synergies. First of all, both the transport of passengers and goods utilize the same infrastructure in all modes of transport. Moreover, the ferries carry both passengers and goods across the Baltic and the income from passenger traffic – including tax free sales – is vital for the economy of the ferry companies. The synergy of passenger and goods transport guarantee high frequencies for the crossing of the Baltic and the straits of Denmark.

Another example of the horizontal synergy can be detected in the manufacturing and distribution of goods. This is the standardization of hardware and software. For example, the use of standard pallets enables their circulation between several companies – even if these companies were competitors. Similarly, it is very important that the data interchange protocols and messages are standardized in electronic data interchange. The public sector has a very important role in the standardization of data interchange message – for one reason there is a possibility to smoothen customs declarations and border operations, and for another, the neutrality of the public administration can help in negotiating a standard that is convenient to as many companies as possible.

Vertical synergy deals with the outsourcing of those activities that do not form the core competence of the company. In manufacturing, the logistics services very rarely form the key competence of an enterprise. Therefore synergy can be achieved by purchasing the logistics services – transport, warehousing and other related services – from an outside company. The emergency of third party logistics operators is a proof of the existence of vertical synergy in the logistics business. As a matter of fact, horizontal and vertical synergies are mixed: the concentration of goods flows to a third party logistics service provider enables the logistics company to attain a high utilization of handling, warehousing and transport equipment. The effects of this concentration are clearly economies of scale. On the other hand, the consignor and consignee do not need to run their own logistics activities and they can concentrate on their core business. Hence, from the logistics service consumer's point of view, the existence of third-party logistics services clearly provides the trade and the industry with vertical synergy.

Competition is an essential feature of all economic activity and therefore it is no wonder that competition exists both among the logistics service consumers and the logistics service providers. Competition inevitably leads to conflicts of benefits. In the transport sector, there are two types of competition: competition between modes and competition between companies. The rail and road modes of transport are in a competitive situation. For example, the Finnish road transport companies argue that the Finnish State Railways exercise unfair competition in the freight transport market.

As regards the competition between the companies, there is only one operator in the rail transport business in every Nordic country. However, according to the directives of the European Union, the liberalization of the rail transport market should lead to the competition between different operators. In the transport markets of the peripheral countries, it is still unlikely that international operators would be interested in entering the business.

The road transport business is very competitive because there are several small operators. A typical size in road transport business is one vehicle per company. The deregulation of the road transport market has increased the competition in the Nordic road transport market. The freedom of the sees is a concept indeed and the maritime transport is perhaps the most liberal business of the world. Very often the national governments support the national shipping companies in order to guarantee the employment of seamen and in order to be self-sufficient in the case of a political conflict. On the other hand, the cost structures of the shipping companies depends very much on the standard of living in the home countries of the shipping companies and subsidies are used to compete with the companies using the flags of convenience for cost reasons. Because the maritime transport is very important in all of the Nordic countries, the competition of ports has particular significance for the foreign trade.

In industry and trade, the logistics service is an important success factor and, using the terminology of this chapter, the vertical synergy between an industrial and a logistics enterprise can be used to gain competitive advantage in the market. The development of infrastructure creates additional horizontal synergy. Therefore it is in the industry's interest to call for more public investment in infrastructure.

Conflicts of value are the most far reaching relations between the actors in the goods transport sector. This kind of conflicts exist in the citizens' relations as regards the consumers and providers of logistics services – i.e. commercial enterprises. The role of the public sector is also very delicate: the public administration acts as a buffer between the conflicting parties. There are different expressions for the conflicts of values. In the lightest form of conflict, the consumers (households) may boycott those products, which are manufactured and distributed in a manner opposite to the consumers' values. This expression of differing opinions normally requires some sort of organization and cordination of the consumers actions. In a more serious type of conflict, the conflicting parties may prosecute each other. Boycotts and prosecutions can be handled through the economic and legal systems of the organized society. Additionally, the political system too can canalize values prevailing in the society.

However, the most extreme expressions of the value conflicts are expressed in civic disobedience, or even terrorist acts. In the transport of goods, civic disobedience would signify the resistance to road projects using methods that are at the limits of the law. Most conflicts of values can be treated using the economic, political and legal structures of the society and, in particular, in the transport of goods there does not seem to be such disagreements that might lead to serious expressions of conflicts.

13.4.2 Conclusions and Guidelines for Further Research

Foreign trade statistics show clearly that the trade between the Nordic countries and the European mainland is concentrated on relatively few commodities. Among these, especially the following articles of foreign trade are worth mentioning:

- export of oil from Norway,
- export of paper, paperboard and articles thereof from Sweden and Finland,
- import of road vehicles to Sweden, Denmark and Norway,
- import of petroleum, petroleum products and related material to Sweden Finland and Denmark,
- import and export of general industrial machinery and equipment to and from all Nordic countries,
- import of electrical machinery, apparatus and appliances to all Nordic countries.

According to the cross-border commodity flow statistics, the Nordic countries can be considered nearly as islands. Two thirds of the international commodity flows leave and enter the Nordic countries by maritime transport.

The following conclusions can be made on this basis: First, there are relatively few actors that make decisions concerning international goods transport on demand side (oil companies, forest industry, and wholesale distributors). Second, the dynamics of industry rather than the dynamics of the consumer market dominate in the foreign trade. And finally, the promotion of international goods transport can be carried out by developing port facilities, by improving infrastructure leading to port areas, and by creating alternative fast transport routes to maritime links. It should be borne in mind that replacing maritime transport by other modes of transport inevitably increases the external costs of goods transport. This may lead to conflicts of values between the organizers of the commodity flows and different interest groups.

On the basis of this desk study, there seem to exist the following opportunities to increase the synergy in the international goods transport:

- development of the infrastructure leading to port facilities,
- guaranteeing the high frequencies of car-ferry traffic, and
- standardization of data interchange.

As to the conflicts of the international goods transport sector, it is important – from the logistics consumers' point of view – that competition exists between the modes of transport and between the transport companies. Moreover, the conflicts of value seem to be solvable using the economic, legal, and political structures of the organized society. In practice, this means the internalization of the external costs of goods transport by means of, for example, emission taxes, which are common to all actors of the international goods transport.

As far as future research in this area is concerned, the strategies of the main actors dealing with international goods transport should be investigated. There are relatively few of these actors and for this reason interviews or Delphi type of panels can be suggested as the research methods.

References

Capineri, C. and Kamann, D.J. (1995), 'Synergy in Networks: Concepts', Paper presented at the European Research Conference, Espinho (Portugal).

Cook, K.S. (1982), 'Network Structures from an Exchange Perspective', in Mardsen, P.V. and N. Lin (eds), *Social Structure and Network Analysis*, Sage Publications, Beverly Hills.

EiE vol II (1994), Enterprises in Europe vol II, Office for Official Publications of the European Communities, Luxembourg.

EiF (1995), Europe in Figures, 4th edition, Office for Official Publications of the European Communities, Luxembourg.

FINRA (1994), Tielaitoksen tavarankuljetustilasto, tielaitoksen tilastoja 3/1994, Helsinki.

Hertz, S. (1993) 'The Internationalization Processes of Freight Transport Companies', Dissertation (Stockholm School of Economics), Stockholm.

Kasanen, E. and Svento, R. (1989) *Arvoristiriidan taloudellista analyysia, in Riittääkö energia, riittääkö järki*, Gaudeamus, Helsinki, pp. 206-231.

Kähäri, P. (1993), Euroopan muuttuva logistiikkatoimiala. Loimaan Kirjapaino Oy.

Palamountain, Jr. J. C. (1955), 'Distribution: Its Economic Conflicts, in The Politics of Distribution', The President and Fellows of Harvard College.

Rothengatter, W. (1992), 'The Internalisation of Positive External Effects of Transport', Paper prepared for the ESTI-conference in Brussels, Karlsruhe.

Scandinavian Link (1987), Industrins kostnader – En dynamisk logistikanalys, Ottilia Trykk ApS.

Schonberger, R.J. (1982), *Japanese Manufacturing Techniques,* The Free Press.

Statistics Finland (1992), Liikennetilastollinen vuosikirja 1992, tilastokeskus, Helsinki.

Stern, L.W. and El-Ansary (1988), *Marketing Channels*, 3rd edition, Englewood Cliffs, New York.
YNS (1995), Yearbook of Nordic Statistics 1995, Nordic Council of Ministers, Århus.
Øystein, H. (1995), Organisering av norske trafikkhavner, TØI rapport 286/1995.

Note

1. Quoted by Susanne Hertz (1993) in The Internationalization Process of Freight Transport Companies, p. 34.

14 Price Effects of Regulation: Stated Offers for Trans-Alpine Freight Transport Services

KARIN MÜLLER AND RICO MAGGI

14.1 Introduction

Liberalization and deregulation efforts characterize current developments of global markets. One observes a gradual liberalization of international trade as well as deregulation of markets for goods and services. As a consequence, worldwide economic interweaving increased over the last decades. Growing globalization of economic activities has been enforced by recent political developments. Political integration in Europe removed borders and increased mobility of production factors, goods and services. Above all, transportation and telecommunication networks are important conditions to meet the needs of a global economy. Freight transport markets in Europe, like other service markets, have been affected by deregulation tendencies. While road freight transport is gradually being liberalized, rail transport is still dominated by national monopolies. This is not only relevant for rail transport but also for intermodal transport which is seen as a future solution to congestion and environmental pollution. Moreover, demanders of freight transport services became more quality oriented due to increased factor mobility and pretentious logistics concepts. The most important qualities for shippers are reliability and transport time. Demanded quality standards have to be met by any competitive provider to stay in the market. Regulative settings affect the competitive behaviour of service providers due to their impact on relative prices.

This chapter concentrates on a highly sensitive part of the European freight transport network to analyse price effects of regulations. We have chosen the trans-Alpine network for our analysis because this part of the European network is under stress from traffic volume high on the one hand and because it covers different regulatory settings, on the other hand. Alpine mountains form natural bottlenecks in the centre of Europe which bundles trans-Alpine freight flows on four major crossings. As a result, some Alpine countries have been implementing regulations to reduce traffic flows and negative external effects of through traffic. The most effective regulations are operating restrictions. The most relevant example in this respect is the weight limit of 28 tons on trucks in Switzerland which, as a non-member of the European Union (EU), does not accept the EU standard of 40 tons per truck. In contrast to this, all neighbouring countries, which are members of the European Union, allow 40 ton trucks. These differences in the regulatory settings of the Alpine network provide us an appropriate framework with which to analyse price effects caused by regulating surface freight transport services.

The objectives of this chapter are threefold. First, we analyse effects of existing regulations on current trans-Alpine freight flows. Second, we try to identify price effects caused by regulations affecting freight transportation services. Third, we discuss possible effects of deregulation, i.e. abolition of the 28 ton limit. Furthermore, we discuss current policy proposals for reregulating the trucking sector by implementing fees on through traffic through Switzerland.

We overcome the lack of sufficient economic data of the freight transport sector by directly enquiring by freight carriers. We enter the market as 'hypothetical' shippers to collect offer prices for freight transport services. We analyse the context of regulation by gathering offers for well defined freight transport services. Our enquiry strategy offers us an appropriate survey instrument to consider the two most important parameters of freight transport services: the quality of freight transport services and the underlying network conditions which are necessary to provide transport services.

The chapter is organized as follows. The first section sets the scene for trans–Alpine freight flows and their interference with network characteristics such as regulations. The second section offers a model for explaining price effects caused by different regulatory settings in the framework of hedonic price analysis. The third section describes the empirical strategy and results of the empirical analysis. Altogether our empirical results reflect short term behavioural responses of freight carriers to regulatory differences in the infrastructure network of Europe.

14.2 Setting the Scene

Economic activities are characterized by increasing international mobility in terms of distance of both production factors as well as finished goods and services. Economic trends towards globalization are based on improved telecommunication and transportation networks. Growing freight flows from major European seaports originates mainly in Northern Europe and cross the Alpine area to reach their destinations in the Centre or South of Europe. Consequently, total traffic volumes through the Alpine countries Austria, France and Switzerland have been increasing over the last decades. Forecasts on traffic volumes confirm that this trend will continue for the coming years. As a result, the Alpine region will be affected by an increasing degree of through traffic in the near future compared to the current level of traffic flows.

The four major Alpine crossings by road and rail are Mt.Cenis/Fréjus (France), Simplon (Switzerland), Gotthard (Switzerland) and Brenner

(Austria). The shortest possible connection for most links between Northern Europe and Italy leads through Switzerland. Given this specific geographical location, Switzerland has historically implemented various regulations to limit and reduce through traffic to prevent destruction and pollution. The most effective regulation in this context is the 28 ton weight limit. This limit does not allow EU-standard trucks of 40 tons to cross Switzerland. As a result, by increasing relative prices of crossing Switzerland, the 28 ton limit has an effect on trans-Alpine route choices of European 40 ton trucks as well on the modal choice to cross Switzerland.

The effect on modal split of transit traffic through the Alpine countries is illustrated in Figure 14.1. It shows that the relative share of freight transport through Switzerland by road is smaller than through France and through Austria, whereas freight transport by rail (including multimodal transport) has a larger share through Switzerland than through France and Austria. Given that the shortest path leads through Switzerland for the majority of links, these figures clearly indicate that Swiss national regulation causes detour traffic of trucks through other Alpine countries.

Main Trans-Alpine Crossings for Road and Rail (in million tons)

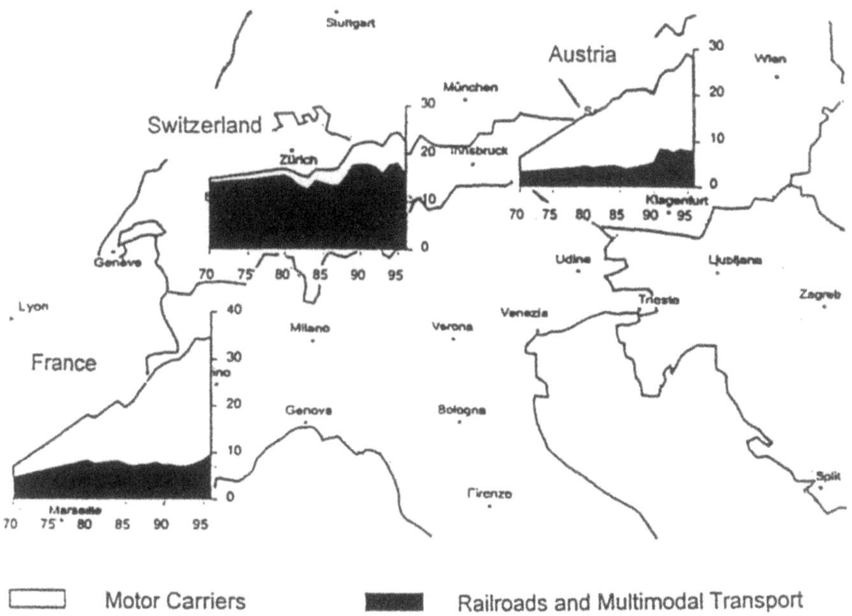

Figure 14.1 Modal split of Trans-Alpine freight flows through Austria, France and Switzerland 1970-1995

Source: GVF (1997).

Switzerland is currently under political pressure from the EU to also permit 40 ton trucks. EU neighbouring countries of Switzerland such as France, Austria, Italy and Germany are affected by detour traffic. The neighbouring countries are mainly interested in a common regulatory setting allowing at least 40 ton trucks to drive in Switzerland as well. Therefore, Swiss weight limit forms an integral part of current bilateral negotiations on land transport between Switzerland and the EU. In return, Switzerland discusses means of reregulation to meet its national environmental policy goals, which are determined by following important plebiscites. In 1994, Swiss voters agreed first to implement a polluter oriented levy on heavy vehicles (LSVA) which will replace a system of lump sum taxes and, second, to allow only through traffic by rail through Switzerland within ten years (Alps Initiative), i.e. by the year 2005. The proposals for implementing the latter plebiscites foresee an additional 'steering charge' per trans-Alpine road freight transport (ATA) of about SFr. 500. The aim of Swiss transportation policy is to shift more freight transport from road to rail, and furthermore to increase the use of multimodal freight transport to cross the country. The implementation of two new levies, i.e. on heavy vehicles (LSVA) and on trans-Alpine transports (ATA), are an integrated part of current and future transportation priorities in Switzerland. The EU requires Switzerland to implement these levies without discrimination. One possibility to prevent discrimination is to provide possibilities for substituting among different modes. The Swiss government is promoting intermodal transport for this reason. Multimodal promotion programmes foresee organizational (e.g. coordination of rail nodes, i.e. 'Bahn 2000'), financial (e.g. subsidies) and technical elements (e.g. construction of a new trans-Alpine corridor, i.e. 'NEAT') which increase the attractiveness of using intermodal transportation.

In conclusion, Swiss regulation of the truck weight limit currently has a significant effect on trans-Alpine freight flows in Europe. Deregulating weight limits in Switzerland means accepting the EU standard of 40 ton weight limit for trucks which would lead to an increased amount of through traffic. At the same time Switzerland discusses means of reregulation to meet its national transport priorities concerning trans–Alpine through traffic.

14.3 The Model

The theoretical framework of our analysis follows a hedonic approach. A hedonic function allows us to consider qualities of freight transport services in our model. In this context, the hedonic function relates prices of freight transport services and the quantities of quality characteristics contained in them. The theory bases of the hedonic hypothesis which assumes that heterogeneous goods or services are aggregations of characteristics, and economic behaviour of individuals and firms, relates to these characteristics (Triplett 1990).

The theoretical framework for our analysis allows the hedonic approach, while we concentrate on the supply side of freight transport services. This allows us to capture quality characteristics in the analysis of a carrier's behaviour. As we have argued in the previously, quality is a decisive argument for the competitiveness of freight carriers. The hedonic approach implies that a transaction of a service is tied to a bundle of characteristics, which is crucial for the analysis of freight transport services. In general, a hedonic function is defined as the relationship between prices of goods or services and the quantities of characteristics contained in them:

$$p = h(\mathbf{z}) \tag{14.1}$$

where p is the price of a good or service and $\mathbf{z}$ is a vector of characteristics.

The theoretical framework of our analysis is a hedonic approach following the theory presented by Rosen (1974). A hedonic function allows us to consider qualities of freight transport services as well as the underlying network structure and production technologies. Following the hedonic theory we are able to formulate an integrated model of price effects of different service qualities, network characteristics and production technologies. In our context, the hedonic function relates offer prices of freight transport services and the quantities of quality characteristics contained in them. We investigate into the supply behaviour of carriers under different restrictions, i.e. the underlying network structure and respective production technologies.

We specify a hedonic offer function for our theoretical purposes. In that case, for one unit (one shipment) of a composite good, e.g. a freight transport service, the supply behaviour of a firm is described with an offer function ϕ (.). An offer function ϕ indicates the offer prices which suppliers are willing to accept for a given design of quality characteristics, $\mathbf{z}$, at profit level π (Rosen 1974). The quality dimension of a transport service is defined by a vector $\mathbf{z} = (z_1,\ldots,z_n)$ where each z_i represents the level of the i-th characteristic of a certain transportation service. Transportation services are completely described by this vector of characteristics. Therefore, we can write the hedonic offer function as:

$$\phi = \phi\,(z_1,\ldots, z_n) \tag{14.2}$$

Furthermore, we can identify implicit offer prices for single characteristics from the offered price for a specific transportation service and respective characteristics related to the service. Implicit prices, i.e. not directly revealed prices on the market are called 'hedonic' prices. Rosen defines 'hedonic' prices as follows: 'Hedonic prices are defined as the implicit prices of attributes and are revealed to economic agents from observed prices of differentiated products and the specific amounts of characteristics associated with them' (Rosen

1974, p. 34). The marginal implicit offer price for a certain quality characteristic z_i is obtained by taking the first derivative ($\delta \phi / \delta z_i = \phi_{zi}$) of $\phi(z_i, z_1^*, ..., z_n^*)$. Thus, while marginal prices for a given level of characteristics are not directly observable, they are implied by offered prices of a requested freight transport service.

We assume competitive markets for long-distance trans-Alpine freight transports. This is a realistic assumption because competition is big on the Alpine network in terms of substitution among different modes of transportation as well as in terms of substitution among different paths. The most important trans-Alpine crossings are relatively closely located compared to the overall transport distance of a trip. Consequently the detour route is only a minor consideration in a long-distance transport from, for example, Northern Europe to the South of Italy.

We previously identified a hedonic offer function which relates offered prices to qualities of provided freight transport services (see Equation 14.2). As we concentrate on the supply side of the market, we adapt the offer function defined by Rosen (1974) for our purposes by introducing additional variables for production technologies and network characteristics. We assume following relation between offer prices, production technology and networks: (1). Offer functions can be shifted in a quality offer price plane by technology, ß, which represent anything that shifts cost or market conditions among firms. Examples which cause shifts are different technologies or different factor prices among supplying firms. (2) Shifts of offer functions may be caused by different network settings, γ. In that case the underlying network structure has an impact on production costs and consequently on offered prices. Network characteristics vary among origin – destination links, which are used for providing services on a given infrastructure network. The most important network characteristics in our respect are regulatory settings. Network related shifters have been identified in literature about hedonic cost function in transportation (Friedlaender and Spady 1981; Callan and Thomas 1992).

We capture previously identified effects on the offer price, i.e., production technologies and network characteristics, respective parameters ß and γ, by rewriting the offer function.

From the above, the offer function ϕ can be specified as:

$$\phi = \phi(z_1, ..., z_n; \pi, \beta, \gamma) \tag{14.3}$$

where:

- γ Offer price
- **z** Vector of freight transportation service qualities
- π Profit
- ß Vector of production technologies
- γ Vector of characteristics of the underlying network structure.

In such a context, a profit maximizing firm solves a maximizing problem with respect to quality vector **z**, where unit revenue is γ, and minimal costs per shipment are C(.). We assume carriers to provide us offer prices at their optimal output level as we enter the competitive market as infinitesimal small customers. The profit function π of a firm can be written as follows in a price taking competitive market:

$$\pi = \Phi(\mathbf{z}) - C(z_1., ..., z_n, \beta, \gamma). \tag{14.4}$$

If we assume $\pi = 0$ for a competitive firm, we can rewrite the zero-profit offer function as following:

$$\Phi(\mathbf{z}) = C(z_1, ..., z_n, \beta, \gamma). \tag{14.5}$$

The above zero profit offer function implies inverse supply functions for the respective quality attributes z_i. The inverse supply function measures the implicit price that must be realized for a firm to find it profitable to supply a given level of quality characteristics **z** (Varian 1992). The inverse supply function for a single quality characteristic z_i is given by

$$\Phi_{zi}(\mathbf{z}) = C_{zi}(\mathbf{z}, \beta, \gamma). \tag{14.6}$$

The inverse supply function allows for endogeneity of prices given exogenous quality vector **z**. Consequently, firms have to state offer prices ϕ, which at least cover the cost of producing a given **z**. In reference to our empirical context, carriers have to state offers prices for well defined requests for freight transport services.

The scope of our analysis lies in the behaviour of freight transport carriers in response to different network settings. For that reason we define hedonic offer functions which reflect supply behaviour of freight carriers on competitive markets. For our empirical purposes, we add an error term ε to the above offer function (14.3) and rewrite it as follows. assuming $\pi = 0$.

$$\phi = \phi\ (\mathbf{z}, \beta, \gamma, \varepsilon) \tag{14.7}$$

This offer function provides the background for the specification of the estimation functions (14.8) and (14.9) for our empirical investigation. The offer function has interesting empirical features. If it is possible to estimate the offer function, inferences can be made with regard to infrastructure characteristics and production technology. Both shifts stemming from different production technologies (ß), as well as shifts caused by varied underlying network structures (γ) are possible sources for shifts of the offer functions. Hence, it is essential to identify empirically the nature of these shifts whose interpretation should be straightforward in terms of cost saving or cost increasing effects.

14.4 The Data

Our survey of freight transport providers is based on offer enquiries for well defined freight transport services. We used a factorial design to define our survey instrument. The design with systematically varied service characteristics is adapted from stated preference technique. Instead of investigating into demand behaviour we use the design to create offer inquiries. We approached several freight forwarders and carriers as 'hypothetical' shippers using offer enquiries to gather offer prices for well defined freight transport services. We were concerned that the lack of credibility in a university institute as a demander for freight transport services might bias our findings. Yet, our empirical results let us assume that carriers treated us as regular new customers. In addition, we completed our data set with secondary market data and network specific information for our empirical purposes.

We selected six large freight forwarders for our enquiry[1]. They represent the most important actors for European surface freight transport. Most of them provide both forwarding services as well as carriage of goods. By selecting six large market actors, we take the market structure of the road transport industry into account with only a few big firms and numerous small companies with less than ten employees and a small number of trucks. Our offer enquiries count for trans-Alpine transports from North to South. The design used covered three characteristics: consignment, weight and link. Consignment has only one attribute level which is general non-food. We decided no to enquire about fresh goods (e.g. fruit) due to comparability reasons. Four weight levels have been selected to check different weights. Varying trans-Alpine regulations are captured by inquiring into 17 links which lead over three major Alpine crossings, i.e. Brenner, Gotthard and Mt. Cenis and cover the most important North-South connections. Thus, we consider the underlying networks i.e. valid regulations on specific links by varying origins and destinations in our design. We assume that regulative settings of a specific transportation network have an effect on costs of freight transport services. By capturing regulatory effects we obtain an important addition to the firm and mode specific cost effects on offered services. Characteristics and levels of the design for enquiries are summarized in Table 14.1.

The selection of weight levels and links reflects our concern about regulations on trans-Alpine freight movements. As noted above, the Swiss weight limit on trucks is 28 tons, which allows a loading of a maximum of about 15 tons while a 40 ton truck is able to load about 24 tons. We assume cost minimizing carriers choose the shortest distance to connect origins and destinations. Carriers minimize their costs among other things, in respect to regulations on certain links. As a consequence, adaptive strategies of freight carriers may cause detour traffic of carriers which do not choose the shortest connection due to regulations on certain parts of the network. Regarding the weight limit in Switzerland, we assume carriers who anticipate the 28 ton limit take a detour around Switzerland because it is more efficient to use a 40 ton truck for the entire distance.

Table 14.1 Characteristics and levels of the design for offer enquiries

	Characteristics		
	Link	*Weight*	*Transported Goods*
Levels	Rotterdam - Bologna	2 tons	General non-food
	Rotterdam - Napoli	15 tons	
	Rotterdam - Torino	30 tons	
	Halle - Bologna	42 tons	
	Halle - Napoli		
	Halle - Torino		
	Hamburg - Bologna		
	Hamburg - Napoli		
	Hamburg - Torino		
	München - Bologna		
	München - Napoli		
	München - Torino		
	Brüssel - Bologna		
	Brüssel - Napoli		
	Brüssel - Torino		
	Karlsruhe - Bologna		
	Karlsruhe - Napoli		

The characteristics shown in Table 14.1 were used to build factorial designs. We enquired about all possible 68 combinations. One example of an offer request is provided in Appendix 14.1. As shown, we tried to use a very simple form which resembles as closely as possible to a genuine consignment. Like this we were able to get as close as possible to a real offer enquiry which increases the validity of our data. Furthermore, we added questions on transport time and punctuality to capture the most important quality characteristic: reliability. Price offers were sought for the three modes, rail, road and multimodal transport which allowed us to compare different technologies.

The survey returned 272 offers which could be used for empirical purposes. All requested offer prices refer to the year 1996. We added secondary evidence in accordance to the above model for all cases. More specifically, we calculated distance of each link. Furthermore, we created dummy variables for BRENNER, GOTTHARD AND MT. CENIS which indicate the shortest trans-Alpine connection for each link. Finally, we introduced dummy variables for road transport (ROAD) and intermodal transport (INTERMODAL) to capture mode specific price shifts with respect to rail. The complete description of variables is presented in Appendix 14. 2.

With regard to the above theoretical model, PRICE is the offered price for a specific freight transport service which has been defined according to our factorial design. In other words the offer price is the dependent variable. The quality of the freight transport service is reflected in following variables: WEIGHT, DISTANCE and TIMEDIFF. They represent the vector of freight transportation service qualities z_i. In our context, reliability is measured in terms of punctuality. We determine a variable TIMEDIFF measuring reliability in terms of expected relative time difference in arrival times. Although final reliability is only to be measured ex post, we define TIMEDIFF as ex ante reliability by the expected difference between earliest and latest arrival time relative to the shortest transport time (TIMEDIFF). Consequently, we expect carriers to have a pricing strategy which depends on reliability, that is, higher prices for freight transport services signify higher expected reliability, ceteribus paribus.[2]

The effects of production technologies on the price, i.e. ß-effects in our model, are captured by following two sets of variables. First, we expect ROAD, RAIL AND INTERMODAL to control technology shifts for different modes of transportation. Second, FIRM dummies capture firm specific differences in production technologies. The underlying network structure is captured by following variables: LIMIT28T, GOTTHARD, MTCENIS and BRENNER. They reflect the γ-effects, that is to say, price effects caused by characteristics of the underlying infrastructure. We expect the LIMIT28T variable to indicate differences of regulation of weight limits. GOTTHARD, MTCENIS and BRENNER which are dummies for the shortest trans-Alpine connection for a specific service, are indicators for the degree of network integration. We expect a positive price effect of relatively poorly integrated networks. Everything else remains constant.

14.5 Empirical Evidence

We performed a two-stage indirect least square estimation due to the endogeneity of the price and reliability variables. The empirical model was estimated using double-log specifications. Note that the coefficients of the continuous variables represent elasticities, while the coefficients of the dummies represent logarithms of the relative price shifts.

We determine in Stage 1 reliability TIMEDIFF as dependent a variable of firm dummies. This model specification is based on our assumption that reliability is a strategic argument of carriers which reflects their optimizing behaviour. We introduce only carriers with no missing values, i.e. FIRM1, FIRM2 and FIRM 3 for explaining TIMEDIFF in Stage 1.

Stage 1

$$\ln(\text{TIMEDIFF}) = \alpha_0 + \alpha_1 \text{ FIRM 1} + \alpha_2 \text{ FIRM 2} + \alpha_3 \text{ FIRM3} + \alpha_4 \varepsilon \tag{14.8}$$

Stage 2

$$\ln(\text{PRICE}) = \beta_0 + \beta_1 \ln(\text{DISTANCE}) + \beta_2 \ln(\text{WEIGHT}) + \beta_3 \text{ROAD} + \beta_4 \text{MULTIMODAL} + \beta_5 \text{LIMIT28T} + \beta_6 \text{INROWEIG} + \beta_7 \text{BRENNER} + \beta_8 \text{MTCENIS} + \beta_9 \text{PRETIMEDIFF} + \beta_{10} \varepsilon \tag{14.9}$$

Predicted values from for Stage 1 reliability are introduced in Stage 2 as the variable PRETIMEDIFF. The variable INROWEIG is an interaction term between the dummy ROAD and WEIGHT. The interaction term is assumed to be positive as prices for road transports increase with increasing weights.

Different network settings are captured by BRENNER, MT CENIS and GOTTHARD. They indicate dummies for the shortest possible connection for all 17 origin and destination links.

Table 14.2 Results of OLS-estimation (total data sample)

Variable	*Coefficient*	t-statistic	*Expected Sign*
ln (DISTANCE)	0.525	7.72	+
ln (WEIGHT)	0.353	10.58	+
ROAD	-1.069	-6.10	-
MULTIMODAL	-0.258	-4.48	-
LIMIT28T	0.376	3.24	+
INROWEIG	0.246	4.03	+
BRENNER	0.135	2.79	?
MTCENIS	-0.107	-1.26	?
PRETIMEDIFF	-0.085	-2.30	-
INTERCEPT	3.020	5.97	
R-square adjusted		0.62	
Observations		272	

The results of the estimation in Stage 2 are shown in Table 14.2. The reference case for the results shown there is a freight transport on rail through Switzerland via GOTTHARD which is represented in the intercept of our estimation. The explained variance is considerable. All coefficients are significant and, whether positive or negative, bear the expected sign.

14.6 Discussion

Results of our OLS estimation are depicted in Figure 14.2 in an offer price and weight diagram. We choose WEIGHT to illustrate our arguments, as the investigated regulation is weight specific. The results in Figure 14.2 refer to transports through the GOTTHARD corridor for an average distance of our sample (1387) and an average reliability (deviation of expected arrival time is 10 percent of total transport time).

The most interesting variable with respect to the price effects of network integration is the regulation of weight limits. The LIMIT28T dummy controls for all road transports which are heavier than 28 tons total weight and for which the shortest way leads through Switzerland. The LIMIT28T dummy allows us to compare equal transports which are not affected by the 28 ton limit. Price effects of the 28 ton regulation are mainly caused by detour traffic, i.e. choosing a longer route to connect origins and destinations to avoid transshipment from 40 ton trucks to 28-ton trucks. We empirically identify a considerable price increase of about 45 percent which is caused by the 28 ton weight limit compared to otherwise equal transports where 40 ton trucks are allowed. Price effects of weight regulation can be seen from Figure 14.2 by an upward shift of the offer function for road transport.

Moreover, our results show that there is a small, but significant difference in price level for otherwise equal transports over Brenner compared to Gotthard which holds as reference for the results shown here. There is no significant price difference between Gotthard and Mt. Cenis. This confirms that all Alpine links are relatively well integrated besides the difference in weight regulation for which we controlled separately with the LIMIT28T dummy.

The distance and weight coefficients, i.e. 0.52 and 0.35 respectively, which are less than 1 indicate the presence of scale effects in respect to offer prices. This is not surprising given the peculiarities of the freight transport service sector with rather high fixed costs and also the fact that we ask for price offers for relatively small shipments.

The price effects of production technology are captured by dummy variables for road, rail and intermodal transport whereas prices for road transport increase at a higher rate than for rail in respect to weight. A significant, positive interaction term between road and weight holds for a sharper rise of costs for road than for rail referring to weight. Furthermore, according to estimated price offers, intermodal transport is about 23 percent cheaper than rail for a given weight. Hence, the combination of road and rail permits the realization of cost advantages. Note that we assume sidings at all origins and destinations while requesting offers for rail modes in the enquiry. In other words, we assume that shippers load directly onto rail cars. On the other hand, using intermodal technology, we assume that there are no sidings either at origins nor at destinations. Shippers who use intermodal transport, load their freight on trucks which ship to the closest terminal where the cargo is transshipped on rail cars. We conclude that the intermodal transport is only used as a road substitute where no sidings exist. Therefore, we compare two different movements, first, those by road or rail, where sidings exist, and second, freight movements using intermodal transport or road where no sidings exist.

According to our results shown in Figure 14.2, we can determine competitive modes for respective weights under different regulatory settings. Consequently, we can say that without the 28 ton limit road is the most competitive mode for transports of less than 30 tons. Conversely, under a regulatory framework of a 28 ton weight limit, the road mode is only competitive for freight transports below 6 tons where the road function cuts the intermodal function in Figure 14.2. This break-even point of road and intermodal transport is surprisingly low. Therefore, intermodal transport is competitive for freight transports of 6 tons and more with weight regulation and again competitive for transports of 30 tons and more without weight regulation.

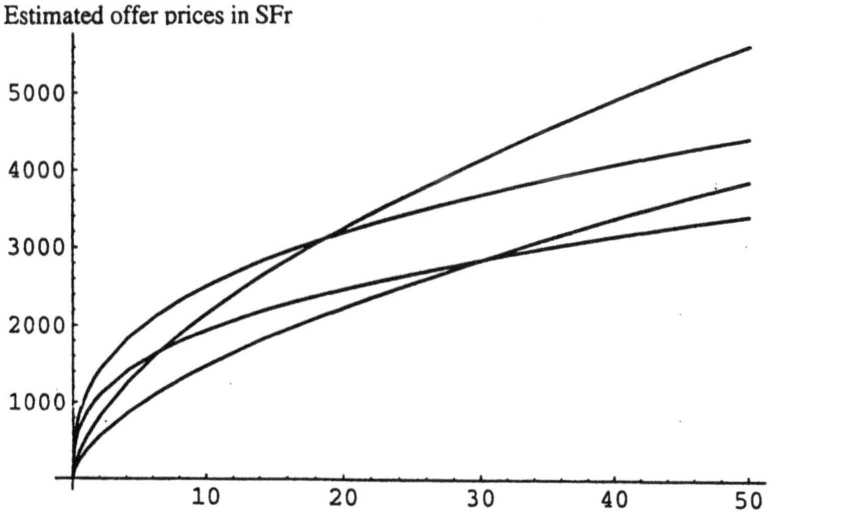

Figure 14.2 Estimated offer prices for Trans-Alpine freight transport services

A further interesting observation is that the rail curve and the regulated road curve cut at 18 tons weight. Interestingly, 18 tons is about the loading capacity of a truck which is allowed to weigh 28 tons in total. This result leads us to assume that the Swiss railways which run rail transportation as a monopoly through Switzerland, has to adapt its price setting strategy to road competitors. Consequently, the railways enter the market for weights which are too heavy for a 28 ton truck by adapting their prices to road competitors.

Moreover empirical results confirm negative price effects of unreliable services, as expected. Thus, our empirical results stress the importance of reliability as a quality characteristic and strategic element for freight carriers.

Regarding the deregulation debate on Swiss weight limitation, the question is raised as to what extent shifts can be expected in respect to Trans-Alpine freight flows if the 28 ton limit will be abolished. We can see from our results that the weight limit helps a lot to keep the railways in the market for larger shipments. An abolition of the weight limit on trucks increases the competitiveness of trucks for heavier weights, and as a consequence, road transport will gain market shares in traditional rail segments i.e. heavy goods and bulk goods. As we have stated earlier, Swiss transport policy aims at opposite goals, i.e. Swiss citizens voted for through traffic on roads not being increased but rather reduced in the coming years. Anticipating the abolition of the 28 ton limit, current national political discussion in Switzerland proposes several means of reregulation. Price effects of future reregulation policies and their impacts on competitiveness of transport modes are subject of the following section.

14.6 Price Effects of Reregulation Policies in Switzerland

The most important international agreement which has a great impact on transport policy of Switzerland is the 'Treaty on Through Traffic' (Transitvertrag) which was agreed between Switzerland and the EU in 1992. In the treaty, the EU agrees to respect the 28 ton limit for trucks and, also, to respect the prohibition of night and Sunday traffic for trucks in Switzerland. In addition, the EU confirmed that it would improve access to terminals for intermodal transport. In return, Switzerland agreed to enlarge capacities for intermodal transport in the short term and to construct a new railway tunnel, the new trans-Alpine corridor (NEAT), in the long term. The treaty is valid for 12 years and will expire in 2005. In other words, the 28 ton limit is currently guaranteed until 2005, yet future weight regulation depends on current bilateral negotiations between Switzerland and the EU.

The system of direct democracy in Switzerland affects transportation policy to a large extent as can be seen by recent examples. In February 1994, the votes on the 'Alps Initiative' (Alpeninitiative) as well as an incentive tax on trucks i.e. 'Levy on heavy vehicles' (Schwerverkehrsabgabe) LSVA were to everyone's surprise, accepted by Swiss citizens. Anticipation of future deregulation of weight limits may have assisted the success of the two bills.

The Alps Initiative demands that after 2004 trans-Alpine freight traffic should only be carried through Switzerland by train. Moreover, the initiative completely prohibits the expansion of trans-Alpine road links.

The government intends to implement these restrictions by introducing market oriented instruments to reduce trans-Alpine freight traffic on roads. The initial proposal for a transit fee was SFr. 500 per Trans-Alpine transport by road (ATA) which has to be paid for all Trans-Alpine transports through Switzerland (INFRAS 1995).

The introduction of an incentive tax on trucks (LSVA) by 2001 will replace the current lump sum tax system where the annual tax for a 28 ton truck is SFr. 2000 per year. The new LSVA system will be a function of driven kilometres and transported tons and will be implemented by 2001. Thus, there are two proposals under discussion which foresee either a SFr. 0.016 tax per tkm or a SFr. 0.025 tax per tkm (NZZ, 12.9.1996). The tax of SFr. 0.025 should cover estimated external effects of freight traffic by road and induce a modal shift from road to rail or intermodal transport. Both the implementation of the LSVA as well as the introduction of the ATA are in a process of legislation.

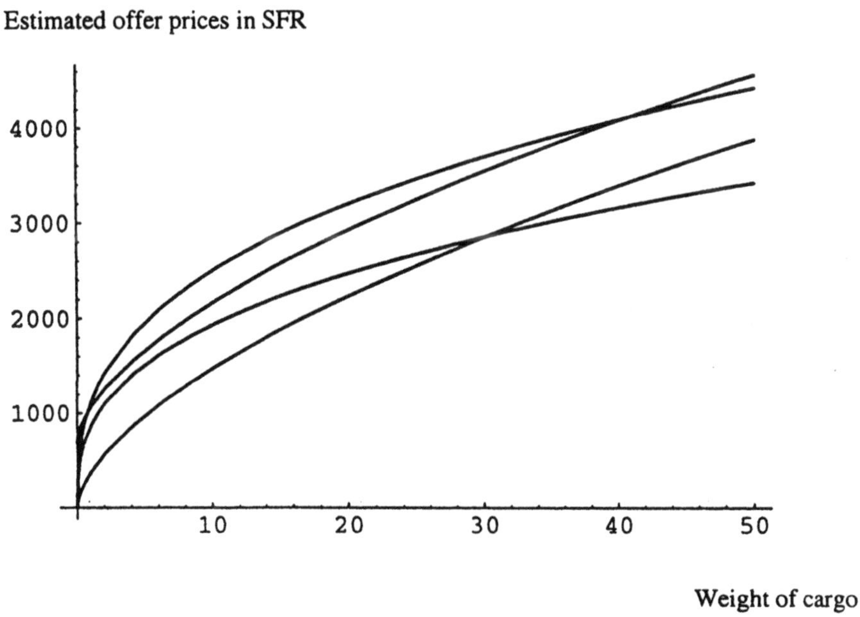

Figure 14.3 Offer prices for freight transport including ATA and LSVA (SFr. 692)

We assume an ATA of 500 and a LSVA of SFr. 0.016, respectively of SFr. 0.025 for our analysis of re-regulatory price effects. The crossing distance for through traffic to pass Switzerland is 300 km from North to South. We calculate a LSVA of total Fr. 192, respectively of Fr. 300, for a full 40 ton truck assuming that the 28 ton limit will be replaced by the LSVA tax system. Furthermore, we assume carriers to charge shippers according to their shipment size (tons). Figure 14.3 shows price effects of re-regulation of through traffic by the levy on through traffic (ATA) of Fr. 500 and the lower variant incentive tax on trucks (LSVA) of Fr. 192.

We can see from Figure 14.3 that the sum of the levies, i.e. ATA + LSVA (total of SFr. 692) shift the offer price function for road upwards. In other words, our results show that under a new system with incentive taxes of SFr. 692 on trucks, the estimated prices for road transports are always higher than offer prices for intermodal transports. According to these findings, the initially proposed regulatory reform would lead to a significant increase of intermodal freight flows because intermodal transport would also be less expensive than using 40 ton trucks (loading capacity: 24 tons of cargo). As a result, current efforts to increase intermodal capacity on trans–Alpine corridors in Switzerland (NEAT) may be needed to meet the resulting growth of intermodal traffic.

On the other hand, if the 28 tons limit will be abolished without reregulating the trucking sector, intermodal transport would only be competitive for cargoes of 30 tons and more. In other words, there would be no incentive to use a different mode than road to cross the Alps for shipments up to 30 tons, because road is the cheapest mode for all shipments which fit on 40 ton trucks (loading capacity: 24 tons plus weight of truck: 16 tons). This of course is rather the opposite outcome than demanded by the 'Alps-Initiative' which foresees carrying all through traffic on rail until the year 2004.

If we compare regulated road transport with rail in Figure 14.3, we can see that the rail mode becomes competitive for heavy loads of 40 tons and more. In other words, this supports the idea that rail has a competitive advantage for moving bulk goods. Again, sidings are assumed for rail movements. However, the estimated offer curve for rail is based on the current regulatory system of the 28 ton limit. As argued previously, we assume that the Swiss railroad monopoly has some power to adapt its prices to road competitors. In other words, it is probable that the rail curve will also shift down after changes in road prices. We assume that the Swiss railroads would be able to provide lower offer prices as a result of, for example, adapting new technologies or implementing operational innovations. It would be probable, thus, that Swiss railroads will adapt their pricing strategy after the re-regulation of the trucking sector. As a result, rail might become competitive for cargoes of less than 40 tons. This holds especially for large volume shippers which are able to negotiate lower rates and tailor-made services.

Currently, there is no movement in the negotiations with the EU, but the latest offer of the EU is to allow the Swiss to impose a total tax (ATA + LSVA) of SFr. 250. The effects of such a tax are illustrated in Figure 14.4.

With this tax, road would be the cheapest mode through the Alps for weights up to 20 tons compared to intermodal transport. This outcome is very interesting. Due to the levy of SFr. 250 on trucks, intermodal transport becomes competitive for weights which are below loading capacity of 24 tons on a 40 ton truck. In other words, the change in relative prices creates an incentive to use intermodal transport for lower weights. This would mean that the proposed regulation by ATA and LSVA of SFr. 250 causes also a shift in the right direction by shifting through traffic from trucks to intermodal transport.

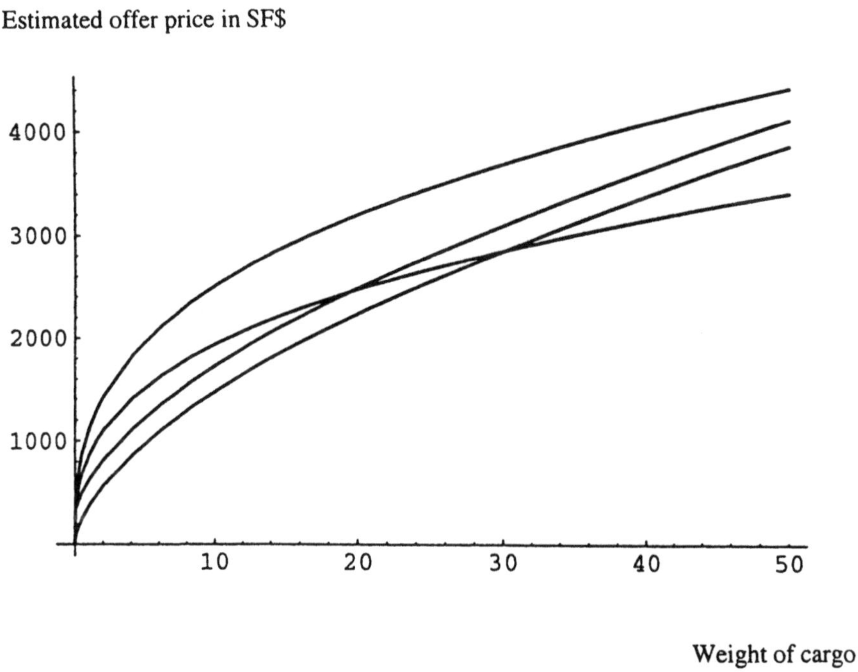

Figure 14.4 Offer prices for freight transport including ATA and LSVA (SFr. 250)

If we compare rail movements (where sidings exist at the origins and destinations) to the reregulated road transport in Figure 14.4, we see that there is no intersection between the two curves. In other words, road transport is more competitive than rail for all cargoes. However, this rather unrealistic outcome is due to the fact that the estimated rail curve is held constant in Figure 14.4. Yet, the Swiss railroads are very likely to adapt their offer prices to changes in relative prices in the road sector as already argued previously. Furthermore, fundamental regulatory changes like separation of operation and infrastructure and free access to third parties are also expected for the trans-Alpine railroad sector. These regulatory reforms would definitely lower offered prices for railroad services and lead to more competitive rail offers than shown in Figure 14.4.

14.7 Conclusions

European transport systems have been heavily affected by liberalization and deregulation trends of international trade. We consider the trans-Alpine freight transportation network which provides a good example of a heavily stressed part of the European transportation system. Different regulatory settings in the Alpine network provide our framework to analyse price offers of carriers and to discuss implications of the Swiss 28 ton limit on trucks as well as alternative regulatory measures.

We conclude that discussed means of regulation have a significant effect on offered prices for well defined freight transport services. The hedonic analysis proved to be an appropriate method to identify price effects of regulation. Selected quality characteristics are relevant elements of carrier's pricing strategies.

The results indicate that the prevailing policy proposal relating to freight transport in Europe, i.e. taxing of heavy vehicles, is a valid alternative to quantitative restrictions for promoting rail and intermodal transport. However, it is difficult to draw straight political implications from our results. The evaluation of policy programmes needs further consideration which goes beyond the present study whose focus is on regulation. Examples of further important conditions which influence the behaviour of freight carriers are other types of regulations in Switzerland or in other countries, such as licenses and driving hours. Moreover technical improvements of the infrastructure and demand behaviour of shippers are important market determinants also.

Though our analysis gives some first insights, further investigation into issues like demand behaviour of shippers as well as impacts of modern logistic concepts is needed. Altogether, investigation into productivity effects and distributional effects of regulation may help to gain a better understanding of overall regulatory effects.

References

Callan, S.J. and Thomas, J.M. (1992), 'Cost Differentials Among Household Good Carriers', *Journal of Transport Economics and Policy*, January, pp. 19–34.

Friedlaender, A.F. and Spady, R.H. (1980), *Freight Transport Regulation,* MIT Press, Cambridge.

Friedli, M. (1996), 'Allgemeine Verkehrspolitik', *Die Volkswirtschaft - Magazin für WirtschaftsPolitik*, pp. 10–9.

Graf, H.G. (1995),'Perspektiven des alpenquerenden Güterverkehrs 1993–2015', GVF-Auftrag Nr. 247, Bern.

GVF (1997), Alpinfo Güterverkehr, *GVF-News*, no. 42, Dienst für Gesamtverkehrsfragen (GVF), Bern, p. 1.

INFRAS (1995), 'Umsetzung der Alpeninitiative. Wirtschaftliche und regionale Auswirkungen einer Alpentransitabgabe', Schlussbericht zuhanden des Bundesamtes für Verkehr, Zürich.

Kinzy, S.A. (1992), 'An Analysis of the Supply of Housing Characteristics by Builders within the Rosen Framework', *Journal of Urban Economics*, vol. 32, no. 1, pp. 1–16.

Lichtenstein, L. and Kern, C.R. (1987), 'The Cost of Quality in Existing Housing: Estimates from an Implicit Market Model', *Journal of Urban Economics*, vol. 22, no. 4, pp. 324–39.

Neue Züricher Zeitung (NZZ), (1996), 'Die Leistungsabhängige Schwerverkehrsabgabe', p. 13.

Rosen, S. (1994), 'Hedonic Prices and Implicit Markets: Product Differentiation in Pure Competition', *Journal of Political Economy*, vol. 62, no. 1, pp.34–55.

Sigmaplan AG (1995), 'Alpenquerender Güterverkehr auf Strasse und Schiene 1994', GVF-Auftrag Nr. 242, Bern.

Triplett, J.E. (1990), 'Hedonic Methods in Statistical Agency Environments: An Intellectual Biopsy', in Berndt, E.R. and J.E. Triplett (eds), *Fifty Years of Economic Measurement*, University of Chicago Press, Chigaco and London.

Varian, H.R. (1992), *Microeconomic Analysis*, 3rd ed., Norton & Company, New York and London.

Wirtschaftsförderung (WF) (1996), 'Gegenwärtiger Stand der Aussenhandelsbeziehungen und der bilateralen Verhandlungen zwischen der Schweiz und der EU', Zürich.

Appendix 14.A.1

Example of an offer request

Commodity:	General Non-Food
Weight:	15 t
Route:	Rotterdam (NL) - Napoli (I)

Shipping time is at 5 pm, day A. Commodities are packed on pallets. There are sidings at the origins and destinations.

Road: Offer Price: Fr. ....

Please indicate below the **soonest** and **latest** possible time of arrival:

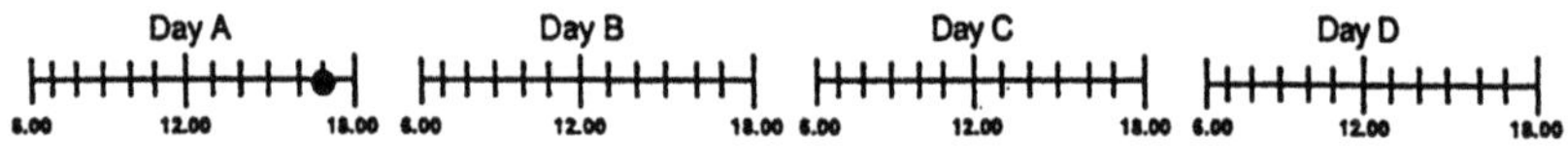

● Ready: Day A, 5 pm

Rail: Offer Price: Fr. ....

Please indicate below the **soonest** and **latest** possible time of arrival:

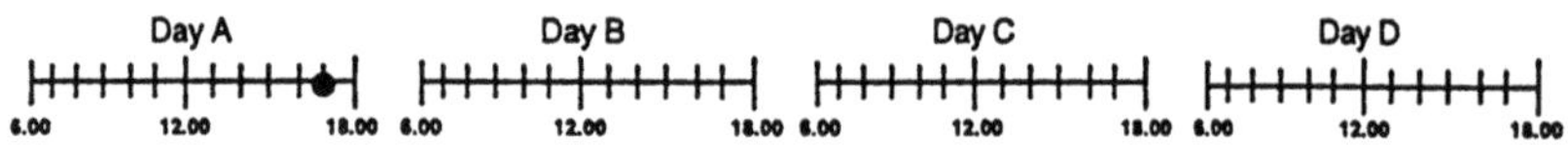

● Ready: Day A, 5 pm

Multimodal Transport: Offer Price: Fr. ....

Which terminals?

....

Please indicate below the **soonest** and **latest** possible time of arrival:

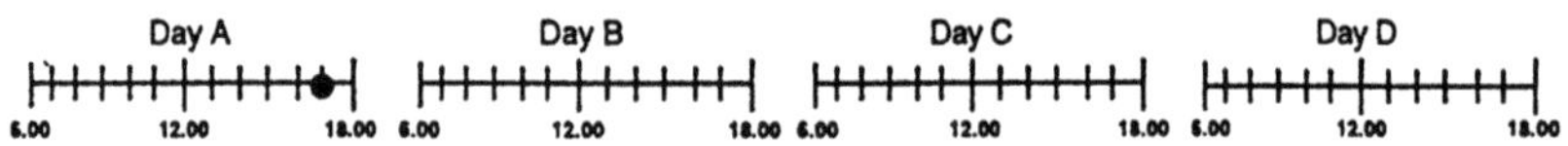

● Ready: Day A, 5 pm

Appendix 14.A.2

List of variables

Variable	Description	
PRICE	Price offer in Swiss Francs (CHF)	
DISTANCE	Distance between origins and destinations in kilometers	
WEIGHT	Weight of load in tons	
TKM	DISTANCE * WEIGHT	
ROAD	Dummy = 1 if road transport	
	Dummy = 0 if rail transport	
MULTIMODAL	Dummy = 1 if multimodal transport	
	Dummy = 0 if rail transport	
LIMIT28T	Dummy = 1	if weight of 30 tons or 42 tons
		and road transport
		and shortest way leads through Switzerland
GOTTHARD	Dummy = 1	if shortes way leads through Switzerland
		(i.e. if path = HAMBURG or ROTTERDAM)
BRENNER	Dummy = 1	if shortest way through Brenner
MTCENIS	Dummy = 1	if shortest way through MtCenis or Montblanc
FIRM1	Dummy = 1	if carrier = Firm 1
FIRM2	Dummy = 1	if carrier = Firm 2
FIRM3	Dummy = 1	if carrier = Firm 3
INROWEIG	Interaction term = ROAD x WEIGHT	
HAMBURG	Dummy = 1	if path Hamburg - Italy
ROTTERDAM	Dummy = 1	if path Rotterdam - Brüssel - Italy
HALLE	Dummy = 1	if path Halle - München - Italy
TIME	Shortest transport time	
TIMEDIFF	Reliability measured as (Expected differerce of shortest and latest arrival) / (TIME)	
PRETIMEDIFF	Predicted values for TIMEDIFF from Stage 1	

Notes

1. Among selected carriers are five Swiss carriers and one Austrian carrier. We are indebted to Wolfgang Koller, University of Economics and Business Administration, Vienna, for doing the Austrian inquiry.

2. We replaced missing values of TIMEDIFF by predicted values regressing shortest transport time TIME on TIMEDIFF.

15 On the Crossing of the Alpine Chain and the Swiss Regulation of Trucking

LAURENT DEMILIE, VALERIE DUPUIS, BART JOURQUIN AND MICHEL BEUTHE

15.1 Introduction

This chapter presents a multimodal freight transportation network model analysis of the problem of trucking regulations in Switzerland. In particular, it aims at assessing the impact of the 40 tons trucks exclusion from Switzerland on the international freight traffic through its territory. The effects of that restriction are measured on the basis of a cost minimizing analysis of transport flows between Italy and the rest of Europe. The paper focuses on the substitution effect between road and rail, and on the choice of itineraries for bypassing Switzerland. The network analysis is based on the trans-European network of roads and railways as defined by the European Conference of Ministers of Transport.

The first section presents the overall international traffic situation of Switzerland and its regulations. The second section explains the methodology of the network analysis, which is based on previous work by Jourquin (1995), the transport cost functions included in the model, the data basis and the calibration of the model. The third section gives the results of the simulation of the present situation and compares them to the results obtained from the simulation of the situation without the present regulation. The conclusion sums up the main results.

15.2 The Problem of the Alpine Passes

Switzerland is an important transit country for freight traffic between Northern Europe and Italy. But the volume of the traffic and the geographic configuration of the country, its circuitous network and mountainous profile, are source of pollution and congestion. In a country where the population gives much attention to preserving a beautiful natural environment, and where tourism is an important activity, these problems raised much concerns, especially since road traffic was continuously expanding. This led to restrictions on trucking over the Swiss territory: since the early seventies transports by trucks of more than 28 tons are forbidden in Switzerland, and trucking is not allowed during the night and on Sunday. But it was decided by referendum that, starting in 2005, all international transit trucks, smaller trucks included, should be banned from Switzerland.

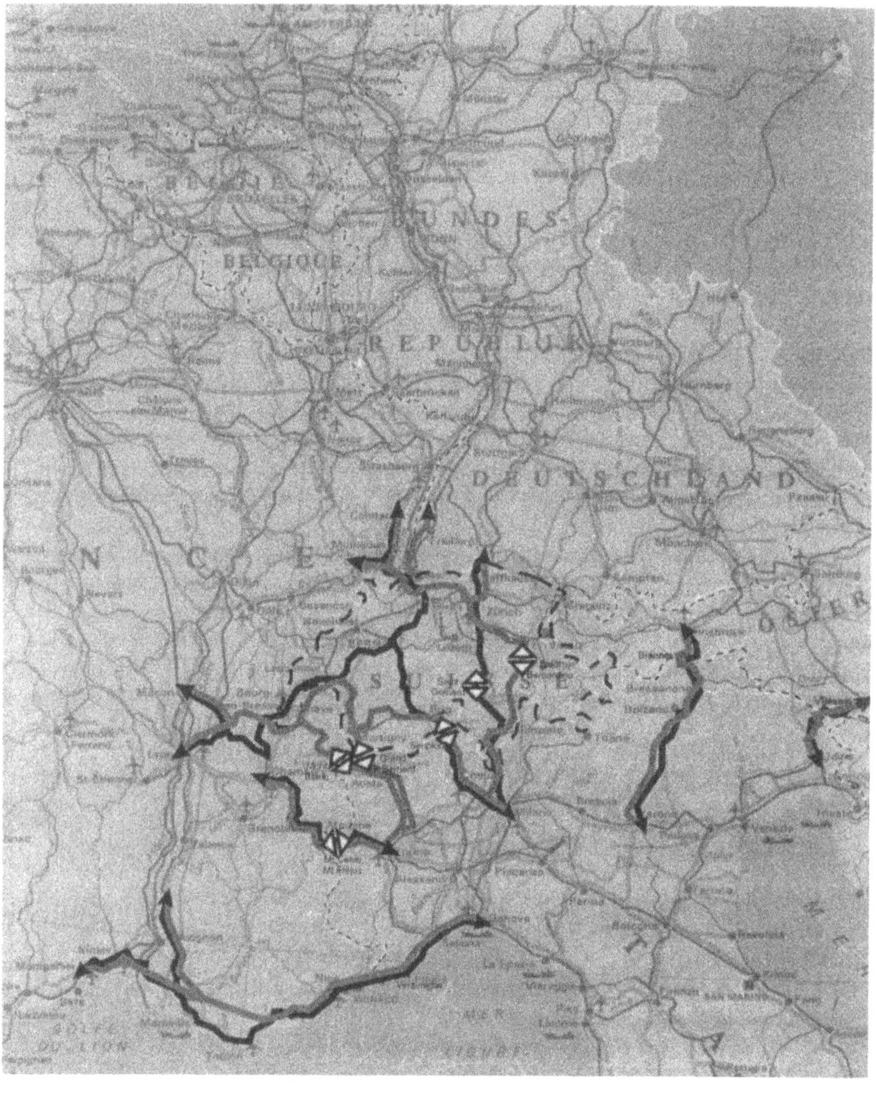

Map 15.1 Main Trans-Alpine passes

A compromise solution to this transit freight problem was negotiated between Switzerland and the European Community and defined in the Transit Agreement of 1990. By this Agreement, Switzerland contracted to develop its railway infrastructures in order to promote combined transports. It is the 'Neue Alpen Transversale' project which includes the boring of new rail tunnels underneath the present tunnels of the St Gotthard and Lötschberg–Simplon links. Note that the decision of completely banning transit transports by trucks is presently under review, and the alternative of penalizing and controlling transit trucking with additional tolls is still considered.

In this chapter, we deal only with the problem of the restriction to 28 tons trucks, analyzing its impact on the cost minimizing transport solutions, on the degree of substitution between rail and road, and on the combined transports which are used. The geographic network which is covered by this analysis includes all the Occidental European countries involved in this international traffic, from Scandinavia to Spain and Italy. This network was digitized on the basis of the list of 'Trunk Lines of International Importance' published by the European Conference of Ministers of Transport (ECMT), updated to the present situation.[1] The map includes roads, railways, inland waterways and short–sea shipping lanes, but, in this application, only the road and railways networks will be used.

Since the Swiss network is at the core of the problem, it is worthwhile to describe the transport corridors which are used for crossing the Alpine chain. Map 15.1 presents the geographic situation of the main Trans-Alpine passes which are used by international freight traffic.

On the Western side, i.e. the French-Italian border:

- At Ventimiglia the rail line has only a single track, but its capacity of 85 trains per day is not fully used, since 25 trains only go through each day;
- The Mt-Cénis/Fréjus pass is made of two tunnels, one for road and the other one for rail. The rail line between Modane and Turin has a capacity of 146 trains per day which is not fully used by the 48 trains per day;
- The Mt-Blanc pass is a road tunnel with a capacity of 250 heavy vehicles per hour.

The main Swiss tunnels are situated along the central segment. Any traffic from Switzerland to Italy necessarily goes through one of them:

- The Gr-St-Bernard Road Tunnel is Part of the E27 towards Aoste. Passengers Traffic is larger than freight Traffic.
- The Lötschberg-Simplon pass is part of the E62 to Milan: the Simplon tunnel links Brig in Switzerland to Domodossola in Italy, by road and by rail with double track; the rail line capacity of 55 trains per day is fully used. On the north side, Brig is connected to Bern and Basel by a double track line through the Lötschberg

tunnel; it is also connected by a double track line to Geneva and Lausanne. On the south side, there are also two access lines from Milan and Novara.

- The St-Gotthard road and rail tunnel is on the National Road 2 between Lucerne and Bellinzona. The rail line which links Zürich and Chiasso allows the loading of trucks on wagons and has a capacity of 179 trains which is close to saturation. A 'rolling road' is also in operation on the line from Basel.
- The San Bernardino road tunnel is on the National Road 13 linking St–Marghreten and Bellinzona.

The Brenner tunnel is part of the central segment (as well as the Reschen) but on the Austrian territory. It is the most important transit point between Italy and Germany and Northern Europe. It provides a road link on the E45 Oslo-Syracuse and a rail link between München and Verona. The rail link is saturated.

Finally, the Eastern segment between Italy and Austria has six main passes. The most important one for the traffic with Eastern countries is the Tarvisio tunnel, but it is also a point of transit for traffic with the Western countries. Its rail link is close to saturation.[2]

Table 15.1 Main Alpine passes

	Road	Acc. combined	Unacc. combined	Rail
Western segment of the Alpine arc				
Ventimiglia	x		x	x
Mt-Cénis/Fréjus	x		x	x
Mt-Blanc	x			
Central segment of the Alpine arc				
Gr-St-Bernard	x			
Simplon	x	(x) 01.01.98	x	x
Gotthard	x	x	x	x
S. Bernardino	x			
Reschen	x			
Brenner	x	x	x	x
Eastern segment of the Alpine arc				
Felbertauern	x			
Tauern	x	x	x	x
Schoberpass	x	x	x	x
Semmering	x		x	x
Wechsel	x		x	x
Tarvisio	x			x

15.2 Methodology

15.2.1 The Geographic and Virtual Networks

For a complete analysis of freight transportation on a network with all its alternative solutions and operating dimensions, it is necessary to identify separately these operations and their characteristics. Thus, transports made by different means on the same infrastructure must be distinguished, and operations of loading, unloading, transshipping and transiting must be separated. This is particularly important if the issue of combined transport is to be dealt with. This can be achieved by creating a fictitious expanded network, or virtual network, linking in a systematic way all the possible successive operations of transportation in the geographic space.[3]

The idea of virtual link in a transportation network was initiated by Harker (1987), who used it in a spatial equilibrium context for modelling different levels of service. It was further developed by Crainic et al. (1990 and 1993) and Guélat et al. (1990) for connecting different modes in the STAN transportation network model. Jourquin's recent contribution (1995), implemented in the NODUS software, was to propose a generalized use of the concept for all the transport operations with an automatic generation of all the virtual links on the basis of a well structured notation of nodes and links. In this way, it is possible to deal with very large networks like the multimodal trans-European network. In the present case, there are about 9,500 geographic links, corresponding to roads and railway tracks, from which something like 180,000 virtual links were generated for this model. The notation also provides a convenient matching of each specific virtual link with the corresponding weight or cost. Additional information on NODUS and the virtual network methodology can also be found in Jourquin and Beuthe (1996), and Demilie et al. (1997).

15.2.2 The Cost Functions

The costs included in the modelling have several components: the costs directly related to the vehicles and their crew, the handling cost and the opportunity cost of time. Together they add up to the shipper's cost. Each mode and means of transportation has its specific cost function. Obviously, for a multimodal transport, the costs of the successive operations of the different modes/means must be added. But, if we consider only a simple unimodal trip by a specific transport unit (e.g. a 40-tons truck), the transport cost per ton is assumed to be a linear increasing function of distance, which can be written as:

$$C^{\theta} = (f^{\theta} + l^{\theta} + o^{\theta}) * H^{\theta} + (m^{\theta} + (f^{\theta} + o^{\theta})/v^{\theta}) * s \qquad (15.1)$$

where θ indicates a particular means/mode combination, H^θ is the time for loading and unloading, and s is the distance. For a particular θ, the first part of the equation (15.1) is a constant, while the second part is proportional to the distance. This general function has been estimated for the different modes and means involved. In the present case, there are two modes, and each mode offers two means: rail transports can be made by a traditional train or by a combined rail/road technique, and road transports can be realized by 28 t. or 40 t. trucks.

The meaning of the different parameters in (15.1) is the following:

- f^θ = F/u*T, per ton and per hour, corresponds to the vehicle cost during the loading and unloading operations:, with F, the vehicle fixed cost per year, (i.e. the capital annuity, the insurance and some of the maintenance costs, plus the crew wages), u, the number of working hours per year, and T, the average load of a vehicle in tons, account being taken of the rate of empty return trips .
- l^θ is the additional labour cost, per ton and per hour, of handling the goods at the points of origin and destination.
- o^θ = R*V/365*24 is the opportunity cost, per ton and per hour, of the capital tied into the goods during one hour, with R, the rate of interest, V, the average value of the goods per ton .
- H^θ, is the sum of loading and unloading times. They are computed by using the formula and the parameters estimated for each mode and each loading or unloading operation by Deming (1978): H = a + b. T^c . It is a non-linear relation between handling time and handled quantity per vehicle:
- m^θ is the variable cost of moving one ton over one km;
- v^θ is the vehicle's average speed, which is the same for the two types of trucks but may vary with the type of road over which they travel.

Besides the initial loading and terminal unloading costs of a transport, multimodal transports also incur transshipment costs. With the exception of rail/road combined transports, for which we have specific figures, transshipment costs are supposed to be the sum of unloading from mode/means θ and loading on mode/means θ'. Transit costs are also included: for the trains, the time cost of waiting at the frontiers, which includes the vehicle cost as well as the opportunity cost, and for the trucks, the road and tunnel tolls.

All the parameters values and their sources are given in the Appendix.

In Figure 15.1, the cost per ton of each mode/means combination is plotted as a function of pier-to-pier journey distance. For instance, the cost for a rail/road combined transport includes the loading at the origin, the trucking to the terminal, the transshipment onto railway wagons at terminal, the railway traction, the transshipment at the end-terminal, and, finally, the transport by truck to the final destination and the unloading. In this figure the cost from origin or destination to the terminal is based on the average distance observed on the network (23 km). We also suppose that the average truck speed is 50 km/h. For this illustration, no toll has been included.

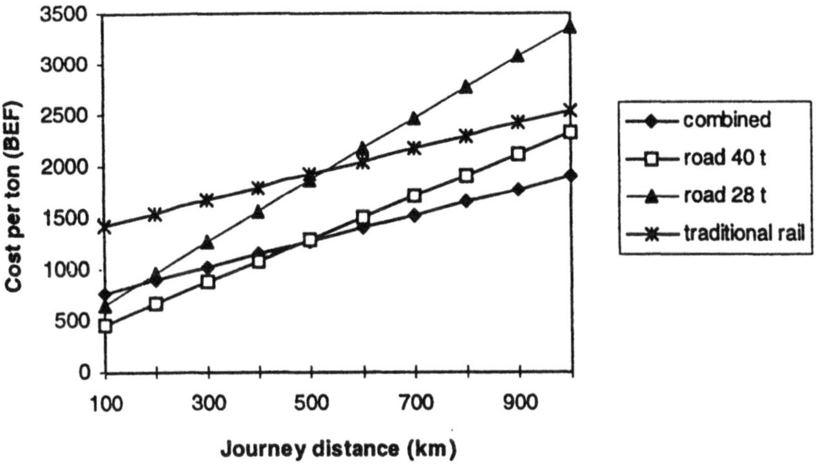

Figure 15.1 Total cost per ton as a function of distance

Thus, it appears that combined transport becomes cheaper than 28 tons truck transport when the distance is longer than 180 km and cheaper with respect to 40 tons truck when the distance is more than 500 km. However, we should be aware that these breaking points may be different from one corridor to another. Indeed, the cost per ton for a transport varies according to the characteristics of the network. For example, it depends on the type of road, which determines the average speed, and on the level of road tolls. For rail transports, it varies with the efficiency of the national railway networks, as explained in the Appendix. Moreover, the cost on a corridor depends also on the specific transit costs which may exist.

15.3 The Database and the Distribution

The database used in this study concerns flows of goods to/from Italy crossing the Alpine Chain in 1994. Regional origin-destination pairs were available for the following countries: Switzerland (12 regions), Italy (6), France (9), Austria (4) and Germany (11). The other relations are aggregated per country.

In order to obtain a point-to-point O-D matrix, a set of centroïds was created as additional nodes of the network. They can be defined as regional centres of gravity, which are taken as points of origin and destination of the goods. Each node of the network was assigned to the closest loading/unloading point. A centroïd was created for each of these clusters of nodes, as a point of unique origin or destination. Moreover, a road link was also created between the centroïd and the nearest loading/unloading point. The distance assigned to that link was the average distance of the nodes in each cluster to that point. It came out that the number of centroids in a region varies from 1 to 20, according to the number of loading/unloading points. The total flows of goods were then assigned among all the centröids, by 5000 random drawings of centröids for small bundles of goods, on a region to region basis. By this Monte-Carlo procedure, a detailed O-D matrix was obtained which can be thought to be very similar to the real one.

Note that, for some countries, such as the Benelux countries, the United Kingdom or the Scandinavian countries, only aggregated data were available. However, the Monte-Carlo procedure in these countries can be justified by the fact that the centröids are not evenly distributed over the network, but are more numerous in industrialized areas where the density of the network is greater. To that extent, it is likely that their distribution over the geographic space corresponds to the distribution of the real origins and destinations. In any case, as these countries are further away from Italy, it is unlikely that this approximation makes any difference.

15.4 Modal Choice and Calibration of the Model

Given the matrix of origins and destinations which defines a set of transportation tasks, the total cost of transportation over the virtual network can be minimized by the choice, for each pair of origin and destination, of the cheapest mode, means and route, the alternatives of combined transport included. Thus, summing up all the costs defined in the previous section, the following total cost is minimized for each origin/destination:

$$TC = \sum_{\text{Origin-Destination}} \; \sum_{\text{Mode/Mean/Route}} \left[\sum_{\text{Unloading}} \text{costs} + \sum_{\text{Loading}} \text{costs} + \sum_{\text{Moving}} \text{costs} + \sum_{\text{Transshipment}} \text{costs} + \sum_{\text{Simple Trasnit}} \text{costs} \right]$$

Naturally, the results of such an exhaustive and detailed analysis can be aggregated in order to compute the modes' market shares; also, all the itineraries as well as the combinations of modes can be identified.

It is worth underlining at this point that the cost minimization is made on the basis of an all-or-nothing procedure for each origin/destination pair, so that all the traffic (of a given commodity) between two nodes is assigned to the same mode/means/route combination. This follows from the specification of the costs per ton which are not increasing functions of the total quantities transported on a particular link. Such an approach supposes normally that there is no capacity constraint. In general, this rather strong hypothesis can be accepted when annual transport flows over a large network are studied. We are aware of the existence of some capacity constraints at a few passes across the Alpine chain. But, the implementation of an equilibrium model in a large network is a difficult task which will require additional work. In the meantime, the results given by an 'all or nothing' assignment procedure are worth considering.

The results obtained can be taken as estimates of transport demand for the different modes and means and itineraries under two hypotheses: that the shippers are actually minimizing the generalized cost of transport, and that the carriers' tariffs bear a close relationship with the operating transport cost, at least at the margin for 'contestable' transports. Both hypotheses can certainly be debated. But, even if they are accepted as a reasonable approximation, the results of this cost minimization have to be assessed with caution, and the model must be calibrated before proceeding further. To begin with, despite the number of cost elements included in the functions, the total cost analyzed does not fully match the definition of generalized cost that is supposed to be minimized by shippers. Decision factors like reliability, safety, information and other services which are provided by the carriers are not included in the functions, because their cost equivalent for the shipper is not known. Moreover, there may be technical or administrative factors which lead the railways to not choose the shortest (and normally the cheapest) route between some origins and destinations. And, then again, the carriers' cost used in the model is only a proxy for the tariff paid by the shipper (and which is generally unknown).

For all these reasons, adjustments will be made to the cost functions, in order to obtain a better fit of the initial simulations to the observed market shares, and to take into account in that way the decision factors which cannot be included formally in the modelling of the costs. The initial simulations which will be used as reference basis are naturally the simulations of the present situation where 28 tons trucks only are allowed in Switzerland. In effect, two distinct basic simulations will be made for the manufactured goods and the non-manufactured goods respectively, in order to take into account the different values of these goods, i.e. 231,000 BEF versus 24,000 BEF, and the corresponding opportunity costs, as well as their specific service requirements. Moreover, since hardly any quantity of non-manufactured goods is transported by combined transport, this transport option is not included in the simulation relative to non-manufactured goods.[4]

Table 15.2 gives the coefficients of adjustments applied to the trucking costs of the two categories of goods.

The decreases of trucking costs should correspond to a large extent to the better relative quality of the road transport services for many goods. This should be particularly the case for the manufactured goods, and we note that the adjustment applied to the manufactured goods is accordingly stronger. An additional adjustment is applied to the 28 tons truck costs for the manufactured goods simulation. Indeed, the lesser weight of these goods and the smaller size of their shipments increase the competitiveness of lighter trucks which can pass through Switzerland.

Table 15.2 Cost adjustments

Manufactured goods	(40 t. truck cost) * 0.68 (28 t. truck cost) * 0.63
Non-manufactured goods	(truck costs) * 0.79

Finally, the railways do not always choose the shortest route. For example, in the case of international transports, the German DB tends to keep the trains as long as possible on its own network, because the revenue of international transports is divided between the different companies in proportion to the distances on the respective networks. Hence, in some cases, the railways do not choose the shortest and, presumably, the cheapest route between an origin and a destination, because the least cost route is not necessarily the one which maximizes their own profit. For that reason, a penalty has been added to the train costs at the Swiss/German and Western Austrian/German borders to force part of the German traffic to remain on the German network and to take the longer route through the Brenner. Another adjustment was made to take into account the particular organization of the French and Belgian railways which concentrate transports from the north to the Mt Cenis tunnel. The train costs over that corridor have been decreased by 15 percent.

The same adjusted cost functions will be used to simulate what would happen if 40 tons trucks were allowed in Switzerland. Then, the comparison of the results obtained in the two situations, i.e. the differences between the modes/means market shares and between the traffic flows over the feasible itineraries, will provide measures of the present regulation's impact.

15.5 The Simulations and Their Results

The basic simulations correspond to the present situation where 28t. trucks only are authorized in Switzerland. Table 15.3 compares the observed modal splits to those resulting from the two basic simulations. As can be seen, the modal distributions given by the simulations are very close to the observed ones, but the rail share of manufactured goods transports is somewhat overestimated.

Table 15.4 gives the modal distribution at the different national borders with Italy. If we compare the estimated 28 tons results to the observed modal splits, we see that road traffic is overestimated in Austria and Switzerland and underestimated in France. This result can be partly explained by the fact that it was difficult to model the full set of road traffic regulations in Austria and Switzerland. Actually, in order to take into account their effect on the traffic, we reduced the trucks' average speed in these two countries. But, regulations like the Austrian restriction to 38 tons trucks or on the number of transit authorizations, for example, have been ignored. Altogether though, despite these imperfections, we think that these results fit reasonably well with the observed data, and that they provide a good basis for analyzing what would happen if the present restriction on trucking in Switzerland was raised.

Table 15.3 Observed and estimated modal splits

	Mode	Observed %	Est. 28 t. %
Manufactured goods	Rail	42	44
	Road	68	66
Non- manufactured goods	Rail	32	32
	Road	68	68

Table 15.4 Observed and estimated modal split by border

		Observed		Est. 28 t		Est. 40 t	
Est 40 t.		Mi. t.	%	Mi. t.	%	Mi. t.	%
Swiss/Italian border	Rail	14.8	78	14.7	67	0.9	2
	Road	4.1	22	7.1	33	46.2	98
French/Italian border	Rail	8.6	20	8.5	25	5.4	23
	Road	34.4	80	25.6	75	17.9	77
Austrian/Italian border	Rail	9.6	32	10.6	29	6.6	31
	Road	20.4	68	25.4	71	14.9	69
Total	Rail	33.0	36	33.8	37	12.9	14
	Road	58.9	64	58.1	63	79.0	86

Table 15.4 also presents the results of the simulations corresponding to the suppression of the 28 tons limit. It shows that allowing 40 tons trucks would have an important impact on the global modal split as the share of road transports would increase from 63 percent to 86 percent. Naturally, Switzerland would be the most affected by the change, since international road transports through its territory would increase from the 7.1 millions of tons estimated by the basic simulation to 46.2 millions. Part of that increase, 20.9 mi.t., would correspond to a switch from rail to road transports, while the rest, 18.2 mi.t., would be the result of a rerouting of road traffic from neighbouring countries. Rail traffic through Switzerland would be reduced to as little as .9 million tons!

As a consequence, the overall traffic through France and Austria would be reduced, but the reduction of road traffic would be particularly strong. In France, the road traffic would decrease by 7.7 mi.t. as against 3.1 mi.t. for the rail, while in Austria, the road traffic would decrease by 10.5 mi.t. as against 4 mi.t. for the rail. In both countries, the rail share would become larger.

The huge impact on the modal split in Switzerland can be explained by the fact that there exists no toll road in this country and no tunnel toll at the Gothard pass. Moreover, the shortest path from the North of France, the Benelux countries and Germany is also going through the Gothard. Nevertheless, it is likely that the modal shift is somewhat overestimated because some restrictions which bear upon road traffic in Switzerland are not fully taken into account in the modelling. Moreover, such an increase of road traffic at some of the passes would create congestion problems which would induce some rerouting of the traffic.

More detailed results are also available for each Alpine pass. Table 15.5 shows the impacts of raising the 28 tons limit in Switzerland on the traffic at each of the Alpine passes, in millions of tons and in number of vehicles.

Table 15.5 Impacts of raising the 28 tons limit on the traffic at the passes

Pass	Rail variations		Road variation	
	mi.t	trains	mi.t.	trucks (1000)
Vintimiglia	-0.1	-221	-	-
Mt-Cenis	-3.1	-6233	-0.6	-36
Mt-Blanc	-	-	-7.0	-422
St-Bernard	-	-	0.5	26
Simplon	-1.4	-2835	1.0	54
Bernardino	-	-	9.38	491
St-Gothard	-12.3	-24858	28.0	1562
Brenner	-3.5	-7032	-9.9	-600
other austrian	-0.4	-810	-0.3	-20

Note: On average, trains carry 497 tons, 28 t.trucks carry 11.1t., and 40t trucks 16.6t.

It can be seen that rail traffic decreases at all the rail passes, and particularly at the Mt-Cenis, the St-Gothard and the Brenner. The road traffic diminishes at the Mt-Blanc and the Brenner, while it strongly increases at the St-Gothard and the San Bernardino passes.

Maps 15.2 and 15.3 present the maps of the main variations of traffic, where the width of the lines is proportional to its increase or decrease.

The map shows that the main decrease of rail traffic will come from Germany and the Benelux countries, along the axis Düsseldorf – Frankfurt – Basel – St-Gothard – Milano. As for the road traffic, the reduction is important on the Metz – Dijon – Mt-Blanc – Torino/Milano axis and the Würzburg – Brenner axis.

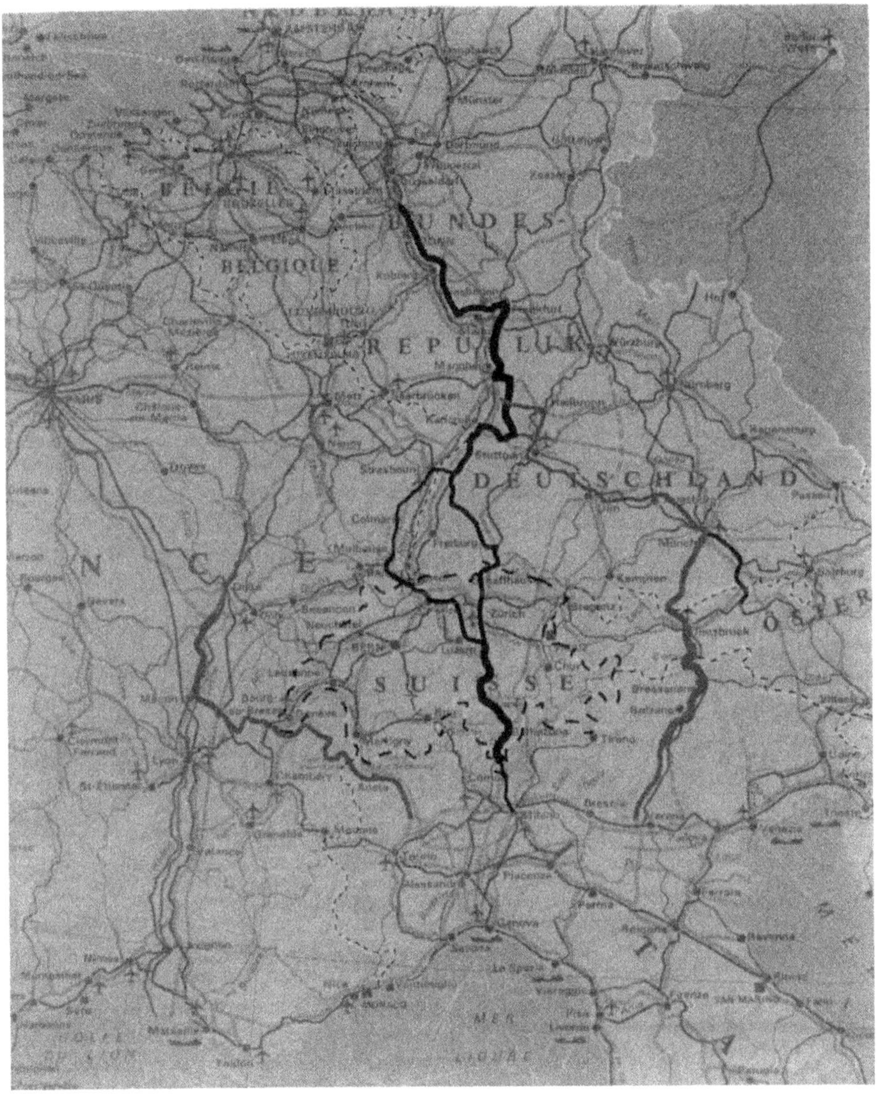

Map 15.2 Main decreases of traffic (Black = rail traffic, Gray = road traffic)

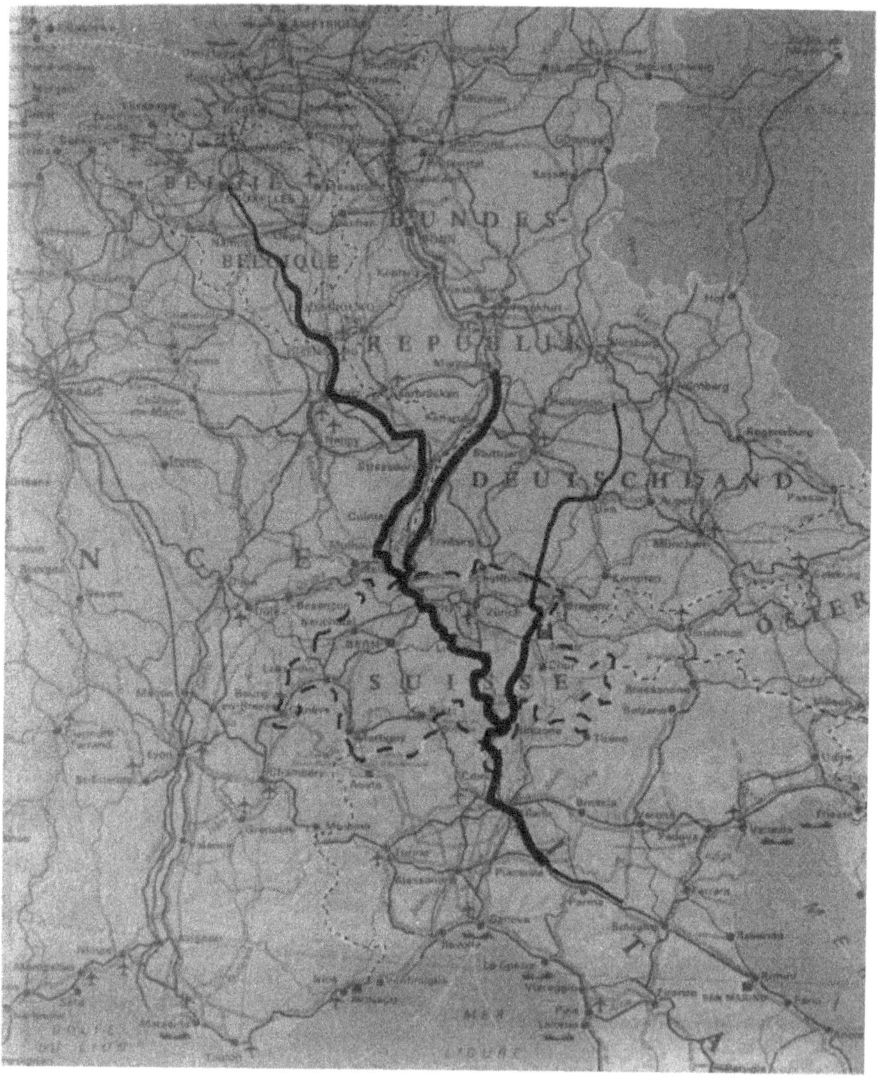

Map 15.3 Main increases of road traffic

In Map 15.4, we can see that two flows of trucks feed the St-Gothard pass, one coming from Belgium and following the Antwerp/Brussels – Metz – Strasbourg – Basel axis, instead of going down through Southern France, the other one coming from The Netherlands and following the Rotterdam – Düsseldorf – Frankfurt – Basel axis. There is also an increased flow from the Eastern part of Germany, which takes the San Bernardino pass instead of the Brenner route.

15.6 Conclusions

This chapter is an attempt to estimate the impacts of the Swiss 28 t. trucks restriction on the transport of goods between Italy and the European countries across the Alpine chain. It uses an extensive model of the trans-European freight transport networks, and relies on a cost analysis rather than on volatile and often unknown tariffs. As far as it was possible, the cost functions were adjusted on the basis of the comparison between the flows estimated by the simulation of the present situation and the observed flows. This adjustment provided a reasonable fit of the model, presumably taking into account some unknown elements of the generalized cost of transport, as well as some traffic diversions which result from technical or administrative requirements and constraints. We think that it offers an interesting basis for assessing the impacts of the Swiss regulation on the choice of modes, means and routes.

When comparing the results of the simulations with the 28 t. restriction to the results obtained without it, it appears that this regulation strongly reduces road freight transports on the Swiss territory: cancelling this restriction would provoke an increase of 39 millions tons transported by road through Switzerland. Part of that increase, i.e. 18 millions tons, would result from the choice of routes through Swiss territory rather than through Austria and France, but the rest of that traffic diversion, i.e. 21 millions tons, would be the result of a modal switch from rail transportation.

The impact of the regulation can also be measured in numbers of trucks using the Swiss roads without the restriction: 2.7 millions trips of 40 t. trucks per year could be expected in place of the .64 million trips of 28 t. trucks. Clearly, the regulation has an important impact from an environmental point of view.

The present chapter focuses on an important specific regulation, but, obviously, the same model and analysis could be applied to measure the impact of some other regulations and means which are under review at the present time, like some different pricing schemes or new technical means and infrastructures.

References

Beuthe, M. and Jourquin, B. (1994), 'L'Influence du Tour de Rôle sur les Coûts de la Navigation Intérieure', *Revue d'Economie Régionale et Urbaine,* no. 3, pp. 417–27.

CEMAT, (1995), *Europe Speaks Intermodal*, booklet, Rome.

CFF (1990), *Le Printemps du Rail*, information booklet of SF, Berne.

Chatelus, G. and Torricelli, G.-P. (1994), *Coopérations Transalpines et Infrastructures de Transport, Une Étude de Cas sur les Relations de l'Italie avec la Suisse et la France*, I.N.R.E.T.S. and I.R.E.

Coleman, R. (1995), *La 'Perméabilité' de la Chaîne des Alpes, Charnière entre le Nord et le Sud de l'Europe,* CEE-Forum dello Sviluppo, Turin

Comité National Routier (1995), *'Coûts de Référence',* Les fiches des cahiers de l'observatoire du CNR, Paris.

Crainic, T.G., Florian, M., Guélat, J. and Spiess, H. (1990), 'Strategic Planning of Freight Transportation: STAN, An Interactive Graphic System', *Transportation Research Record,* 1283.

Crainic, T.G., Florian, M. and Larin, D. (1993), 'STAN, New Developments', Centre de Recherche sur les Transports, Université de Montréal, Research paper no. 942.

Demilie, L, Jourquin, B. and Beuthe, M. (1997), 'A Sensitivity Analysis of Transportation Modes Market Shares on a Multimodal Network, The Case of Dry Bulk Transports between Benelux/Germany and Spain', in Capineri, C. and P. Rietveld (eds), *Networks in Transport and Communications*, Ashgate, Aldershot, pp. 235–51.

Deming, W.E. (1978), 'On a Rational Relationship for Certain Costs of Handling Motor Freight over the Platform', *Transportation Journal*, vol. 17, pp. 5-11.

DFTCE-Sigmaplan (1991), *Transalpiner Güterverkehr, Auswirkungrn des Gotthard-Strassentunnels auf den Güterverkehr, Schlussbericht über die Entwicklung 1980-1989*, Bern.

DFTCE-Sigmaplan (1995), *Alpenqueneder Güterverkehr auf Strasse und Schiene 1994, Alpenbogen Ventimiglia bis Wien*, GVF-Auftrag nr.242, Dienst für Gesamtverkehrsfragen, Bern.

Gathon, H-J., (1991), 'La Performance Relative des Chemins de Fer Européens: Gestion et Autonomie', PhD thesis, University of Liège.

Guélat, J., Florian, M. and Crainic, T.G. (1990), 'A Multimode Multiproduct Network Assignment Model for Strategic Planning of Freight Flows', *Transportation Science*, vol. 24, pp. 25–39.

Harker, P.T. (1987), *Predicting Intercity Freight Flows*, VNU Science Press, Utrecht, The Netherlands.

Jourquin, B. (1995), 'Un Outil d'Analyse Économique des Transports de Marchandises sur des Réseaux Multi-modaux et Multi-produits: Le Réseau Virtuel, Concepts, Méthodes et Applications', PhD Thesis, Facultés Universitaires Catholiques de Mons.

Jourquin, B. and Beuthe, M. (1996), 'Transportation Policy Analysis with a Geographical Information System: The Virtual Network of Freight Transportation in Europe', *Transportation Research C*, vol. 4, no. 6, pp. 359–71.

Ministero dei Transporti e della Navigazione (1995), Conto Nazionale dei Transporti, Roma, Italy.
Reggiani, A. and Bolis, S. (1998), *Methods and Models Analysing Transalpine Freight Transport: An Overview*, in Beuthe, M. and P. Nijkamp (eds), *Dynamic Networks and Spatial Change*, Ashgate, Aldershot (forthcoming).
Russo, R. (1995), *Combined Transport through the Alps, A Comparative Analysis at the Austrian-Italian Border,* Vienna University of Economics and Business Administration.
Sandonnini, P.P. (1991), *Ricerca Sulle Problematiche dello Scambio Internazionale delle Merci Attraverso i Valichi Alpini*, Unione Regionale delle Camere di Commercio Industria Artigianato e Agricoltura del Veneto.
Senn, L. (1995), *Il Trasporto Attraverso le Alpi, Nuove Infrastrutture di Trasporto nelle Alpi: la Necessità di un Approccio Globale e Sistemico*, Uniontrasporti, Milan.
U.I.C. (1994), *European Infrastructure Master Plan,* Paris.

Appendix 15.A.1

In this annex the values of the parameters – with reference to equation (15.1) – are shown.

The values in Table 15.A.1 are expressed in 1994 BEF: f, l, and o are in BEF per ton and per hour, m in BEF per ton/km.

Table 15.A.1 Values of the parameters[5]

	Railway		Truck	
Parameters	Combined	Classic	40 tons	28 tons
f	13	9	63	95
l	-	2.05	60.28	90.42
o (manufactured)	2.64	2.64	2.64	2.64
o (non manufactured)	0.27	0.27	0.27	0.27
m	0.80[a]	0.78[a]	0.75[b]	1.05[b]
Average loading (tons)	496.8	488.8	16.6	11.1
% empty	20	17	21	21

a: includes fuel, part of maintenance and various administrative costs.
b: includes fuel, maintenance and repair, and the cost of the tires.

Table 15.A.2 Adjustment coefficients

Railway company	Productivity index	Relative index to Belgium
SJ	1	0.592
NS	0.762	0.777
SNCF	0.7	0.846
RENFE	0.69	0.858
VR	0.675	0.877
CFF	0.667	0.888
CH	0.666	0.889
BR	0.653	0.907
CFL	0.637	0.929
SNCB	0.592	1
FS	0.583	1.015
CP	0.563	1.052
DB	0.528	1.121
TCDD	0.352	1.682

The parameters for the railways are based on the published statistics of the Belgian railway company (S.N.C.B.). As there exists a large number of possible engine-carriage combinations, we have defined a standard traditional train and a standard train for combined transport. Note that the Belgian cost data have been adjusted for each national railway company, in order to take account of their varying efficiency. The adjustment coefficients, which are given in Table 15.A.2, are based on the work of Gathon (1991). Jourquin (1995) gives more details on the computation of the parameters.

Notes

1. From information collected from various sources. Among them: U.I.C. (1994); DFTCE–Sigmaplan (1991,1995); CEMAT (1995).

2. Useful references on the crossing of Switzerland can be found in CFF (1990); Chatelus and Torricelli (1994); Coleman (1995); Russo (1995); Sandonnini (1991); Senn (1995).

3. An interesting review of alternative approaches can be found in Reggiani and Bolis (1998).

4. Practically, the manufactured goods correspond to the NSTR category 9. No category of non-manufactured goods uses combined transport by more than 5 percent.

5. The road data are from the Comité National Routier, France (1994) and FEBETRA, Belgium. The traditional railway data are based on statistics provided by the Belgian railway company (S.N.C.B.), adjusted in order to take into account the relative efficiency of the various national railway companies: see Jourquin (1995) and Gathon (1991). The specific combined railway data are provided by INTERCONTAINER, EUROTRANS and TRW.

16 External Effects Evaluation and Environmental Impact Reduction in Freight Transportation

DOMENICO CAMPISI, MASSIMO GASTALDI AND PIERFRANCESCO REVERBERI

16.1 Introduction

Transportation plays a fundamental role in the organization of modern societies, given that wide and dense communication networks definitely lead towards the social and economic integration of the different countries. Though the substantial benefits that a well-developed transportation network is capable to provide to the system of human activities are highly appreciated, there is a growing awareness of the significant inconveniences which may be attributed to its considerable growth rates as registered in recent decades. Actually, economy and trade expansions encouraged by a more extensive transport system than the past determine a transport demand growth which heavily reflects in traffic congestion and air pollution.

At present, the transportation sector burden far exceeds the environmental carrying capacity and the risk exists that ecological sustainability is seriously endangered by economic development. The social costs of road transport are estimated to amount to approximately 5 percent of Gross Domestic Product (GDP) in most developed countries. Such costs are largely due to air and noise pollution caused by vehicle circulation and the lack of safety of the road network (Himanen et al. 1992; Gastaldi et al. 1996).

It goes without saying that comprehensive and yet articulated strategies are needed in order to keep transportation sector growth within the bounds imposed by a sustainable development. Scientific research is highly contributing to pursue this aim through the starting-up of a large number of projects that study the whole set of transportation and environment interactions. These projects are expected to introduce significant innovations both in the technological context (e.g. by producing electric vehicles, alternative fuels, catalytic converters, efficient and silent engines) and in the strategic decision making process (including policy measures directed towards transport demand modal and space-time restriction and redistribution, as well as transport supply operational improvement).

Researches undertaken in the field of transportation/environment interactions are evolving from a transport mode-oriented approach, that analyses independently the environmental impacts of each transport mode, to an integrated approach that tries to elicit the complex set of interrelationships both between the transport and environmental systems and within each of the two systems.

Freight transport impinges on the environment in several important ways, yet not considered a decade or so ago: in particular, it severely contributes to acoustic and atmospheric pollution, accidents, low level ozone concentration, vibration and visual intrusion. Environmental damages caused by transportation (particularly by road users) are stimulating political intervention for remedial actions, that are coming about through the introduction of new regulations and standards and the tightening of existing laws. Fairly drastic measures have been proposed by governments in various countries (e.g. Canada, Denmark, Japan, the Netherlands and Sweden) to curb the ever increasing trend of road freight transport by means of economic and technological incentives, regulations and prohibitions. These actions are leading to the definition of taxes and fees for transport users that are intended to diminish the gap between payments and marginal costs. The pressures of increasingly congested road infrastructures and environmental protection on the one side, together with the needs of modern industry and the globalization of markets on the other, impose that production delivery should be shifted away from road networks to high quality rail and integrated road-rail transport services.

In this framework, Italy suffers from a peculiar handicap, because its geographical and geological patterns, together with the inadequacy of its physical railway network, create an impedance to the movement of goods. Thus, it seems to be difficult to switch road freight transport to the apparently more ecological rail mode over the short run. The main aim of this paper is to give some insights relative to the current situation in Italy and verify the possibility of switching increasing rates of truck transport towards the less pollutant railway system.

This paper is structured as follows. Section 16.2 briefly reviews state of art methodologies for socioeconomic evaluation of transport impacts on the environment, with particular regard to freight transport. Section 16.3 includes the econometric model. A Barnett translog cost function for a three-input transportation model is estimated and extensive numerical simulations are carried out which aim at evaluating environmental benefits from introducing a given pollution tax in the Italian rail-truck competition case. Finally, Section 16.4 contains some concluding remarks.

16.2 Socioeconomic Evaluation of Environmental Impacts

Transportation system impacts on the environment are of various nature and strength, depending on the different transport modes. Thus, the negative effects of the latter should be assessed and compared according to the following environmental quality criteria (EEC 1992):

- operational pollution, originating directly from vehicular traffic, which greatly affects air, water and vegetation quality and produces noise and vibrations;
- soil intrusion by transportation infrastructures, that often determine permanent and irreversible detriments;
- traffic congestion, which is a recurring phenomenon of increasing significance in urban and metropolitan areas, not only for road but also for rail, air and waterway transport;
- risk of possibly devastating accidents due to hazardous freight transport.

It has been assessed that road transport is the cause of the most severe impacts of operational pollution, soil intrusion, traffic congestion and hazardous freight transport; therefore, a large amount of research project resources have been employed to improve its performances. Results achieved by these projects and their socioeconomic implications largely influence transport policy measures adopted by the different countries.

It was quickly recognized that the technological progress contribution, which consists of efficient and silent engines, catalytic converters, alternative fuels and electric vehicles aiming at reducing vehicle emissions below acceptable levels imposed by the authorities, is not enough by itself to curb the adverse environmental effects due to the rapid transport and mobility demand growth (DRIVE 1990). This means that it must be supported by the adoption of a comprehensive strategy including policy measures directed towards transport demand modal and space-time restriction and redistribution, as well as transport supply operational improvement.

Due to the wide range of possible interventions, it is necessary to set up a methodology for identifying proper transport policy measures, on the basis of a correct forecast of their connected impacts. In particular, several models have to be used for such different areas as transport system planning and management (including both demand/supply and transport system/land use interaction models: see e.g. Meyer and Miller 1984), air pollution modelling (including combined modules for assessing emission and dispersion phenomena: see e.g. Matzoros and Van Vliet 1992), noise pollution modelling (including manual methods, on-scale simulation of physical models and numerical simulation by automatic computation codes: see e.g. DRIVE 1989). It does not comply with the aims of this chapter to analyse in detail any of the abovementioned models. What is more relevant here is focusing the attention on economic evaluation of transportation impacts on the environment.

Socioeconomic evaluation of traffic pollution is necessary to assure equity between polluters and those suffering from pollution, by determining the amount of transfer price for a proper incentive policy.

The Dublin Declaration on the Environment in 1990 documents the need to take account of the external effects due to transportation. The transport sector produces both internal and external effects. Recall that internal effects consist of immediate economic consequences of an action that are directly perceived by the agent, while external effects are related to benefits or inconveniences to other people or firms caused by an economic agent who does not bear the economic consequences of his action, that often are not part of a market transaction. However, it is often difficult – and sometimes even not possible- to distinguish clearly among internal and external effects. For instance, accident costs are partly internal (through insurance fees) and partly external (through expenses sustained by the welfare system); likewise, infrastructure costs are partially external in sofar as specific taxes and tolls paid by users are not directly related to marginal costs. Therefore, Table 16.1 must be seen as a tentative initial classification.

Table 16.1 Social costs scheme

SOCIAL COSTS	EXTERNAL COSTS	ECOLOGY COSTS	FAUNA & FLORA
			ENERGY
			NOISE
			AIR, WATER, LAND, POLLUTION
			LANDSCAPE EFFECTS
			VIBRATION
		CONGESTION	
		ACCIDENTS	
		USE OF SPACE	
	EXTERNAL COSTS / INTERNAL COSTS	INFRASTR. COSTS	
	INTERNAL COSTS	PRIVATE COSTS	FUEL
			MAINTENANCE
			REPAIRS
			INSURANCE
			TAX
			VEHICLE AMORTIZATION

Source: Gastaldi et al. (1996).

Figures 16.1 and 16.2 show the physical effects of transportation on the environment, depending on time interval and spatial size. Clearly, it is difficult to forecast environmental effects of transportation when these concern a long term horizon and/or remote geographical areas. Moreover, some effects are not fully identified by those who suffer from them: generally, people do not perceive a causal relationship between diseases and environmental pollution.

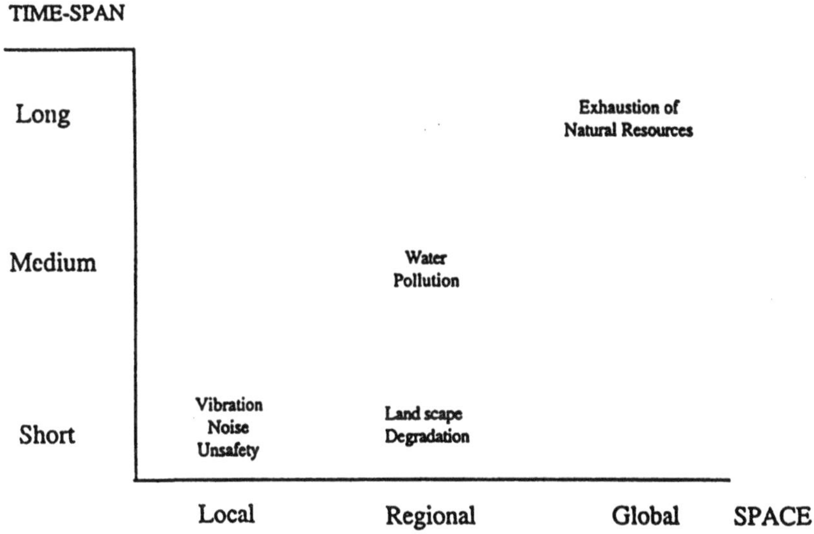

Figure 16.1 Physical effects of transportation on the environment (except air pollution)

Source: Gastaldi et al. (1996).

An important market principle is the internalization of external effects of the transport system (primarily due to traffic accidents, air pollution, noise annoyance and recurring congestion) through pricing of the external costs for society. If these effects are not considered properly, an allocation of resources will result that produces and consumes too much transportation, favouring transport modes that create significant negative effects at the expense of those that cause only minor negative effects. Studies conducted in Sweden demonstrate that, at present, only private cars with catalytic converters, rail traffic on the main line system and domestic aviation pay according to the current evaluation of external costs (Hansson 1991).

The problem is that external costs such as environmental impacts cannot be easily estimated nor evaluated in financial terms, since in most cases there are no market prices; consequently, a cost responsibility cannot be easily determined. Nevertheless, any fully rational decision making process concerning environmental problems should be based on monetary valuations, so that it is a duty for economists to make them explicit and precise as far as possible. The value of environmental goods that have no market price can be assessed either on the supply side or the demand side (Gastaldi et al. 1996). On the supply side, two methods are currently in use: a) the abatement cost for alleviating harm caused by the environmental degradation, such as the cost of noise protection by anti-noise screens; b) the damage cost, such as productivity losses or health care expenses due to air pollution. Also on the demand side two methods are currently in use: a) willingness to pay (WTP), namely, the amount of money that would be paid in order to have a better environment, as for reducing air pollution; b) willingness to accept (WTA), namely, the amount of money that would compensate environmental condition worsening.

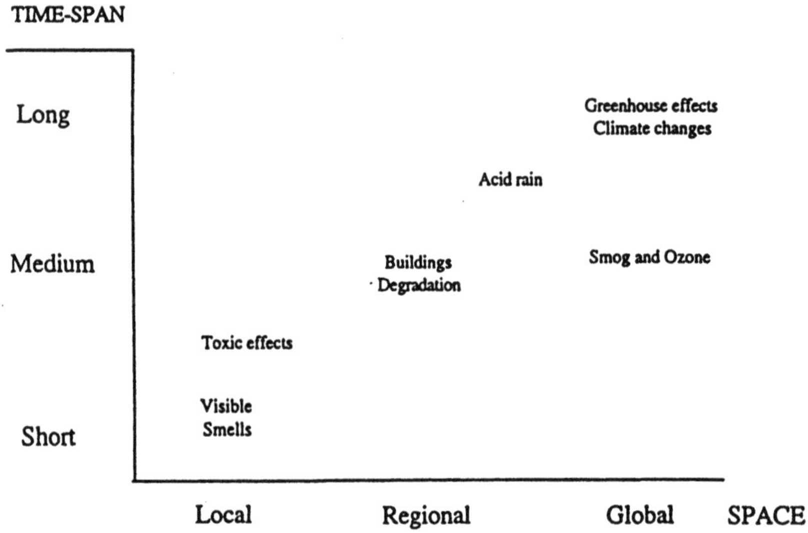

Figure 16.2 Transportation effects on atmospheric pollution

Source: Gastaldi et al. (1996).

Even if an optimal charge cannot be defined, policy measures are compelled to establish restrictions, regulations and economic incentives to reduce detrimental effects, in light of the fact that nature cannot manage current pollution level. Once an environmental objective is formulated, e.g. as a specified limitation for an emission, the question is how to reach this goal. In this framework, external effects pricing can be used as an economic instrument to reach any specified limitation as cost efficiently as possible. Without a charge, there are only costs for measures reducing the emissions, while, with emission charges, there would be counteracting reductions in the total charges paid for emissions. Charge levels will determine whether it is favourable or not in specific cases to take measures to reduce emissions. Imposing taxes and fares on infrastructure use, miles travelled, fuel consumption, pollutant emissions, car ownership, driving licence and/or encouraging the purchase of unleaded-fuelled cars with catalytic converters may represent effective means to achieve the established government standards for emission levels. Thus, environmental constraints may be capable of stimulating technological progress. Some examples of in force or proposed charges for road, rail, air and navigation traffic emissions are reported in the literature (see, for example, Hansson 1991).

It has been stated that external costs are not easy to measure according to economic-financial tools (e.g. cost/benefit analysis); nevertheless, social costs of road traffic in several countries have been assessed in a OECD report (1989). It has been obtained that noise annoyance and air pollution costs, including both damage costs (e.g. productivity losses, health-care costs, decline in property values) and abatement costs (e.g. adjusted vehicle technology and antinoise screens or barriers), when added to damage and recovery costs resulting from incidents due to lack of safety of the road network, range from 2.5 percent to 3.2 percent of GDP. This is, however, only a conservative estimate: if congestion and land consumption (e.g. road and parking space building) would also be included, the non-internalized social costs of transport might amount to about 5 percent of GDP in most developed countries.

A number of further studies have been carried out on this topic. Table 16.2 presents average monetary values for some of the main external effects of transportation as provided by such studies, that have been subjectively weighted according to their relative importance and year of appearance (it has to be specified that the reported values are calibrated for France and standardized in 1992 ECU). Based on the presented table, it is possible to derive that environmental impacts attributable to railways are far less severe than those produced by roadways. In particular, the following remarks can be drawn (for further details and extended references about the considered studies, see Gastaldi et al. 1996):

- Acoustic pollution. Road traffic noise cost results to be more than three times the cost produced by railway traffic.
- Air pollution. No external costs are estimated for freight trains, since these are electric-powered for the most part and release a very slight amount of polluting substances directly in the atmosphere.
- Safety. External cost reported in the table is half the total social cost, while the rest is assumed to be covered by insurance companies. Accident costs are generally evaluated on the basis of estimates of the monetary value of a human life.

- Congestion. Travel time losses due to congestion phenomena are monetized based on the use of standard traffic flow-speed curves and evaluation of time. Note that railway congestion cost has a null value.
- Greenhouse effect. Average vehicle fuel consumption and occupancy rates as well as estimates of emission cost per ton of carbon have been used to determine a total cost per passenger/km associated with the different transport modes. Note that railway impacts are again considered to be negligible.

Table 16.2 External costs, freight transport (ECU x 1000 tons/km)

	ROAD	RAIL
NOISE	3.07	0.74
AIR POLLUTION	11.98	0
UNSAFETY	Highway 1.51 Main Road 1.56	0.04
CONGESTION	Highway 3.23 Main Road 16.20	0
GREENHOUSE EFFECT	5.38	0

Source: Gastaldi et al. (1996).

16.3 Environmental Benefits from Rail-Truck Competition: The Italian Case

In this section, an experimental study is presented which attempts to provide useful insights in light of defining suitable policy measures for improving the efficiency of the Italian freight transportation system. In particular, it is stated that this objective can be achieved by stimulating the competition among alternative technologies, which is necessary for congestion reduction and environmental quality improvement. An analysis of the current situation is carried out by means of a suitable econometric model that estimates substitution and demand elasticities on both a set of ten productive sectors and the twenty Italian regions. This allows to highlight productive sectors really benefiting from increasing inter-modal competition as well as the effectiveness of forthcoming infrastructural interventions in the Italian railway system.

Moreover, such a framework is used to compute harmful emission levels due to freight transportation and simulate the effect of a tax on air pollution. These results are still partial, since environmental impacts of production processes are not considered, but they can be seen as a starting point in view of applying a sustainable development model for production delivery. Note that the environmental tax is introduced without taking into account the social costs of pollution by the transport sector, so that obtained results tend to underestimate this complex phenomenon (for a detailed discussion see, for example, Gastaldi et al. 1996; Campisi and Gastaldi 1996).

It has already been stated in the preceding section that various environmental issues have to be considered when defining policy measures for a sustainable development of freight transportation systems. Up to now, the most important effect has been air pollution by noxious gases, but there do exist other significant impacts, such as noise pollution, traffic congestion (which has demonstrable adverse psychological effects on health), land and aesthetics deterioration (that also are quite important but do not seem to have priority in public policy consideration) as well as the contribution of automotive emissions to greenhouse warming (that is now just an emerging effect, but potentially an enormous one). In our model, we only address air pollution produced by CO_2 and NO_x emissions. Our main purpose is to evaluate the possibility of switching road freight transport to the apparently more ecological rail mode by simulating the effects of introducing a given pollution tax in the Italian case. Therefore, we consider a (simplified) three-input model with the following cost function:

$$C = (p'_R, p'_T, p_P, W, L, E) \tag{16.1}$$

where:

$p_R' = p_R + A_R$, $p_T' = p_T + A_T$;
A_R = pollution tax on rail freight transportation, £/ton;
A_T = pollution tax on truck freight transportation, £/ton,
while p_R and p_T are the rail and truck rates (£/ton) respectively, p_P is the price of delivered product (£/ton.), W is the weight of shipment (tons), L is the length of haul (km) and E is the pollutant emission level (gr/km).

In this model, the product being produced is transportation of some weight of a given commodity. Output is measured by a three element vector that includes the delivered product amount (in tons), the number of kilometres that it was shipped and the environmental impact. Production and transport of a given commodity are the only inputs of our simplified production process. Thus, product is included as an input into the production of the delivered product, along with rail and truck transportation, while environmental impact is directly evaluated. Tests reported in Buckley and Westbrook (1990) confirm that inclusion of the product as an input significantly enhances the performance of such a model.

Following Buckley and Westbrook (1989, 1990), we model the movement of goods from a given set of origins to a given set of destinations. Recall from economic theory that, given a set of factor prices $P = (p_1, p_2, \ldots\ldots, p_m)$, it is possible to obtain the cost-minimizing set $X=\{x_1, x_2, \ldots\ldots, x_m;\ x_i=x_i(Y, P)\}$ of factor demand levels that allow to produce a given output Y. The total cost of production is given by:

$$C = p_1x_1(Y, P)+p_2x_2(Y,P)+\ldots.+p_mx_m(Y,P)=C(Y,P)$$

The cost-minimizing factor demand levels are obtained by applying Shepard's Lemma (Shepard 1970), which states that, if C(Y, P) is the minimum cost of production, then the cost minimizing set of factor demands is:

$$x_i^* = \partial C(Y, P) / \partial p_i$$

Alternatively, by taking the logarithms of the involved quantities and differentiating, we obtain the cost minimizing factor cost shares:

$$s_i = \partial \ln C / \partial \ln p_i = (\partial C / \partial p_i)(p_i / C) = p_i x_i^* / C$$

Recall that factor i is said to be (Hicks-Allen) substitute to factor j if:

$$x_{ij} = (\partial x_i / \partial p_j) > 0$$

whereas it is said a (Hicks-Allen) complement of factor j if $x_{ij} < 0$. Therefore, if a rise in the j-th factor price that reduces the use of j-th factor ($x_{jj} < 0$), increases (reduces) the use of the i-th factor for each fixed Y, then i is a substitute (complement) to j. Since $x_{ij} = x_{ji}$, the above definition is perfectly symmetric. Moreover, the price elasticity of factor demand is defined as:

$$\varepsilon_{ij} = (\partial x_i / \partial p_j)(p_j / x_i) \qquad i,j = 1,2,\ldots.m$$

where ε_{ij} is not symmetric. We may also define:

$$\sigma_{ij} = \varepsilon_{ij} / s_j \qquad i,j = 1,2,....m$$

where coefficients σ_{ij} are called the (Allen-partial) elasticities of factor substitution. Clearly $\sigma_{ij} > 0$ ($\sigma_{ij} < 0$) if factor i and j are substitutes (complements) to each other, so that the sign of σ_{ij} can be used to determine whether a given pair of factors are substitutes or complements. Note that coefficients σ_{ij} are symmetric.

In order to estimate the Allen elasticities of substitution (AES) in the framework of our model (16.1), we adopt the following procedure (see Bianco et al. 1995):

- define the Barnett Translog cost function on the basis of duality theory;
- derive a set of input-share functions by means of the Shepard Lemma;
- estimate the share function;
- measure the AES coefficients in accordance with the standard formula.

Our methodology is based on an input cost function expressed by a Barnett Translog approximation (BTL – Barnett 1985) which extends the Translog specification (TL – Christensen et al. 1973) for the computation of substitution elasticities. The application of the transformation proposed by Barnett improves the translog models' performances. In fact, while the elasticity values are not very different from those obtained by applying TL, their standard errors decrease markedly. Moreover, it can be proved that the three input cost function (16.1) expressed by a BTL approximation satisfies the regularity conditions (non-negativity of the fitted shares and concavity of the estimated cost equation) required by economic theory (see Bianco et al. 1995). Actually, negative fitted shares produce results with no economic or statistical sense. Hence, observations producing negative fitted shares or concavity violations must be considered as errors and omitted from the estimation process (see Campisi and Gastaldi 1996).
Therefore, we transform the relative prices to improve the concavity of the estimated cost function (Barnett 1985). In our three-input case, this transformation yields:

$$p'_i / p_P \rightarrow (p'_i / p_P) + \theta_i \quad \text{for } i = R, T \text{ (Rail, Truck)}$$

where θ_i assume negative values bounded by:

$$-\min (p'_i / p_P) < \theta_i < 0 \quad \text{for } i = R, T \text{ (Rail, Truck)}.$$

Given these bounds, it is feasible to perform a grid search over (θ_R, θ_T), choosing as optimal the values (θ_R^*, θ_T^*) that minimize the number of concavity violations (maximize the number of used observations). Let $V_i = p_i' / p_P$ and $\omega_i = V_i + \theta_i$ (i = R,T). By defining $LP_i = \ln(\omega_i)$ for i = R, T, our BTL cost function becomes:

$$\begin{aligned}\ln(C/p_P) = {} & a_0 + a_R LP'_R + a_T LP'_T + a_W \ln W + a_L \ln L + a_E \ln E \\ & + 1/2\, a_{RR} (LP'_R)^2 + a_{RT} LP'_R LP'_T + a_{RW} LP'_R \ln W \\ & + a_{RTL} LP'_R \ln L + a_{RE} LP'_R \ln E + 1/2\, a_{TT} (LP'_T)^2 \\ & + a_{TW} LP'_T \ln W + a_{TL} LP'_T \ln L + a_{TE} LP'_T \ln E \\ & + 1/2\, a_{WW} (\ln W)^2 + a_{WL} \ln W \ln L + 1/2\, a_{LL} (\ln L)^2 \\ & + a_{WE} \ln W \ln E + a_{LE} \ln L \ln E + 1/2\, a_{EE} (\ln E)^2 \\ & - b_R LP_R^{'-1} - b_T LP_T^{'-1} - 1/2\, b_{RR} LP_R^{'-2} - b_{RT} LP_R^{'-1} LP_T^{'-1} \\ & - 1/2\, b_{TT} LP_T^{'-2} \end{aligned} \qquad (16.3)$$

and the cost shares are given by:

$$\begin{aligned} s_R = \delta \ln C/\delta \ln p'_R = {} & a_R + a_{RR} LP'_R + a_{RT} LP'_T + a_{RW} \ln W \\ & + a_{RL} \ln L + a_{RE} \ln E + b_R LP_R^{'-2} + b_{RR} LP_R^{'-3} + b_{RT} LP_R^{'-2} LP_T^{'-1} \\ s_T = \delta \ln C/\delta \ln p'_T = {} & a_T + a_{RT} LP'_R + a_{TT} LP'_T + a_{TW} \ln W + a_{TL} \ln L \\ & + a_{TE} \ln E + b_T LP_T^{'-2} + b_{TT} LP_T^{'-3} + b_{RT} LP_T^{'-2} LP_R^{'-1} \\ s_P = \delta \ln C/\delta \ln p_P = {} & 1 - s_R - s_T \end{aligned} \qquad (16.4)$$

Coefficients a_0, a_i, a_{ij}, b_i and b_{ij} for i, j = R, T are parameters to be estimated. Since the Allen-Uzawa elasticities of substitution are defined as $\sigma_{ij}=C_{ij}/C_iC_j$, where $C_i = \delta C / \delta p_i$ and $C_{ij} = \delta C_i / \delta p_j$, according to our BTL specification AES are defined as:

$$\sigma_{ij} = (V_i * V_j / \omega_i * \omega_j) * (a_{ij} - b_{ij} LP_i^{-2} LP_j^{-2} + s_i s_j)/s_i s_j$$

for i,j = R, T

and

$$\sigma_{ii} = (V_i/\omega_i)^2 * \{[a_{ii} - 2b_i LP_i^{-3} - 3b_{ii} LP_i^{-4} - 2b_{ij} LP_i^{-3} LP_j^{-1} + s_i^2 - s_i * (V_i/\omega_i)] / s_i^2\}$$

for i = R, T (16.5)

Analogous expressions for σ_{RP}, σ_{TP} and σ_{PP} can be easily derived. Recall that conventional demand elasticities can be related to the elasticities of substitution (Allen 1956), as the following relations can be obtained from (16.2):

$$\varepsilon_{ij} = s_j \, \sigma_{ij} \quad \text{and} \quad \varepsilon_{ii} = s_i \, \sigma_{ii} \qquad \text{for i,j} = \text{R, T} \tag{16.6}$$

which represent the cross-price demand elasticities between rail and truck (ε_{RT}, ε_{TR}) and the own-price demand elasticities for rail (ε_{RR}) and truck (ε_{TT}) respectively.

16.3.1 Data Base

For our purposes, a large body of the ninety-nine physical commodities classified by NST/R (Nomenclature Statistique du Traffic provided by the Observatoire Economique Statistique du Traffic) have been aggregated into the following 10 sectors (the numbers of the corresponding commodities in the NST/R classification are reported in parentheses):

1 Agricultural products and livestock (1–9)
2 Forage and food-stuffs (11–18)
3 Solid mineral fuels (21–24)
4 Oil products (31–37)
5 Minerals and junks for metallurgical industry (41, 44–47)
6 Metallurgical products (50–59)
7 Raw and manufactured minerals, building materials (61–65, 69)
8 Compost and chemical fertilizer (71–72)
9 Chemical products (81–84, 89)
10 Machinery and vehicles (91–99)

The disaggregate interregional trade flows data (W) among the twenty Italian regions have been provided by Progetto Finalizzato Trasporti 2, a research project on transportation funded by the Italian National Research Council, while transport rates (p_R, p_T) have been provided by the Italian Confederation of Truck Operators (CONFETRA) and the Italian Railways (FS). On the other hand, delivered product prices (p_P) have been appropriately derived from the Italian Input-Output table (ISTAT 1987). All data refer to 1985.

16.3.2 Numerical Results

This section is devoted to analyse the Italian freight transport system by assessing the substitution and price elasticity coefficients between rail and truck. In particular, we give a detailed profile of the interregional movement of goods by considering the aggregated ten productive sectors and the twenty Italian regions assumed as production and consumption places. Note that air, pipeline, inland waterways and sea transportation are not considered in our framework, since they account for a limited transport share. Furthermore, in the case of inland and sea waterways data are generally too aggregated, whereas data on shipment characteristics (i.e. vessel type, dimension and capacity) and relative rates are not fully available. Interregional trade flows data set allows to compare the tonnages shipped by rail and truck for the ten sectors as listed in Section 16.3.1. In Italy, sectors 6 (metallurgical products) and 10 (machinery and vehicles) account for more than 2/3 of rail interregional transport. At the same time, sector 10 alone amounts to about 1/4 of the road movement of goods, followed by sectors 7 (raw and manufactured minerals, building materials) and 2 (forage and foodstuffs).

The implicit cost of pollution was more difficult to estimate. Table 16.3 shows that transportation in general is a large contributor to air pollution. Carbon dioxide (CO_2) from transportation alone represents 22.5 percent of the total emission rate (Lucas 1990; Faiz 1993); other pollution sources are carbon monoxide (CO), hydrocarbons (HC), nitrogen oxides (NO_x), sulphur oxides (SO_x), suspended particulate matter (SPM) and lead (Pb). Note that CO becomes CO_2 when released into the atmosphere, while HC becomes oxidated as aldehydes and eventually also becomes CO_2. Table 16.4 indicates transport emissions in gr/km.

In an interesting study dedicated to freight transportation (Ferrovie dello Stato 1993a), the European Commission suggested to introduce a pollution tax comprised between 0.01 and 0.06 ECU (19 and 117 £) per t-km to cover the environmental costs of transport. Gastaldi et al. (1996) obtain a similar result, since a tax amount that falls within the proposed range can be suitably derived from Table 16.2. However, in our analysis, this tax would increase freight transportation rates by 50 percent to 100 percent, so that this proposal is not feasible. Actually, the relevant demand redistribution caused by such a rate increase would imply that significant changes be achieved in both current infrastructures and technologies, which however cannot be implemented in the assumed short run (5–10 years). Moreover, given that we focus our attention on air pollution in the Italian case, we are allowed to choose a modest short term freight tax amount of 0.005 ECU (10£) per t-km. Then, we distribute such an amount between rail and truck rates proportionally, according to CO_2 emissions in gr/km as well as weight and distance of the shipment for each mode. Rates change by 0.1 to 0.8 percent for rail and 2.5 percent to 9.4 percent for truck.

For each productive sector and each region, we estimate the unknown parameters in (16.3) and (16.4). Note that it is necessary to estimate a system of three non-linear equations, since only two of the three relations drawn up in (16.4) are statistically independent (in fact, $s_R + s_T + s_P = 1$). Sectoral data fit better than regional ones for both sectoral and regional cases; however, high R-square values and significant t–ratios correspond to both applications. Furthermore, the regularity conditions hold (Campisi and Gastaldi 1996).

Table 16.3 Contribution of transport to conventional pollutant emissions in Italy, 1985 (1000 tons/year)

	CO_2	CO	HC	NO_x	SO_x	SPM	Pb
Total	1520889	5500	800	1500	2000	400	7
Transport Sector	342200	4510	448	645	140	92	n.a.
%	22.5	82.0	56.0	43.0	7.0	23.0	n.a.
Passenger Transport	197200	3192	n.a.	239	45	n.a.	n.a.
Freight Transport	145000	1318	n.a.	406	95	n.a.	n.a.
Passenger Transport %	57.7	70.8	n.a.	37.1	32.1	n.a.	n.a.
Freight Transport %	42.3	29.2	n.a.	62.9	67.9	n.a.	n.a.
Rail Freight Transport	6127	7	n.a.	7	11	n.a.	n.a.
Truck Freight Transport	126439	1232	n.a.	399	84	n.a.	n.a.
Rail Freight Transport % a)	4.2	0.005	n.a.	1.7	11.6	n.a.	n.a.
Truck Freight Transport %	87.2	93.5	n.a.	98.2	88.4	n.a.	n.a.

Note: a) Percentages do not sum to unity because other transportation modes are not included.

Sources: FAIZ (1993); FERROVIE DELLO STATO (1993a).

Table 16.4 Emissions of pollutants in Italy, 1985 (gr/vehicle km)

	CO_2	CO	HC	NO_x	SO_x	SPM	Pb
Rail	56.13	1	0.3	2	0.3	n.a.	n.a.
Truck	1158	8	2.8	17.5	1.59	n.a.	n.a.

Sources: COMMISSION OF THE EUROPEAN COMMUNITY (1991); FERROVIE DELLO STATO (1993a).

In order to measure factor substitution possibilities, we estimate the Allen elasticities of substitution (σ_{ij}) and the price elasticities (ε_{ij}) in (16.6). Table 16.5 reports the substitution elasticities between rail and truck ($\sigma_{RT} = \sigma_{TR}$), the own-price demand elasticities for rail (ε_{RR}) and truck (ε_{TT}) and the cross-price demand elasticities between rail and truck (ε_{RT} and ε_{TR}) and the pollution variation due to the introduction of a pollution tax ($\Delta P\%$). Coefficients have been calculated corresponding to productive sector-specific data mean values. Since $\sigma_{RT} >> 0$, rail and truck carriers are highly substitute for all productive sectors. In the present situation, when a pollution tax is applied, coefficients vary among sectors with values that range from 1.11 (sector 6, metallurgical products) to 23.37 (sector 10, machinery and vehicles). Notice that higher levels of substitution coefficients are related to movement of goods requiring special trucks and wagons, where a large amount of the Italian Railways' efforts are concentrated (Ferrovie dello Stato 1993b). The demand own price elasticities vary considerably among sectors, with values ranging from –0.890 (sector 8, compost and chemical fertilizer) to –2.363 (sector 3, solid mineral fuels) in the case of rail transport and from –0.298 (sector 4, oil products) to –1.771 (sector 9, chemical products) in the case of truck transportation. Then, whereas the estimated elasticities of demand for rail services are sufficiently high to suggest the efficacy of selective rate cutting, the estimated truck elasticities do not appear to be sufficiently high to warrant this conclusion. In addition, since $|\varepsilon_{RR}| > |\varepsilon_{TT}|$ for all sectors, the demand for rail is more sensible to a change in rail price than the demand for truck with respect to truck price, thus showing the superiority of truck services.

Thus, from a sectoral point of view, the estimated substitution and demand elasticities indicate a vigorous intermodal competition mainly in sectors 2 (forage and food-stuffs), 8 (compost and chemical fertilizer), 9 (chemical products) and 10 (machinery and vehicles). Since in Italy a large amount of goods is delivered by truck, the sectoral results show how the rail carrier could increase its market share by selecting appropriate fare policies. The lowest levels of inter-modal competition are reached in sectors 3 (solid mineral fuels), 4 (oil product) and 6 (metallurgical products), which are at the core of road transportation.

The cross-elasticities of demand for rail with respect to changes in truck rates ranges from 0.005 (sector 6, metallurgical products) to 0.680 (sector 2, forage and food-stuffs), whereas the elasticities of demand for truck with respect to changes in rail rates ranges from 0.001 (sector 6, metallurgical products) to 0.238 (sector 10, machinery and vehicles). Note that, for each productive sector, an increase in truck rates produces a larger change on rail demand level than vice versa (since $\varepsilon_{RT} > \varepsilon_{TR}$), except for sector 5 (minerals and junks for metallurgical industry), that is the only sector characterized by $W_T < W_R$. The last column of Table 16.5 indicates percentage changes in pollution emissions ($\Delta C\%$, $\Delta P\%$) when a cost rationalizing policy based on the substitution process is applied. Then, it seems that freight rates and the corresponding pollution reduction are very sensitive even to a minimal pollution tax of 10£ per t-km.

Table 16.6 reports the same outcomes of Table 16.5 relative to the regional level, where each region is considered both as a production site (origin) and a consumption site (destination). Coefficients have been calculated corresponding to regional data mean values. The adopted methodology fails to converge for Val d'Aosta and Molise regions only; this is due to the low number of observations (less than 20) considered in the estimation procedure. Since σ_{RT}>>0, rail and truck carriers are highly substitute goods in all Italian regions. These coefficients, however, vary significantly among regions, taking values that range from 6.89 (destination) and 7.04 (origin) for Basilicata to 34.09 (destination) and 27.40 (origin) for Lombardia. Demand own - price elasticities also vary considerably among regions, taking values that range from –0.395 (destination) and –0.389 (origin) for Puglia to –2.098 (destination) and –2.025 (origin) for Lombardia in the case of rail transport and from –0.215 (destination) and –0.236 (origin) for Puglia to –1.173 (destination) and –1.109 (origin) for Lombardia in the case of truck transportation. Note that, as already shown in the sectoral case, $\varepsilon_{RR} > \varepsilon_{TT}$. It follows that the superiority of truck services is confirmed at the regional level. Moreover, this pattern becomes more evident by applying a pollution tax, because of the higher environmental truck impact.

Table 16.5 Substitution elasticities, demand elasticities and pollution variation – sectoral results

	σ_{RT}	ε_{RR}	ε_{TT}	ε_{RT}	ε_{TR}	ΔP%
SECTOR 1	6.26	-1.512	-0.791	0.171	0.027	-4.92
SECTOR 2	22.60	-1.373	-0.302	0.680	0.029	-17.88
SECTOR 3	2.65	-2.363	-1.052	0.079	0.027	-2.06
SECTOR 4	2.32	-1.189	-0.298	0.162	0.004	-1.84
SECTOR 5	5.55	-1.322	-1.461	0.123	0.170	-4.09
SECTOR 6	1.11	-1.017	-0.920	0.005	0.001	-0.88
SECTOR 7	2.10	-2.180	-1.395	0.071	0.006	-1.66
SECTOR 8	21.73	-0.890	-0.516	0.137	0.014	-17.12
SECTOR 9	14.80	-2.080	-1.771	0.226	0.023	-11.69
SECTOR 10	23.37	-1.631	-0.660	0.502	0.238	-18.52

Table 16.6 Substitution elasticities, demand elasticities and pollution variation – regional results

		σ_{RT}	ε_{RR}	ε_{TT}	ε_{RT}	ε_{TR}	ΔP%
PIEMONTE	destination	28.55	-1.320	-0.765	0.958	0.227	-17.60
1	origin	25.63	-1.510	-0.726	0.896	0.239	-14.97
VAL D'AOSTA	destination	-	-	-	-	-	-
2	origin	-	-	-	-	-	-
LOMBARDIA	destination	34.09	-2.098	-1.173	0.132	0.035	-19.93
3	origin	27.40	-2.025	-1.109	0.110	0.022	-16.98
TRENTINO	destination	15.18	-0.509	-0.395	0.536	0.114	-8.89
4	origin	17.02	-0.531	-0.355	0.571	0.179	-10.61
VENETO	destination	21.67	-1.498	-0.669	0.125	0.095	-12.81
5	origin	21.78	-1.553	-0.712	0.142	0.104	-12.95
FRIULI	destination	10.75	-0.510	-0.229	0.516	0.093	-6.93
6	origin	10.89	-0.495	-0.246	0.274	0.075	-6.95
LIGURIA	destination	17.19	-0.972	-0.727	0.626	0.379	-10.86
7	origin	16.95	-1.111	-0.619	0.586	0.199	-10.63
EMILIA ROM.	destination	18.01	-1.402	-0.445	0.491	0.087	-10.96
8	origin	18.19	-1.378	-0.689	0.419	0.101	-11.38
TOSCANA	destination	17.21	-0.980	-0.742	0.756	0.197	-10.54
9	origin	15.75	-0.979	-0.526	0.908	0.237	-9.65
UMBRIA	destination	12.21	-1.001	-0.409	0.461	0.169	-8.24
10	origin	12.35	-1.041	-0.556	0.484	0.132	-8.17
MARCHE	destination	9.85	-1.001	-0.860	0.118	0.014	-5.86
11	origin	10.37	-1.025	-0.828	0.142	0.015	-6.23
LAZIO	destination	13.35	-1.240	-0.899	0.628	0.141	-8.23
12	origin	13.09	-1.198	-0.823	0.755	0.173	-8.00
ABRUZZO	destination	8.21	-0.985	-0.693	0.541	0.106	-4.88
13	origin	8.44	-1.035	-0.784	0.598	0.073	-5.36
MOLISE	destination	-	-	-	-	-	-
14	origin	-	-	-	-	-	-
CAMPANIA	destination	15.10	-1.298	-0.980	0.900	0.191	-8.31
15	origin	13.78	-1.069	-0.797	0.793	0.255	-7.68
PUGLIA	destination	9.17	-0.395	-0.215	0.326	0.102	-5.60
16	origin	8.79	-0.389	-0.236	0.288	0.061	-5.36
BASILICATA	destination	6.89	-0.750	-0.533	0.466	0.059	-3.97
17	origin	7.04	-0.685	-0.512	0.447	0.057	-4.04
CALABRIA	destination	10.29	-1.301	-1.042	0.430	0.255	-6.55
18	origin	10.39	-1.256	-1.098	0.440	0.275	-6.65
SICILIA	destination	13.36	-1.753	-1.053	1.030	0.451	-8.94
19	origin	11.32	-1.675	-1.023	0.964	0.389	-7.65
SARDEGNA	destination	10.75	-1.068	-0.545	0.685	0.268	-6.18
20	origin	11.04	-1.256	-0.595	0.755	0.292	-6.32

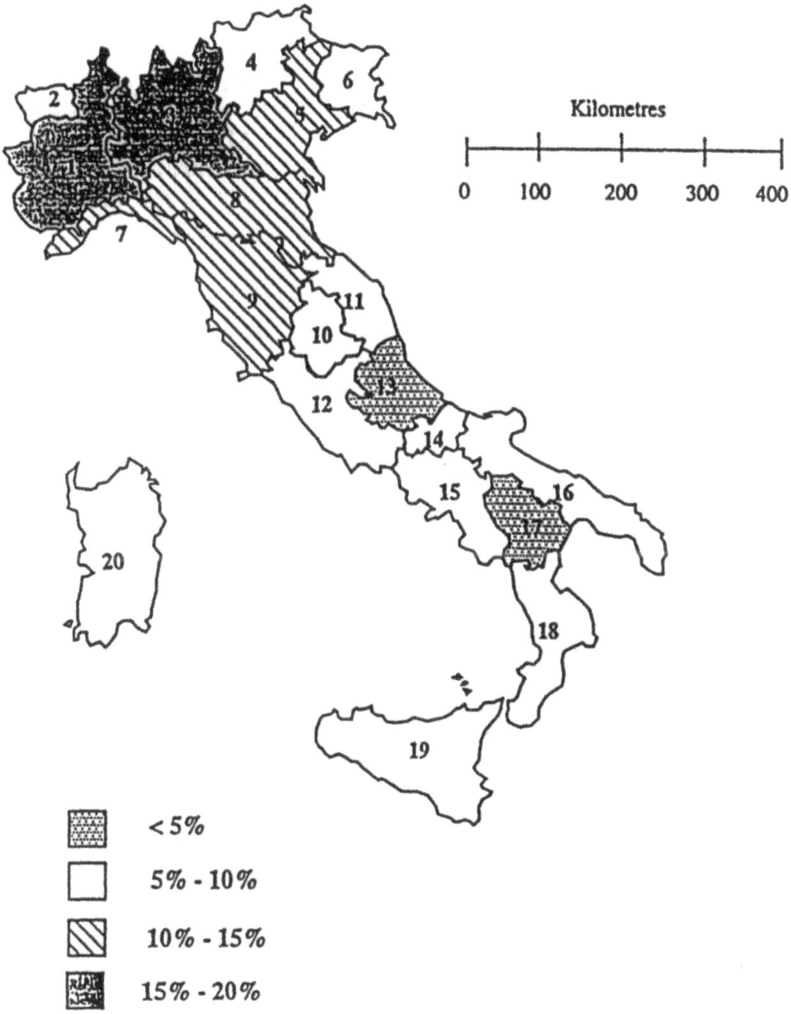

Map 16.1 Regional pollution reduction

When considering a region as the destination of freight flows, the cross elasticities of demand for rail with respect to changes in truck rates range from 0.118 (Marche) to 1.030 (Sicily). On the other hand, when considering a region as the origin of freight flows, the same values range from 0.110 (Lombardia) to 0.964 (Sicily). The elasticities of demand for truck with respect to changes in trail rates range from 0.014 (destination) and 0.015 (origin) for Marche to 0.451 (destination) and 0.389 (origin) for Sicily. Both the last column of Table 16.6 and Map 16.1 show that regions in the Padanian area (that is, Lombardia, Piemonte, Emilia Romagna and Veneto) could effectively benefit from a West-East railway corridor joining Torin – Milan – Venice, as it has been proposed at a policy level, when this is accompanied by a suitable environmental policy. In fact, the estimated vigorous intermodal substitution process in this area could determine a relevant decrease of pollutant emissions (that amounts to about 14 percent). Note that, because of the peculiar geomorphic configuration of the Padanian area, a significant air pollution decrease could help in reducing both accidents caused by fog (that is a particularly heavy phenomenon in this area) and physical as well as psychological diseases due to the presence of smog.

16.4 Conclusions

Scientific research plays a fundamental role in the solution process of the serious problems associated with the transport system impacts on the environment. In the expected scenario of a considerable increase of mobility and traffic congestion, it is essential to identify proper tools and methodologies aiming at the restriction of both non-renewable resource consumption and pollutant emissions by the transport sector, in order to preserve the carrying capacity of the environmental system and keep within the bounds imposed by a sustainable development.

Measuring the complex relationships between rail and truck freight transport in terms of their environmental impacts is a hard task. Moreover, the ongoing technologies and existing infrastructures do not allow significant policy changes over the short run. Yet, what we learn from our simulation exercise is that there are intermodal substitution possibilities, so that including pollution costs of freight shipping through a suitable pollution tax can affect transport modal choice in the direction of reaching social objectives.

A number of key variables affect the demand for road and rail freight transport: distance, cost, quality of service, existing alternatives, economic and environmental conditions. In all developed countries, rail is the most successful mode over medium distances, while road is more attractive over short distances since it offers a level of flexibility that rail cannot provide. On the contrary, rail freight rates are usually set at a too high amount with respect to the truck ones, thus switching 'long-distance' potential customers away from rail. In addition, customers are not only influenced by transport rates and speed, but also by the perceived service quality level of rival transport modes. This issue is particularly striking today, because new production systems require more efficient and reliable transport services.

From a social point of view, sustainable development requires to take account of environmental impacts for each economic activity. A pollution tax is a partial response to this requirement. Other policies, such as fines, permits, prohibitions and regulations, could be efficient as well, but they would represent more punitive approaches that are also more difficult to implement. It has been shown here that a pollution tax could influence transportation mode choice and thus indirectly environmental quality without significantly hurting the economic growth process. This in itself satisfies the intrinsic intergenerational tradeoff when considering sustainable development (Nijkamp 1994).

From a policy point of view, we investigated the effects of introducing a given pollution tax in the Italian rail-truck competition case, emphasizing the benefits achieved in terms of pollutant emission reduction. In short, the proposed tax policy produces a pollution reduction that is equal to 10.13 percent at a sectoral level and to about 11 percent at a regional level.

References

Allen, R.G.D. (1956), *Mathematical Analysis for Economists*, Macmillan & Co., London.

Barnett, W.A. (1985), 'The Miniflex-Laurent Translog Flexible Functional Form', *Journal of Econometrics*, vol. 30, pp. 33–44.

Bianco, L., Campisi, D. and Gastaldi, M. (1995), 'Which Regions Really Benefit from Rail-Truck Substitution? Empirical Evidence for Italy', *Papers in Regional Science*, vol. 74, no. 1, pp. 41-62.

Buckley, P. and Westbrook, M.D. (1989), 'The Importance of Market Definition in the Assessment of the Competitive Relationship between Rail and Truck Transportation', Mimeo, Georgetown University.

Buckley, P. and Westbrook, M.D. (1990), 'Flexible Functional Forms and Regularity: Assessing the Competitive Relationship between Rail and Truck Transportation', *The Review of Economics and Statistics*, vol. 72, pp. 623-30.

Campisi, D. and Gastaldi, M. (1996), 'Environmental Protection, Economic Efficiency and Intermodal Competition in Freight Transport', *Transportation Research C,* vol. 4, no. 6, pp. 391–406.

Caves, D.W. and Christensen, L.R. (1980), 'Global Properties of Flexible Functional Frontiers,' *The Review of Economics and Statistics*, vol. 70, pp. 422–32.

Christensen, L.R., Jorgenson, D.W. and Lau, L.J. (1973), 'Transcendental Logarithmic Production Frontiers', *The Review of Economics and Statistics*, vol. 55, pp. 28–45.

DRIVE Project V1005 (1990), 'PREDICT – Pollution Reduction by Information and Control Techniques', *Working paper*, Deliverable n.1.

DRIVE Project V1036 (1989), 'EVA- Evaluation Process for Road Transport Informatics', *Working Paper 3.4* on 'Operating Cost, Air and Noise Pollution'.

EEC (1992), 'L'impatto dei Trasporti sull'Ambiente', *Libro Verde*, Rome.

Faiz, A. (1993), 'Automotive Emissions in Developing Countries – Relative Implications for Global Warming, Acidification and Urban Air Quality', *Transportation Research A*, vol. 27, no. 3, pp. 167–86.

Ferrovie dello Stato (1993a), *Linea Treno*, vol. 36, no.8, Rome.

Ferrovie dello Stato (1993b), 'Il Trasporto delle Merci in Italia', *Libro Bianco*, Area Trasporto, Rome.

Gastaldi, M., Pradayrol, J.P., Quinet, E. and Rega, M. (1996), 'Valuation of Environmental Externalities: from Theory to Decision-making', *Transportation Planning and Technology*, vol. 19, nos. 3–4, pp. 207–19.

Hansson, L. (1991), 'Pricing of Air Pollution in the Swedish Transport Policy', *Transportation Research Record 1312* on 'Energy and Environmental Issues', TRB, USA.

Himanen, V. , Nijkamp, P. and Padjen, J. (1992), 'Environmental Quality and Transport Policy in Europe', *Transportation Research A*, vol. 26A, no. 2, pp. 147–57.

ISTAT (1987), *Tavola Intersettoriale dell'Economia Italiana 1982*, Rome, Italy.

Lucas (1990), *Motive Power for the Passenger Car*, Lucas Diesel, Blois, France.

Matzoros, A. and Van Vliet, D. (1992), 'A Model of Air Pollution from Road Traffic Based on the Characteristics of Interrupted Flow and Junction Control', *Transportation Research A* , vol. 26A, no. 4, pp. 315–55 (Parts I and II).

Meyer, M.D. and Miller, E.J. (1984), *Urban Transportation Planning*, McGraw-Hill, New York.

Nijkamp, P. (1994), 'Roads towards Environmentally Sustainable Transport', *Transportation Research A*, vol. 28, no. 4, pp. 261–71.

Organisation for Economic Cooperation and Development, OECD (1989), 'The Social Costs of Land Transport', *Environment Directorate*, Paris.

Shepard, R. (1970), *The Theory of Cost and Production*, Princeton University Press, Princeton, N.J.

17 European Freight Transport Analysis Using Neural Networks and Logit Models

AURA REGGIANI, PETER NIJKAMP AND WAI FAI TSANG

17.1 Changes in the European Freight Transport Scene

After the completion of the European market and with the widening of Europe towards an easterly direction, mobility in general has shown a steady increase in Europe. In particular, cross-border transport has been at a rising edge with annual growth rates exceeding 10 percent, a process reinforced by the current globalization trends. The integration of former segmented markets – and the related liberalization in the European space – has led to drastic changes in both goods and passenger transport.

The European Commission recognized this restructuring phenomenon several years ago, an observation which can also be found in the Maastricht Treaty. European networks are seen as the backbone of integration forces, while changes in the morphology of the networks are expected to generate system-wide impacts. Clearly, the emphasis on the potential of these networks for competitiveness and cohesion provokes various questions on the relative efficiency and substitutability of the different modes of this network. This issue is particularly important, as the competition between different modes and the social acceptability of modal choices are not only determined by the direct operational costs, but also by environmental externalities.

As a result, there is increasing interest in the issue of intermodal competition and complementarity. For surface transport in Europe, especially the competitive position of rail vis-à-vis road is at stake. This holds increasingly also for commodity transport. It needs to be added however, that the analysis of freight transport in Europe is fraught with many difficulties, as freight is not a homogeneous commodity, but is composed of an extremely diversified set of goods with specific haulage requirements and logistic needs. This means that a commodity specific approach is necessary to analyse in depth implications of changes in network configurations. This approach will also be adopted in the present chapter.

The aim of this chapter is to investigate freight flow patterns in Europe from a multiregional perspective, by looking into the modal choice for these goods from the viewpoint of freight costs and transport time. Two competing models, viz. a discrete choice model and a neural network model, will be employed to map out the spatial flow patterns in an explanatory context. This also offers a possibility to compare the relative performance of those models. A selection of Dutch regions and Italian regions will be used to test the predictive power of the models concerned. Next, a sensitivity analysis will be carried out in order to investigate the expected consequences of a rise in transport costs, e.g. as a consequence of a European environmental tax on freight costs.

17.2 The Models Used

This chapter aims to analyse interregional freight transport movements in Europe as well as to forecast resulting spatiotemporal flow patterns on the basis of new transport economic scenarios. For this purpose, a modal split analysis will be carried out by means of two statistical models, namely the logit model and the neural network model. A binary logit model will be discussed in Section 17.2.1, while a feedforward neural network model will be presented in Section 17.2.2.

17.2.1 The Logit Approach

A widely adopted approach for modal split analysis is the logit model (see e.g. Ben-Akiva and Lerman 1985). Recent experiments using logit models/spatial interaction models in order to map out the freight transport in Europe have been carried out by Tavasszy(1996), who showed the suitability of logit models also for the goods transport sector (where data are more 'fuzzy' and incomplete compared with the passenger sector). Logit models are discrete choice models which are used for modelling a choice from a set of mutually exclusive and exhaustive alternatives. It is assumed that the decision maker chooses the alternative with the highest utility among the set of alternatives. The utility of an alternative is determined by a utility function, which consists of independent attributes of the alternative concerned and the relevant parameters. In a logit approach the concept of random utility is adopted, which means that the true utilities of the alternatives are considered to be random variables, i.e.

$$U_{in} = f(X_{i,m}) + \varepsilon_{in} \qquad (17.1)$$

where

U_{in} = the utility of alternative i for individual n
$f(X_{i,m})$ = a function of attributes m related to alternative i
ε_{in} = a random disturbance term.

By maximizing then the stochastic utility (17.1), the probability that an alternative is chosen is defined as the probability that it has the highest utility among all relevant alternatives (see e.g. Ben-Akiva and Lerman 1985; Cramer 1991; McFadden 1977).

Since in our case two discrete choices – rail (t) and road (c) – will be considered, a binary logit model is adopted. Then the following assumption is made concerning the random term:

$$F(\varepsilon_n) = \frac{1}{1 + e^{-\mu\varepsilon_n}}, \qquad \mu > 0, \;\; -\infty < \varepsilon_n < \infty , \tag{17.2}$$

$$f(\varepsilon_n) = \frac{\mu e^{-\mu\varepsilon_n}}{(1 + e^{-\mu\varepsilon_n})^2} \tag{17.3}$$

For the sake of convenience, also the following assumption is made: $\mu = 1$. Thus the logit model for modal split choice of the rail versus road between two regions i and j has the following formulation:

$$P^t_{ij} = \frac{\exp(U^t_{ij})}{\exp(U^t_{ij}) + \exp(U^c_{ij})} \tag{17.4}$$

where

$$U^t_{ij} = \beta_1 * X^t_{1,ij} + \beta_2 * X^t_{2,ij} \tag{17.5}$$

and

$$U^c_{ij} = \beta_3 * X^c_{1,ij} + \beta_4 * X^c_{2,ij} \tag{17.6}$$

and where:

P^t_{ij} = the probability of choosing the train from region i to region j ($i \neq j$);

U^t_{ij} = the utility connected with the rail mode (t) on the link ij;

U^c_{ij} = the utility related to the road mode (c) on the link ij;

$X^m_{1,ij}$ = the attribute 'time' for mode m in the utility function for the link ij;

$X^m_{2,ij}$ = the attribute 'cost' for mode m in the utility function for the link ij;

β_1,β_2 = the parameters related to the attributes time and cost, respectively, for the mode train;

β_3, β_4 = the parameters related to the attributes time and cost, respectively, for the mode road.

The binary logit model has in the meantime become a standard analytical tool in discrete choice modelling. The results of this logit model for an empirical case on European freight transport will be given in Section 17.3.

17.2.2 The Neural Network Approach

Neural network (NN) analysis has in recent years become a popular analysis tool (see for reviews Himanen et al. 1998). NNs replicates human brain functions and are thus considered as 'intelligent', since they learn and generalize by examples (see e.g. Reggiani et al. 1998). NNs have been widely applied to the area of transport engineering, in particular in relation to traffic control problems and accidents (see Dougherty 1997; Himanen et al. 1998). However, only a few experiments exist in the field of transport economics or transport route/mode/destination choice (see e.g. Nijkamp et al. 1996; Schintler and Olurotimi 1998). Our experiments aim to explore also this novel research direction.

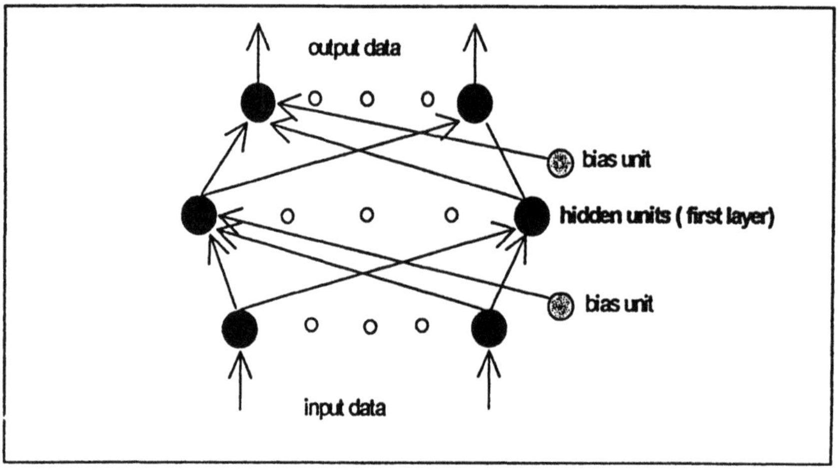

Figure 17.1 Feedforward neural network architecture

Following the majority of applications on NNs, in this study a two-layer feedforward, totally connected NN will be used in order to analyse the freight transport modal split problem. The methodological structure of the main steps related to the application of a feedforward NN is described in Reggiani and Tritapepe (1998) (see also Figure 17.1). Concisely, it consists of three stages: a) definition of network architecture; b) learning phase; c) forecasting phase. It is necessary to define the right architecture of the network, i.e. the number of units on the relevant levels. Usually, the input and output units depend on the number of input and output variables which define the problem. In our application one possible NN architecture contains four input units which correspond to the attributes time and cost related to each transport mode (rail and road) and one output unit corresponding to the probability of choosing one mode[1] (e.g., the rail mode). In the past years we have witnessed an increasing acceptance of NN models in social science research, including transportation science. Section 17.3 will offer empirical results obtained by applying an NN model to European freight flow data.

17.3 Empirical Application

In this section, experiments with the logit and the neural network approach (see Subsection 17.2.1 and 17.2.2) will be presented and discussed. In Subsection 17.3.1 a concise description of the data set will be given. The experiments carried out by means of the logit approach and the neural network approach are presented in Subsections 17.3.2 and 17.3.3, respectively. Then the two approaches will be mutually compared in Subsection 17.3.4.

17.3.1 The Data

The data set[2] contains the freight flows and the attributes related to each link between 108 European regions[3] for the year 1986. The attributes considered are *time* and *cost* between each link (ij) with reference to each transport mode. In particular, each observation of the data set pertains to variables related to each link (ij). Furthermore, the flow distribution in the matrices concerned refers to one particular kind of goods, viz. food.

Since 108 areas have been considered, the data set should ideally contain 11664 observations (according to the previous remarks on our observations). However, our data set contains finally 4409 observations because of the following considerations (by analysing the data set):

- the intra-area freight flows are zero;
- for each link, only the transport movements towards one direction i → j have been considered;
- only the links where the flows and the attributes (of both road and rail) are different from zero have been considered (i.e., empty cells are excluded).

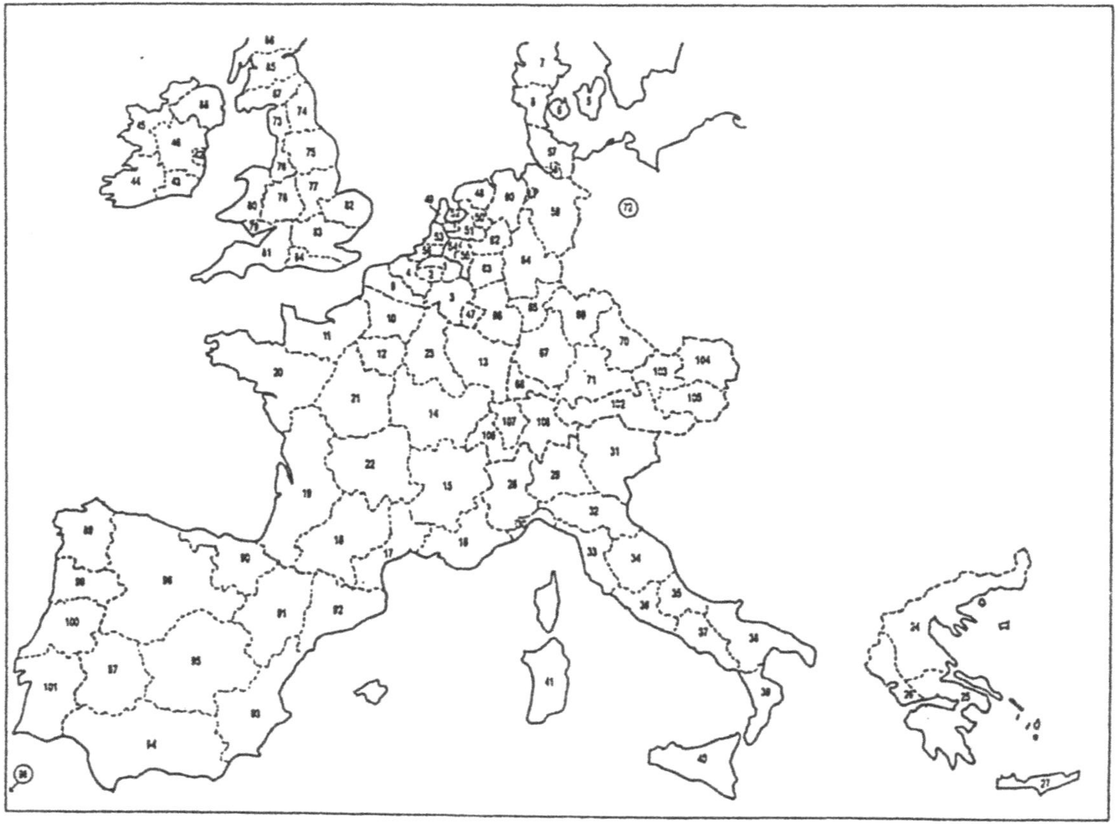

Map 17.1 Map of the 108 European regions considered

The data set has been randomly subdivided into three subsets:

- a *training set* containing 2992 observations, i.e. about 68 percent of the data set;
- a *cross-validation set* containing 447 observations, i.e. about 10 percent of the data set;
- a *test set* containing 970 observations, i.e. about 22 percent of the data set.

17.3.2 Experiments by Means of a Logit Approach

As mentioned before, a binary logit model has been used in order to analyse a modal split problem between road and rail in relation to the interregional food transport between 108 regions in Europe. First, the calibration results and an evaluation of the logit model will be presented. The spatial forecasting of the calibrated logit model will subsequently be performed and evaluated.

Calibrating the binary logit model First, the logit model has been calibrated in order to estimate the unknown parameters in the utility function. For this purpose, a data set, which is the learning set combined with the cross-validation set, has been used. Concerning the logit model structure, two cases are considered; in Case A, the two competing transport modes rail and road are supposed to have the same parameter for a given attribute (i.e. = $\beta_1 = \beta_{2,}\ \beta_2 = \beta_4$), while in Case B each transport mode has different parameters for a given attribute. The logit model has been calibrated by using the LIMDEP software. The estimated parameters resulting from the calibration stage are presented in Tables 17.1 and 17.2 for Case A and Case B, respectively.

Table 17.1 The results related to Case A

Variables	coefficient		std error	t - ratio
time	β_1	-0.00952	0.3514E-05	-2707.83
cost	β_2	-0.06493	0.1535E-04	-4229.71
Log likelihood	= -0.2750E+08			
$\chi^2(2)$	= 0.1348E+09			
ρ^2	= 0.71023			

Next, the goodness-of-fit of the model has been evaluated using two statistical indicators: the likelihood-ratio (ρ^2)[4] and the t-test. The related results are also presented in Tables 17.1 and 17.2.

Table 17.2 The results related to Case B

variables	coefficient		std error	t - ratio
time	β_1	-0.00806	0.4825^E-05	-1670.67
	β_3	-0.00802	0.5258^E-05	-1525.31
cost	β_2	-0.06208	0.2303^E-04	-2696.35
	β_4	-0.05567	0.6843^E-04	-813.498
log likelihood	= -0.2739^E+08			
$\chi^2(2)$	= 0.1350^E+09			
ρ^2	= 0.71138			

The t-test indicates that the two parameters are significantly different from zero in both cases (see Table 17.1 and Table 17.2). Also the value of ρ^2 indicates that the calibrated logit models perform reasonably well for the two cases. Table 17.2 also indicates that β_1 has almost the same value as β_3. This is also the case for β_2 and β_4. However, the calculated ρ^2 for Case B is slightly better than for Case A, which suggests that Case B performs slightly better than Case A.

Spatial forecasting performance of the binary logit model The binary logit model, as calibrated in the previous subsection, can be used to make spatial forecasts on the basis of various transport economic scenarios. For this predictive purpose, both the data set used in the calibration stage and the test set which is not used in the calibration stage, are employed.

In order to analyse the spatial forecasting performance of the binary logit model, the statistical indicators R^2 and ARV will be used. The coefficient of determination R^2 is usually adopted in the calibration procedure for logit models, while the Average Relative Variance[5] (ARV) is more commonly used for neural network models (see e.g. Fischer 1998; Fischer and Gopal 1994). However, we will consider here the indicator ARV also for our logit model in order to carry out a comparison with the NN approach. Both the R^2 and the ARV indicators have been calculated for the two cases, as well as for the test set. Especially the test set shows significant results. It will be also used subsequently to explore the NN's performance. The probabilities of choosing the rail and road modes is used in calculating the statistical indicators. The results are presented in Table 17.3 and Table 17.4 for case A and B successively.

Table 17.3 The results related to Case A

size of data set	**3439 observations**	**970 observations**
ARV	0.302	0.203
R^2	0.816	0.835

Table 17.4 The results related to Case B

size of data set	**3439 observations**	**970 observations**
ARV	0.267	0.185
R^2	0.865	0.887

It should be noted that the ARV measure should ideally approach zero, while the R^2 measure should approach one, if the estimates tend to be accurate. Concerning the general results presented in Table 17.3 and Table 17.4, the binary logit model appears to have a good predictive ability; in particular, Case B turns out to perform better than Case A for different numbers of observations. Therefore, only the results of Case B will be illustrated in Subsection 17.3.4 and in Section 17.4 where the logit model will be compared with the NN model.

17.3.3 Experiments by Means of a Neural Network Approach

As mentioned in Subsection 17.3.2, the modal split problem will also be analysed by means of a more recently developed statistical model, viz the feedforward neural network model (see Subsection 17.2.2).

It has already been mentioned that the whole data set contains 4409 observations (examples or patterns). The following general considerations apply to the experiment undertaken here:

- The training for the neural net model (and the calibration for the logit model) has been carried out by using the *training set.*

- The performance measure has been evaluated by using the *test set* (spatial forecasting).
- The attributes (time and cost denoted by V_j) have been transformed (in a value range between [0-1]) by means of the following functions:

$$V_j^f = \exp(-0.002\, V_j) \qquad (17.7)$$

The variables are defined as follows:

TC_{ij}^f : transformed rail cost cor link (ij);

TT_{ij}^f : transformed rail time for link (ij);

RC_{ij}^f : transformed road cost for link (ij);

RT_{ij}^f : transformed road time for link (ij);

T_{ij} : total freight flow related to link (ij);

T_{ij}^{road} : total road flow related to link (ij);

p_{ij}^{road} : road mode probability for link (ij), in relation to the following relationship

$$T_{ij}^{road} = p_{ij}^{road} \cdot T_{ij}\,. \qquad (17.8)$$

Concerning the number of hidden units, they have empirically been defined by taking into account the number of observations in the data set as well as by carrying out a large number of experiments. With regard to the parameters defining the neural architecture, they have been determined after several empirical experiments. Finally, the parameters of the NNs are set as follows:

- number of hidden units: 8
- learning rate a = 0.9
- momentum factor l = 0.05
- epoch size: 1
- initial weight values: randomly between [-0.1; 0.1]

It should be noted that by using a feedforward NN it is necessary to cope with the overfitting problem. Consequently, in the experiments the cross-validating technique (by using the cross-validation subset) has been used in order to avoid such a problem (for details on the overfitting problem and the cross-validating technique, see e.g. Fischer 1998; Fischer and Gopal 1994; Reggiani and Tritapepe 1998).

The results related to the above mentioned experiment will now be presented. In general, by using a statistical model for forecasting, the first step is to evaluate the predictive quality of the model, i.e. to determine how well the model learned to approximate the unknown input-output function for arbitrary values of input units, while the final aim of our work is to evaluate the freight transport movements in Europe in order to forecast spatiotemporal patterns on the basis of new transport economic scenarios. The present section will particularly analyse this first research stage, i.e. the spatial forecasting of the model adopted. The predictive quality will be evaluated - by means of a performance measure - by using the test set which had been set apart and not yet used for the calibration (learning) phase, as mentioned above.

The predictive performance of an NN can be judged by means of the statistical indicator ARV (see Nijkamp et al. 1996 and Subsection 17.3.2); the result of the test statistic is the following:

$$ARV_{NN} = 0.176$$

It is then evident that the above ARV indicator, emerging from NN, gives a better result than the ARV indicator emerging from the logit analysis. Tables 17.3 and 17.4 present also the values of ARV = 0.203 and ARV = 0.185 – both greater than 0.176 – and show thus a better performance of the NN approach. This result is rather promising and gives sufficient confidence in the validity of the NN approach for spatial analysis.

17.3.4 Comparison of the Logit and Neural Network Approach

In this subsection, the spatial forecasting performance of the two alternative approaches adopted will be compared and evaluated.

By using the test set, which was not used for the calibration procedure, in our procedure both the binary logit and the NN model have been employed to predict the freight flows for link (ij). This performance has been evaluated using the statistical indicator ARV.

In light of the enormous number of commodity flows we will not present the estimates for all interregional flows in Europe, but only for three illustrative types of flows, viz. from Dutch regions to Europe as a whole and vice versa, and from Europe to Italian regions. Tables 17.5, 17.6 and 17.7 illustrate the predictions made by the two distinct approaches.

Table 17.5 Food transport flows from Dutch regions to Europe

Regions	Food Transport Flows LOGIT	real	NN	rel. prediction error LOGIT	NN
Breda	170981	181032	176781	-5,6%	-2,3%
Eindhoven	904321	968534	945732	-6,6%	-2,4%
Maastricht	252429	264424	255930	-4,5%	-3,2%
Total	1327732	1413990	1378442	-6,1%	-2,5%

Table 17.6 Food transport flows from Europe to Dutch regions

Regions	Food Transport Flows LOGIT	real	NN	rel. prediction error LOGIT	NN
Breda	15837	15922	15634	-0,5%	-1,8%
Eindhoven	121918	119772	122434	1,8%	2,2%
Maastricht	59550	59880	60010	-0,6%	0,2%
Total	197304	195574	198077	0,9%	1,3%

Table 17.7 Food transport flows from Europe to Italian regions

Regions	Food Transport Flows LOGIT	real	NN	rel. prediction error LOGIT	NN
Ancona	898	921	888	-2,5%	-3,6%
Bari	16722	16925	16040	-1,2%	-5,2%
Bologna	71272	68916	72920	3,4%	5,8%
Cagliari	4072	4019	4010	1,3%	-0,2%
Florence	27052	27488	26756	-1,6%	-2,7%
Milan	60781	59977	59482	1,3%	-0,8%
Naples	55916	54720	57807	2,2%	5,6%
Palermo	29344	29221	29018	0,4%	-0,7%
Pescara	8939	8895	8471	0,5%	-4,8%
Reggio di Calabria	1384	1375	1324	0,6%	-3,7%
Rome	13879	14504	13756	-4,3%	-5,2%
Turin	106438	105414	108563	1,0%	3,0%
Venice	8776	9280	9155	-5,4%	-1,4%
Total	405472	401655	408189	1,3%	-0,2%

Table 17.5 presents the predictions for the export flows of foodstuff from three regions in the Netherlands (Breda, Eindhoven and Maastricht). Both approaches predict a slightly smaller transport flow

than the observed flow; however the predictions made by the logit model are less accurate than those predicted by the NN model.

Analogously, the predicted import flows from Europe to the same three regions in the Netherlands are presented in Table 17.6. This table indicates that the logit results are slightly more accurate than the NN results. In the case of Maastricht, the logit prediction is slightly smaller than the observed value, while the neural network prediction is slightly higher.

Next, we have focused our attention on the import flows from Europe to Italian regions. The predicted import flows to thirteen Italian regions are shown in Table 17.7. The NN model again appears to make on average slightly more accurate predictions than the binary logit model, although at the individual (regional) level the logit model also gives a good approximation.

Finally, Table 17.8 shows the ARV indicators, which have been calculated for both the logit and the NN approach (see also the previous sections).

Table 17.8 Comparison of logit and NN performance

	ARV
NN	0.176
Logit	0.185

According to the ARV indicator, the NN approach for forecasting spatial flows performs overall slightly better than the logit approach.

17.4 Policy Scenario Experiments

As mentioned above, freight transport causes high social costs, which might be charged to the transportation sector. We will now investigate the consequences of varying the transportation costs for freight flows. A sensitivity analysis of the previous results based on some economic scenarios will now be carried out in this section by using again both the binary logit model and the NN model. Two policy scenarios based on different external costs assignments will be used; they will be concisely discussed here. Later on, we will present the results related to the sensitivity analysis for the logit and the neural network approach.

At present, because of severe problems on the road transport network (for example, congestion), governments are trying to reduce the road usage by imposing policy measures that serve to increase the cost of road usage (see Verhoef 1996). An example of a Pigouvian policy for coping with environmental externalities is the recently increased tax on fuel in the Netherlands. In so doing, the usage of the road transport network is made less attractive than other transport networks. In the light of these recent developments, two scenarios have been developed and considered for an sensitivity analysis; these are based on the observations in the test set. In Scenario 1 we assume that a uniform European tax policy for freight transport is adopted and that the cost attribute related to the road mode is increased by 25 percent for all links (ij). Scenario 2 assumes only a national environmental policy, which means that same cost increase is made exclusively for links (ij) which start or end in Dutch regions.

The conditional predictions for the three Dutch regions are presented in Tables 17.9 and 17.10 for the binary logit and the neural network model, respectively. The relative prediction error (see Tables 17.9 and 17.10) is defined as the difference between the predicted flow and the real flow as a percentage of the real flow. These tables indicate that the binary logit model is relatively more sensitive to changes in the cost attribute than the NN model. Table 17.9 also shows that the binary logit model gives the same predictions in the two scenarios, which is caused by the independence of irrelevant alternatives feature (IIA) of this discrete choice model. The NN model estimates appear to give the lowest prediction error.

Table 17.9 Results of the sensitivity analysis for the binary logit model (columns b and c)

	Food Transport Flows				Relative Prediction Error		
From NL to Europe	*real flow*	*pred. flow*					
Regions		a) test set	b) scen. 1	c) scen. 2	a)	b)	c)
Breda	181032	170981	161327	161327	-5,6%	-10,9%	-10,9%
Eindhoven	968534	904321	861082	861082	-6,6%	-11,1%	-11,1%
Maastricht	264424	252429	245336	245336	-4,5%	-7,2%	-7,2%
TOTAL	1413990	1327732	1267745	1267745	-6,1%	-10,3%	-10,3%
From Europe to NL	*real flow*	*pred. flow*					
Regions		a) test set	b) scen. 1	c) scen. 2	a)	b)	c)
Breda	15922	15837	15599	15599	-0,5%	-2,0%	-2,0%
Eindhoven	119772	121918	119056	119056	1,8%	-0,6%	-0,6%
Maastricht	59880	59550	58363	58363	-0,6%	-2,5%	-2,5%
TOTAL	195574	197304	193018	193019	0,9%	-1,3%	-1,3%

It is interesting to note that in the neural network case, and particularly in the case of inflows from Europe to the Netherlands, the model shows – in the mean value – a slight increase of flows, despite the cost increase. This result may be plausible by taking into account the increasing amount of interaction among regional flows as a result of increased efficiency. It would certainly be relevant to compare these results with more updated data in order to better evaluate the 'forecasting' analysis of the two models, since we have used – as a starting point – a test set related to the year 1986.

Table 17.10 Results of the sensitivity analysis for the neural network model (columns b and c)

	Food Transport Flows				Relative Prediction Error		
From NL to Europe **Regions**	*real flow*	*pred. flow* a) test set	b) scen. 1	c) scen. 2	a)	b)	c)
Breda	181032	176781	175783	171600	-2,3%	-2,9%	-5,2%
Eindhoven	968534	945732	941847	930447	-2,4%	-2,8%	-3,9%
Maastricht	264424	255930	255261	254181	-3,2%	-3,5%	-3,9%
TOTAL	1413990	1378442	1372891	1356228	-2,5%	-2,9%	-4,1%
From Europe to NL **Regions**	*real flow*	*pred. flow* a) test set	b) scen. 1	c) scen. 2	a)	b)	c)
Breda	15922	15634	15598	15508	-1,8%	-2,0%	-2,6%
Eindhoven	119772	122434	122117	121270	2,2%	2,0%	1,3%
Maastricht	59880	60010	59832	59368	0,2%	-0,1%	-0,9%
TOTAL	195574	198077	197548	196148	1,3%	1,0%	0,3%

However, the above results may be considered valid in the absence of updated data that would be able to test our hypothesis of a 25 percent increase in the costs, given the good performance of the calibration/test phase. Moreover, these results may offer a 'range of values' to policy actors aimed at evaluating the impact of cost changes on flows, given the intrinsic limits of both adopted models.

On the one hand, the large amount of data at an aggregate level, hampers a behavioural perspective inherent in logit models. On the other hand, the type of architecture adopted in NN models seems critical for the validity of the results. Consequently, the results of our model may be used as a benchmark for the results of other models, by offering a more 'flexible' output to policy actors.

17.5 Concluding Remarks

The aim of this chapter has been to depict transport flows of commodities in an interregional European setting. Based on an extensive (NEA) data set, various estimates of the impacts of costs on transport movements have been made. The test results show that both the logit and the NN approach are giving fairly favourable results. In general, NN models seem to perform slightly better. After this exploratory comparative study of two modelling approaches, it is certainly opportune to investigate more thoroughly the differences in background of these two research paradigms. It is well known that the logit model is a particular spatial interaction model that has its roots in social behaviour of actors, however with the limit of assuming certain properties, like the well known IIA (Independence from Irrelevant Alternatives) assumption. The NN model is based on similarly of learning experiments and has certainly a behavioural adjustment potential, but is less easily interpretable from social science motives, even though recent results show a compatibility between feedforward NNs and binary logit models (see Schintler and Olurotimi 1998), feedforward NNs and spatial interaction models (see Fischer and Gopal 1994) and feedforward NNs and logistic regression models (see Schumacher et al. 1996). Given its predictive ability, more research is needed to better investigate the behavioural roots of NN models.

Acknowledgement

The authors wish to thank NEA Transport Research and Training (Rijswijk, The Netherlands) and particularly Dr. Philippe Tardieu for providing an extensive data set for the experiments. The Italian CNR project PFT2 no. 97.000.264.PF74 is also gratefully acknowledged.

References

Ben-Akiva, M. and Lerman, S.R. (1985), *Discrete Choice Analysis: Theory and Application to Travel Demand*, MIT Press, Cambridge, Massachusetts.

Cramer, J.S. (1991), *The LOGIT Model: an Introduction for Economists*, Routledge, Chapman and Hall Inc., New York.

Dougherty, M. (ed.) (1997), 'Special Issue on "Neural Networks in Transportation"', *Transportation Research C* (forthcoming).

Fischer, M.M. (1998), 'Computational Neural Networks. An Attractive Class of Mathematical Models for Transportation Research', in Himanen, V., Nijkamp, P. and A. Reggiani (eds.), *Neural Networks in Transport Applications* (forthcoming).

Fischer, M.M. and Gopal, S. (1994), 'Artificial Neural Networks: A New Approach to Modelling Interregional Telecommunication Flows', *Journal of Regional Science*, vol. 34, no. 4, pp. 503–27.

Himanen, V., Nijkamp, P. and Reggiani, A. (eds.) (1998), *Neural Networks in Transport Applications*, Ashgate, Aldershot (forthcoming).

McFadden, D. (1977), 'Econometric Models of Probabilistic Choice', in Mansky, C.F. and D. McFadden (eds), *Structural Analysis of Discrete Data with Econometric Applications*, MIT Press, Cambridge, Massachusetts.

Nijkamp, P., Reggiani, A. and Tritapepe, T. (1996), 'Modelling Inter-Urban Transport Flows in Italy: A Comparison between Neural Network Approach and Logit Analysis', *Transportation Research C*, vol. 4, no. 6, pp. 323–38.
Reggiani, A. and Tritapepe, T. (1998), 'Neural Networks and Logit Models: A Comparative Analysis with Reference to Commuters' Mobility in the Metropolitan Region of Milan', in Himanen, V., Nijkamp, P. and A. Reggiani, (eds.), *Neural Networks in Transport Applications*, Ashgate, Aldershot (forthcoming).
Reggiani, A., Romanelli, R., Tritapepe, T. and Nijkamp, P. (1998), 'Neural Networks: An Overview and Applications in the Space Economy', in Himanen, V., Nijkamp, P. and A. Reggiani (eds.), *Neural Networks in Transport Applications*, Ashgate, Aldershot (forthcoming).
Schintler, L.A. and Olurotimi, O. (1998), 'Neural Networks as Adaptive Logit Models', in Himanen, V., Nijkamp, P. and A. Reggiani (eds.), *Neural Networks in Transport Applications*, Ashgate, Aldershot (forthcoming).
Schumacher, M., Roßner, R. and Vach, W. (1996), 'Neural Networks and Logistic Regression', *Computational Statistics & Data Analysis*, vol. 21, pp. 661–82.
Tavasszy, L.A. (1996), *Modelling European Freight Transport Flows*, PhD Thesis, Delft University of Technology, Delft.
Verhoef, E.T. (1996), *The Economics of Regulating Road Transport*, Edward Elgar, Aldershot.

Annex: Table 17.A.1 List of the 108 European regions considered

1 Antwerp
2 Bruxelles
3 Liege
4 Gent
Denmark
5 Copenhagen
6 Odense
7 Aarhus
8 Fredericia
France
9 Lille
10 Amiens
11 Rouen
12 Paris
13 Metz
14 Dijon
15 Lyon
16 Marseille
17 Montpellier
18 Toulouse
19 Bordeaux
20 Rennes
21 Tours
22 Clermont-Ferrand
23 Reims
Greece
24 Thessaloniki
25 Athens
27 Patras
Italy
28 Turin
29 Milan
30 Genoa
31 Venice
32 Bologna
33 Florence
34 Ancona
35 Pescara
36 Rome
37 Naples
38 Bari
39 Reggio di Calabria
40 Palermo
41 Cagliari
Ireland
42 Dublin
43 Rosslare
44 Cork
45 Galway
46 Athlone
Luxemburg
47 Luxemburg
The Netherlands
48 Groningen
49 Amsterdam
50 Almelo
51 Arnhem
52 Utrecht
53 Rotterdam
54 Eindhoven
55 Maastricht
56 Breda
Germany
57 Kiel
58 Hamburg
59 Hannover
60 Oldenburg
61 Bremen
62 Essen
63 Koln
64 Kassel
65 Frankfurt
66 Ludwigshafen
67 Stuttgart
68 Freiburg
69 Nurnberg
70 Regensberg
71 Munchen
72 Berlin
United Kingdom
73 Carlisle
74 Newcastle
75 Leeds
76 Manchester
77 Nottingham
78 Birmingham
79 Cardiff
80 Holyhead
81 Bristol
82 Cambridge
83 London
84 Southampton
85 Glasgow
86 Aberdeen
87 Dumfries
88 Belfast
Spain
89 Lugo
90 Bilbao
91 Zaragoza
92 Barcelona
93 Valencia
94 Sevilla
95 Madrid
96 Valladolid
97 Caceres
98 Canary Islands
Portugal
100 Coimbra
101 Lisbon
Austria
102 Innsbruck
103 Linz
104 Vienna\
105 Graz
Switzerland
106 Geneva
107 Bern
108 Zurich

Notes

1. The choice probability of the other mode is just the complement.

2. The data set has been kindly provided by NEA Transport Research and Training, Rijswijk.

3. See Map 17.1 and Table 17.A.1.

4. The definition of the statistical indicator ρ^2 is: $\rho^2 = 1 - (\lambda_{(0)} / \lambda_{(\beta)})$, where $\lambda_{(0)}$ = the value of the log likelihood function when all weights are zero and $\lambda_{(\beta)}$ = the value of the log likelihood function at its maximum (see Ben-Akiva and Lerman 1985).

5. The definition of the statistical indicator ARV is:

$$ARV = \frac{(y - \hat{y})^2}{\Sigma(y - \bar{y})^2}$$

while the definition of the statistical indicator R^2 is:

$$R^2 = \frac{\Sigma(\bar{y} - \hat{y})^2}{\Sigma(y - \bar{y})^2}$$

where y = the observed transport flow using road, $\bar{y}$ = the transport flow using road, predicted by the adopted model, and y= the average of the observed transport flow using road (see Fischer and Gopal 1994).

For Product Safety Concerns and Information please contact our EU representative GPSR@taylorandfrancis.com
Taylor & Francis Verlag GmbH, Kaufingerstraße 24, 80331 München, Germany

www.ingramcontent.com/pod-product-compliance
Ingram Content Group UK Ltd.
Pitfield, Milton Keynes, MK11 3LW, UK
UKHW022207190926
475702UK00003B/239
* 9 7 8 1 1 3 8 3 5 1 3 9 4 *